THE SOCIOLOGY OF DEVIANCE

THE SOCIOLOGY OF DEVIANCE

Differences, Tradition, and Stigma

By

ROBERT J. FRANZESE, Ph.D.

CHARLES C THOMAS • PUBLISHER, LTD.
Springfield • Illinois • U.S.A.

Published and Distributed Throughout the World by

CHARLES C THOMAS • PUBLISHER, LTD.
2600 South First Street
Springfield, Illinois 62704

©2009 by CHARLES C THOMAS • PUBLISHER, LTD.

ISBN 978-0-398-07855-3 (hard)
ISBN 978-0-398-07856-0 (paper)

Library of Congress Catalog Card Number: 2008044159

With THOMAS BOOKS *careful attention is given to all details of manufacturing
and design. It is the Publisher's desire to present books that are satisfactory as to their
physical qualities and artistic possibilities and appropriate for their particular use.*
THOMAS BOOKS *will be true to those laws of quality that assure a good name
and good will.*

Printed in the United States of America
CR-R-3

Library of Congress Cataloging-in-Publication Data

Franzese, Robert J.
    The sociology of deviance : differences, tradition, and stigma / by
Robert J. Franzese.
        p. cm.
    Includes bibliographical references and index.
    ISBN 978-0-398-07855-3 (hard) -- ISBN 978-0-398-07856-0 (pbk.)
    1. Deviant behavior--Case studies. I. Title.

HM811.F73 2009
302.5'42--dc22

                                                            2008044159

I dedicate this book to those professors who instilled in me a love of sociology, and by doing so are responsible for a 40-year career in sociology and higher education. These individuals believed in me and gave me "the shot in the arm" that launched me through three degrees, and provided me with an understanding of and respect for the sociological enterprise and imagination. They are Dr. Kenneth Root, who I took for three undergraduate courses, and who was the first to "turn me on" to sociology in "Introduction to Sociology." I'll never forget the day I was walking across the campus of the University of Nebraska-Omaha and encountered Dr. Root who informed me the Sociology Department was going to ask me to attend graduate school. This lifted me about 10 feet off the ground, and inspired me to think more seriously about a graduate education. The late Dr. Wayne Wheeler took the baton from there, and during my senior year was my mentor in two courses in independent study. Dr. Wheeler had an uncanny knowledge of sociology and shared many of my same interests in the discipline, including social stratification and social change. In April of my senior year he too encouraged me to enroll in graduate school (I had yet to make that decision) eventually becoming my thesis advisor, and one semester I was his graduate teaching assistant. "Wayne," as I would grow to call him, was a powerful influence on my career and along with Dr. Root is deserving of my fondest memories, respect and gratitude. Other professors deserving mention here are Philip Vogt, whom I consider the finest professor I had during my undergraduate years, and Pete Kuchel who taught me a great deal about criminology and juvenile delinquency. Professor Vogt was a masterful and inspiring teacher of social problems, and minority and ethnic group relations. "Pete" as his students called him, possessed an amazing sense of humor, while offering a practical and experienced-based approach to the study of criminology and criminal justice.

PREFACE

The Sociology of Deviance: Differences, Tradition, and Stigma is dedicated to a sociological analysis of deviance, a term reframed to imply *differences*. Deviance is approached from the outset as meaning *differences*: differences in attitudes, behaviors, lifestyles, and values of people. The terms "deviance" or "deviant behavior" are understood as labels themselves, and are used sparingly, such as in the title, and in Chapter 14 "Elite and Power Deviance" ("deviance" appears with frequency in the theory chapters since it is a term used by the theorists addressed). "Deviance" is employed in the title to draw attention to the fact this is a deviance text. "Deviance" is used in the heading for Chapter 14, since much of the chapter derives from the works of David Simon's *Elite Deviance*, and in order to introduce a new concept, *power deviance* that is an extension on the concept of elite deviance. Part of the title of the text is *Tradition* and this means the book assumes a traditional approach to the study of differences. Traditional topics are covered such as suicide, mental disorders and physical disabilities, addictions and substance abuse and use, criminal behaviors, and sexual behaviors and differences. The book has one chapter devoted to criminal behavior in order to avoid duplicating criminology and criminal justice texts, with emphasis placed on violent and property offenses. The term *stigma* appears in the title for two reasons: it is to honor the contributions of Erving Goffman to the study of differences, and it is used to accentuate the importance of societal reaction to attitudes, behaviors, lifestyles, and values that are varied and different in a heterogeneous society. Nowhere is this more evident than in Chapter 12 "Societal Reaction and Stigmatization: Mental Disorders and Physical Disabilities" where mental disorders and physical disabilities are approached from understanding them in light of labels and stigma.

The Sociology of Deviance: Differences, Tradition, and Stigma includes case studies or examples relevant to every chapter, and "In Recognition" where individuals who have made contributions to related subject matter are honored. These recognitions are toward the end of every chapter, and the case studies are found at the beginning of most chapters, but are placed elsewhere in several instances. A major part of the book includes analyses and empirical assessments of the theories discussed in Chapters 4 through 8. In this respect the book offers one of the most comprehensive and specific discussions of the theories, and their empirical viability. Four of the five theory chapters present discussions of tests of major theories, thus providing students with more detail on the efficacy of deviance theories than usually is the case. An intent of this book is not to duplicate other texts in deviance, and to show variety in the manner in which different substantive topics are covered. For example, attention is given to historical developments when discussing mental disorders and physical disabilities, but this is not generally the case in Chapter 13 where sexual behaviors and differences are presented. Chapter 11 has coverage of gambling as a form of addiction, an area generally not addressed in other texts on deviant behavior.

R.J.F.

ACKNOWLEDGMENTS

Several individuals were instrumental in producing the final product. One of my colleagues, Dr. Lorraine Latimore provided significant insights and materials into updating empirical studies of many theories addressed in this book, in particular strain and social control theories, as was the case for Carolyn Vinyard, a graduate teaching assistant who also played a major role in identifying major and recent empirical tests of deviance and crime theories, especially social learning theories. Meredith Denney, an undergraduate teaching assistant at the time and now a blooming and promising graduate student undertook the tedious duty of researching and then copying journal articles that are used throughout the book. As always, Meredith went above and beyond the call of duty and located additional materials that are cited in the text. Another colleague, Dr. Susan Sharp introduced me to *Feminist Criminology*, a journal she helped to establish, and by doing so expanded the horizons and coverage of feminist theories addressed in the book. Last are Virginia Franzese-Olin, my daughter and Rick Fry, artist extraordinaire who painstakingly and with great patience helped immensley with computer-related typing and graph/chart issues. Corey Helms and Dr. Craig St. John are deserving of mention. Corey is an outstanding undergraduate student who undertook the difficult task of indexing. As the Chair of the Department of Sociology, Dr. St. John provided me with resources essential to completing the book. The contributions of the above individuals are deeply appreciated and bigger than what I have stated in this brief paragraph. A special thanks goes to my wife Patty who encouraged and supported me throughout the writing of this book, not to mention throughout my entire professional career.

CONTENTS

SECTION 3: SUBSTANTIVE AREAS

THE SOCIOLOGY OF DEVIANCE

Section 1

BACKGROUND

Chapter 1

THE NATURE OF DEVIANCE

CASE STUDY: THE HUTTERITES

Occasionally, societies experience the settlement of successful communal organizations, or subcultures. Over the years the United States has seen the emergence of numerous communes, and to this day few exist. However, several communal organizations have survived and even flourished. One such group is known as the Hutterites, one of three Annabatists religious communes with origins in central Europe who immigrated to North America in search of religious freedoms during the nineteenth century. Most of the 30,000 Hutterites in North America reside in Canada, and some communes dot the plains of the north central states, such as North and South Dakota.

The Hutterites are an agricultural-based society which partially explains their success and durability. With total focus and in-depth attention of each commune on farming as the major economic mode of production, the communes are well-known for their successful harvests and acquisition of adequate financial resources and security. Notwithstanding, one of the most important values of the Hutterites is communal ownership of wealth as opposed to individual hoarding of wealth, power and income. In this respect

the Hutterites have been referred to as the "Christian Communists of Canada."

The Hutterites adhere to rigid understanding of the bible, meaning they interpret it literally. From this derives all of the values and practices so deeply followed by the group, including traditional sex roles and corporal punishment for misbehaving children. In respect to traditional sex roles the Hutterites maintain sex role segregation relative to work, family structure and power in the communes. Men undertake physical labor associated with farming and other outside-type chores, while women cook, sew, shop, and take on the primary responsibilities of child-rearing. In addition, Hutterite male and female dress reflects their strong preoccupation with avoiding sins of the flesh, since women wear long dresses that reveal no skin, and they wear head coverings. Male dress is also conservative and like that of women does not vary from man-to-man. All of this spills over to male leadership in each commune, where elected male elders make the major business and religious decisions. Women in essence are in the background and are not allowed an equal status with men.

Although there is evidence of change most Hutterite communes stress education up to but ending with high school. Mastery of the three "r's," reading, writing and arithmetic is the focus of Hutterite education, along with Hutterite religious and cultural education. Some modern communes allow gifted individuals to matriculate to college but this is rare. Experiencing the outside world does occur with Hutterites especially when they go into neighboring towns on business, but to encourage the young to attend college is seen by most Hutterites as a threat to their traditions and lifestyles. Attending colleges or universities would expose young Hutterites to the very issue of greatest concern for their salvation: sins of the flesh. What is more, Hutterites youth might be more likely to leave the life once they found more about the outside world, its opportunities, and many diversions.

Hutterite life appears simple and uncomplicated. Dress style is the same for men and for women, and homes do not allow pictures on the walls, even pictures of flowers or mountains, because once again this is considered worldly and antithetical to Hutterite interpretation of the bible. So day by day, year after year, Hutterite life and culture remains essentially unchanged, centered around religious dogma, farming, and a quiet, peaceful existence.

Deviance Defined

Consider this for a moment: a way of life in twenty-first century America that embraces sex role inequality, and communal as opposed to individual acquisition of wealth. Add to this a very strict adherence to the bible and living miles away from the modern social world with no televisions, radios, DVD players or Ipods. The questions for you may be "what do I make of this" and "would I trade places with the Hutterites" (or would they switch lifestyles with us).

Our first impression may be that the Hutterites are weird or strange, or just not with it. We may even question their mental health. However, we are reminded that they have chosen to live a much secluded way of life, one reminiscent of the nineteenth century. This type of example is the essence of the study of deviance since sociologists interested in this field often find themselves studying people and lifestyles much different than what most of us have experienced, *or will ever experience.* The study of deviance is the study of differences, and in this book the definition of deviance presented is atypical of those found in other similar texts, and which has been offered by other sociologists. Here deviance is defined in terms of *differences,* with the full definition *"deviance is the differences in behaviors, values, attitudes, lifestyles, and life choices among individuals and groups."* What separates this definition from others is its lack of value judgment that can emanate from the word deviance itself. Deviance implies a value judgment, and begs the question "according to who?" To say the Hutterites are different means something much different than to identify them as deviant. "Deviance" is a label and carries with it the potential for stigmatizing individuals and groups.

Multiple Definitions of Deviance

Listed are definitions of deviance that have been offered over the years. These are presented here for the purpose of contrast, with each other and with the definition to be employed in this text. The definitions are those that were developed by major scholars in the study of deviance.

Ronald Akers: We consider here only behavior which deviates in a disapproved direction. More specifically, attention is directed primarily to instances of disapproved behavior considered serious enough to warrant major societal efforts to control them, using strong negative sanctions or treatment-corrective techniques. (1977:11)

Howard S. Becker: The deviant is one to whom the label has successfully been applied; deviant behavior is behavior that people so label. (1963: 9)

Kai T. Erickson: Deviance is not a property inherent in certain forms of behavior. It is properly conferred upon these forms by the audiences which directly or indirectly witness them. (1962: 308)

Robert K. Merton: . . . deviant behavior refers to conduct that departs significantly from the norms set for people in their social statuses. (1966: 805)

John Kitsuse: Forms of behavior per se do not differentiate deviants from non-deviants; it is the responses of the conventional and conforming members of the society who identify and interpret behavior as deviant which sociologically transforms persons into deviants. (1962: 253)

John A. Humphrey: In short, the process of defining behaviors as deviant or not, and the public response to the act and the actor established a boundary between acceptable and unacceptable behavior in a given society. Norms and values have been established; social organization and culture have been defined. (2006:6).

Marshall B. Clinard and **Robert F. Meier:** Deviance constitutes departures from norms that draw social disapproval such that the variations elicit, or are likely to elicit, if detected, negative sanctions. (2004: 6)

Alex Thio: Deviant behavior, we may say, is any behavior considered deviant by public consensus, which may range from the maximum to the minimum. (2006: 12)

Commonalities Across the Definitions

Although the above definitions of deviance are different from one another, there are some striking similarities among them. First, there is concern for behavior, or behavior that departs from social norms, or societal approved ways of doing things. Of course, in the study of deviance something must be earmarked in order for there to be purpose to the field of study, and this is usually behavior. Second, several authors use the words "applied," "conferred," and "transforms" as indication that those considered deviant become so through social processes and communication. In these definitions there is an almost mystical or religious conversionary notion, in as much as the deviant is "anointed" as such by others, for whatever reasons. Third, societal reaction emerges from the definitions through use of phrases or words such as "label," "control," "social disapproval," and "sanctions". The implication here, and it is ubiquitous among students of deviance, is that much of what is considered deviant is about *reaction*, or recognition of behaviors that stand out and are annoying, disturbing, and even threatening to people.

Student Definitions

For years the author of this text has asked students enrolled in his deviance classes to offer their own meanings of deviance. Normally this is done as an "ice breaker," and as the opening activity in the class. Listed are some of these definitions and they are unedited, meaning they are presented as given in class.

- Any form of behavior that is not socially, culturally or economically accepted.
- Deviance is an action that is consider not acceptable to society.
- Deviance is anything a person can do that another sees as wrong.
- Any behavior outside the social norm.
- What you do when you want to be out of the ordinary-mix things up.
- Any thought, behavior or action that is immoral or lawful.
- Immoral and unethical actions against norms of society.

- Any behavior that can potentially be harmful.
- An act a person commits that a society reacts to negatively.
- Acting as a rebel.

Students quite often define deviance in terms of violations of social norms, and they also see deviance as representing immorality. However, as a semester evolves, quite often students will broaden their horizons, implying they understand the meaning of deviance from multiple perspectives.

Models of Deviance

Deviance can be conceptualized in a number of ways, and two such conceptualizations are presented in this section. The first is a model developed by Alex Thio, a leading contemporary scholar in the study of deviance. The second model was developed by Ruth Shonle Cavan some decades ago, and is a model designed to apply to juvenile delinquency. Cavan's bell-shaped curve method of understanding delinquency is adaptable to the study of deviance.

Alex Thio (2006) has posited an idea that divides the way sociologists study deviance into two distinct categories: the positivist and constructionist perspectives. Thio's conceptualization is both interesting and instructive in that it sheds significant light on the challenges involved in *defining* deviance, as well as issues involved in the ways that sociologists go about *studying* deviant behavior.

The *positivist perspective* owes its origins to early sociology, and assumes a scientific stance to understanding deviance. From this perspective deviance can and must be examined and understood using the research methods available to social scientists, such as field and survey research. Positivists argue (when studying deviance) it is the responsibility of sociologists to discern the causes

and consequences of deviant conduct. The positivist perspective has three elements or parts: *absolutism, objectivism* and *determinism. Absolutism* means deviance is real in the social world; the behavior does exist and is worthy of study. Using an example, if marijuana smoking is a topic to be studied, the person doing the research does not question whether or not it's deviant: he or she just goes on and studies it, period. *Objectivism* is an old idea of science, involving the notion that behavior is observable, or measurable. In other words, if it can be sensed, it can be studied. *Determinism* is to be understood to mean deviance has causes that must be unraveled, requiring the development of theories that explain the behavior (2006: 5–8).

The *constructionist perspective* takes a very different, if not diametrically opposite position as that just discussed. This conceptualization assumes the position that nothing is deviant unless it is *defined* as such, or *nothing in-and-of itself is deviant.* Thus using the marijuana example from before, constructionists argue that smoking pot is only illegal or deviant because it has been *defined that way* and, in short, some people clearly do not lend it approval. Similar to the positivist perspective, constructionism has three elements: *relativism, subjectivism* and *voluntarism. Relativism* concerns *labels and labeling.* It is the notion individuals become labeled by others, with the labels originating from definitions or connotations of deviance developed in society. Consequently, the marijuana smoker who gets caught smoking pot or is known to be engaged in the use of the drug may become labeled as a deviant. *Subjectivism* is the opposite of objectivism, and implies that the way to knowing the social world comes from immersing oneself in it, therefore if a social scientist wanted to understand marijuana smoking, this would entail the need to be in the presence of those smoking pot. There is an underlying assumption and it is for sociologists to truly capture all that encompasses the act of smoking marijuana–the behaviors, values, attitudes and interaction surrounding the use of the drug–then it is imperative they be on the scene observing and documenting the actual behavior. *Voluntarism* implies deviant behavior is derived from the conscious decisions *(free will)* by individuals to engage in the behavior, and is the idea there are *no causes* of deviance, meaning if you or I become deviant, it was our decision to do so. Many people say they smoke pot to reduce stress, or as a result of peer influence. Not so say the constructionists. Smoking marijuana is a personal decision that is derived from a conscious decision to do so, minus any causes (2006: 9–10).

Over four decades ago Ruth Shonle Cavan (1961) developed a model to explain juvenile delinquency that is quite applicable to understanding deviance. Cavan took the bell-shaped curve and divided it into seven areas, each one representing some degree of behavior related to delinquency. As you can see in Figure 1:1, the middle area "D" is that of normal conformity, and does not involve delinquent behavior. Moving to the left the behavior is *negative*, and the areas further left represent more serious delinquency. Moving right from area "D" the behavior is positive, and becomes more so the further right one goes, and both ends of the bell-shaped curve are considered *contracultures*, or points of no return, and in the jargon of criminologists include individuals who are incorrigible, or who will not change. Those furthest left (Area A) would be serious juvenile offenders, for which there is little hope, and those on the far right (Area G) are more like saints, but also are mired in a state of inflexibility, or never expected to change. Close inspection of Figure 1:1 shows dotted lines that separate the seven areas. This is important since it implies that people drift from one area to another, and most return back to area "D." Solid lines would indicate that passage across the seven areas was infeasible, and would signify once crossing the lines deviance would become a permanent status.

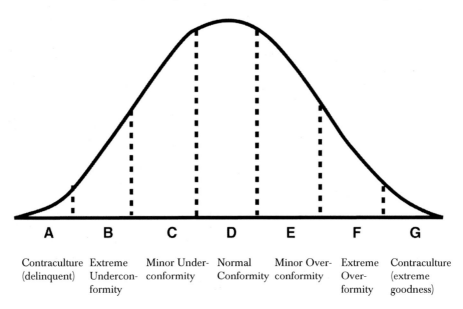

A	B	C	D	E	F	G
Contraculture (delinquent)	Extreme Underconformity	Minor Underconformity	Normal Conformity	Minor Overconformity	Extreme Overformity	Contraculture (extreme goodness)

Figure 1:1. Ruth Cavan's Delinquency Model.

However, the human condition is malleable, and just because some 14-year-old decides to steal a car once does not mean he or she is on the path to a career in deviant behavior. On the contrary, the time spent in area "B" would most likely be short-lived, with eventual reentry back into area "D" (1961: 243–258).

Ruth Shonle Cavan's concept of the contraculture is applicable to understanding deviance. Area "D" can still be referred to that as normal conformity, however the labels for the other areas now change. For example, minor under conformity becomes minor deviance, and extreme under conformity is now extreme deviance (and the same logic applies to the "positive" side of the curve). The extremes on the curve still remain contracultures and for all areas the examples change to reflect the focus on deviance.

What should stand out with the revised Cavan model is not only the malleability of the human condition, but also the vitality involved with deviant behavior. Most of us the majority of the time exist within area "D," but every now and then we drift into one of the other places on the curve, most likely areas "C" or "E." But this does not mean we live a life of deviance. Instead, it implies we are human beings who occasionally engage in deviance, both negative and positive. Over 70,000,000 Americans have smoked marijuana, and 30,000,000 have had extra marital relationships. However, the great majority of people who smoke pot have done so no more than six times, and most individuals who have affairs do not make a habit of it. This conjures up an important piece of the deviance puzzle, and that is labeling. Smoke marijuana 500 times in your life and never get caught, and guess what? You may escape the label "marijuana user." Smoke it once and get caught, and guess what? Well, let's leave that as an rhetorical question. Cavan's model is simple, yet powerful, conveying an important message, which is as human beings we may

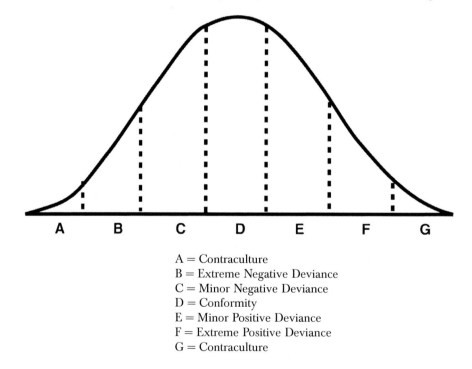

A = Contraculture
B = Extreme Negative Deviance
C = Minor Negative Deviance
D = Conformity
E = Minor Positive Deviance
F = Extreme Positive Deviance
G = Contraculture

Figure 1:2. Ruth Cavan's Model Applied to Deviance.

experiment as we go through life, and this experimentation may involve behaviors perceived to exist outside socially acceptable norms. For most of us the experimentation is short-lived, but if detected can have life-changing consequences.

Case Study: The Gangster Disciples

In the United States there are between 23,000 and 30,000 gangs depending on who is doing the counting (National Youth Gang Center, 2006; National Gang Crime Research Center, 2006). The great majority of these gangs are no more than youth street gangs (Franzese, Covey, and Menard, 2006) but some are super gangs with membership into the thousands (National Gang Crime Research Center, 2006). One such mega gang is the "Gangster Disciples" (GDs), who in Chicago alone number 30,000 members. Formed during the 1960s the GDs have spread to 35 states and have amassed significant financial resources through drug trafficking. One of the founders of the GDs, Larry Hoover was serving a 200-year sentence at Joliet State Prison in Illinois for a gang-related murder committed in 1973, but has since been transferred to the federal correctional facility in Terre Haute, Indiana after being convicted on federal charges, including drug conspiracy and extortion. In case you're asking: Yes, for years Hoover managed to run the GDs and its criminal enterprises from his prison cell (National Gang Crime Research Center, 2006).

Critical to the GDs are its *symbols* that take on particular importance to sociologists. The major symbol of the GDs is the *six-pointed Star of David*, and moving clockwise the points on the star stand for *love, life, loyalty, knowledge, wisdom* and *understanding*. The common citizen may mistake the points to stand for something much different, such as blood, violence, mayhem, and so forth, thus the significance of the symbol not only for the gang, but for sociologists. Sociologists frequently examine the symbolic world of culture, attempting to understand the meanings behind symbols, and the ways people relate, interpret, and react to the symbolic life of the group under study. It is possible to understand the six-pointed Star of David in Durkheimian terms, as a source of social solidarity and unity among a very large and diverse criminal organization. The Gangster Disciples have a second set of symbols known as *signing to the right*, allowing them to communicate with each other, as well as a means to identify themselves as members of the Gangster Disciples when in an unfamilar neighborhood or city. Signing to the right includes crossing legs and arms to the right, and wearing a cap tilted to the right.

The GDs have immersed themselves into the fabric of the legitimate social life of Chicago. Over the years they have managed to gain control over public housing projects, were used as monitors in the school system to prevent gang wars, reaped the benefits of a $500,000 government grant known as "Save the Children," and had significant influence in the Illinois correctional system, characterized by intimidation of prison guards by incarcerated GDs. In prison GDs formed alliances with other gangs that spilled over to the outside world, lessening the chances of inter-gang rivalries, especially over drug trafficking.

Gangster Disciples are basically males, however women play important roles in the life of the gang through partnering with male gang members, having their children, and helping with criminal activities such as drug trafficking. It is not clear if women have equal status to that of their male GD counterparts, but what is evident is females are an important element to the overall existence and stability of the gang (National Gang Crime Research Center, 2006).

Criminal v. Non-Criminal Deviance

Before concluding the chapter in honor of Emile Durkheim, brief mention should be made concerning criminal and noncriminal deviance. In this text the focus is on *noncriminal deviance*, although there are times when separating the two categories will be somewhat difficult, and this will occur when discussing theories (Chapters 4 though 8) and in Chapter 10 where physical, emotional and sexual abuse is covered. Many theories addressed in deviance texts are also covered in criminology and criminal justice publications, *and most were developed to explain crime and juvenile delinquency, not specifically deviance.*

Many texts on deviance include chapters on violence, property offenses, and organized and white-collar crime, but only violence and property crimes are covered in this text. Organized and white-collar crime are not addressed specifically, although the last chapter is devoted to coverage of elite and power deviance that on occasion will carry themes close to organized and white-collar criminality. The focus will be on areas of long term study in deviance that are generally *noncriminal* in content, such as mental illness and sexual deviance, and by doing so the goal is not to duplicate criminology and criminal justice texts.

In Recognition: Emile Durkheim

Perhaps the most intriguing figure in the history of sociology is Emile Durkheim (1858–1917), who was versatile in his interests, and in what he published. What is more, he was one of several early sociologists who would advance the young discipline through the use of empirical research, and the development of theory that still has significance today. Durkheim's life spanned a time when sociology was in its earliest stages, but on the move. His life overlapped with that of other great social thinkers such as Karl Marx, Max Weber, Georg Simmel and Herbert Spencer. The nineteenth and early part of the twentieth centuries were a time ripe with the enthusiasm and energy surrounding the development of sociology.

The recognition addressed here is on two grounds: the first is to do as just concluded, and that is to honor Emile Durkheim as a powerful founding figure in sociology; and second to recognize his influence on the field of deviance. In this respect several of his works are of paramount importance. *The Division of Labor in Society* (1956, first published in 1893), *The Rules of Sociological Method* (1950, first published in 1894) and *Suicide: A Study in Sociology* (1951, first published in 1897) all entail contributions to the study of deviance. It is in the first two works Durkheim wrote crime is a normal and inevitable social fact in society, because he viewed crime as a central component of societal evolution, and the development of law and morality (1982:98). His classic work on suicide also has important relevancy to the study of deviance, since Durkheim saw suicide as a social fact, one strongly connected to the extent of social organization and integration in society. Rather than identifying suicide as abnormal, which would relegate it as a psychological phenomenon, Durkheim attempted to understand it in terms of social facts, including marital status, religion and economic conditions (which are discussed in Chapter 9).

Over the years it has become commonplace among sociologists to paraphrase Durkheim and to extend his earlier observation about crime to become "deviance is normal in society." What Durkheim did for the study of both crime and deviance was critical to the establishment of deviance and criminology as subfields in sociology, and the debt to Durkheim cannot be underestimated, neither as a student of crime and deviance, or as a theorist.

SUMMARY

Deviance can and does mean different things to different people, even those who study it professionally. *In this text deviance is defined in terms of differences; differences in behaviors, values, attitudes, life styles and life choices among individuals and groups.* The field of deviance is into its second century, and has come a long way since the time of Durkheim. It is a field with much diversity, and a myriad of studies investigating numerous aspects of social life. But perhaps the most salient issues facing sociologists when they study deviance concerns *how* it is examined, and the need for ethics and objectivity that are required for accurate data collection and its interpretation. It is to these issues and others that we now turn our attention.

Chapter 2

STUDYING DEVIANCE

RESEARCH METHODS IN SOCIOLOGY: AN OVERVIEW

First time students in the study of deviance or sociology may ask "how is it that sociologists know what they know?" "Does their knowledge come from intuition or did it just drop from the sky?" The answer to these questions comes from understanding the methods sociology uses to collect its data. The major research methods in sociology are *field studies, survey research* and *secondary analysis.*

Field Studies

Field studies are known by several names including observation research and ethnographic studies. Regardless of what they are called, field research involves going into a social setting and observing firsthand what is taking place. There are many great examples of field research in sociology and anthropology, with a common thread running across the immersing of the researcher in the environment under study. In order to collect field data social scientists employ various techniques such as taking notes, recording conversations, and videotaping people as they interact. The example of field research

to be discussed in this chapter is that undertaken by Laud Humphreys who in the early 1970s observed men in homosexual relationships in a park in St. Louis, Missouri. Although this study is to be delineated in some detail, suffice it to say here that Humphreys used key tools of the field scientist by relying on his eyes and his note-taking to record the behaviors under study (also note that his methodology was tainted by violation of ethics, to be discussed).

Social scientists who engage in field research must answer important questions before venturing out to do their research. *One question* deals with the issue of anonymity, or whether or not the researcher will be known to those under observation. The answer depends much on what is being studied. If it is deviant criminal lifestyles that are to be observed such as drug users or prostitutes, undertaking the research anonymously may be the best way to go, and there are risks involved in such research, including danger to life. In the 1980s a sociologist from Northern Illinois University was murdered while studying male prostitutes in Miami, Florida. "Snoopers" may be perceived as undercover police and this clearly places them at risk. A *second question* concerns entrance into the social setting, especially when it involves being a known observer who intends to use an insider to gain access to the group or situation under study. This is tricky business since it entails befriending an individual who (because he or she is assisting the researcher) may ultimately be perceived as a traitor to the group or social setting, especially if the observations reveal things that people do not want known to the world. When Howard Becker (1961) undertook his now famous field study of medical students he discovered they and physicians developed derogatory attitudes toward patients, such as calling them "crocks" referring to those people who were in frequent need of medical care. Certainly medical doctors or even aspiring medical students do not want that information about them revealed to the public.

Toward the end of the chapter the three research methods discussed will be compared, but for now understanding field research places social scientists in the midst of those being observed is essential to having a working grasp of what it entails.

Survey Research

Survey research is the way of the sociologist. Like it or not, the successes sociologists have had with the survey method have spilled over to other fields, such as marketing and telemarketing. Through the last half of the twentieth century sociologists were actively involved doing surveys and became the expert survey researchers in the United States, helping to pave the way for other professionals (and perhaps some not so professional) in becoming competent users of the survey method.

Survey data is used widely in the study of deviance. For example, The National Center for Child Abuse and Neglect has undertaken major survey research on child abuse in the United States, and The National Survey on Drug Use and Health (NSDUH) is an annual calibration of the nature and extent of drug and alcohol use in America. The results of both surveys are addressed in their respective chapters, and NSDUH is the example of survey research used in this chapter. Additionally, survey research has been an important way that social scientists and others have learned about the sexual behaviors and attitudes of Americans. Although there are more recent examples (discussed in Chapter 13), the studies undertaken by Alfred Kinsey (1948, 1953) and Shere Hite (1976) stand out as groundbreakers in the study of the sexuality of Americans (Kinsey's research receives brief attention in Chapter 13).

Like any research method, survey research has its limitations and drawbacks. But in order to understand survey research, it is necessary first to address the ways survey research is undertaken. The most effective method is person-to-person survey research, which can yield up to a 70 percent response rate. Next is the telephone survey which has a response rate of about 50 percent, followed by the mail survey technique which on a good day may result in a 30 percent return rate. Obviously, when anywhere from 30 to 70 percent of a sample does not answer survey questions, this poses significant methodological issues. One of these issues is who responds, or better posed who did not respond. If not carefully and scientifically undertaken, groups such as minorities and members of the upper social strata can be easily left out of survey research, and groups such as the elderly and women may be overrepresented, therefore skewing the results; big time. In order to address this issue, professionally undertaken survey research uses sophisticated random sampling statistical techniques, that can reduce error in the estimation of a population to no more than three or four percent. While not perfect, a small percentage of error in sampling is much better than missing the mark by as much as 30 or more percent. When the latter occurs it simply is not possible to generalize any findings to the broader population from which the sample was drawn, bringing one to question the value of the research in the first place.

The old expression "garbage in and garbage out" also applies to the limitations involved with survey research. Poorly designed research instruments basically yield worthless information. Included are bad questions or items that individuals asked to respond to, and that may be vague or just plain irrelevant. One might be surprised as to how many survey instruments have been designed that include items that were not pretested to determine their worthiness, which brings up a point. Well-designed surveys can be of great value and this requires pretesting of items on a population similar to the one that will receive the actual survey. When this occurs the survey instrument can have high credibility and will yield data that can be taken to the bank, meaning the instrument has validity and has the potential of producing reliable results over time (if longitudinal research is undertaken). For our purposes it is important to understand much data in the study of deviance is derived from survey research, and there is so much data out there that has been collected over the years social scientists will never be wanting for the opportunity to crunch numbers, which brings us to the discussion of secondary analysis.

Secondary Analysis

Secondary analysis implies using data collected elsewhere by others. As noted secondary data is available on just about any topic of interest to sociologists, and others. Sources of these data include but are not limited to the Bureau of the Census, The Bureau of Justice Statistics, The National Crime Victimization Survey, The Denver Youth Survey, and the Oklahoma City Survey at the University of Oklahoma. If one desires to analyze data on issues including crime, gender, political opinions, demography, sexuality and sexual orientation, drug and alcohol use and abuse, social mobility, and so forth, it is available for the asking, or in some instances the buying. Much of these data can be downloaded onto a computer, making research quite amenable and easier to undertake. Data from the major survey institutions or organizations are quite valid and reliable largely because they employ professional statisticians and researchers who expend significant time on creating and testing questions and items.

The value of secondary research cannot be underestimated. Earlier it was stated there are mounds of data that can be tested and retested, and so much secondary data have yet to be analyzed. What is more, it is quite common for researchers to test the same data set in ways not done previously, therefore secondary analysis allows for reanalysis and critical evaluation.

The three research methods discussed share both strengths and weaknesses, and can be compared on the basis of *validity, reliability, generalizability* and *depth*, and for our purposes the terms are defined as follows. *Validity* means the researcher studied what he or she set out to analyze. For example, if it is a study of drug and alcohol addiction, the term addiction would need to be defined in ways that can be measured unambiguously (of course other terms would also need to be tightly operationalized). *Reliability* is the test of consistency over time, meaning using the same data set or instrument would produce the same results, from study to study (ceteris paribas). *Generalizability* infers the ability to project the results from a smaller population or sample to larger ones, *depth* means richness of the data, or the quality of the information collected.

Discussed are three examples of the research methods. The examples are a reflection of specific research methods: homosexuality in public places; field research; drug and alcohol use; survey research; and, priests and pedophilia; secondary analysis.

Field Research:
Studying Homosexuality

It was only during the past three decades that homosexual behavior has been studied extensively, although earlier studies (Kinsey 1948, 1953) did examine it with limited samples and public uproar. Perhaps the groundbreaking research on homosexual behavior was undertaken by Laud Humphreys (1970) when he observed homosexual contact between men in parks in St. Louis, Missouri and other cities. Humphreys spent several years during the 1960s undertaking his research which basically involved actually observing men seeking homosexual contact in public bathrooms (called tearooms in the gay subculture). Since significant risks were involved for the men observed, Humphreys acted as a "watchqueen," or a lookout especially wary of the police. Humphreys' explanation for his watchqueen role that was he was a voyeur who gained sexual gratification from watching other men engage in homosexual activity.

Initially Humphreys chose not to identify himself as a researcher, and over time he observed 134 men having sex in public bathrooms, basing his final analysis largely on 100 subjects, due to attrition. He did eventually reveal his research identity to some of the men, and interviewed them extensively. From these interviews Humphreys gathered a significant amount of data, but wanted to get the bigger picture, and proceeded to concoct a method of collecting more information, using *unethical practices*. Humphreys was

able to gain access to the "straight" lives of 50 men he observed by faking to be a health surveyor, going to their homes to interview them. While there he discovered, as he did with the other men to whom he revealed his research identity, many of the men were married with children, and were not necessarily gay, instead they enjoyed the nature of the anonymous sex they had with other men.

To gain access to the residences of the 50 males Humphreys recorded their license plates numbers and tracked them down through the departments of motor vehicles. In this respect he used deception to the nth degree, which would become a major criticism of his research. It should be noted that while undertaking the research, Humphreys was a doctoral student at Washington University in St. Louis, and because of the severe concerns registered by faculty in the Department of Sociology over his lack of ethics, he was not allowed to complete his Ph.D. A member of the Department of Sociology assaulted Humphreys upon learning about his research, especially how it was conducted. In addition, Humphreys was an ordained Episcopalian minister, married with children, who "came out of the closets" in the 1970s which also raised concerns, not only about his ethics, but also his motives and objectivity. Humphreys was able to publish based on his field research and his interest in and involvement as a homosexual. Two books now considered classics in the study of homosexual behavior are *Tearoom Trade: Impersonal Sex in Public Places* (1970) and *Out of the Closets: The Sociology of Homosexual Liberation* (1972).

Laud Humphreys can be both commended and despised for his research. On the one hand, Humphreys attempted to scientifically unravel and understand the world of male homosexual behavior, a world largely ignored previously. In this respect, Humphreys research was groundbreaking and led the way for greater discourse about gay and lesbian issues, as well as study of them. On the other hand, there is the concern for ethics. Humphreys used deception (the bogus health survey), and by acting as a lookout clearly placed his subjects and himself at risk of being arrested and harassed by the police. It should also be noted it was the 1960s when Humphreys was in the field, a time in American society when there existed far more hostility and less tolerance toward homosexuals than exist today, not to mention the study of homosexuality was several years away from being acceptable to professional sociologists.

Survey Research: Studying Drug and Alcohol Abuse

Each year a major survey of drug use in the United States is undertaken by the Substance Abuse and Mental Health Services Administration (SAMHSA) and is known as the National Survey on Drug Use and Health (NSDUH) (formerly The National Household Survey on Drug Use). Typically 65,000–70,000 Americans, 12 years of age and older are interviewed in person, and the sampling design is complex, known as *multistage area sampling* (MSAS), where the sampling process begins with larger units and is narrowed down to smaller, more refined segments of the American population. MSAS accounts for differences in population sizes of the 50 states by use of *statistical weighting adjustment techniques*, and over sampling of some cohorts by age is undertaken to reach a representative sample. The random sampling of the American population results in small error (around 3%), assuring data from the sample can be generalized to the total population (please keep in mind the 65,000–75,000, 12 years of age and older individuals sampled are intended to be representative of the millions of people in those ages).

It would be an exercise in futility if the sampling processes resulted in a biased or not representative picture of drug use in the United States. Thus, the first step in the research is to make sure the selection of respondents is accurate, then it is time to undertake the actual in-person interviews at the residences of those selected through the sampling process. The data collection method involves the use of computers by the interviewers and respondents referred to as *computer assisted interviewing* (CAI) where the subjects take questions directly from the interviewers, and *audio computer-assisted self-interviewing* (ACASI) in which respondents answer part of the survey by themselves in the presence of the interviewer. To assure confidentiality, the names of respondents are not recorded, with each interview lasting one hour, and all respondents are paid $30.00 for participating. It is to be noted the interviewers do not just show up at the doorsteps of respondents, unannounced and ready to go. Letters of introduction are mailed in advance, and before the actual interviews begin, the interviewer spends several minutes discussing the procedures with respondents.

The survey instrument is lengthy and detailed, too developed to identify fully in this discussion, but as an overview the questions on the instrument include, but are not limited to demographic-identifier items (age, race, gender, location, etc.), and focus on the percentage of respondents who have *used drugs in the month prior to the interview*. The questions inquire into the types of illicit drugs used (i.e., marijuana, cocaine, inhalants); nonmedical use of prescription drugs (i.e., pain relievers, stimulants, sedatives); alcohol use, broken down to include any use-binge drinking and heavy use; use of tobacco; age-initiation of drug use; perceived risk of drug use; substance dependence, abuse and treatment by types of drugs; and, mental health items, including questions about depression, and serious psychological distress related to substance abuse. The final report presents a comprehensive picture of prevalence and frequency of drug use and abuse, and the results are detailed in Chapter 11.

Secondary Analysis: Priests and Pedophilia

In recent years the most embarrassing and shocking news relative to religion in America has been the issue of Roman Catholic priests and pedophilia. When victims of priestly pedophilia began to emerge in numbers during the late 1990s, concern for a full accounting of this tragedy was voiced by many Americans and Roman Catholics. In light of the ever-increasing accounts of child molestation by priests, the Roman Catholic Church agreed to conduct a major study, the goal of which was to get to the bottom of the nature and extent of priests and pedophilia in the country. Accordingly, in June 2002 at the general meeting of the Catholic Bishops of the United States, the "John Jay College of Criminal Justice of the City University of New York" was commissioned to study the problem. The report, popularly called "The National Review Board Study" was released in spring 2004, and it is to the *research design* that this discussion is directed (for discussion of the results please consult the actual report).

Immediately, the research team was faced with difficult questions and decisions, and. one such obvious question was how to undertake the research. Given the fact extremely sensitive issues were to be examined, it was apparent from the beginning that to ask victims or priests about their experiences with pedophilia would place many of them at significant psychological and emotional risks. Another difficulty was the issue of subject selection and just how to go about it given the years singled out for study

(1950–2002), and the strong likelihood that a number of priests may be deceased or have left the priesthood. Add to this the challenges involved with identifying and getting victims to respond, the John Jay team chose a different research route: *church files.* No one was interviewed. One-hundred percent of the findings came from files stored by the various Roman Catholic entities under analysis (dioceses and religious order).

A major decision .also concerned the breadth and depth of the scope of the study. The Catholic Bishops directed the John Jay team to study dioceses and many religious orders in the United States. Initially, some Bishops were opposed to such scrutiny, but eventually John Jay was able to proceed with a research design that entailed the examination of files from across the country. However, another question needed to be resolved and involved who would read the files. The decision was made by the Bishops to appoint one person from each diocese to read the files and to record data from them. In order to achieve this, the John Jay team developed *three separate research/survey- type instruments* to guide the assigned recorders through the process. The first instrument was structured to inquire into the *big picture* as it related to a particular diocese or religious order, meaning getting a count on *all known* incidences of pedophilia existing in the files from 1950–2002, and two other instruments were used to gather a diversity of information on the accused *priests, and the victims.* Included on the *priest survey* were items such as when the priest was ordained, his total number of victims, his age when he first molested a child, if the priest had been molested as a child, and the actions the Church took to deal with the claims of abuse. The *victim survey* included questions about age when first victimized, the gender of the victim, where the alleged abuse occurred and the actions taken by the Church on behalf of the victim. Of course, all three surveys included a number of other items and are included in the appendix of the report on data. The recorders canvassed the files and completed the instruments based on what was available in them, discovering missing or incomplete data for a number of items on all three instruments from across the United States. For example, of the 4,311 priests the files associated with pedophilia, there were data on only 178 who had been sexually assaulted as children themselves.

To assure confidentiality the completed survey instruments were sent to an auditing firm prior to being received by the John Jay team. The auditing firm took great measures to protect the confidentiality of the data by removing any indication which diocese or religious order had completed the instruments. A special coding procedure was implemented that hid the true identity of the respondents (diocese or religious order) and the instruments were mailed to John Jay College for analysis.

Although the case of The National Review Board Study is not your typical example of secondary analysis, it does describe the concerns and procedures that are involved with this type of research, which is quite important in a study that entails the lives of people as victims and perpetrators.

CASE STUDY: DONNIE BRASCO

On occasion this book will use examples that are not necessarily the direct product of sociological research, but are used to illustrate points concerning deviance, as well as to make comparisons with how social scientists undertake data collection to the ways other professionals gather information. Thus is the case with this discussion of Federal Bureau of Investigation (F.B.I.). Special Agent Joseph D. Pistone, who for six years went undercover to investigate the world of Italian organized crime, using the alias Donnie Brasco (Pistone and Woodley, 1987). From 1976–1981, Pistone infiltrated one of America's most notorious mafia families, the Joseph Bonanno crime family. By doing so he placed himself in harms way and became the first F.B.I. agent to undertake long-term undercover work (long-term was considered six months at the time Pistone went undercover). Pistone cleverly adopted the name Donnie Brasco, the name of the high school he attended years earlier while living in Pennsylvania. The undercover life Pistone led is detailed in *Donnie Brasco: My Undercover Life in the Mafia*, but is not repeated here with nearly the depth. What is covered are examples of his investigation that are used to highlight and to compare what he did (and *how* he did it) with that of field research.

Pistone's successful entry into the Bonanno family was greatly enhanced by growing up in neighborhoods where there were elements of organized crime, as well as his recognized and respected intelligence. Pistone was a tough customer who knew about and understood the ways of Mafioso, which enhanced his ability to go undercover and to deceive members of the Bonnano crime family. Initially Pistone (Brasco) frequented bars and restaurants in Manhattan, New York and gradually came to know members of organized crime, posing as a wise guy from out-of-town (1987, 36–37). Of course, Pistone's main job was to gather intelligence on mobsters that would be used to prosecute them, therefore he had to be shrewd and careful about how he gained access to and develop the trust of members of the Bonnano family. At stake was not only the most serious investigation of organized crime ever attempted by the F.B.I., but also his life. To become careless would destroy the investigation and result in the death of Pistone. To protect himself and the investigation, Pistone never wrote down notes, but relayed intelligence back to the Bureau by telephone and secretive meetings with other agents (1987, 38). During the six years Pistone discovered significant information on the Bonnano crime operations, in particular drug trafficking. In order to do this he was successful in partnering with Benjamin "Lefty Guns" Ruggiero an integral player in the Bonnano crime machine (1987, 124). Pistone spent numerous hours with Ruggiero and other mobsters learning in detail about their criminal activities. One way Pistone avoided blowing his undercover identity was occasionally moving about to other cities, usually under the alibi he had work to do with mobsters in those locations. When the heat was on, Pistone would conveniently disappear, and in the end, fearing that a contract might be out on his life, the F.B.I. decided it was time to curtail the undercover operation. Toward the conclusion of his undercover work it was rumored that Pistone had a contract on another Mafioso, and this too quickened the pace at which his undercover investigation was concluded. The results of his work are astounding, resulting in hundreds of indictments, and over 100 convictions. In addition, some members of the Bonnano family met with death, and "Lefty" Ruggiero was sentenced to 20 years incarceration (1987, 383).

Joseph Pistone was involved in a different type of "field research" and "data collection." The objective was to use the information he collected *against* those he observed. This is a much different strategy and philosophy than adopted by social scientists. When the latter take to the field, it is their highest obligation to remain objective and detached, and never to use the data against those observed, or to engage in deceit (even Pistone himself stated that it was difficult not

to develop a relationship with those he betrayed). If social scientists observe crime or deviance, they are placed in a very precarious situation, and it is a matter of ethics as to what they do with information, especially criminal activity. Put simply, Pistone's task was to break up a group, and to do significant legal harm to its members. By comparison, the charge to social scientists is to understand and to build knowledge about a group or social setting, *without intentionally disrupting or destroying it, or its participants.*

The Weberian Dichotomy: Value Relevance v. Value Neutrality

Max Weber's discussion of *value neutrality v. value relevance* has significance for the study of deviance (Shils and Finch, 1949). What social scientists decide to study may emanate from their personal interests and backgrounds, a notion Weber referred to as *value neutrality.* In sociology it is quite common for African American sociologists to devote most of their research to African American issues and problems, as it is also common for female sociologists to undertake research on topics that are predominately about women. The question then concerns objectivity, and can be framed: "is it possible to study social issues or groups and to be a member of or part of the very thing we are studying?" Weber's answer to this lies in *value relevance,* a term he used to denote the need for social scientists to be guided by the ethos and standards of science when involved in studying the social world. In other words, for Weber it mattered less if one is motivated to research some aspect of social reality for which he or she has direct involvement and interest, than it is for social scientists to be able to separate their personal lives and experiences from how they go about researching and evaluating both. In the final analysis it is paramount that sociologists interpret data with the highest standards of objectivity and science, even if what they discover runs counter to their personal interests and concerns (and perhaps even wanted to find out). Enter Laud Humphreys. Humphreys has been widely criticized for his lack of ethics, and questions could also be raised about his objectivity, since years after the publication of *Tearoom Trade* Humphreys became active in the gay liberation movement, leaving one to question if he was objective when undertaking his research. A question is "was Humphreys cognizant of and serious about the Weberian duality, or did he draw his conclusions based on his own homosexuality, especially since he not only was active in the Gay Liberation Movement, but was passionate about it?" Social scientists, regardless of their sensitivity and relationship to issues, must remove their emotional attachments to whom and what they study, in order to derive unbiased and uncontaminated interpretations of data.

In Recognition: Laud Humphreys

Hindsight is always 20/20 and it is quite easy to criticize the works of others, but Laud Humphreys' field research must be understood in the context of time and intolerance. The 1960s represented a hodgepodge of political, social and philosophical attitudes and ideals, often stereotyped as "the Age of Aquarius," manifested by liberalism and social change. Yet that era was still in close juxtaposition to the 1950s which was arguably more conservative. During the 1960s there were social changes and events that would lead one to believe, to sound like Bob Dylan "the times they were a changing" which they were. There were riots and demonstrations, the growing popularity of marijuana and hallucinogenic drugs, and there was the so called "new morality." But amidst all these events there was still intolerance toward some social issues such as

homosexuality. It would not be until the 1980s that "coming out" became a choice for many gay Americans (although some had done so earlier) and it was still feared by gays that being openly homosexual could result in physical injuries (gay bashing) and discrimination in searches for employment. It is in this context that *Tearoom Trade* must be understood. To undertake research on homosexuality 40 years ago was considered in-and-of-itself unnecessary and offensive to the scientific community, not to mention that homosexuality was looked down upon by the majority of the general public. Add to this the fact that Laud Humphreys undertook field research that involved observing male homosexual behavior, and there existed a recipe for professional and personal disaster. Humphreys placed himself in great jeopardy as a doctoral student, citizen (possible police harassment and arrest) and future professional. It has already been noted that Humphreys was not allowed to continue his doctoral studies at Washington University in St. Louis, and that he was physically assaulted by a tenured faculty member because of his lack of ethics, as well as the disgust that particular professor felt over what he studied, and how he did it. The point is that 40 years ago studying homosexuality was still largely unacceptable using any methodology, and what we knew about it was derived largely from psychiatry and bigotry. Laud Humphreys took a major step in the direction of validating study of the gay lifestyle, opening the door for future research. Today, in sociology there is "Queer Sociology" or "Queer Theory Sociology," which at first glance may not sound at all flattering, but is a segment of sociology dedicated to greater understanding of homosexuality. There is no question about it, Laud Humphreys gave us two looks: one involved his lack of ethics, yet the other involved his groundbreaking and door opening research. On both fronts his research is not to be forgotten or overlooked.

Humphreys' professional career included faculty positions at Southern Illinois University in Carbondale, Illinois and Pitzer College in Southern California. Humphreys' challenges to the establishment were not restricted to his strong gay rights philosophies and activism, but also included participation in anti-Viet Nam War, rallies and the destruction of a picture of President Richard M. Nixon that was hanging in the draft board office in Carbondale, for which he served three months of a one-year prison sentence. Later in his life Humphreys' turned to counseling, and ironically consulted with police departments relative to gay and lesbian due process issues.

SUMMARY

Studying deviance is no simple task, and requires a professional grasp of research methodology, and it also demands objectivity. This latter point cannot be stressed enough. Whether it is survey research, field research, or secondary analysis, it is of paramount importance that in the final analysis what is reported is done so in a way that reflects *impartiality* and *detachment*. This is not easily accomplished since social scientists are also human beings with feelings, values, personal experiences and philosophies. But the call is still for truthful scientific discovery, or as Weber wrote, value neutrality.

Section 2

THEORIES

Chapter 3

AN OVERVIEW OF AND INTRODUCTION TO SOCIOLOGICAL THEORIES OF DEVIANCE

OVERVIEW

This chapter will outline *sociological theories* of deviance. Many texts cover theories from other disciplines, such as biological and psychological/psychiatric theories of deviant behavior. It is the aim of this text to focus on the *major sociological theories* of deviance that have been developed since the time of Durkheim. By no means will this be an exhaustive coverage of these theories, instead the leading and most popular theories are to be addressed. Before overviewing different categories of deviance theories, a brief discussion of sociology and sociologists is presented.

WHAT IS SOCIOLOGY AND WHO ARE SOCIOLOGISTS?

Many people have taken at least one sociology course, usually in college, and a fair number walk away from the course asking a rather pertinent question "what good is sociology, and what the heck does one do with a degree or degrees in the field?" One way to approach this two-part question is to suc-

cinctly discuss what sociology is and then to address the "who" aspect. Sociology dates back to the mid-nineteenth century with origins in England, France and Germany (there are scholars who date sociology's founding to much earlier, such as Alvin Gouldner's 1965 classic book *Enter Plato: Classical Greece and the Origins of Social Theory*). Since this is not an introductory course in sociology the readers will be spared names and dates of early works and authors in the discipline. For our purposes sociology was a product of the times, and an outgrowth of other intellectual endeavors including economics, history and philosophy. As for the times, the nineteenth century in Europe represented a period of great and gradual social evolution, with the ever-present influence of industrialization and urbanization. Both of these major processes were changing the landscape of agrarian-based Europe and led to questions about how they were affecting social life. Early sociologists were concerned about the transition from simple social life centered around farming, to the more complex existence found in cities. Among other issues, the founding figures in sociology asked questions about crime, the nature of law in changing societies, and the types of organizations that would emerge in urbanized and industrialized social milieus. Some even went as far as asking about who was best suited to survive major social changes, a Darwinian style approach to analyzing society and social organizations. In a major way the earliest sociology was concerned with social change, and sought to develop theories that would explain it. As time went on and sociology aged, the discipline underwent significant alterations and today it is comprised of many subfields. The subfields include but are not limited to: gender; social inequality; crime and delinquency; family; demography; social problems; race and ethnicity; religion; education; the polity; government; sport; urban sociology; and, of course, deviance. The "rigorous" areas are typically considered to be statistics and research methods, and the diversity found in sociology has a little of something in it for different people, which leads us to a brief discussion of the "who."

It is a truism to say that sociologists are not among the most highly paid professionals, and it is equally accurate to write they are among the most passionate about their discipline. "Getting hooked" on sociology is quite common for students from all backgrounds and talent levels, normally occurring in the undergraduate years, and probably without premeditation. A number of sociologists stumbled into the field, meaning they were introduced to it in an introductory or elective course that really caught their attention, and the rest is history, or should it be said, sociology. Today sociology is a discipline comprised of African Americans, Hispanics, Asians, whites, and a growing number of women, after many years of being dominated by males. The demographic make-up of the field started to undergo significant changes during the 1980s, and today American sociology is a reflection of the broader culture, with diversity the name of the game as evidenced across sociology

departments in the United States. For sociology this means empowerment. Contemporary sociological research is rich with information engendered by people from all walks of life, which has greatly enhanced the quality of findings reported by sociologists. It was not that long ago the majority of sociological data was collected and analyzed by white males, but today the world of sociology has been broadened to include the perspectives of a multitude of experiences and backgrounds. Sociology is a discipline on the move, as well as one that requires future professionals in the field to have strong skills in mathematics and the sciences. It is not, and has never really been a field of study for those seeking refuge from   rigorous and demanding subject matters.

THE BIRTH OF THE STUDY OF DEVIANCE

In Chapter 1, the emergence of the subfield of deviance was stated to be a product of the works of French sociologist Emile Durkheim. Although Durkheim wrote over 100 years ago, it was not until the 1960s that courses in deviance started to become common in sociology departments, and those courses were quite different than what passes today as the study of deviant behavior. Earlier courses in deviance were heavily focused on crime, mental illness, suicide, alcohol abuse and sexual deviance, usually minus the study of homosexuality. Contemporary classes in deviance include a broader and more expanded number of topics, with perhaps the area of sexual deviance the one that has undergone the greatest transformation. Until the 1970s coverage of sexual orientation, incest, and pedophilia were uncommon in deviance classes. Today they are an integral part of such courses, as is the study of drug abuse (earlier courses had less broad coverage of drug abuse), disabilities, and violence.

One other area that has seen significant change is *theories of deviance*. During the last 25 years a number of new theories have been developed and some are addressed in this book. A word of caution is offered here: *many theories of deviant behavior are the same theories covered in criminology and criminal justice courses and texts*. It is difficult not to duplicate these theories in a course in deviance, and it is also a challenge to adapt them to topics or examples for which these theories were not originally intended or tested. Although an intent of this book is not to duplicate criminology courses or texts, the presentation of theories is one area where there is repetition. It is also noted theoretical development in deviance has largely taken the form of *integrated theory*, or the inclusion of previous theories into a new one. Many theories of deviance are like an old-fashioned recipe where one adds a little of this and a little of that arrive at something different. This should be quite evident as theories of deviance are covered in the text.

Theoretical Categories: Classifying and Categorizing Theories of Deviance

There is *no one theory* of deviance, and there are *many types* of theories of deviance. What is more, from author to author, book to book, and in the academic journals, the classification of theories of deviance is quite diverse, and even within a type of theory there can be significant variations in theoretical scope, and no where is this more true than conflict theories. In this text, six ways of classifying deviance theories are presented: anomie and structural theories; anomie and structural theories extended: strain theories; control theories; societal reaction and other social processes theories; and conflict and

feminist theories. A brief explanation of each conceptualization is now presented, and far more detail follows in the next six chapters.

Anomie and Structural Theories

Anomie and structural theories of deviance are traced to the works of Emile Durkeim, and explain deviance as a result of social breakdown and social change, or *strains* in the social fabric of groups. More specifically, these theories hold deviant behavior is likely to occur when the social cohesion or solidarity in society is threatened or diminished, and when individuals are blocked from achieving societal goals through legitimate means. These are early *strain theories*, meaning deviance is viewed as resulting from strains in groups or in the social structure of cultures. An analogy may help. We have all experienced *personal strain*, and at times this may have led to involvement with deviance, such as the decision to abuse alcohol and drugs, or even to contemplate suicide. Now, extending this analogy beyond the unit of the individual, anomie and structural theories locate the etiology of deviance within the inner workings of society, and in this respect the first anomie and structural theories were *macro sociological* explanations of deviance and criminality.

Anomie and Structural Theories of Deviance Extended

More recent anomie and structural theories of deviance are an extension of those developed at the turn of the twentieth century, and explain deviance in terms of adaptations to society, and multiple forms of *strain* that may lead individuals to commit crimes and acts of deviance. Emphasized less in these theories is the role of social cohesion as a cause of deviance, and gaining greater recognition are social psychological principles as correlates of nonconformity, including the inability to achieve desired goals, and personal issues such as the death of a loved one, or the break-up of a romantic relationship. The most recent strain explanations are *micro sociological* in nature, representing a break with traditional theorizing about deviant behavior.

Control Theories

Control theories also date back some years, and trace deviance and criminality to improper socialization at early ages. Control theories begin with the assumption human beings need to be constrained (controlled) because of their orientation toward self-preservation, and that within society there are various forms of control that emerge to keep us all in line. However, at times these mechanisms of control fail or are inadequately applied to individuals, resulting in deviant and even criminal behavior. Bonding to the social order plays big into the picture of social control theories, typically assuming the form of identifying the bonds to society that are critical to conformity.

Societal Reaction and Other Social Processes Theories

Of all theories addressed in deviance texts and courses, labeling theory, a societal reaction theory, is among the most popular, controversial, and scientifically questionable. Yet given its faults, labeling theory remains a topic of considerable discussion in deviance. Social reaction theories, such as labeling theory emanate from symbolic interactionism (a major theoretical perspective in sociology) and place emphasis on *definitional issues* involved in the *construction of deviance designations*, and the *interactions* that occur among

deviants, and the *meanings* actors attach to behaviors and events. These types of theories examine the impact of labels on deviance and how deviance and criminality are learned. Fairly recent to this tradition is shaming and restorative justice that approach deviance and crime differently than the labeling perspective. A major assumption of shaming theory is deviant individuals will begin to conform when shamed in ways that do not further marginalize and alienate them from society. Informal shaming and restorative processes are advocated, strategies that get the message across to deviants, while at the same time acting to reintegrate them into the social mainstream.

Social processes theories also include theories about learning deviant behavior that are applicable to a variety of deviant behaviors, such as white-collar crime, drug and alcohol use, and disabilities.

Conflict Theories and Feminist Theories

Conflict theories are perhaps the most diverse of the theoretical categories or "schools" in deviance and in criminology, and therefore it can be said *there is no one type* of conflict theory. The conflict approach owes its origins to the eighteenth century philosopher Karl Marx, who argued private ownership of property was the root cause of social and economic inequality, and the myriad of injustices that emerged from them, such as crime, sexism, and poverty. The conflict tradition is concerned with the nature of relationships between people, and how the human condition is shaped by the economic mode of production. In Marx's scheme of things capitalism creates great rifts in society, benefitting those few who own and control the means of production, while greatly disenfranchising and dehumanizing the remainder of the population. It is from this thinking numerous conflict theories have emerged, with their seminal commonality the tie to Karl Marx. Depending on the style of conflict theory, conflict itself can be viewed as a means to progressive social change, or can take the form of advocating hostile revolution to achieve social and economic injustice.

Feminist theories examine and explain deviance from the perspectives of women, and may not approach it using the same data collection and statistical analysis techniques commonly found in academic journals. Feminists take the position *gender is the central organizing principle in societies*, a point they argue has been ignored by sociologists until recently. Similar to the conflict approach, there is *no one feminist theory* of deviance or crime, instead there are feminist *theories*.

CASE STUDY: THE KIBBUTZ

The Kibbutz is a communal system that dots the plains of Israel, and like many other communes throughout history, the Kibbuzt distinguishes and separates itself from the dominant society. A major philosophical underpinning of the Kibbutz system is *equalitarianism*, which is the belief in gender equality that plays itself out in all areas of Kibbutz living, including positions of power and leadership in the communes. Men and women see themselves as equals, a development that starts very early in life, and in order to engender sex role equality, children are reared away from their parents for a good portion of every week, returning to them in the evenings and on weekends. The idea is to socialize boys and girls from young ages by learning, playing, and sleeping together with the goal of instilling in children a lifelong belief in and support of equalitarianism.

Many Kibbutzi are economically independent and successful with agriculture as the hallmark of the Kibbutzi way of life. Men and women share equally in the farming enterprise, performing tasks such as driving tractors and repairing equipment and motor vehicles. In addition, women and men perform leadership roles as managers and financial officers, all of which is augmented by a deep belief in education. The children of the Kibbutz are among the most educated in western nations, receiving rigorous elementary and secondary school educations, and many matriculate to colleges and universities, returning to the Kibbutz upon completing postsecondary education. While in college young adults major in fields such as agronomy, education, business administration and the sciences, and some further their education by receiving graduate degrees and attending medical college.

The Kibbutz way of life is not without its issues. At times men and women have a difficult time practicing equalitarianism (especially men) and child-rearing becomes problematic to the point that some families leave the Kibbutz altogether. What is more, the acquisition of individual wealth and material goods is downplayed in the communes, and this too becomes a reason for attrition. But what remains of great interest to sociologists and other scholars is the Kibbutz system is rare among social experiments, since it has been able to maintain a strong emphasis on sex role equality in a world that often pays little more than lip service to it.

In Recognition: Talcott Parsons

At first glance, to recognize Talcott Parsons in a deviance book may seem somewhat out of context, and given the scholars who are typically covered in deviance courses, a discussion of Parsons is quite unusual. But Talcott Parsons remains a central figure in American sociology, and is the case elsewhere in this book, other important scholars, some of whom are not sociologists will be recognized for their contributions to knowledge in general. What is more, Parsons did exact a *major indirect influence* on deviance theory, discussed shortly.

Parsons' contributions to the development of sociology cannot be underestimated. The central focus of his work is on social action which he attempted to unravel and to explain within the context of the broader social system. Unlike other early twentieth century American sociologists such as Charles Horton Cooley and George Herbert Mead, who made interaction in-and-of-itself the purview of their interests, Parsons work involved very detailed and complex assumptions about human action, which he sought to use as building blocks for understanding the social whole. Parsons had a number of important publications, with two of the most noted *The Structure of Social Action* (1937) and *The Social System* published in 1951. The intention is not to cover in detail these two complicated and prestigious works, but it is important to note in *Structure of Social Action* Parsons sought to unravel the essence of human actions in terms of their origins and sources of motivation. *The Social System* built upon this by connecting action to the level of systems, a task Parsons felt was important to understanding the building blocks of societies, and what makes them work.

Two of Parsons' most cited ideas are found in *The Social System*, and are briefly explained. The *pattern variables* were created by Parsons as a scheme to explain and to classify human action, and his concept of *the social system* is conceived of as a system involving individuals seeking optimal gratification from interaction situations. Parsons' focus on systems and the interaction occurring within them is known as *structural functionalism*, or the tendency of social organisms to be stable and orderly.

Talcott Parsons had an indirect but important influence on the study of deviance through one of his prized students at Harvard University, Robert K. Merton. *Social Structure and Anomie* (1938) by Merton is a reflection of the professor-student relationship, in that it outlined five modes of adaptation available to *human actors* in societies (detailed in the next chapter). Although the "master" Talcott Parsons did not himself develop a theory of deviance, his contribution to the intellectual development of Robert K. Merton is duly noted.

SUMMARY

There are many theories of deviance, and a number of paradigms used to group or to categorize them. This book presents its own typology of deviance theories, both different from while similar to how other deviance texts order and structure them. What is important is sociologists develop and apply theory to explain deviant behavior, rather than assuming a shotgun approach, without any attempt at formally explaining deviance in a logical and consistent manner. The next six chapters are devoted to greater coverage of leading theories of deviance.

Chapter 4

ANOMIE AND STRUCTURAL THEORIES

CASE STUDY: THE 1960s

The Beatles; the assassination of an American president; race riots; antiwar demonstrations; the feminist movement; the gray power movement; the environmental movement; the assassination of a civil rights leader; the gay power movement; the assassination of a presidential candidate; sending federal troops to major southern universities to guarantee African Americans could enter them without harm; the murder of civil rights protestors; the age of Aquarius; the New Frontier and the Great Society, and the list goes on and on. The 1960s represented an era of massive social change; of what Alvin Toufler called future shock. The decade began somewhat slowly and ended 180 degrees opposite. Initially it was an era of enormous promise; the election of a young and dynamic president whose youthfulness, beautiful wife and little children added energy to a White House that had seemingly aged so much during the 1950s. There was the promise of a moon landing before the end of the decade made at a time when the United States could barely get a rocket launched without exploding in mid-air, and there was the captivating race between two New York Yankees to see who would be the first baseball player to go over

the top in what was the most revered sports record in the United States, if not the world. Slowly the promise began to disappear. There was the embarrassment of the failed Bay of Pigs invasion in spring 1961 followed by the frightening Cuban Missile Crisis in October 1962. For 13 days the world was on edge as the United States and the former Soviet Union stood toe-to-toe in a drama never before seen or experienced since. Nuclear confrontation was more than possible, and backing down was not an option for either side. Saving face was, and eventually brought both nations' leadership to their senses, ending, at least publicly the threat of destroying the planet. Approximately one year later the world was once again put on edge as President John F. Kennedy was assassinated in Dallas, Texas on November 22, 1963. What would follow after that would forever paint the 1960s as a generation lost in itself as racial disturbances marred city after city resulting in billions of dollars of losses, not to mention violence and historically unmatched manifestations of hatred and alienation. By 1967 the war in Viet Nam began to look unwinnable to some Americans, especially to its youth, and peaceful and unpeaceful anti-war demonstrations, marches and riots occurred across America, assuming one of its worse forms at the 1968 Democratic Convention in Chicago, Illinois when police officers and anti-war protestors clashed, with physical injuries to both, and a deepening sense that the young and the old had built insurmountable bridges between them. For many Americans, the United States was falling apart at the seams. It's stability, predictability, and stoic identity seemed to have gone down the drain, as dearly-held values, traditions, and patriotism were questioned, doubted and rejected. Enter anomie. Anomie is the term introduced by Emile Durkheim that can be used to explain situations such as the 1960s. Anomie means normlessness, or a condition in society when the established norms, rules and ways of life are in dynamic fluctuation and appear to have lost their hold on and importance to people. This was how so many Americans saw and now see the 1960s, as a time when "do your own thing" replaced "ask not what your country can do for you, but what you can do for your country" (Inaugural Address, President John F. Kennedy, January 1961). By 1968 the United States was ravaged by internal disruptions and a very unpopular war. To make matters worse, in April and June, 1968, Civil Rights Leader Martin Luther King and presidential candidate Senator Robert F. Kennedy were murdered, and Americans once again were placed into shock and dismay. The questions became "who are we?"; "what have we become?"; and, "where are we headed?" It appeared momentarily that anomie had replaced the hopes, promises and caring for others that had marked the beginning of the decade.

Emile Durkheim and Deviance

Emile Durkheim set the stage for what eventually would become the field of deviance in sociology. In *Division of Labor in Society* (1893), *The Rules of Sociological Method* Durkheim (1894), and *Suicide* (1897) Durk-

heim addressed the ubitiqous nature of crime in society, and analyzed homicide and self-destruction using theoretical and methodological frameworks that would become trademarks for sociological research. In his classic work *Division of Labor in Society* Durkheim introduced the term *anomie*, which means normlessness, a concept that is as famous to sociology as the notion of id is in psychology. Durkheim argued that deviance can result when the norms and rules of society become less clear and ambiguous resulting in the weakened regulation of human conduct. In this respect the term anomie took on wide applicability applying not only to instances of criminality but also to suicide, which Durkheim argued was associated with the degree of social cohesion within a group. The topic of suicide is addressed in chapter 9 as is Durkheim's theory of suicide, but here it is important to note that Durkheim theorized about the role of *the social* in the decision of individuals to take their own lives.

The concept anomie is the pivotal notion from the works of Durkheim that is of paramount importance in *theories* of deviance. Contemporary leading deviance theories are a take-off from Durkheim's anomie, and what Durkheim offered as anomie's explanation for crime and deviance is important in itself. To comprehend this last statement one must grasp Durkheim's sociology which is *structural* in nature, meaning Durkheim was the quintessential early sociologist who looked at the role of society and its relationship to behavior. Critical to this idea are his notions of solidarity, especially *mechanical* and *organic solidarity, the types of law associated with the two types of solidarity,* and *social cohesion.* In *Division of Labor in Society*, one of his two doctoral dissertations (the other is *The Rules of Sociological Method*), Durkheim identified two types of social solidarity that characterize societies at different stages of their evolution or development, and their corresponding legal structures. By *mechanical solidarity* Durkheim meant societies that were less developed and more agrarian in social and economic structure. Societies characterized by mechanical solidarity are a far cry from what so many of us today have experienced; they are simple, homogenous in origin, meaning people are intensely alike morally, religiously and socially, and *repressive law* is used as the means for regulating social conduct. *Repressive law* can be thought of as the law of crimes, based on notions of punishment employed to maintain social order and obedience, with a powerful presence of the collective conscience. Mechanical solidarity is solidarity based on the similarities among individuals with the "glue" or *social cohesion* based on strong homogeneity (*Division Of Labor in Society*, 1893). On the other hand, *organic solidarity* exists when societies become more heterogeneous or diverse, and is based on the law of contracts, or *restitutive law.* Here social solidarity draws its strength from the differences among individuals, with social order and stability derived from the contractual obligations among people. *Social cohesion* develops from the strength of ties among people that are commanded and regulated by law, and the influence of collective conscience is less pronounced. For many of us this is the type of social organization we have grown up with and understand.

Durkheim's theorizing about crime and deviance emanate directly from that just discussed, since both are viewed by him as violations of the two types of law, and the relationship of crime and deviance to social cohesion and social solidarity. On this latter note, Durkheim observed that crime and deviance are intricately interwoven with the degree of belongingness the individual has to the group; if the degree of belongingness (cohesion or solidarity) is strong such as that found with mechanical solidarity then the likelihood of deviance and crime is reduced; if it is weak there is an increased risk of crime and deviant behavior. Durkheim connected this to "division of labor" in which he wrote that the transition from mechanical to organic solidarity was anything but smooth. The division of labor in advancing societies is likely to be associated with abnormal social behavior, as a result of the weakened collective conscience and moral consensus that evolves from the transition from more "tight" social organizations to organizations that experience greater diversity and diffuseness. This brings us full circle to *anomie.* Anomie is a condition associated with this transition from the simple to the more complex; from a condition where repressive law and punishment kept people in line to situations where the law of contracts had less total influence and control over human conduct, thus opening the door for increases in individuality. Stated more simply, bigger isn't necessarily better. However, it is important here to restate Durkheim's now famous exclamation about crime in society and that is ". . . crime is normal because a society exempt from it is utterly impossible. Crime, as we have shown elsewhere, consists of an act that offends very strong collective sentiments. In a society in which criminal acts are no longer committed, the sentiments they offend would have to be found without exception in all individual consciousness, and they must be found to exist with the same degree as sentiments contrary to them. Assuming that this condition could actually be realized, crime would therefore not disappear; it would only change its form, for the very cause which would thus dry up the sources of criminality would immediately open up new ones" (1893, 67). Durkheim's insistence on the "normality" of crime in society goes one step further in what is perhaps the most recognized commentary in all his writings: "Crime, then is necessary; it is bound up with the fundamental conditions of all social life, and by that very fact is useful, because these conditions of which it is a part are themselves indispensable to the normal evolution of morality and law" (1893, 70). In Durkheim's scheme of things, crime does occur in any type of social arrangement, one based on mechanical or organic solidarity. In addition, Durkheim also recognized the notion of the *relativity* of crime and deviance when he stated "Imagine a society of saints, a perfect cloister of exemplary individuals. Crimes, properly affirmed, where there be unknown; but faults which appear venial to the layman will create there the same scandal that the ordinary offense does in ordinary consciousness . . . For the same reason, the perfect and upright man judges his smallest failings with a severity that the majority reserve for acts more truly in the nature of an offense" (1893, 69). Durkheim is observing that humans are normative creatures, and norms do and will vary across different social conditions. This notion of the relativity of behavior is an integral part of the sociology of deviance and has a major place in what Thio identified as the constructionist perspective (discussed in Chapter 1) and a number of leading theories of deviance, especially labeling theory (discussed in Chapter 7).

Robert K. Merton: "Social Structure and Anomie"

Explaining the Theory

Robert K. Merton is one of the greatest American sociologists and a student of the "master", Talcott Parsons. Merton too was a structural functionalist, but one who deviated in major ways from the writings of his profound mentor. It is not the intent here to address the differences between these two scholars, instead it is to Merton's contribu-

tion to the study of deviance attention is directed. It should be noted that Merton was a social theorist, and not a student of deviance or criminology, but in *Social Structure and Anomie* (1938) Merton laid out what has become one of the most famous statements on deviance published to date. ("Social Structure and Anomie" is also a chapter in one of the greatest American treatises on sociological theory, *Social Theory and Social Structure*, by Merton published in 1968). Merton's central notion in his theory of deviance is anomie, which he integrates into his discussions of culture and social structure. Merton defined culture as "that set of normative values governing behavior which is common to members of a designated society or group" and social structure as "that set of social relationships in which members of the society or group are variously implicated" (1968, 216). Merton theorized anomie is directly related to culture (which includes goals) and social structure (which includes means) and observed deviance occurs when there exists a disconnect or disjunction between the two. For example, some individuals believe in society's goals (i.e., material success; prestige) but lack the approved means of acheiving them (i.e., hard work; education). When this occurs, deviance occurs. Others downplay or do not believe they will achieve the goals, but still work within society's approved methods of survival. Yet others embrace both the dearly held goals and means and are not deviant. Merton developed a typology that identified five modes of adaptation to society and their relationships to socially acceptable goals and socially acceptable means of achieving them. The + *sign* indicates agreement with the goals or means; the - *sign* indicates deviating from the goals or means. The typology demonstrates Merton's debt to Talcott Parsons via his use of adaptation (actors) and to Durkheim (anomie). The typology is presented below.

Mode of Adaptation	Culture Goals	Institutionalized Means
1. Conformity	+	+
2. Innovation	+	—
3. Ritualism	—	+
4. Retreatism	—	—
5. Rebellion	—	—
	+	+

Conformists and ritualists represent opposite ends of the spectrum, conformity the *most* common and ritualism the *least* common of the modes of adaptation, with the adaptations based on the relationship of individuals to economic activity, and as Merton wrote, "Our task is to search out some of the factors which exert pressure upon individuals to engage in certain of these logically possible alternative responses" (1938, 677). Adaptations 2, 3, and 5 result from *frustrations* derived from the inability to achieve economic success or other manifestations/indications that one has made it in a competitive society. The innovator simply gives up on the institutional means, but still places high stress on cultural goals; ritualists drop the goals but remain living with society's normative structure; and rebellion entails total frustration with the legitimate goals and means, coupled with the objective of replacing them with a new social order (1938, 678). At first glance this appears to be quite a simplistic explanation of deviance, and in a sense it is. To be sure there must be many more than five ways individuals adapt to society, and that included as goals and means can be far more extensive than outlined by Merton. But the question about theory always comes down to its validity and scientific soundness, a concern now addressed.

Analysis and Empirical Support

In Chapters 5 through 8 there is discussion of analysis and empirical support of the theories under consideration. It is imperative from the outset to mention that testing of the theories is never perfect or comprehensive. Most saliently, it is *that which was tested, and how it was tested* that determines if theory stands up to scientific scrutiny. In the fields of criminology and deviance, it is unusual for all major propositions of a theory to be tested in one full swoon, and more common for segments of them to be placed under the microscope, so to speak. Therefore, when examining empirical analyses of theories *four issues* should be considered: "the questions that are being asked?" the operational definitions of the variables being tested; sampling designs; and the statistical techniques employed to analyze the data. The theory chapters will not necessarily address all four issues specifically (especially statistical tests), however they will detail major findings relative to many theories under study (some of the theories have received limited testing) while identifying key elements of the research designs, including sampling issues and major variables. One note about discussing statistical analyses: this is a deviance text and as such it is written to reach a diverse student constituency, some of who might not have taken or successfully/enthusiastically completed a course in statistics. Therefore, limited coverage of the statistical methods used to analyze data is presented, but it is important for all of us to remember that quite frequently, ceteris paribus (other things being equal) it is the statistical designs used that will determine if a theory has stood up to the test. This point cannot be stressed enough, nor can the fact that exact replication of tests is rarely undertaken in studies of crime and deviance. In academic journal articles where most of what we are addressing is found, multiple regression is the technique most frequently used to analyze data, and there are many variants of it, which can and does lead to different findings and conclusions concerning the validation of a theory (or segments of it). Sometimes this is a necessary evil since a major criticism of a study may be that inappropriate statistical techniques were used, with the critics recommending other statistical designs as alternatives. Enough said on this matter, and now it is time to turn attention to a major example of what we have just discussed, "A Developmental Test of Mertonian Anomie Theory," by Scott Menard.

Scott Menard (1995) offers the best test to date of "Social Structure and Anomie." Menard argued that previous tests fell short of an accurate measure of Merton's typology, since few if any are tests of the modes of adaptation which are central to Merton's thinking (1996, 169). Earlier empirical tests of Merton's theory generally focused on the relationship between the failure to achieve socially acceptable goals via acceptable means, and structural-based variables such as social class, race and gender, as evidence of support or non-support for Merton's explanation for deviance (1995, 136). Recognizing the shortcomings in the way that "Social Structure and Anomie" has been tested, Menard proceeded to examine multiple facets of Merton's typology by looking at the relationship of the modes of adaptation (ignored in previous studies), social class, race and gender (overemphasized in test of Merton) to deviant and criminal behavior, thus assuming a broad-based approach to Merton's work.

Menard's sample consisted of five Waves taken from the National Youth Survey (NYS) with sample sizes ranging from 1,725 (Wave 1) to approximately 1,500 in Wave 5 (NYS is a national probability sample of youth between the ages 11–17 which was implemented in 1976). Menard divided his sam-

ples into early adolescence (11–14), middle adolescence (14–17) and late adolescence (17– 20). Over the five Waves, subjects responded to Likert-scale type items that would indicate the degree to which they agreed or disagreed with statements that would determine their relationship to or involvement with criminal behavior and deviance (i.e., drug use). The demographic variables employed are: gender, coded male or female; race was white or nonwhite; socioeconomic status (ses) was ses of parents; and academic success was measured by respondent grade point average (GPA). Merton-specific variables were attained by asking questions such as "What do you think your chances are of completing a college degree?", and the measure of educational and economic opportunity was obtained by asking "What do you think your chances are for getting the kind of job you would like to have after finishing school?" Criminal behavior was indicated by involvement in minor offenses such as petty theft and vandalism, and more serious index offenses including gang fighting, sexual assault, aggravated assault and robbery. Illicit drug use included drugs such as heroin, cocaine, marijuana and alcohol. Menard hypothesized along the lines of Merton's typology by expecting to find that innovators would have the greatest involvement with minor and index offenses and retreatists would report the highest use of illicit drugs (1995, 144). Most salient to this discussion is the measurement of the modes of adaptation, again central to Merton's theory but overlooked in previous studies. For example, subjects who responded that it was wrong to engage in crime and illicit drug use would be expected to conform to social norms and those who identified themselves as being involved in crime or deviance would be expected to fit into one of the other modes of adaptation, such as innovation and retreatism (1995, 144–145).

Some of Menard's many findings include early adolescence had the highest percentage of respondents who believe in the importance of getting a good job (economic opportunity) and the importance of receiving a college education (educational opportunity). In addition, regardless of parental ses, academic success and a positive outlook on future educational chances were significantly correlated with perceived economic opportunity (1195, 149). What is more, during mid-adolescence females were reported to have the greatest chances of being ritualists, and lower involvement with drugs during late adolescence (1995, 160;165). What about illegal behavior? For both males and females early adolescence was found to include involvement with less serious criminality, with mid-adolescence more likely to be associated with more serous crime and deviance, including drug use. *Menard concluded his research is in support of Merton.* For example, lower rates of offending are found with conformists and ritualists, with innovators and retreatists having higher rates of offending. When it came to drug use, retreatists were the more likely to use illicit drugs, also consistent with Merton's typology.

In Recognition: Robert K. Merton

The debt owed to Emile Durkheim for his role as a founding figure in sociology and the study of deviance cannot be overstated. Neither can the importance of Robert K. Merton be underestimated in his place in American sociology, and to theories of deviance which even Merton could not foresee would emerge from *Social Structure and Anomie.* What Merton placed into motion in this seminal work has had lasting influence in the study of deviance, but we are reminded that Merton was social a theorist first and foremost, one of the greatest in American intellectual inquiry. He was a modern struc-

tural functionalist breaking ways with his teacher and friend Talcott Parsons. Merton would come to emphasize middle range theories as opposed to the grand arching theory proposed and advocated by Parsons. Merton extended and advanced Parsons, and by doing so helped to bring sociology to the next level. Many of us may have forgotten that the following terms come from the middle range theorizing of Merton: manifest and latent functions. Merton's structural functionalism made room for the importance of social change and social conflict within society, two areas in which Parsons has received major criticism for decades. Merton also questioned the notion of the interrelationships of society's major parts put forth by Parsons, thereby taking the position that societies are not the tightly structured organisms that resist social change, remaining intact even when faced with great challenges and disruption. Merton established a functionalism that grabbed hold of that proposed by Parsons and placed it within the context of changing times, and the ever increasing presence of conflict theory in sociology.

"Social Structure and Anomie" will be a major force in the study of deviance for years to come. Merton's wisdom and keen insights into the inner workings of cultures allowed him to develop a theory of deviance that legions of sociologists and criminologists have followed for over 70 years, and many others have integrated into their own conceptualizations of deviance and criminality. Robert K. Merton is truly a giant in sociological thinking.

SUMMARY

Emile Durkheim is the critical figure in the development of theories of deviance. His concept "anomie" is one of the most well-known terms in sociology, and it is of paramount importance in the study of deviance and in criminology. For over 100 years sociologists have worked with, renewed, reinvented and integrated anomie in many theories and empirical tests. Anomie is one of those concepts that will have long-lasting value to the study of the social world: it is a time honored idea that continues to receive the awe and respect of generations of sociologists. Robert K. Merton saw its value in his now famous theory, and from that work came a life for anomie that is still important and going strong in the twenty-first century. The next chapter is an extension—an *evolution* of Durkheim and Merton.

Chapter 5

ANOMIE AND STRUCTRUAL THEORIES EXTENDED:
STRAIN THEORIES

CASE STUDY:
ROBERT HANSSEN

Consider the following:

- compromising the United States "Continuity of Government Plan" or the plan developed to ensure the survival of the president and the government in case of nuclear attack.
- divulging the identities of at least nine Soviet spies who were recruited to spy for the United States (against the Soviet Union).
- revealing the existence of a spy tunnel underneath the Soviet embassy, used to spy electronically on the Soviets.
- revealing "The National Intelligence Program" that included all elements of intelligence the United States planned for a year, and how the funding would be spent.
- revealing worldwide double agent information.

The above represents the tip of the iceberg involving the most serious espionage ever initiated against the United States. To this day, more than seven years after the spying stopped, the United States intelligence community and game plans are still feared compromised, and perhaps have fallen into the hands of rogue states and despots motivated to destabilize and to destroy America. But who would engage in this level of spying against the United States and more importantly, why? The answer to the first part of the question is Robert Phillip Hanssen, a career agent with the Federal Bureau of Investigation (F.B.I.), the nation's most prestigious and powerful domestic law enforcement organization. For nearly 20 years, Hanssen used his position of trust and top secret clearance to sell highly classified documents to America's arch enemy and world rival, the Soviet Union. Why? The first thought is money, after all it is believed Hanssen earned at least two million dollars through his spying activity, which doing the math turns out to be an average of $100,000 annually. But there is more to the life of Bob Hanssen that holds alternative explanations for his treasonist conduct. All information reported is derived from *The Bureau and the Mole* (2002) written by Pulitzer Prize winning author David A. Vise, who is a national staff writer for the *Washington Post* newspaper.

Robert Hanssen was born in 1944 to Howard and Vivian Hanssen, and after World War II Howard became a police officer in Chicago, Illinois, a position he did not want his son ever to hold. Howard Haansen was an abusive parent, and mother Vivian either did not attempt to prevent the abuse or was incapable at stopping its occurence. Through his formative years, Robert faced significant abuse from his father, although apparently he only received physical abuse twice as a young child. Most of the abuse was emotional, and assumed the form of ridicule and embarrassment. One area where this was prevalent was course grades, where Robert was unable to satisfy his father. Good grades were not good enough, and that included "B's" in rigorous courses such as chemistry. When attending parent-teacher conferences Howard Hanssen would belittle the teacher for giving his son grades he did not think Robert had earned. This pattern continued into the college years, when Howard would question Robert's professors about giving his son good grades. It should be noted Robert was a very bright student, who as a child read spy novels and engaged in challenging and mind developing games such as rubric cube, usually with his childhood and lifelong friend Jack Hoschouer.

After high school Robert attended Knox College, a private four-year institution in Illinois where his undergraduate major was premedicine. Howard wanted his son to become a physician, and when Robert was denied entry to medical school he opted instead for a dental education that he left after just two years, much to the displeasure of Howard. Shortly before quitting dental school, Robert married Bonnie Wauck a devout Roman Catholic, a point that will be revisited. His career path after dental college included working for an accounting firm in Chicago, and (in 1971 he received the Masters Degree in Business Administration MBA), eventually leaving that position to become a Chicago police officer, a decision flying right in the face of his father. Right out of the police academy Robert was assigned to the Special Internal Affairs Unit (C-5),

that investigated corrupt police officers. It was here that Robert distinguished himself as a shrewd and intelligent police officer, one who might be suited for a more prestigious career in law enforcement. Hanssen remained in Chicago police work until 1976 when he began his training to become a special agent with the Federal Bureau of Investigation. Upon graduating from the F.B.I. Academy he was assigned to Indiana where he was successful investigating white-collar crime, then in 1978 as a result of his continued successes in law enforcement Robert was transferred to New York City where he worked in Soviet counterintelligence. It is here where Hanssen began spying for the Soviets. While assigned to New York City, Robert and his growing family resided in upscale Scarsdale living beyond his means, which meant that he would need to borrow money from his father, a task that was humiliating to Robert, yet psychologically rewarding to Howard, who was always quick to remind Robert although he was an F.B.I. agent, he was a failure who would have no need to frequently borrow money from his parents had he not quit dental school. Rather than continue to ask his father for financial support, Robert began selling secrets to the Soviets, and in 1980 his wife Bonnie caught him examining classified documents in his basement he intended to sell to Russian agents. This led to a meeting with their Catholic priest (Robert was a protestant who converted to Roman Catholicism) and Robert pledged to give back what he had earned to Mother Teresa, a promise he did not fulfill. Robert's spying involved completely duping the Soviets as to his true identity, and began by mailing secrets to Soviet agents in New York City, and continued with drop-offs in parks in Washington, D.C.

In 1981, Robert Hanssen was assigned to counterintelligence at F.B.I. headquarters in Washington, D.C., where he would continue spying until he was caught in February 2001. Ironically, Hanssen had been considering retiring from the Bureau and accepting a lucrative offer of $200,000 a year to work in corporate America. But the heat was on since even after the arrest of CIA officer Aldrich Ames by the F.B.I. in the late 1990s for spying, it was apparent there was still espionage taking place that was compromising America's security. The F.B.I. did not really have its man, yet. The Bureau moved into full gear, and was able to identify the master spy it had been seeking for years as its own Robert Phillip Hanssen. Hanssen was sentenced to life in federal prison without parole, and his wife was allowed to collect a lifetime retirement from the Bureau of $30,000 annually.

But there is even more to Hanssen than espionage. For 18 months in the early 1990s, Hanssen carried on an "adulterous" relationship with stripper Priscilla Galey. During the 18-month period Hanssen showered her with gifts totaling $500,000, and took her on expensive trips. However, it is unclear if they ever engaged in sexual activity, although reports are that she wanted to and Robert declined. It was only after Galey had used a credit card to purchase cigarettes provided by Hanssen that he discontinued seeing her, permanently. In addition to this rather bizarre relationship, Hanssen had other sexual aberrations. On occasion, Hanssen's lifelong friend, Jack Houschour would stay with the Hanssen's, and Robert would offer Jack the opportunity to have sex with his wife Bonnie, or at least to allow Jack to view Bonnie and Robert engaging in sexual intercourse. Jack declined.

Lives such as that of Robert Hanssen beg the questions of why and how? Why did he engage in various forms of deviance, and how was this possible? Perhaps some of the answers lay with general strain theory as proposed by Robert Agnew.

The Work of Robert Agnew: General Strain Theory (GST)

Perhaps there is no bigger name in criminological theory today than Robert Agnew, who initially in 1985 and then in 1992 set the world of theory on fire with what is labeled as General Strain Theory (GST). GST is an extension of the works of Emile Durkheim, but most saliently of Robert Merton's "Social Structure and Anomie." Whereas the latter is the landmark theory in criminology/deviance, Agnew's general strain theory is one of the most significant of its time, as witnessed by the numerous attempts at testing it.

Explaining the Theory

Undergraduate students in sociology are probably familiar with GST, most notably its three types of strain. Since the publication of *Foundation for a General Strain Theory of Crime and Delinquency* (1992), Agnew has expanded and elaborated on the theory. However, what is most known and most frequently cited about it are the *three* major types of strain, the *first which is the inability to achieve positively valued goals, a direct link* to Robert Merton. The *second and third types of strain* are extensions on Merton, and it is these latter types that have gained the most attention from sociologists and criminologists. The *second type* of strain occurs when positively valued stimuli are removed, or there is the threat of removing them. Two examples are the death of a loved one, and the ending of an important relationship. The *third type* of strain involves the introduction of negative or noxious stimuli, and includes negative relations with parents and negative relations with schools (1992, 50). Accordingly, if the theory is correct, any one of the above types of strain should correlate with involvement in crime and delinquency. Three examples are: the failure to achieve an important societal goal such as success would lead one to commit antisocial acts (*strain type 1*); the divorce of parents may lead to criminality (*strain type 2*); or being victimized by child abuse could drive an individual to engage in delinquency or crime (*strain type 3*).

But there is more to Agnew's work concerning its empirical viability, including his discussion of *equity and distributive justice*, derived from social psychology, behavioral psychology, and medical sociology. Critical is the notion of equity, or the assumption individuals may be driven to criminality as a result of the unjust allocation of resources, or because in interaction situations justice has not been actualized (1992, 55). It is in the notion of equity/justice that Agnew truly modifies Merton's focus on strain as a failure to achieve positively valued goals (1992, 51–56). According to Agnew, there are *three types* of strain that fall under this category. The *first* is the disjunction between goals and expectations, or committing deviant or criminal acts because one cannot reach important societal goals, such as getting a good job or completing a college education. The *second* type of strain occurs when individuals fail to match their expectations with their achievements, meaning they fall short of the expectations. For example, individuals may be seeking all "As" in their classes, instead they earn a combination of "As", "Bs", and "Cs", or perhaps they fall short of acquiring the job they really wanted. The *third* type of strain deals directly with distributive justice, and occurs when individuals perceive they have been unfairly treated, or have not received the benefits from an interaction situation they initially sought. An example may be when individuals enter into relationships, and expect greater affection and attention than that actually received, or their inputs into the relationships exceed what they get

out of them. Therefore, in Agnew's theory there are *three major types of strain*, but the first type of strain–failure to achieve positively valued goals–*is further subdivided into three other types of strain*, a part of the theory that is often overlooked or forgotten (especially in textbooks).

A question that emerges is "what then are the social psychological sources of deviance and criminality that clarify why individuals become antisocial?" The answer is in the emotions of *anger and frustration* that Agnew argues derive from the removal of positive stimuli, and the introduction of negative stimuli. Agnew writes "Anger . . . is the most critical emotional reaction for the purposes of general strain theory. Anger results when individuals blame their adversity on others, and anger is a key emotion because it increases the individual's level of felt injury, creates a desire for retaliation/revenge, energizes the individual action, and lowers inhibitions, in part because individuals believe that others feel their aggression is justified" (1992, 59–60). For Agnew, it is the latter two major types of strain that are central to his theory; but there is more. Agnew developed his theory to account for the effects of the *magnitude, recency, duration,* and *clustering,* all of which fuel anger and frustration, resulting in delinquency and crime. Each is addressed briefly.

Magnitude involves the size in the discrepancy between goals and expectations; the size of the loss of positive stimuli; and, the magnitude of the pain incurred from negative/noxious events. *Recency* is a mater of how close in time adverse conditions have occurred, and *duration* implies the length of time negative events last in the lives of individuals. *Clustering* means a double or triple whammy or more, when several negative stimuli cluster together at roughly the same time period, thus exacerbating anger and frustration (1992, 64–66). An example of this latter point may be an adolescent who is a victim of child abuse, whose self-concept is depleted as a result of his victimization, and whose parents have recently filed for divorce.

In his 1992 groundbreaking publication, Agnew also addressed *adaptations* (coping) to strain, which entail *cognitive, emotional* and *behavioral strategies* that can be actualized though either legitimate or illegitimate channels. *Cognitive* strategies may be thought of as "mind-game techniques" such as telling oneself things could be worse; the goal was not that important anyway, and stressing what has gone well in one's life as opposed to accentuating what hasn't. *Behavioral* coping strategies involve making positive/constructive changes, such as changing schools or even engaging in delinquent activities such as revenge. *Emotional* coping techniques could include antisocial conduct including the use of drugs, or legitimate behaviors such as meditation and physical exercise (1992, 69–70).

Agnew continues to refine GST as a response to numerous tests done on it, including modifying the definition of strain, as well as identifying the types of strain that are weakly and strongly correlated with crime (2001; 2002). As other social scientists have tested general strain theory, Agnew has responded by examining some of its key conceptualizations. One example is his discussion of the types of strain with strong correlations to crime, an area he needed to clarify and expand upon in the 1992 classic article (2001, 343–347). Reflecting on research undertaken on his theory, Agnew has written factors such as parental rejection, inappropriate parental supervision and discipline, child abuse and neglect, negative secondary school experiences, unsatisfying work, homelessness, criminal victimization, and prejudice and discrimination are reported to be associated with delinquency and crime.

What is more, Agnew also identified the conditions in which the failure to achieve core goals leads to antisocial conduct, occurring most often when individuals seek immediate gratification, such as the need for money in the short term (2001, 343). It is to be noted in his earlier work Agnew played down the role of failure to achieve positively valued goals, and its effects on deviance and criminality.

Having laid out the key aspects of Agnew's theory, it is now time to address the issues of analysis and empirical support.

Analysis and Empirical Support

Reiterating an important conversation from the last chapter, it is important to state that empirical support for any theory has a great deal to do with the following: the questions asked–the slant of the research; operationalizations of variables; sampling techniques employed; and, statistical techniques used to analyze data. All four issues are of paramount importance when putting theory to the test, and therefore play a major role in assessing the efficacy of theory. What is more, it may not be possible or even prudent to test an entire theory, instead "pieces" of theories may be tested, allowing limited examination of their ability to predict outcomes.

Thus is the case with Robert Agnew's general strain theory. As noted earlier, there have been many tests done on it, representing multiple slants (the questions asked), with most tests offering moderate support. For example, a number of studies have found at least some support for the effects of strain on delinquency, when mediated by negative emotions including anger and frustration (Agnew, 1985; Agnew and Brezina, 1997; Agnew and White, 1992; Agnew, Cullen, Burton, Jr., Evans, and Dunaway, 1996; Colvin, 2000; Katz, 2000; Mazerole and Maahs, 2000; Piquero and Sealock, 2000). Other research supports, again to a modest extent, the effects of factors such as coping skills, self-esteem, family attachment, moral beliefs and association with delinquent peers as conditioning factors in the effects of strain on delinquency (Agnew, Brezina, Wright, and Cullen, 2002; Agnew and White, 1992; Aseltine, Gore, and Gordan, 2000; Mazerolle and Maahs, 2000; Paternoster and Mazerolle, 1994; Piquero and Sealock, 2000). Agnew and White (1992) and Paternoster and Mazerolle (1994) reported a positive correlation between strain and delinquency and drug use, and Hoffman and Miller (1998) reported after controlling for other factors such association with delinquent peers and low self-esteem, strain still increased involvement in delinquency.

The above represents a small portion of research testing GST, but hopefully it makes the point: pieces of it have been tested, offering partial but encouraging support for it. But does this make the theory "bad" or without viability, since the tests are not comprehensive and conclusive? Not really, since these studies were all undertaken differently, positing a variety of hypotheses and analyzed by multiple statistical techniques. Two important studies tests of GST are now discussed in detail, hopefully providing further insight into the strengths of the theory, and the significance of the methodology used when examining it.

Broidy (2001) offers one of the best tests of general strain theory to date. Employing a nonrandom convenience sample of 896 undergraduate students at Northwestern University in Evansville, Illinois and using self report data, Broidy found support for the effects of strain on negative emotions (anger), the effects of negative emotions on legitimate coping (i.e., cognitive coping), and the effects of negative emotions and legiti-

mate coping on deviant outcomes (i.e., stealing, vandalism). Broidy reported strong and statistically significant relationships of unfair outcomes, blocked goals, stress, and self-esteem on negative emotions such as anger, frustration, and feeling depressed, and she reported emotions other than anger (i.e., depression, frustration, guilt) had a strong and statistically significant effect on legitimate coping (cognitive, behavioral and emotional). Her tests also revealed the following variables had powerful effects on deviant outcomes: anger; other negative emotions; stress, deviant peers; deviant opportunities; and, membership in social clubs (2001, 21–27). Another important finding was sex is an important predictor of delinquency, meaning males more than females have a greater probability of engaging in deviant outcomes (2001, 28).

Robert Agnew and colleagues have undertaken a number of tests of GST. One of the most recent is an extension on the theory that includes personality and constraint variables as possible effects on juvenile delinquency (2002). Agnew et al. drew a sample of 1,423 children from "The National Survey of Children" (NSC) that encompasses many items relevant to GST (such as those just reviewed). The children were asked to respond to items directly related to strain including: family relationships; conflict with parents; school hatred; bullying by other children; and, safeness of the neighborhoods in which they resided. Agnew also included measures of social control and learning, such as attachment to parents, parental firmness, school attachment, and troublesome friends (2002, 50–53). Parents and teachers were asked to respond to items related to the personality of children, that Agnew identified as "negative emotionality." These items asked if the child was impulsive, acted without thinking, and if the child has a strong temper (2002, 54). Interestingly,

Agnew et al. found only minor support for strain, learning and social control on delinquency, with the strongest effects reported to be for "troublesome friends" and "school attachment" (it should be noted that his research included 25 variables subsumed under three categories: strain variables; social control/learning variables; and demographic measures). Additional tests of the same variables, some coded differently revealed similar results. Few variables had statistically significant or strong effects on delinquency, and ironically the few that did were not strain variables specifically. School attachment and troublesome friends, classified by Agnew et al. as learning and social control variables, exerted the strongest influences on delinquency, and "age of child" and "African American" were the demographic variables found to have the most powerful effects on delinquency. Although the results do not verify the *direct and unmitigated* effects of strain on delinquency, Agnew et al. wrote "These data support the central hypothesis of this study: People high in negative emotionality and low in constraint are more likely than are others to react to strain with delinquency" (2002, 60–61), implying an interaction of strain, control and learning on antisocial conduct.

So where does this leave us? GST theory remains an important theory in the study of crime and deviance, and this is reminiscent of the pattern once found with labeling theory (discussed in Chapter 7). From the 1960s to the early 1980s, labeling theory enjoyed great popularity while experiencing spotty empirical support, and in sociology and criminology today it is still addressed in various courses, even though it hit its peak years ago, given its lack of scientific verification. This is not to imply that strain theory is in the same boat. On the contrary, the testing of it is not finished, and an entire generation of young and aspiring criminologists and

deviance theorists will undoubtedly continue to place it under the microscope, and perhaps in doing so and using more sophisticated methodologies and statistical techniques, will unravel and tease out the specific conditions under which strain is found to be a more powerful predictor of delinquency, deviance and crime. Attention is now turned to another recent strain theory, C*rime and the American Dream* by Stephen F. Messner and Richard Rosenfield.

The Work of Stephen F. Messner and Richard Rosenfield: Crime and the American Dream: Institutional-Anomie Theory

Although less popular than general strain theory, *institutional-anomie theory*, proposed by Stephen F. Messner and Richard Rosenfield, is a relatively recent extension of Robert Merton's "Social Structure and Anomie." In *Crime and the American Dream* (1994) Messner and Rosenfield posited what they call institutional-anomie theory, to be explained shortly. But ask yourself two basic sociological/anthropological questions: first, "what are the social institutions found in all known societies?"; second, "how would you rank order them, from most to least important, and why?" The answers to the first question probably include the family, education, religion, the polity, and government. Of course, there are other social institutions and they include sport and the law. But in your answer did you also mention the economy? This brings us to the second question. The guess here is that many ranked family first, religion second, education third (or some close facsimile), and there is a scatter gram effect after that. The "why's" will undoubtedly vary, but family is the first social group most of us experience, and it is important in shaping our personalities and values. Some might have put religion as number one, and the reason given may be its place in providing individuals with values, and conformity to social norms and the law. Education as number one and the explanation may include its long-term role in shaping our beliefs, values and attitudes, and in providing the essential skills required to succeed in society. But how do others see the same questions? The "others" in this case are Messner and Rosenfield. These authors rank the economy as the most powerful and dominant social institution in capitalist societies, in particular the United States. Their reason is the emphasis placed on material success in Western societies. With such overpowering focus on materialism, the economy surges ahead of all other social institutions, with the latter reduced to the role of follower, and "monkey see, monkey do" (author's emphasis). The family, education, the polity, religion, and so on all play second fiddle to the economy, and begin to *mimic* it. The family assumes a form analogous to the economy, as does religion, education, law, and so-on-and-so-forth. According to Messner and Rosenfield "the cultural message that comes through with the greatest force is the one most compatible with the logic of the economy: the competitive, individualistic, and materialistic message of the American dream" (1994, 86).

Messner and Rosenfield have a name for the emphasis on materialism: *the American dream*, which is ubiquitous and hard to escape in American society, permeating every aspect of our lives and culture. The authors define the American dream as a" commitment to the goal of material success to be pursued by everyone in American society under conditions of open, individual competition" (1994, 62). It is interesting what the authors conclude about this level of competition and pursuit of materialism. On the one hand, some might suggest that incessant competition and the acquisition of worldly status symbols would result in a society that keeps improving because we all push ourselves to be better, to get more and more and more, perhaps with a trickle-down effect, where even the least fortunate in society pull themselves up by their bootstraps, becoming successful participants in the capitalist way of life. But Messner and Rosenfield see it differently. The stress placed on materialism forces people into criminality, into a state of competitivism that pits them against each other. The resulting cutthroat mentality results in anomie, with behavior becoming unregulated, because the economy is dominant and other social institutions so weakened. Economic success through whatever means necessary comes at the expense of social institutions such as the family and religion, that we are reminded take a back seat to capitalism. To remedy this issue the authors wrote:

> The structural changes that lead to significant reduction in crime are those that promote a rebalancing of social institutions. These changes would involve reducing the subordination to the economy of the family, schools, the polity, and the general system of social stratification. . . . More specifically, social roles such as parenting, "spousing," teaching, learning and serving the community will have to become, as ends in themselves, meaningful alternatives to material acquisition. (1994, 103–104)

Analysis and Empirical Support

Crime and the American Dream has not come close to generating the magnitude of empirical studies testing Robert Agnew's general strain theory, however, the relatively few studies that have tested institutional-anomie theory have been encouraging, with more tests needed to be undertaken in order to assess its efficacy. Part of the issue is institutional-anomie which is a *macro level theory*, and in the past 20 years macro theories of crime and deviance have fallen out of favor, partially out of the long history of attempting to validate them with minimal success, and the popularity of newer theories such as GST and Ronald Akers (the later is covered in Chapter 7). The history of sociology and criminology is rich with macro level theories that explain crime and delinquency as a product of industrialization, poverty, immigration, urbanization, race/ethnicity, and socioeconomic status. Two major studies testing institutional-anomie theory are presented as examples.

Messner and Rosenfeld offer one of the most prominent tests of institutional-anomie theory (1997). The authors tested the theory employing a sample of 45 nations, and hypothesized factors such as access to and the quality of social welfare programs are correlated with a decrease in the rate of homicide (1997, 1,394). The concept under study *decommodification of labor*, is policies that protect citizens from market forces, including entitlement programs and social security, policies often associated with the empowerment of people. Protective social policy does not leave citizens to the ebb and flow of the economy, that can result in large portions of society at risk of poverty and unemployment. Messner and Rosenfeld wrote ". . . decommodification signals that the balance of institutional power in market society has shifted from the economy toward the polity; it implies that purely economic values and criteria are accommodated to collective, political considerations. . . . Given the general logic of institutional-anomie theory, then, the decommodification of labor should vary inversely with societal levels of crime, including the most serious crime-homicide" (1997, 1,393–1,394). Thus their hypothesis: ". . . levels of homicide will vary inversely

with the decommodification of labor" (1997, 1,393). To be more specific, Messner and Rosenfeld argue in societies where the economy rules, there will be large amounts of anomie, and as a result, high crime rates (here to be identified as homicide rates).

The independent variables in this study are income inequality; economic discrimination defined as intentional economic discrimination against certain groups; the sex ratio of populations; and the degree of development of the 45 nations under analysis (1997, 1,401–1,403). The data analysis indicates decommodification of labor had a statistically significant relationship to lower levels of homicide, and sex ratio, or the percentage of a population 64 years of age or older was found to effect lower rates of homicide, largely because elderly people are recipients of entitlement programs, reinforcing Messner and Rosenfeld's assumption that decommodification policies result in lower rates of murder (1997, 1,407–1,409). The authors conducted four different tests of their hypotheses, and in three models the degree of development was found to have an inverse relationship with homicide rates (the greater the degree of development of nations, the lower the homicide rate). Income inequality was not reported to effect rates of homicide, and economic discrimination was reported to be associated with higher rates of homicide in two of the four tests performed (in one test where it did not impact the homicide rate, the effect of economic discrimination was undertaken before the decommodification variable was included, and in a second test Syria, was left out as one of the 45 nations because it is "an outlier on homicide" (1997, 1,405–1,406). It should be noted the United States had by far the greatest rate of homicide of any of the 45 nations under study.

A second major study of institutional-anomie theory, undertaken by Mitchell B. Chamlin and John Cochran (1995) examined the impact of structural (macro) level variables on rates of instrumental crime (property offenses), which included robbery, burglary, larceny, and auto theft. Working from their hypothesis "The effect of economic conditions on instrumental crime rates depend on the vitality of noneconomic institutions" (1995, 415), the authors tested the impact of economic depravation (percentage of families below the poverty line), family structure (divorce rate), religious participation (church membership rate), and political involvement (actual voting) on the dependent variable, property offenses (another way of understanding the hypothesis is strong noneconomic institutions, such as the family, religion and the polity should offset the dominating effect of the powerful economic institution, as proposed by Messner and Rosenfeld). Chamlin and Cochran used the following data sources to measure property offenses: The Uniform Crime Reports published annually by the Federal Bureau of Investigation; *The State and Metropolitan Area Data Book* for measures of economic depravation and political participation; and, church membership data published by Bernard Quinn et al. (1995, 417–419). In addition, the authors also used the percent of the population African Americans, and the percent of a total population 18–24 years of age as demographic variables to be tested on property offenses.

As is the case in many studies, the authors ran several tests of their hypotheses, using different arrangements of the independent or predictor variables, a strategy often undertaken for the purposes of comparison. By incorporating some variables in one test, and changing them in other statistical analyses, it became possible to see how the different variables individually, and collectively effected the dependent variable. The four different tests reported the following predictor variables had the strongest influence on property crime: percent of the population

18–24; church membership; poverty; voting behavior; and, family structure. Chamlin and Cochran concluded the presence of noneconomic institutional variables on property offenses supported their hypothesis, implying a powerful economic institution is not a slam-dunk when it comes to predicting property crime. On the contrary, strong noneconomic institutions can have a mediating/weakening influence on instrumental crime, individually and collectively.

The Work of Albert K. Cohen: Delinquent Boys

We are reminded many theories in criminology and deviance were developed to explain juvenile delinquency. Thus is the case with the final two strain theories discussed in this chapter. Albert Cohen's *Delinquent Boys* (1955) represents one of the most influential delinquency theories, and is discussed here since it is an extension on the work of Robert Merton and a precursor of future Mertonian-type theories, such as Robert Agnew's general strain theory. Cutting to the chase, Cohen theorized delinquency among working class boys is a direct product of strain, in particular the strain associated with *not being able to achieve middle-class goals*. Working class neighborhoods develop subcultures comprised predominantly of young people, and these subcultures serves as a source of adjustment to issues such as strain. Out of these subcultures arises juvenile delinquency, that Cohen wrotes is an reaction formation against middle-class values: juvenile delinquency is ". . . an "irrational," "malicious," "unaccount -able" hostility to the cnemy within the gates as well as without: the norms of the respectable middle-class society" (1955, 133). Cohen's proposition working class boy delinquency represents striking back at the middle class is natural, because working-class parents accept middle-class standards, and pass these down to their children who proceed to internalize them (1995, 125). What about middle-class delinquency? According to Cohen, it is a matter of sex role identification, or boys heavily socialized by their mothers, who as a result go overboard, so to speak, by engaging in delinquent acts just to prove their masculinity (1955, 164). So when it comes to delinquent behavior there exist a duality: working-class boy delinquency is a reaction formation; middle-class boy delinquency is an attempt by boys to prove their manliness. Cohen also observed working class boy delinquents take delight in harming others, engage in short-term goals (hedonism), and their crimes reflect versatility, meaning they commit a variety of offenses, all aimed at getting even with middle class society because they cannot be a part of its legitimate success structures (1955, 24–28). This brings us to working-class girl delinquency which Cohen states represents an attempt to gain status via establishing rapport with delinquent boys, and is specialized in context, meaning it is sexual oriented. As Cohen notes "boys collect stamps, girls collect boys" (1955, 142–143).

Analysis and Empirical Support

Over the years *Delinquent Boys* has been assessed more on theoretical than empirical grounds. Moyer (2001) has written Cohen's work does not meet the standard criteria for what constitutes theory, instead represents middle range theory, which tends to be based on data. Kitsuse and Dietrick (1959) commented Cohen placed too much emphasis on the relationship between middle class values and the delinquent behavior of working class boys, and Yablonsky (1962) criticized Cohen because he had failed to consider personality traits of delinquent boys,

such as sociopathy, that could explain their criminal activities. Perhaps most saliently, feminists have criticized *Delinquent Boys* on the grounds of gender bias implying Cohen overemphasized male delinquency, while failing to understand the nature of female delinquency, which constitutes more than sexuality and status seeking through relationships with boys (Leonard, 1982; Naffine, 1987), a point well-established through recent research on females in gangs and female gangs (Campbell, 1984; Esbensen and Winfree, 1998; Petersen, Miller, and Esbensen, 2001; Schallet, A. G., G. Hunt, and K. Joe-Laidler, 2003) But a point must be made at this juncture: Albert Cohen's *Delinquent Boys*, regardless of its flaws, remains a seminal work in criminology and the study of deviance. It preceded the emergence of the modern feminist movement by a decade, and was written at least that many years before the social sciences began to engage in and emphasize rigorous statistical designs as part of theory testing and empirical research.

The Work of Richard A. Cloward and Lloyd E. Ohlin: Delinquency and Opportunity: A Theory of Delinquent Gangs

Rarely in sociology is there a work that has influence outside of the disciplne such as *Delinquency and Opportunity: A Theory of Delinquent Gangs* (1960), published five years after Cohen's *Delinquent Boys*, building on it and the works of Emile Durkheim and Robert K. Merton. It first appeared at the start of a volatile decade, the 1960s, and just prior to the election of John F. Kennedy as the thirty-fifth president of the United States. This is no small point since *Delinquency and Opportunity* and Michael Harrington's *The Other America: Poverty in the United States* (1962) had profound impact on Kennedy's

The New Frontier, and eventually President Lyndon Johnson's *The Great Society*, arguably two of the most ambitious social and political programs in American history. Both President Kennedy and his younger brother, Attorney General Robert F. Kennedy read the books and were moved to attack poverty and crime, partially as a result of the information contained in them. Yet it was still only the early 1960s, and racism and other social ills ran rampant, social problems President Kennedy would seek to remedy during his administration which was cut short by his assassination in November 1963.

Delinquency and Opportunity introduced *"differential opportunity theory"* which placed the explanation for crime and delinquency squarely at the feet of the uneven distribution of legitimate opportunities in American society. Cloward and Ohlin wrote: "Our hypothesis is the disparity between what lower-class youths are led to want and what is actually available to them is a source of a major problem of adjustment. . . . When pressures from unfulfilled aspirations become sufficiently intense, many lower class youth turn away from legitimate channels, adopting other means, beyond conventional mores, which might offer a possible route to success goals. . . . The sense of injustice cancels out the individual's obligation to the established system" (1960, 86–118). The authors concluded in American society there exists a segment of the population that is unable to achieve the American dream through legitimate means, and as a result turns to illegitimate channels to acquire highly valued goals such as money, prestige and esteem. However, the illegitimate means themselves are not evenly distributed, resulting in three different subcultural routes: *the criminal subculture*; the *conflict subculture*; and, the *retreatist subculture*. The *criminal subculture* is the most successful of the three illegitimate subcultures, and is represented by age grad-

ing, modeling after older adult criminals, and disciplining of its members, meaning "there is no place in organized crime for the impulsive, unpredictable individual" (1960, 161–186). The youth in the criminal subculture stand the greatest chance of achieving money and status since this subculture is organized and exercises social control over its members. A step down from this is the *conflict subculture*, made up of fighting male youth who engage in violence as a result of feeling frustrated, and blocked opportunities. Youth who belong to the conflict subculture are unlikely to move upward into the criminal subculture because they lack discipline, and act out of emotion, rather than using savvy. The *retreatist* subculture is the third rung on the ladder of illegitimate subcultures and it is for the ultimate losers in society such as alcoholics and drug addicts. The youth in this subculture are so bad off that not only are they total failures according to legitimate society, but they have also failed in the illegitimate world. Most interestingly, Cloward and Ohlin wrote: "deviance and conformity generally result from the same kinds of condition" (1960, 37), meaning the genesis of both is to be found in society's goals, and the ability (or inability) to achieve them.

Analysis and Empirical Support

Delinquency and Opportunity has been largely evaluated on the basis of its theoretical and social policy implications, similar to that of Albert Cohen's *Delinquent Boys*. David Matza and Gresham Sykes stated a weakness of the theory is the overemphasis placed on middle class values, and suggested delinquency among working class youth was a product of the search for thrills, which also applied to middle class delinquency. Schrag (1962) commented delinquency is more diverse than suggested by Cloward and

Ohlin, and that *Delinquency and Opportunity* failed to explain why many working class and lower class boys do not engage in criminal acts. Lilly, Cullen, and Ball (1989) paid homage to *Delinquency and Opportunity* by recognizing that it and other strain theories were the most prominent explanations of delinquency of their era. Finally, Martin, Mutchnick, and Austin (1990) noted Cloward and Ohlin were asked to develop youth-related services and programs for the Lower East Side in Manhattan, New York City, a clear show of respect for and belief in their work. On a personal note, the author of this book found differential opportunity theory so interesting and dynamic that it helped to cement his interest in sociology and criminology as an undergraduate major.

In Recognition: Robert Agnew

Robert Agnew is a scholar who has played an important role in taking the study of crime and deviance to the next level. After years of marco theorizing in sociology and criminology/deviance, Agnew helped to blaze a path toward micro-social psychological thinking about crime and deviance, thus moving it out of the 1980s and early 1990s, when there were many evolving and competing theoretical developments (do not be mistaken, there still are today). Agnew's general strain theory surfaced to the top of the heap, and has been widely tested and evaluated for nearly two decades. It is rare for any one scholar to have such influence on a discipline or subject area but Robert K. Merton, Albert Cohen, Richard A. Cloward and Lloyd E. Ohlin, Ronald Akers and Meda Chesney-Lind did, to name a few. But these individuals are far and few among all those who have attempted innovations in theory, and who have challenged long-standing paradigms. Robert Agnew's work is so important that it represents the state-of-the-art of

theories of crime and deviance in the early part of the twenty-first century.

It seems Robert Agnew was destined for prominence from the earliest stages of his study in sociology. He graduated with highest honors and highest distinction from Rutgers University in New Brunswick, New Jersey in 1975, and received the doctorate (Ph.D.) in sociology from the prestigious Department of Sociology at the University of North Carolina-Chapel Hill in 1980. His dissertation "A Revised Strain Theory of Delinquency" would become the basis of his life's work, and itself was a take-off from his maters degree thesis "Anomie and Success: A Study of the Effects of Goals on Anomie," completed in 1978. After receiving the doctorate, Agnew accepted a faculty position at Emory University in Atlanta, Georgia where he is currently Professor of Sociology. He has held multiple positions in numerous professional societies in sociology and criminology, and needless to say he has been the recipient of many awards. When it comes to publishing, Agnew has a record like Ty Cobb (an legitimate one at that) with pages of refereed journal publications, and several outstanding books, including *Pressured into Crime: An Overview of General Strain Theory* published in 2006.

SUMMARY

Strain theories have occupied an important place in the history of sociology, owing much of their debt to the earlier works of Emile Durkheim. Robert K. Merton extended the tradition of strain theories in the 1930s, followed by Albert K. Cohen, Richard A. Cloward, and Lloyd E. Ohlin in the 1950s and 1960s, respectively. In recent years Robert Agnew, Stephen F. Messner, and Richard Rosenfeld have provided new life to strain theories, Agnew through his general strain theory and Messner and Rosenfeld's institutional anomie theory. GST is a microsociological perspective, and institutional anomie theory is macrosociological in nature. However, both theories offer promise, and with additional testing will be refined, perhaps giving birth to newer theories, in the tradition of Durkheim and Merton.

Attention turns now to control theories, another set of explanations for crime and deviance.

Chapter 6

CONTROL THEORIES

Control theories represent an interesting diversion from other theoretical traditions since the emphasis is on *why individuals do not* commit crimes or become deviant. Perhaps Robert Agnew says it best when he writes: "Social control theory . . . focuses on the absence of significant relationships with conventional others and institutions" whereas the previous theory discussed, the strain approach focuses on "negative relationships with others: relationships in which the individual is not treated as he or she wants to be treated" (1992, 48–49). With this in mind we turn attention to the leading control theories, beginning with that proposed by Travis Hirschi.

The Work of Travis Hirschi:
Causes of Delinquency

The year was 1969 and the tumultuous decade of the 1960s was coming to an end. Whereas the 1960s began with considerable promise and hope, it was ending on a greatly different note than anticipated: with much anger, frustration, sadness and disappointment; extreme disappointment. But sociology was riding a high, and the areas of criminology and deviance contributed to the popularity of sociology. During the 1960s, sociology contributed significantly to theories of

and research in criminology and deviance. No place was this more evident in *Causes of Delinquency* by Travis Hirschi, one of the most prominent criminologists in American sociology. In this classic work, Hirschi extended the concept of social control discussed by Emile Durkheim years earlier, and in doing so developed a theory although since modified, is still respected and tested. The four key elements of his theory (to be explained shortly) are: attachment; commitment; involvement; and belief, all which Hirschi theorized acted as mediating influences on delinquent behavior.

Explaining the Theory

The heart and soul of Hirschi's theory is as follows: strong positive bonds to conventional society will reduce the chances youth will become juvenile delinquents. At first glance this appears like the proverbial common sense statement, but we are reminded common sense told us the world was flat. Hirschi's four types of positive bonding to the social order are explained as follows. *Attachment means* being close to positive, significant others, such as parents, peers and the school. For example, when discussing attachment to parents Hirschi writes: "As is well known, the emotional bond between the parent and the child presumably provides the bridge across which pass parental ideals and expectations" (1969, 86). *Commitment* is conforming to social norms and to conventional society. When addressing commitment Hirschi writes: "One is committed to conformity not only by what one has but also by what one hopes to obtain. Thus "ambition" and/or "aspiration" play an important role in producing conformity" (1969, 21), implying there are certainly awards for playing by society's rule. *Involvement* entails spending positive time in conventional activities including work, sport, recreation, hobbies and doing homework, as is exemplified by the statement: "The child playing ping-pong, swimming in the community pool, or doing his homework is not committing delinquent acts" (1969, 187). *Belief* is supporting and upholding the laws and the legal system, and as noted by Hirschi: "We have not suggested that delinquency is based on our beliefs counter to conventional morality . . . but the meaning and efficacy of such beliefs are contingent upon other beliefs and, indeed, on the strength of other ties to the conventional order" (1969, 26). In addition to the four bonds addressed individually, Hirschi theorized three combinations of bonds would strengthen the antidelinquent response: attachment and commitment; commitment and involvement; and, attachment and belief.

Causes of Delinquency is more than just an expose of theoretical conceptualizations. It is also a test of these assumptions. Hirschi collected data to test social bonding theory from 5,545 public junior and senior high students enrolled in the Richmond County School District in the San Francisco Bay area in 1964. The sample included Caucasian and African American boys and girls, with complete data available for 4,077 students (1969, 35–36). The data were derived from three sources: school records that included infor-

mation on standardized test scores; police records that detailed what crimes youth in the sample had committed; and, an elaborate and lengthy questionnaire that included numerous school-related items, personal items, such as information on work and relationships with parents, and self-report questions, such as those asking about theft and fighting. (Appendix C in *Causes of Delinquency* has all of these items, and is well worth examining, since it has questions that would seem both ridiculous and inappropriate today, such as "Have you ever danced with a Mexican?" and "Have you ever gone to a party where most people are white?").

The results of the test of social bonding theory are generally supportive and encouraging. Identified below is a sampling of the areas reporting support for the theory *by types of social bond*, with page references in parentheses:

Attachment to Parents

- strong supervision by mother and low levels of delinquency (89)
- low involvement with delinquency by intimacy of communication with father (91)

Attachment to School

- low levels of delinquency by high standardized test scores (114)
- low self reporting of delinquency by positive self rating of school abilities (118)

Attachment to Peers

- low levels of delinquency by involvement with noncriminal friends (146)
- low self reported delinquency and respect of peer opinions (147)

Commitment to Conventional Lines of Action

- low involvement in smoking, drinking and dating by college aspirations (165)
- low level of involvement in delinquency by high achievement orientation (179)

Belief

- low self reporting of delinquency by respect for the police (201)
- low self reported delinquency by belief in individual responsibility (206)

The data analysis undertaken by Hirschi indicates strong and consistent support for social bonding theory. Now it is time to turn attention to other studies testing the theory.

Analysis and Empirical Support

Social control theory has been one of the most widely-tested theories in criminology and in the study of deviance. The results of the tests have usually been supportive, and this is quite interesting, since Travis Hirschi abandoned the theory in its original format during the 1990s (to be discussed in the following section). As is the case with tests of any theory, some parts of a theory may find more positive support than other aspects of the theory. As we have seen, Hirschi identified four bonds to conventional society: attachment, commitment, involvement and belief. Each bond has found at least some empirical support, depending upon who did the research, and what questions were asked. As Brown, Esbensen and Geis noted "The theory has been buttressed by empirical testing undertaken by many criminologists. . . . The basic framework of the theory has been challenged by only a few criminologists" (1991, 373). Support for social bonding theory has been reported for the *relationship*

between attachment, commitment and delinquency by a number of criminologists, including Agnew (1993), Akers and Cochran (1985), Cernkovich and Giordano (1987, 1992), Hirschi (1969), Junger and Marshall (1997), and, Sampson and Laub (1993). Agnew (1985) and Dunsmore and Kaplan (1997) found support for the *relationship between social bonds and minor forms of delinquency*, while other researchers have found support for the *connection between belief in the law and delinquent behavior* (Akers and Cochran, 1985; Jensen and Rojak, 1998; Krohn and Massey, 1980). It is to be stressed the above represents the tip of the iceberg when it comes to tests of social control theory and to gain a more in-depth look at such testing, two important studies of the theory are analyzed in detail.

Marianne Junger and Ineke Haen Marshall (1997) undertook a detailed test of social control theory using a sample of 814 boys of four ethnic backgrounds who resided in the Netherlands (the 814 boys represented completed questionnaires). Junger and Marshall wanted to apply social control theory to a different cultural setting since they noted almost all tests of criminological theories are undertaken in the United States (1997, 83). The four ethnic backgrounds represented in the study are boys of Turkish, Surinamese, Moroccan and Dutch heritage. In essence, the authors wanted to determine if Hirschi's four bonds to the social order predicted involvement in juvenile delinquency, with the data sources including a self-report instrument and police records. The tests of social control theory yielded the following results. First, weak belief in the law was found to be a strong predictor of involvement in delinquency, for all four ethnicities. Second, bonding to family and to school also was reported to predict involvement in delinquency, and was especially strong for low supervision and weak communication (in the family), and when it entailed many conflicts in school and bad school performance (except for the Moroccan sample). Leisure time was the primary measure of involvement, and for all four groups involvement in unconventional activities was highly predictive of juvenile delinquency. A critical finding concerning the bond of attachment was friends with police records play a major role in becoming active in antisocial conduct, and this too was reported for all four ethnicities (1997, 100). Junger and Marshall concluded the traditional Hirschi theory was useful in understanding delinquency from a cross-cultural perspective.

In a demonstration of the strength of Hirschi's theory, Longshore, Chang, Hsieh, and Messina (2004) tested the relationship of all four bonds to substance abuse, and employed a sample of 1,036 male probationers who were participants in Treatment Alternatives to Street Crime (TASC), a program established as an alternative to incarceration. The sample consisted of African American, Caucasian and Latino males who were asked to complete a questionnaire that included items relevant to the bonds of attachment, belief, commitment, and involvement. In a change of direction from other tests of social control theory, the authors' measure of commitment was *religious commitment*, or the importance of religion in the lives of the respondents. Additionally, Longshore, et al. tested for the effects of peer association in the abuse of alcohol and illegal drugs. The results supported their initial assumption that weak bonds to conventional society were predictive of substance abuse, with moral belief the bond with the strongest link to abusing drugs and alcohol. Associating with substance abusing friends also predicted use of drugs and alcohol, but this relationship occurred in conjunction with and was strengthened by

weak beliefs in the law and other rules, contributing to the body of literature that has found support for the power of Hirschi's bonds as predictors and correlates of delinquency (2004, 553).

The Work of Michael R. Gottfredson and Travis Hirschi: A General Theory of Crime

With the publication of *A General Theory of Crime* (1990), Michael R. Gottfredson and Travis Hirschi made three important contributions to criminology and to the study of deviance: first, although all but abandoning social bond theory, they readdressed and repackaged it, thus giving it a "new look" and by doing so created a new interest in the social control perspective; second, they returned to a time in the study of juvenile delinquency when there was research on the role of parents in the etiology of delinquent behavior; and third, *A General Theory of Crime* became part of a "wave" of new theories in criminology having surfaced during the last 20 years, which have helped to energize the fields of criminology and deviance.

Explaining the Theory

Ask yourself several questions. If you are not a criminal or deviant, why is that the case? Are you just simply better than some others? By luck of the draw do you just happen to have friends who do not violate social norms? Or is there something more, did you have parents or guardians who laid down the law when you were younger (and perhaps still do)? Gottfredson and Hirschi broke away from Hirchi's earlier thinking that crime was a result of weakened bonds to conventional society. Instead, they argue crime is a result of low self-control, and go one step further by arguing their *General*

Theory of Crime applies to *all* types of crime, ranging from the basic predatory crimes, such as theft and assault, to white-collar crime (thus the "general" in the title of their book). How is this possible? Gottfredson and Hirschi propose all criminals lack restraint: they lack control over their inhibitions, and they desire immediate gratification (1990, 90). Who then, or what is responsible for low self-control, and the inability to restrain oneself from criminality and deviance? Mom and dad. That's right! Parents are responsible for low self-control and the criminality of their children. Gottfredson and Hirschi stated that:

> All that is required to activate the system is affection for or investment in the child. The person who cares for the child will watch his behavior, see him doing things he should not do, and correct him. The result may be a child more capable of delaying gratification, more sensitive to the interests and desires of others, more independent, more willing to accept restraints on his activity, and more unlikely to use force or violence to attain his ends. (1990, 97)

It comes down to child-rearing practices for Gottfredson and Hirschi, and they go on to note that "The minimum conditions seem to be these: in order to teach the child self-control, someone must (1) monitor the child's behavior; (2) recognize deviant behavior when it occurs; and (3) punish such behavior" (1990, 97). Crime and delinquency are explained as the absence of points one through three. Interestingly, the authors do not conclude crime is a slam-dunk for those individuals who are not disciplined in the formative years. Gottfredson and Hirschi state there must be opportunity to commit crime, and when this is mixed with low self-control, individuals have a high probability of engaging in criminal or deviant acts (1990, 91–94).

So what are the characteristics of low self-control? It is not a long list, but included are: (1) seeking immediate gratification; (2) taking risks, being physical and adventuresome; (3) unstable social lives, including marriages, friendships, unstable work history; (4) poor academic skills; and (5) self-centeredness, even to the point of not caring about others, especially people who criminals victimize (1990, 89–90).

One of the most important and criticized aspects of *A General Theory of Crime* is the assumption that all types of crime can be explained as a result of low self-control, with many types of crime committed by roughly the same types of people. According to Gottfredson and Hirschi individuals who commit burglaries, robberies, homicides, car theft, and rapes tend to be young African American males seeking immediate gratification from committing crimes. The common denominator among these men? Lack of restraint and self-control (1990, 27–35). Even embezzlers and white-collar criminals also seek immediate rewards. The more sophisticated-type criminals lack restraint and have the opportunity to commit crimes, meaning they have available target(s) to victimize (1990, 38–39).

Analysis and Empirical Support

A General Theory of Crime has undergone significant testing, and depending on the focus of the research, has received consistent support (Barron, 2003; Finkel and Campbell, 2001; Gibbs, Giever, and Higgins, 2003; Grasmick, Bursik, and Arnelev, 1993; Longshore, Chang, Hsieh, and Messina, 2004; Mason and Windle, 2002; Nagin and Paternoster, 1994; Pratt and Cullen, 2000; Tittle and Botchkovar, 2005; Tittle, Ward, and Grasmick, 2003a, 2003b; Vazsonyi and Crosswhite, 2004). Studies have found support for the *relationship between low social control and delinquency* (Arnelev et al., 1993;

Gibbs and Giever, 1995; Lagrange and Silverman, 1999; Tremblay, Boulerice, Arsenauly, and Niscale, 1995) and the *connection of poor parenting to criminal activity* (Feldman and Weinberger, 1994; Gibbs, Geiver, and Martin, 1998; Hay, 2001; Perrone, Sullivan, Pratt, and Satenik, 2004; Unnever, Pratt, and Cullen, 2003). A few studies have examined Gottfredson and Hirschi's assumption *that individual rankings of self-control remain stable after age 10*, with one study rendering it support (Arneklev, Grasmick, Tittle, and Bursik, 1999), another study neither confirming or rejecting the assumption (Turner and Piquero, 2002), and one study (to be addressed below) rejecting the stability hypothesis (Burt, Simons, and Simons, 2006). The empirical examinations of *A General Theory of Crime* affirm its popularity and respect, and two studies putting it to the test are now examined.

Burt, Simons and Simons (2006) have undertaken a recent in-depth study of *A General Theory of Crime*. The objective of their research was to test the different facets of the theory, using a sample of African American adolescents and their caregivers. The sample for the research was derived from the Family and Community Health Study (FACHS), which analyzes the effects of neighborhood and family on the health and development of children over time (2006, 361). Two Waves of children between the ages of 10–12 (Wave 1) and 12–14 (Wave 2) were drawn, and included 867 African American boys and girls in Wave 1, and 779 African American boys and girls in wave 2. The authors employed several different scales to test important elements of Gottfredson and Hirschi's theory. The scales were for: *low self-control*, which included 39 items such as "you enjoy taking risks" and "you often feel frustrated"; *delinquency*, measured by use of a self-report instrument; *parenting practices* included items about parental monitoring of

children, consistency of disciple, inductive reasoning, problem solving and positive parental reinforcement. There were also scales for *deviant peer affiliation, positive peer association*, and *attachment to teachers*. The multitude of scales used made it possible to undertake a comprehensive test of the theory. In addition, Burt et al. included two control variables: age and sex (2006, 364–368).

Their major findings were older males are most likely to be involved in delinquency, a finding consistent with years of research in the study of juvenile delinquency. Burt et al. also found low self-control was strongly related to delinquency, and authoritative parenting (firm and decisive parenting) was associated with low levels of criminality in children, findings supporting key premises of the theory. In addition, the authors reported little support for Gottfredson and Hirschi's assumption that detached or uninvolved parenting working solely through low self-control causes delinquency (2006, 372–373). Perhaps the major finding concerns the *stability postulate*, or that after age 10 individual rankings of control remain stable over the life span. Burt et al. found that from Wave 1 to Wave 2 there were consistent shifts in the self-control stability rankings of respondents, another departure from that reported by Gottfredson and Hirschi. However, major aspects of the theory still received support, consistent with the literature.

A study undertaken by Gibbs, Giever and Higgins (2003) tested the efficacy of the "general theory" using a nonrandom sample of 422 university students enrolled in liberal studies courses. Students were asked to complete a 129-item questionnaire that included scales for low self-control, parental management and deviance. The authors sought to study the direct effect of low self-control on deviance, and the effect of parental management working through low self-control on deviance, in order to ascertain which had the strongest effect. The 422 respondents engaged in retrospective research whereby they were asked to recall their experiences with parental management when they were in the ninth grade (2003, 446). Their research confirmed the "general theory" by reporting a statistically significant but modest direct effect of parental management on deviance, and a stronger mediated effect of parental management working through low self-control on deviant behavior. In addition Gibbs et al. reported low self-control itself exerted a strong direct effect on deviance.

CASE STUDY: THE BRANCH DAVIDIANS

The Branch Davidians are most known for the tragedy that occurred after a 51-day standoff on April 19, 1993, when agents of the Federal Bureau of Investigation attacked the Branch Davidian compound, resulting in the deaths of 75 followers, including 21 children (much information in this section is adapted from *Waco-Inside Story*, 1995). But little is generally known or understood about this organization and its various leaders, including David Koresh.

The Branch Davidians (BD) are an extension of the Church of the Seventh-Day Adventists (SDA), and were originally founded by Victor Houteff in 1935, who broke from the SDA after disagreement with some of its doctrines. The first name of the BD was The Shepard's Rod, and Houteff believed his role was to amass 144,000 Christians and eventually take them to Israel, based on prophecy from the Book of Revelation. In order to accomplish this prophecy and to prepare for the trek to Israel, Houteff founded the Mount Carmel Center in Waco, Texas in 1935. Houteff

eventually changed the name from The Shepard's Rod to the Davidian Seventh-Day Adventist Association (DSAA), based on the belief he and his followers would establish the Davidic Kingdom, and wait out the second coming of Jesus Christ, and the end of the world. But he never came anything close to recruiting 144,000 followers, falling way short and probably never having more than 125–150 believers at the Compound. Houteff died in 1955 and his wife Florence assumed leadership over the group, but it splintered after her prophecy failed that God would return and render judgment on April, 22, 1959. One of the key followers of the DSAA, Benjamin Roden assumed control of one of the groups, declaring himself an angel of God, and changed the name to the Branch Davidian SDAs (BDDSAs). Roden died in 1978, and his wife Lois ascended to the leadership of BDDSAs by anointing herself angel status, while preaching that God was really feminine in form. Eventually she married Vernon Howell who joined the group in 1981. Howell was in his twenties and Lois Roden in her late sixties, with Howell assuming leadership over the BDDSAs in the late 1980s after the death of Lois. A power struggle ensued between Howell and Lois's son George, with Howell the eventual victor, but only after a court trial in which Howell and other followers were acquitted of charges of attempting to gain control over the BDSAAs through the use of violence (Roden was shot in the chest and hands). In 1990, Howell changed the name to the Branch Davidians, reestablishing the compound at Waco, and convincing its members they were living in the end times, and should be preparing for the apocalypse by stockpiling food and weapons. It is during this time that Howell changed his name: to *David Koresh* (Bromley, D. and E. Silver, 1995; Anthony, D. and T. Robbins, 1997).

The Work of Charles R. Tittle: Control Balance Theory

Once again, ask yourself several questions. Who is control of you? How much control do others exert over you? How much control do you have over yourself? Control over our lives has been a question posed over the years by a number of areas of study including religion, philosophy, psychology and sociology. From the previous discussions of social control theory it is evident the question of control has played an important role in the study of crime and deviance, with scholars such as Travis Hirschi explaining deviations from laws and social norms in terms of bonds to conventional society. But perhaps this is just too simple with regard to approaching the issues of crime and deviance, meaning there may be more to the story than nonnormative conduct resulting from attenuated bonds to the social order. Maybe it has much to do with perceptions of control over our lives; maybe it is linked to opportunities to commit acts of deviance; maybe it is as a result of strain; or, maybe it is a result of choice. Enter Charles R. Tittle.

Explaining the Theory

Charles R. Tittle has been a prominent criminologist for over 40 years, who in 1995 published *Control Balance: Toward a General Theory of Deviance*, representing one of the newer and "pure" theories of deviance to emerge in the last several decades. By "pure" is meant the theory is not necessarily a criminology-specific theory, but one that can be applied to a multitude of types of deviant behavior, criminal or noncriminal. The theory is a combination of fairly easy to understand, yet complex and at times quite vague ideas and concepts (this latter problem has led to limited empirical testing of the theory,

to be discussed in the next section). The crux of the theory is all individuals experience some form of control over their lives. *Control balance* occurs when the control individuals have over their lives is *equal* to the amount of control exerted over them. Others experience *control imbalance*, and in this situation individuals either (a) control more than they are controlled or (b) are controlled more than they control, thus resulting in deviance. It is in the following statement Tittle clarifies this latter distinction and introduces the notion of *control ratio*: "The central premise of the theory is the amount of control to which an individual is subject, relative to the amount of control he or she can exercise, determines the probability of deviance occurring as well as the type of deviance likely to occur (1995, 135). Of interest is Tittle's approach to control imbalance and its relationship to deviance and crime. Control imbalance is to be conceptualized as a continuum (a straight line) with control balance (conformity) in the middle and control imbalances on both sides of conformity. At the left side is *repression*, comprised of three categories of deviance, each indicative of *control deficit*, or when individuals are controlled more than they control. The three categories are submission, defiance, and predation. On the right side is *autonomy*, also comprised of three types of deviance, but representing *control surplus*, a situation where one controls more than he or she is controlled: The three types of autonomy are decadence, plunder, and exploitation (1995, 136–140). Both control deficit and surplus (control imbalance) are related to deviance, but differ as to its nature and degree. Let's summarize to this point. *Tittle is arguing deviance is related to social control; control balance* where deviance is absent, and *control imbalance* when deviance occurs. But imbalance is characterized by different types of deviance, some criminal, others noncriminal; some violent, others not violent, thus offering flexibility to the theory. More specifically, the six types of deviance (subsumed under their proper category) are (1995, 136–140):

Repression (Control Deficit)

- *Predation:* includes acts of violence, such as homicide, rape and robbery, as well as crimes such as theft, fraud and price gouging. Also included is parental use of guilt to intimate or control their children.
- *Defiance:* these can be acts that have little reward for the deviant, such as vandalism, political protests, and moodiness by a marital partner.
- *Submission:* individuals submit themselves to various types of abuse, such as physical and sexual abuse.

Autonomy (Control Surplus)

- *Exploitation:* these acts involve taking advantaged of others, such as corporate fraud, influence peddling, and can include murder for hire.
- *Plunder:* Included are environmental destruction and ethnic cleansing.
- *Decadence:* Sadistic torture, sexual abuse of children, and humiliating others for the pure joy of it fall into this category.

Tittle's theory also addresses the *motivations* for deviance, which he identifies as *predispositional* and *situational* factors. *Predispositional* motivating factors include: the control ratio which will vary according to race, social class, status and gender; those factors that meet physical and psychic needs; and, the desire for autonomy learned in early childhood. *Situational* factors include being provoked by racial slurs and other unkind words and insults, and displays of weakness that may provoke criminal victimization (1995, 162). Both types of motivations can be a means of rectifying, remedying, or responding to situations. This latter point is seen clearly in the case of individuals who respond violently to insults, and those that exploit others for profit. Encompassed within this theory are elements of classical and contemporary *strain theory* (i.e., negative relationships as exemplified by insults and racial slurs); *routine activities theory*, or explanations of crime that focus on opportunities for criminal acts (i.e., being out late at night when predatory crimes may occur); personal decisions to commit violations, or aspects of *rational choice theory*; and, *conflict theory*, explaining deviant actions as a result of repression and exploitation.

Analysis and Empirical Support

Compared to other theories, Control Balance Theory (CBT) has not been widely tested, mostly as a result of its complexity. However, when tested it has received some empirical support (Curry and Piquero, 2003; Delisi and Hochstetler, 2002; Hickman and Piquero, 2001; Higgins and Lauterbauch, 2004; Piquero, Macintosh and Hickman, 2001; Piquero and Hickman, 1999, 2002, 2003; Tittle,- 2004). One major test of CBT is now addressed by applying it to white-collar crime.

Piquero and Piquero (1996) are the first scholars to apply CBT to white-collar criminality, and sampled 87 adults ranging in ages from 21–54, who were enrolled in university level business courses in the mid-Atlantic region of the United States (1996, 406–412). The focus of their research was to ascertain, assuming hypothetical situations, if the respondents would be likely to engage in exploitative behavior–if they would engage in white-collar-type criminality. The authors hypothesized exploitation (defined in this case as lying about or inflating sales statistics) would be more closely linked with control surplus, and would have little or nothing to do with control deficits. Several scales were developed to measure exploitation, and included questions such as "What is the chance you would act as the manager did under these circumstances?" (asking a subordinate to lie about sales data); "What is the chance you would be arrested for a criminal offense if you did what the manager did under these circumstances?"; and, "how exciting or thrilling would it be to engage in the act portrayed in the scenario?"

Piquero and Piquero included a number of variables, in addition to their measures of control surplus and control deficit including age, race, moral beliefs, perceived risks of committing the offense, and benefits to be derived from the crime. The findings are consistent with their hypothesis that control surplus is more likely to predict white collar criminality (as operationalized in this study). Of all the variables tested, control surplus had the only statistically significant relationship to committing the illegal act of inflating sales statistics (1996, 418). This finding is consistent with one of the main premises of CBT, and that is individuals characterized by control surplus are more likely to experience self-control and to be exploitive, whereas those characterized by control deficits experience being controlled, and are more likely to be the exploited.

The Work of John Hagan: Structural Criminology

As noted when discussing *A General Theory of Crime*, the past 20 years have been ripe for the introduction of new theories in criminology and the study of deviance. Tittle proposed "Control Balance Theory" in 1990, and Gottfredson and Hirshi developed

their "General Theory of Crime" in 1995. One year earlier than the work of Tittle, criminologist John Hagan published *Structural Criminology* (1989) and introduced "power control theory" (PCT), an interesting and exciting integrated theory that combines elements of classical Marxist theory, feminist theory, and elements of control theories. Of interest, and not to be ignored is PCT was put forth by a male (Hagan), showing the emerging influence of feminism in criminology, and in the field of deviance.

Explaining the Theory

Most Americans are raised in nuclear families, and many of these individuals are reared in environments with brothers and sisters, who are different from each other as a result of the ways they are socialized. Please recall, Gottfredson and Hirschi placed the onus of responsibility of having well-behaved children squarely on the shoulders of parents. In their case, the socialization of children by parents is prima facie in how their offspring turn out. In a similar vein, Canadian criminologist John Hagan also sees parents in a prominent role concerning the delinquency of children, only Hagan makes his arguments on the macro sociological ground that western cultures, such as those found in Canada and the United States, are characterized by the powerful social institution of the family that greatly affects if children will conform or not conform.

Central to Hagan's theory is boys and girls experience different types of socialization, depending upon the type of family structure; *patriarchal* or *egalitarian*. In *patriarchal families* traditional gender role socialization is stressed, and in *egalitarian families* equality between males and females is more pronounced. This in turn has a major connection to juvenile delinquency, as will be discussed later. In order to more clearly understand the importance of the types of socialization between the two family structures, Hagan states that in advanced western societies *an instrument-object relationship* exists between parents and children, with parents being the instruments of control, and children the objects of their power, or the recipients of parental control (1989, 157). What transpires from this type relationship between parents and their children is the ways that boys and girls are raised. In traditional patriarchal families, the father-husband is the authority figure who works outside the home, and has supreme power over all family members, including the wife-mother. Why? She is not economically productive, or not economically active outside the home: she stays at home and has primary responsibility for socializing children. The father-husband derives his power from the workplace, since he is the only family member who "brings home the bacon," to use an old expression, and therefore emerges as the central power figure in the family. Meanwhile, the mother focuses her energies on child-rearing, and when it comes to daughters, firmly instilling in them their future roles as mother-wife. This is what Hagan refers to as the *"cult of domesticity,"* or girls being *socialized* for becoming mothers and wives (1989, 156–158). On the other hand, children brought up in families where sex role equality is the norm, view their futures in an entirely different light. These children are socialized by parents who work outside the home, and who are *both* economically productive. Sons and daughters alike experience the same signals and direction from their parents, and are raised to see the world is full of multiple options and opportunities. So what then is the link of all of this to delinquency? In *patriarchal families*, daughters are more severely controlled by their mothers and therefore do not take many risks, including not committing acts of delinquency. Daughters are taught to be feminine and to accept their limited roles in life. Boys on the other hand are not nearly as closely monitored or supervised, and do engage in a fair amount of risk taking, that can entail involvement in juvenile delinquency.

In *equalitarian families* both boys and girls are taught by their parents that risk taking is acceptable, and since mothers also work full-time outside the home and spend less time supervising their children, both girls and boys may engage in juvenile delinquent behaviors. Hagan writes "Daughters become more like sons in their involvement in such forms of risk taking as delinquency" (1989, 158), and "as mothers gain power relative to husbands, daughters gain freedom relative to sons" (1989, 157). Both patriarchal and egalitarian families are involved in reproducing gender roles, or to state this differently, parents from both family structures reproduce themselves.

Analysis and Empirical Support

Power Control Theory has undergone a fair amount of empirical testing and receives backing (Blackwell, 2000; Grasmick, Hagan, Blackwell and Arnelev, 1996; Hagan, 1989; Hagan, Gillis and Simpson, 1990; Hagan and Kay, 1990; Jensen and Thompson, 1990; McCarthy, Hagan and Woodward, 1999). Other scholars have raised issues concerning PCT relative to its spotty support outside of Canada (Jensen, 1990, 1993a, 1993b), and Chesney-Lind and Shelden (1992) have questioned the theory's emphasis on the roles of mothers in producing juvenile delinquents, although they recognized John Hagan for explicating the importance of gender and patriarchy as causal factors in delinquency (1992, 97). An example of a study in support of PCT follows directly below.

Harold Grasmick, John Hagan, Brenda-Sims Blackwell and Bruce J. Arneklev (1996) *extended* PCT beyond its original boundaries by applying it to 416 adults from Oklahoma City, Oklahoma by inquiring into risk-taking behaviors they engaged in as *adults*. Two measures of patriarchy were developed: *occupational patriarchy*, or the parent(s) that had power in the family as derived from the workplace. An example of a Likert-type item concerning occupational patriarchy is "For most of the time growing up: Mother and father were both employed with or without authority in workplace." Their research also included Likert-type items on *attitudinal patriarchy*, or how the respondents viewed the gender roles of parents, especially mothers. Two examples of questions here are: "it is okay for mothers to work full-time when their youngest child is under age five"; and, "men are by nature better leaders for the family than are women." The research also included measures of maternal and paternal parental control, or items about parental supervision of the respondents when they were teenagers. The risk preferences items (i.e., getting into trouble for excitement) measured the degree of risk respondents had engaged in as adults (1996, 184–187). The study was partially retrospective in nature since it entailed asking respondents to recall past familial experiences, such as how closely they were supervised by parents, and which parent possessed power in the family.

The findings reported by Grasmick et al. are supportive of PCT. Respondents from less patriarchal families were almost equally involved in risk-taking behaviors as adults, and males from patriarchal families were significantly more likely to have engaged in taking risks in their adult years. In addition, the authors reported fathers had far greater influence on risk taking of both sons and daughters in patriarchal families, a finding that runs counter to one of the basic tenets of PCT (1996, 188–192). Grasmick et al. concluded "Parental control in patriarchal families, therefore, is a key factor in shaping gender differences in subsequent adult risk preferences, as power control theory predicts, but, contrary to the theory's initial formulation, fathers have a bigger impact than mothers" (1996, 193).

In Recognition: Michael Gottfredson

One of the most distinguished criminologists of the last quarter century is Michael Gottfredson, who is currently the Executive Vice Chancellor at the University of California-Irvine. Prior to his current position, he was the Vice President for Undergraduate Education and Professor of Management and Policy, Law, Sociology, and Psychology at the University of Arizona in Tuscon. Dr. Gottfredson has also held positions at the Claremont Graduate School, the University of Illinois at Urbana, and the State University of New York at Albany. Although Dr. Gottfredson's research accomplishments are many, he is most widely known for his collaboration with Travis Hirschi in their renowned *A General Theory of Crime* published in 1990. Dr. Gottfredson has made significant contributions to self-control theory, and his publications also include articles and books in the areas of social policy, deviance, victims of crime, pretrial release, prisons, causes of crime, and discretion in the criminal justice system.

Dr. Gottfredson has acted as a consultant on criminal justice policy, and he held the title of the Director of the Criminal Justice Research Center in New York City. Additionally, he was on the Board of Directors of "The Parent Connection" and "The Crime and Justice Research Center."

SUMMARY

Control or social control theories represent an important cog-in-the-wheel in theories about deviance and crime. Travis Hirschi was instrumental in the late 1960s in advancing a concrete control theory, and once again in 1990 along with Michael Gottfredson. Control theories are unique in that they question why individuals do not violate social norms, a position different from other theoretical traditions in sociology that focus on the causes and correlates of crime and deviance. Over the years other social control-oriented theories have been proposed, including John Hagan's power control theory and Charles R. Tittle's control balance theory. Both have received empirical support, but will need further testing to better assess their theoretical efficacy.

The next set of deviance theories to be discussed are concerned with societal reaction, and learning nonconformity.

Chapter 7

SOCIETAL REACTION AND OTHER SOCIAL PROCESSES THEORIES

CASE STUDY: STUDENT IDEAS ABOUT LABELING

For years the author of this text has engaged his classes in an exercise concerning labels. It is a simple assignment whereby students are asked to identify both positive and negative labels. They are not told in advance this exercise will take place, instead the author arrives in class the first day labeling theory is to be addressed, and gives a basic charge, and that is every student is to spend a few minutes jotting down what they believe to be both positive and negative labels. After the task is completed, the author asks the students to state their examples of positive and negative deviance. A recorder jots down the contributions, and the notes are collected. Listed is a sampling of student ideas about both positive and negative labels:

Positive Labels

- ambition
- benevolent
- attractive
- studious
- popular
- talented
- doctors
- rich/wealthy
- perfect
- comedian
- teachers
- nurse
- leader
- trustworthy
- beautiful

Negative Labels

- child molester
- idiot
- prostitute
- ex con
- terrorist
- alcoholic/addict
- mentally ill
- poor
- ugly
- stupid
- deviant
- adulterer
- liar
- lazy
- gay/homosexual

Not to anyone's surprise, students appear to have little difficulty arriving at negative labels, but they are more pressed to conjure up positive ones. What is more, discussion does ensue, and there is often debate over what is negative and what is positive. A case in hand is "gay/homosexual," connotations that certainly have changed in the eyes of students over the years, with some students recognizing these as negative labels, and others arguing the exact opposite. During the 1970s when the author undertook this same exercise, students were likely to view gay/homosexual negatively, and they were hesitant to discuss sexual orientation, period. By the 1990s this had changed, however, today students find themselves on both sides of the coin, with little standing in their way in terms of open discussion. Case in hand two, the term deviant itself. As noted in the first chapter, the words deviant or deviance constitute a label, usually negative. Contemporary students will vary on how they react to the terms since in their minds this may mean occasional smoking of marijuana or premarital sex, neither which may be perceived as deviant or negative by some students, yet for others both smoking marijuana and engaging in premarital sex is considered wrong, even seriously deviant.

The disagreements do not begin and end with negative labels but also extend to positive ones, such as leader and rich/wealthy. For some students leader is not necessarily a superlative, since in their lifetimes they have known leaders who fall short of integrity, such as former President Clinton's lying about his relationship with Monica Lewinsky, and the leaders who took down Enron. Rich/wealthy meets with debate, with some students recognizing wealth as an extension of hard work, diligence and belief in the American way. Yet other students view wealth and prosperity as signs of corruption, greed, and the willingness of individuals to walk over others, no matter the cost. The exercise, as simple as it is, gets students to think as well as to reflect on their values and upbringing.

The Societal Reaction Tradition

Ask yourselves a few basic questions starting with "what is it that you know and remember about others"? Change this question a bit and ask yourselves "what is it that you will continue to know and remember about others for years"? In your lifetime you have probably encountered individuals who are alcoholics, criminals, mentally ill, school drop outs, and sexual deviants. One rather interesting place to test what is being asked is high school reunions: carefully observe what takes place. In all likelihood the popular people from years back will probably hang with each other; the athletes will tend to gather around one another and recant old "war stories"; the class scholars will undoubtedly move in the same circles; and the less-than popular, and those with questionable high school histories will either be out-of-the-loop, or not come at all to high school class reunions, even though years later they may have gone on to be successful at their careers, and to have solid families and marriages. An example is a friend of the author's who was expelled from high school just two months prior to graduating for committing the "heinous" offense of playing basketball in the high school gym on a Sunday morning, before official supervision arrived. An intramural game was to be played by senior boys from the town's two high schools, and the school officials who were to referee the event were late, so my friend decided to "shoot around" while waiting for the referees to arrive. The next day he was summoned to the office of the principle and expelled. It was his third "offense" in four years, and the third time was not the charm. His first two offenses involved being late one morning for school when he was a freshman, and getting caught sneaking out at lunch time to play eight ball at the local pool hall his junior year. How is he remembered? As the kid who got kicked out. He is not invited to class reunions, although he not only attended high school with many of his peers, but also went all the way from kindergarten with the same class mates, getting expelled just 60 days short of receiving his high school diploma. Sixty days cost him 12 years in the eyes of the graduating class. By the following August this friend was serving his country in Viet Nam. Forty years later he is a successful business and family man, who owns an expensive house on a beautiful golf course. As for the author of this text, well he was only suspended for three days for the same violation, and graduated with his classmates (it was only his second offense).

In the study of deviance attention has been placed on issues such as those addressed above. Many individuals are "marked" for their past indiscretions, real or perceived, and carry with them the memories of their pasts, if for no other reason than others will not let them forget about who and what they once were (and may still be). Attention is now directed toward this type of stigmatizing processes, which for some years has been called *labeling theory*.

attempt to unravel and to explain the symbolic nature of cultures, in order to piece together the lives, values, beliefs and behaviors of people who reside in them (Cooley, 1902, 1909; Mead, 1934). The major data collection method used with labeling theory is field research, which was discussed in the second chapter. If undertaken properly, field research allows the scientist time to become immersed in a social setting, and to be able to learn a great deal about much of what takes place there, especially the meanings humans attach to their interactions and social milieu.

It is to this tradition that labeling theory (LT) owes its origins. Labeling theorists emphasize the role of interaction in the construction of social labels (whatever they may be) and how individuals apply and react to labels. We begin with the early work of *Frank Tannenbaum.* "Analysis and Empirical Support" will not be presented after the three authors individually. Instead it will follow the discussion of the works of Frank Tannenbaum, Edwin M. Lemert, and Howard S. Becker.

THE WORKS OF FRANK TANNENBAUM, EDWIN LEMERT AND HOWARD S. BECKER: LABELING THEORY AND THE SOCIETAL REACTION PERSPECTIVE

Labeling theory, also sometimes referred to as the *societal reaction* school, has its origins in symbolic interaction (SI) theory, one of the leading general theories in sociology. SI focuses on human interaction, and the meanings and interpretation associated with human communication. As such, it is an

Frank Tannenbaum and the Dramatization of Evil

Frank Tannenbaum is considered one of the first, if not the original labeling theorist. His 1938 work, *Crime and the Community* laid the foundation for what would eventually become the labeling perspective. Tannenbaum was concerned with societal reaction to juvenile delinquents after they are caught committing antisocial acts, and the consequences this portends for young people who were formally processed by the criminal justice system. Tannenbaum wrote: "Only some of the children are caught . . . although all may be equally guilty" (1938, 19). The formal processing results in the "dramatization of evil," whereby society actually worsens the situation concerning delinquents by formally labeling them. In another statement Tannenbaum observed: "He becomes classified as a thief, perhaps, and the entire world about him has suddenly become a different place for him and will remain different for the rest of his life" (1938, 19).

Tannenbaum recognized the importance of official processing, and coined the term *tagging* to refer to the official stamp or mark that is placed on young people when they are arrested and processed through the criminal justice network: "The process of making the criminal, therefore, is a process of tagging, defining, identifying, describing, emphasizing, making conscious and self-conscious; it becomes a way of stimulating, suggesting, emphasizing, and evoking the very traits that are complained of. . . . The person becomes the thing he is described as being. . ." (1938, 19–20). It is this type of thinking that forms the basis of labeling theory, and as you will see puts forth the position that labels are long-lasting, potentially devastating to those who have been labeled, and perhaps impossible to eradicate. The labeled person becomes a self-fulfilling prophecy, or one who as a result of the label continues a life of deviance and crime.

The Work of Edwin M. Lemert: Primary and Secondary Deviance

Chronologically, Edwin M. Lemert is the next major figure in labeling theory whose major publications *Social Pathology* (1951) and *Human Deviance, Social Problems, and Social Control* (1967, 1972) expanded on the work of Tannenbaum and his concern for the long-term effects of labels. Lemert introduced two of the most important concepts, not only as they related to labeling theory, but also for the entire field of deviance. The concepts are *primary* and *secondary deviance*, as Lemert envisioned deviance as a continuum.

Primary deviance is a type of deviance that most of us have experienced, such as *occasionally* drinking alcohol underage, and driving over the speed limit. The key here is primary deviance is *infrequent* behavior, and most saliently individuals who occasionally engage in it do not think of or define themselves as a deviant, nor do others. Lemert wrote primary deviance "does not lead to symbolic reorganization at the level of self regarding attitudes and social roles" (1967, 17).

On the other hand, *secondary deviance* is of a much different and serious nature, since it entails immersion into a life of deviance, largely as a result of *societal reaction*. Deviants, in a sense, dig themselves into a deeper hole, and are unable to change how society perceives them, and how they have come to see themselves. In short, they become the label (i.e., alcoholic; criminal/ex-con; crazy). Lemert wrote: "Secondary deviance refers to a special class of socially defined responses which people make to problems created by the societal reaction to their deviance. These problems are essentially moral problems which revolve around stigmatization, punishments, segregation and social control. . . . The secondary deviant, as opposed to his actions, is a person whose life and identity are organized around the facts of deviance" (1967, 40–41).

Lemert outlined the process involved in becoming a secondary deviant (1951, 77):

1. primary deviation;
2. societal penalties;
3. further primary deviation;
4. stronger penalties and rejections;
5. further deviation, perhaps with hostilities and resentments beginning to focus upon those doing the penalizing;
6. crisis reached in the tolerance quotient, expressed in formal action by the community stigmatizing the deviant;

7. strengthening of the deviant conduct as a reaction to the stigmatizing and penalties; and;

8. ultimate acceptance of deviant and social status and efforts at adjustment on the basis of the associated role.

Lemert extended labeling theory by applying it to check forgers, and distinguished between naïve and secondary check forgers (1972). Naïve check forgers are those individuals who do not get hooked on the crime of forgery, meaning they do it on occasion, and fail to develop an identity as a career criminal (1972, 165). Secondary check forgers mirror the idea of secondary deviance; they accept their deviant status, and build their lives around it, to the point that they evade long-term relationships because their crimes keep them on the run (1972, 180).

The Work of Howard S. Becker: Moral Entrepreneurs

"The deviant is one to whom that label has been successfully applied; deviant behavior is behavior that people so label" (1963, 9). This sentence from one of the most famous works in sociology, *Outsiders: Studies in the Sociology of Deviance* (1963) represents some of the most important words in labeling theory, and emanates from the mind of Howard S. Becker, who is often identified as the most important figure in the history of the labeling perspective. Becker is also a noted methodologist, (in addition to his interest in deviant behavior), and his earlier study of marijuana use among jazz musicians in Chicago, Illinois was influential in how he would come to approach the subject matter of deviance.

Becker parted ways with other students of deviance by disagreeing with their more functionalist view that what is considered deviant results from societal consensus. Becker argued, on the contrary only a few individuals have the power and legitimacy in society to determine what is deviant (1963, 8). He called these individuals *moral entrepreneurs*, who are generally from the upper social classes (1963, 149). Given their power and status in society, the moral entrepreneurs determine what is deviant and not deviant, directly impacting who will get labeled. Becker did not see the moral entrepreneurs as necessarily mean or evil, instead he wrote that they are moved to help the less fortunate, and are taking society's best interests to heart. But in doing so, those in lower social class positions and without power become labeled via the formal actions taken by those people intending to help them. Becker wrote "Moral crusaders typically want to help those beneath them to achieve a better status. That those beneath them do not always like the means proposed for their salvation is another matter. But this fact–that moral crusaders are typically dominated by those in the upper levels of the social structure–means they add to the power they derive from the legitimacy of their moral position, the power they derive from their superior position in society" (1963, 149). Becker observed rule enforcers are necessary in order to carry out the wishes and values of the moral crusaders, and are individuals most likely to have direct contact with those in need of salvation, meaning the ones doing the official labeling.

Becker created what he called the "Sequential Model of Deviant Behavior" which depicts more clearly his thinking about deviance and labeling (1963, 20).

The model is instructive of Becker's approach to labeling, since becoming labeled as a result of getting caught is accentuated in the model. "Falsely Accused" individuals are those who have been labeled, did nothing wrong, yet they have been labeled.

Table 7:1.

HOWARD BECKER'S SEQUENTIAL MODEL
OF DEVIANT BEHAVIOR

	Obediant Behavior	Rule-Breaking Breaking
Perceived as Deviant	Falsely Accused **Labeled**	Pure Deviant **Labeled**
Not Perceived as Deviant	Conforming **Not Labeled**	Secret Deviant **Not Labeled**

"Secret deviants" are those who do engage in deviance, are not apprehended, and receive no official labels. "Pure deviants" get caught and have labels slapped on them. Finally, "Conforming" individuals are not deviant, and unlike the "falsely accused" are not labeled, which takes us back to Becker's famous assertion: "The deviant is one to whom that label has been successfully applied; deviant behavior is behavior that people so label" (1963, 9).

Analysis and Empirical Support

Labeling theory was ripe for the times. Those times were the 1960s when the establishment was under heavy scrutiny, especially by the young. This was an era of civil rights and anti-war demonstrations. It represented the origins of the modern feminist movement, and other social causes such as "the Gray Power" and Gay Liberation Movements, and the efforts of Caesar Chavez in California with the Mexican grape pickers. It is in this context that labeling theory thrived. It was new and refreshing to undergraduate students taking sociology classes, and to young and aspiring sociologists (like the author of this text). Labeling theory did not explain deviance as done previously. Labeling theory focused on the *cre-*

ation of social labels and the role of those with affluence, influence, and power in the development and application of deviance designations. It appeared to have wide applicability, including criminals and the mentally ill. It was and still is a fun perspective to present to students, but is has met with a fair number of powerful critics (Akers, 1968; Gibbs, 1966; Heidensohn, 1968; Leonard, 1982; Liazos, 1972; Mankoff, 1971; Plummer, 1979; Shoemaker, 1996; Taylor, Walton, and Young, 1973; Ward, 1971; Wellford, 1975; Young, 1981). Perhaps the most serious criticisms of labeling theory were not levied against it directly, but *indirectly*, and those will be discussed at the end of this section. At this juncture, it should be noted actual empirical tests of the theories (i.e., Becker, Lemert) just addressed are rare, therefore attention is focused on criticisms of their content.

All authors cited above have basically enunciated the same concerns about labeling theory, and a summary of the most important of these criticisms is now presented.

1. A common criticism deals with *origins*, or can be stated as "the chicken or the egg" argument. The concern is as follows, stated as rhetorical questions: "What comes first, the label or the behavior?" "Does the label create the deviant behavior?" "What are the origins of the deviant behavior?" For example, alcoholics usually drink before facing an official (or unofficial) label, so in this case the alcoholic already existed, therefore the behavior preceded the label. But we are reminded about Becker's "secret deviant," so in some limited respect this has been addressed by labeling theorists.

2. A second common critique strikes much at the human condition, and can be referred to as the *slam-dunk* criti-

cism, or "here's the label, so here's the behavior." Using alcoholism as an example again just because individuals may be labeled as alcoholics does not mean that they will actually become alcoholics, especially in the meaning of secondary deviance (we are reminded they may have been alcoholics prior to the application of the label). Human beings are hopefully far more malleable than getting slapped with and becoming the label. This deterministic/fatalistic notion of labeling is quite oversimplified and limited.

3. A third observation rendered by critics of labeling theory is its overemphasis on *formal labels*, such as those that emanate from the police, school officials, and mental health experts. Many individuals have been formally labeled, and just simply moved on with their lives in normal ways. A concern then becomes what are the effects of *informal* labels, such as those stemming from parents, siblings, peers, and coworkers? This aspect of the labeling process has not been widely addressed. Another issue is the effects of *self-imposed* labels, or how individuals perceive themselves, and the effects of these perceptions on self-concept. It may very well be the most poignant labeling may come from *within*, and from those who care about us the most, not to mention individuals for whom we care deeply. This goes back to the first criticism. It is possible labeling may have already occurred prior to the introduction of formal labels. *Self-labeling* may well have taken place, and labels from significant others may have been imposed long before the existence of formal labels. The process of secondary deviance may already be in effect prior to formal labeling.

4. The fourth criticism deals with *who* gets labeled. Sociologists have long studied the underdog, such as drug users, ex-convicts, the mentally ill, and the poor, who represent easier subjects to study since they lack power. But what about studying the powerful? There has been considerable research undertaken on white-collar and other types of middle class to higher social class criminality, but not necessarily from the labeling perspective. In recent years there has been discussion of *shaming* (to be addressed in the next section) and this may apply to the deviance and criminal actions committed by the more fortunate. But attention has been placed on the powerless, not only from the labeling perspective, but from other theoretical slants.

5. The last common criticism addressed deals with *structure*. Labeling theorists are descendants of the interactionist tradition, and focus on the meanings attached to human interaction. But interactions occur within the broader social structure, and labeling theorists tend to neglect structure, which entails variables of long-term and enduring interest to sociologists, such as social class or socioeconomic status, race and ethnicity, gender, and type of community organization (urban, suburban, rural). It should be noted that contemporary studies of deviance and crime are heavily social psychological in nature, placing emphasis on interaction and personality variables, while deemphasizing the role of structure. In this case labeling theory is not alone.

The most important criticism of labeling theory is more *indirect* than direct, meaning the criticisms do not target the theory, per se. Instead, the all-important issue arises concerning *whether or not it is a theory*, or just a *perspective* or approach. According to the standards of theory construction, labeling theory is not formally stated: it lacks propositions; it does not involve the logical ordering and interconnections among variables; and, it fails to have sound definitions of concepts, which makes testing any theory a huge challenge (Homans, 1962; Stinchcomb, 1968; Turner, 1991).

Labeling theory has fallen on hard times for over two decades, although it is still covered in many criminology and deviance texts. In recent years, new directions in the labeling approach have emerged, and it is to these conceptualizations attention is now directed.

The Work of John Braithwaite: Shaming and Restorative Justice

Consider the following. Judge D. William Simpson from Salisbury, Maryland ordered an 18-year--old youth, Sherrele Purnell to spend three hours walking and wearing a sign that read "I was caught stealing gas." In Florida, one court ordered individuals convicted of driving under the influence of alcohol (DUI) to place DUI stickers on their license plates. Judge Joe Brown, a Memphis, Tennessee judge, made it possible for victims to go to the homes of the burglars who had victimized them, and told them they could take anything they wanted, and keep it. In California, a purse-snatcher was ordered by the court to wear tap-dancing shoes when he went out in public which would make the preverbal Fred Astaire-type sounds. In Arkansas, shoplifters were ordered to wear signs describing the crimes they committed, and to walk in front of the stores they had victimized. One reaction to the examples just described is "how embarrassing." But innovations in sentencing and the formal processing of offenders is occurring across

the nation, under the belief that incarceration is not a successful method of dealing with criminals, instead, embarrassing them may be more effective and rehabilitative. Rather than calling this labeling, it is now referred to as shaming and restorative justice *(in this section both terms will often be used simultaneously)*.

Labeling theory in its original forms has become yesterday's news. However, there are scholars who have expanded on the traditional labeling perspective by focusing on two related notions: *shaming* and *restorative justice.* Ironically, whereas labeling theory clearly questioned the impact of official processing by criminal justice authorities, shaming and restorative justice theorists and practioners see benefits that derive from societal reaction to antisocial behaviors, as long as they are not devastating or destructive to those being shamed. The work of Australian social scientist John Braithwaite is central to this perspective.

Explaining the Theory

Who would ever conclude being embarrassed might actually have positive benefits, for both those who victimize others, and for society in general? Thus is the argument put forth by John Braithwaite (1989). Braithwaite's thinking is individuals who violate laws should not go without punishment. On the contrary, they should be made to face up to those they have harmed, and to the community around them. Think about this for a moment. People sentenced to prison get a bye, so to speak. They are warehoused away from the public, and as a result do not have to reside with others, possibly encountering them and experiencing comments, frowns, and possibly even aggressive types of responses. As President George W. Bush said repeatedly about terrorists; "they can run but they can't hide." In the same vein criminal offenders, when kept within society and not incarcerated, must live in a world where people will know who and what they are about.

Braithwaite identified two types of shaming, one destructive in nature and the other more positive and rehabilitative. The first type of shaming is *disintegrative shaming* and involves humiliating and stigmatizing offenders to the point that they are unable to find employment and other positive avenues within society. Disintegrative shaming deepens secondary deviance thus forcing offenders into a life of criminality and deviance, or as Braithwaite states creating a "class of outcastes" (1989, 55).

Reintegrative shaming (frequently identified as Reintegrative Shaming Theory or RST) is the exact opposite. It is shaming with positive outcomes for all concerned, since it is intended to straighten out offenders and reintegrate them back into society, as productive law abiding citizens. But this is not a walk in the park. Condemnation and disapproval are aimed at making offenders aware of their undesirable conduct, and less invasive reactions follow in order to "reintegrate the offender back into the community of law abiding or respectable citizens through words or gestures of forgiveness or ceremonies to decertify the offender as deviant" (1989, 100–101).

Similar to shaming is the concept of restorative justice (RS), an important and popular notion that has its roots in several scholars (Bazemore and Walgrave, 1999; Braithwaite, 1989, 1998, 1999; Hahn, 1998; Harris, 1998; Quinn, 1998; Van Ness and Strong, 1997). Restorative justice parts ways from the traditional view that the state represents the interests of victims by punishing offenders. Instead, the argument with RS is victims must be made whole again by reducing the harm that has been done to them, and offenders too must be restored by rein-

tegrating them back into the community. But the question becomes how does restoration occur? The answer lies in face-to-face encounters of victims with offenders in the hope of making positive changes in both. Quinn (1998) suggested the aim of RS is to maximize the chances offenders will be rehabilitated, while strongly focusing on the needs of victims through use of one or more of the following strategies:

- **Victim impact panels.** Where victims talk to offenders about their experiences and feelings concerning their victimization.
- **Family group conferences.** Entails family members of both victims and offenders concerning the oft frightening and demeaning experiences faced by victims.
- **Sentencing circles.** Involves the friends and relatives of both offenders and victims, once again in situations in which victimization is discussed and feelings are expressed.
- **Citizen reparative boards.** Where conditions of probation are established by regular citizens as opposed to formal authorities.

The hope of such meetings is that offenders must face their victims, and learn firsthand about the harms they perpetrated upon them. In this type of process offenders cannot hide from those they have harmed. They must look the victims in the eyes, and they must view their emotions and perhaps even feel the pain for which they are responsible. These meetings can be intense and highly emotional for all concerned. But keep in mind, the goal is restoration *for all concerned.*

Restorative Justice is practiced across the nation, where over two dozen states have enacted legislation implementing RJ with juvenile delinquents (Levrant, Cullen, Fulton and Wozniak, 1999). Maryland has adopted RJ with delinquents that is aimed at holding offenders accountable for their crimes, and Vermont has initiated reparative probation boards comprised of five volunteers from the community, who develop agreements with offenders directed at making victims whole again, rehabilitating offenders and holding them accountable for their crimes (1999, 4–5)

Analysis and Empirical Support

Empirical tests of shaming theory and restorative justice are in short supply. Most that have been conducted have examined the effects of shaming on delinquency (Hay, 2001; Makkai and Braithwaite, 1991; Vagg, 1998; Wong, 1999; Zhang, 1995) with at least one study examining the relationship between the effectiveness of treatment for alcoholism and shaming (Houts, 1995). One study is discussed that will shed light on the validity of shaming theory and how research is undertaken.

Carter Hay (2001) surveyed 197 high school students from the southwest United States who were enrolled in physical education classes. His objective was to "focus on the relationship between parental sanctioning and adolescent delinquency" (2001, 137). In order to do so, Hay constructed three scales, one to measure shaming, and the other two to measure reintegration and delinquency. The shaming scale was designed to tap into what Hay (and Braithwaite) referred to as moralizing, which included items concerning parental reactions to child wrongdoing. Reintegration was basically a measure of parental forgiveness when children engaged in delinquency. Child involvement in delinquency included self-report items, and items that measured projected delinquency such as "If you found yourself in a situation where you had the chance to

do the following things (seven delinquency items, such as stealing and vandalism) how likely is it that you would do each one?" The self-report scale included nine items that asked respondents the earliest age they committed delinquent acts, such as breaking into a building or a house, stealing and getting into fights (2001, 139). Again, please keep in mind the research question concerned the relationship between shaming, reintegration and participation in delinquency.

The first part of Hay's analysis investigated the relationship between demographic variables and reintegration, and then shaming. The variables were age, race/ethnicity, sex, family structure, childhood antisocial behavior, and several measures of attachment between parents and children. The results for reintegration revealed four variables- race/ethnicity, childhood anti-social behavior—and two measures of parental attachment were had statistically significant relationships to reintegration. However, only one variable, a measure of parental attachment, was reported to have a statistically significant relationship to shaming (2001, 142).

Hay then analyzed the main question, and reported parental shaming and reintegration did affect involvement in delinquency, contingent on how the shaming/reintegration measure was constructed. Three combinations of the two variables were found to have statistically significant relationships to delinquency: high reintegration/high shaming; high reintegration/low shaming; and, low reintegration/high shaming. The strongest of the three relationships was for high reintegration/high shaming, implying parental forgiveness (allowing the child back into the fold) and parental moralizing (disapproval of child involvement in delinquency and shaming children) did impact antisocial behavior of children. Parents who made it obvious and apparent they disapproved of delinquent behavior were less likely to have children who violated the law (2001, 144). The findings by Hay provide support for shaming theory, however, concerns about shaming and RJ have been registered, and attention is now turned to this issue.

Sharon Levrant, Francis T. Cullen, Besty Fulton and John F. Wozniak (1999) have offered some of the most insightful criticisms of restorative justice, and in their analysis they state their objective "is not simply naysaying" but note their "essay, however, is a cautionary reminder that jumping on the bandwagon may be premature" (1999, 22). The bottom line for these scholars is RJ has yet to prove itself, and in cases where it has been practiced, RJ has met with minimal successes, at best (1999, 21). Levrant et al. made a number of observations concerning restorative justice, and several of these are now discussed.

One concern is RJ programs limit the constitutional rights of offenders, since mediation programs often exclude defense counsel. RJ may proceed without the input of defense attorneys, and the subsequent actions decided by mediation boards may actually result in more severe penalization of offenders. Following from this is the concern for "widening the net," whereby juvenile offenders are brought into the criminal justice system for minor offenses. In short, RJ may not be needed for youth who commit non-threatening violations of the law. Another issue is RJ may actually increase punishment, because those enacting it may shame offenders in ways that go beyond the scope of restorative justice (such as carrying signs identifying one as a thief, etc.). Other issues addressed by Levrant, et al. include the failure of RJ programs to come anything close to full restitution, and case loads of probation officers are high to begin with, and adding RJ efforts to their plate makes it unreasonable to expect it will be effective (1999, 7–13).

The most telling criticism deals with the structure of restorative justice efforts themselves. Levrant et al. state RJ programs fail to achieve their objectives because they lack intensity. The authors note effective intervention programs occupy up to 70 percent of the time of offenders, and last for nearly one-half a year. In addition, effective strategies entail close monitoring of offenders, and employ individuals who possess the skills required to work with their clients, interpersonally and constructively. Also of concern to the authors is the lack of attention paid to the cognitive levels of offenders, meaning most are lumped together and not evaluated in terms of their individual differences in cognitive maturity. RJ programs do little of the above, and what is more, if they do succeed it is because their clients are low-risk offenders who may never again violate the law anyway. Success with high-risk offenders is a different issue, and RJ efforts are rarely directed toward serious offenders (1999, 7–19).

Social Processes Theories

Ponder the following questions. When individuals begin to use marijuana, how is it they know *how* to use the drug? Or when individuals experiment with cocaine for their first time, *how* is it that they know how to use the drug? Nearly two dozen former employees at Enron were involved in a scandal that took down one of America's largest corporations. *How* is it that they all became involved in this tragedy? *How* is it that American soldiers could partake in the abuses at Abu Ghraib? *How* is it many professional baseball players would use illegal steroids? At first glance these questions may appear quite basic, if not downright irrelevant. But let's return to the first question. Smoking marijuana does not come about naturally. How to hold a marijuana cigarette (or roach clip, etc.), how to smoke it, and how to recognize its euphoric effects are *learned*. Likewise, how to use cocaine and how to recognize its effects are *learned*. Every question posed above has one common answer: *learning*. When professionals engage in embezzlement, insider trading, fraud and conspiracy, like the Enron example, it just does not happen by default. There is a process involved that entails bringing individuals into the fold, and teaching them *how* and *why* they should violate the law, even though they are making six figures or above annually. The same logic applies to professional athletes who will risk their health, and perhaps careers to use performance enhancing drugs. Illegal steroids do not drop out of the sky. They are made available for athletes (and others such as police officers), and their use spreads like hot cakes because these athletes learn of their potential value for boosting their stats and salaries. For example, Abu Ghraib? *Learning* (of course there are other theories that could be used to explain the above examples).

One of the long-standing and most important theories in the study of deviance relates to learning. Now, as just mentioned, the above examples/questions may have other theoretical explanations, but in this section attention is turned to learning as the cause or strongest correlate of deviant behavior. The prominent theory developed by Edwin Sutherland represents the starting point.

Edwin Sutherland: Differential Association Theory

The time was the 1930s, and two dominating explanations for criminal behavior were Freudian-based psychology and biology. Enter Edwin Sutherland. Sutherland posed a much different approach to the standard-bearers of the day as they attempted to explain the causes of antisocial behavior. Sutherland did not believe deviance was a

product of deep-seated personal conflicts, or something off, or haywire in the biological make-up of people. Instead, he assumed a more pragmatic approach and theorized deviance was a result of *learning*.

Explaining the Theory

Sutherland's classic theory is most known for its nine central propositions, that are listed below (1947, 6–8). *Direct quotes are included to clarify the propositions*:

1. Criminal behavior is learned. "Negatively this means that criminal behavior is not inherited . . ."
2. Criminal behavior is learned in interaction with other persons in a process of communication. "This communication is verbal in many respects but includes also 'the communication of gestures.'"
3. The principal part of the learning of criminal behavior occurs with intimate personal groups. Movies and newspapers contribute little to criminal behavior.
4. When criminal behavior is learned, the learning includes (a) techniques of committing the crime, which are sometimes very complicated, sometimes very simple (b) the specific direction of motives, drives, rationalizations, and attitudes.
5. The specific direction of motives and drives is learned from definitions of the legal codes as favorable or unfavorable. People are surrounded by individuals who support laws and those who violate them.
6. A person becomes delinquent because of an excess of definitions favorable to violation of law over definitions unfavorable to violation of law. "This is the principle of differential association. . . . When persons become criminal, they

do so because of contacts with criminal patterns and because of isolation from anti criminal patterns."

7. Differential associations may vary in frequency, duration, priority, and intensity. This means that learning criminality entails deep immersion into interactions with individuals who favor violation of the law.

8. The process of learning criminal behavior by association with criminal and anticriminal patterns involves all of the mechanisms that are involved in any other learning.

9. While criminal behavior is an expression of general needs and values, it is not explained by those general needs and values, since noncriminal behavior is an expression of the same needs and values. "The attempts by many scholars to explain criminal behavior by general drives and values, such as the happiness principle, striving for social status, the money motive, or frustration, have been, and must continue to be, futile, since they explain lawful behavior as completely as they explain criminal behavior."

Sutherland's theory is one of the most direct and easy to understand of all theories of deviance and criminality. It is right to the point, and leaves little doubt in one's mind how he sees the etiology of antisocial conduct. However, a rarely discussed and perhaps forgotten important piece of differential association theory concerns that which preceded the nine propositions, *and addresses how criminological theory should be developed.* This is significant since the *nine statements emanate directly* from Sutherland's thinking concerning how theories about criminality should come about.

Sutherland argued in order to develop sound criminological theory it is imperative that scientists employ an organized process that captures and integrates the different assumptions and elements of a body of knowledge (Traub and Little, 1980). In order to accomplish such a feat, Sutherland identified two complimentary processes that can be used in the development of criminological theory (*please remember although the terms "criminological" or "criminology" are used here, differential association theory has a prominent and fixed place in the study of deviance, as do many of the theories discussed in this book that were developed to explain crime and delinquency*). The first process is logical abstraction in which the factors that cause criminality are identified, and then applied to both the rich and the poor. The second step involves *differentiation of the level of analysis,* which means there must be a step-by-step development and identification in a logical manner of the factors that are common to explain criminality (1980, 110–116).

Extending on this later discussion, Sutherland identified *scientific explanations,* which distinguish between processes operating at the time of a crime–*situational factors*–and those that exist over a *period of time,* which Sutherland referred to as "*genetic,*" or *historical.* In this respect, Sutherland recognized there are causes of crime on the spur of the moment, and those that emerge given time. The latter has particular importance for differential association theory, since Sutherland labeled the section of his book that describes it as "Genetic Explanation of Criminal Behavior." The more precise meaning of this is to be found in his groundbreaking works *The Professional Thief* (1937) and *White Collar Crime* (1949).

Analysis and Empirical Support

A tribute to any theory is that it is tested, even if the results may not support it. A common criticism of many theories in the study of deviance and crime has centered around defining and then measuring key variables.

This is the case with differential association theory, in which ambiguity in operationalizing variables (such as association; techniques, drives and rationalizations) has been recognized as a major problem in validating it (Short, 1960). Other issues is the theory's ignoring of the role of parents and siblings in learning criminal definitions (Jensen, 1972), and the failure of the theory to clearly specify the learning processes involved in becoming deviant or criminal (Akers, 1996; Akers and Sellers, 2004). But there is empirical support for differential theory, and one example is now discussed.

Charles R. Tittle, Mary Jean Burke, and Elton F. Jackson (1986) undertook one of the most important tests of differential association theory (DAT) to date, and surveyed 1,953 individuals 15 years of age and older from Iowa, New Jersey and Oregon. The authors developed separate scales designed to measure critical DAT variables. Likert-type scales were created to measure associations; attitudes and rationalizations concerning deviance and criminality; perceptions of crime-favorable expectations; fear of legal sanctions; motives and drives; and predicted future of criminal behavior. For example, items used to tap into association included "How many people do you know personally who ever got into trouble because they did (each of) the things we have been talking about?" (i.e., assault and illegal gambling), and "Of all the people you know personally, how many of them do these things (i.e., theft and illegal gambling) at least one a year?" To measure the "perceptions" item, one question was asked: "If tomorrow you were to (commit a criminal act), how much respect would you lose among people you know personally if they found out about it?" An example of the measurement of fear of legal sanctions is the item "How upset would you be if you were arrested?" One item was created to measure motives and drives, and

it is "There are a lot of things that people would like to do, even if they may not do them, for one reason or the other. . . . I'd like you to tell me whether you would like to do these things almost always, a lot of the time, once in a while, or never" (1986, 412–414). The study was designed to examine the influence of learning on committing criminal offenses, and smoking marijuana. Criminal offenses in this research ranged from theft-related items, assault to illegal gambling, and the study included the normal array of independent or control variables such as age, education, race, gender, family income, and employment status.

The results of this research support DAT. Association, perception of crime-favorable normative expectations, and the motive variable interacted together to influence criminality (motive had the only direct effect on crime), and association increased use of marijuana by operating indirectly through motive (1986, 422–423). The research undertaken by Tittle et al. demonstrated more clearly *how differential association works*, since it identified key variables that operate *independently of one another and together*, to increase deviance and criminality.

One additional study is addressed, and represents a recent development in understanding the connection between deviant associations and involvement in antisocial conduct. The study by Dana L. Haynie (2001) entails the question of friendship networks and their influence on criminality and deviance.

Data from the National Longitudinal Study of Adolescent Health (Add Health) were employed with a final sample of 13,000 adolescents to test for the influence of peers on involvement in delinquency and deviance. Three characteristics of friendship networks were used to examine their effects on antisocial behavior: *density*, which is the degree of cohesiveness in a group; *centrality*, the position an individual holds within friendship networks; and, *popularity*, the number of nominations adolescents receive from others in the network that are indicative of their standing in the group. The three variables were calibrated using *simple counts*. The measure for popularity included the number of times respondents were nominated by others, and density was a product of the number of ties in a friendship network. Centrality was determined on the basis of the perceptions held by others of a respondent's position in a network. Fourteen items were used for self-reporting of delinquency, and included questions common to self-report instruments, such as those inquiring about theft, selling drugs, assault, and drug and alcohol abuse (2001, 1,030–1,034). Age, gender, race and measurements of attachment to peers, school, and parents were used as control variables.

The results are generally supportive, but once again the findings point to the *combined* or *interactive* effects of variables on delinquency/deviance. *Individually*, centrality, density and popularity had insignificant effects on antisocial conduct. However, when *mixed together* in different combinations, their effects were stronger and statistically relevant. For example, *high density combined with delinquent peer associations, and centrality in combination with delinquency associations*, increased the likelihood of involvement in undesirable conduct (2001, 1,041). However, Haynie was unable to report the mixture of centrality and density was correlated with, or predictive of delinquency or deviance (2001, 1,040).

Over the years scholars have modified or moved beyond DAT's assumptions about how learning influences deviant choices. Haynie's use of social network theory serves as one example. The works of Ronald Akers represent yet another attempt at modernizing DAT.

The Works of Ronald Akers: Social Learning Theory and Social Structure and Social Learning Theory

Edwin Sutherland's differential association theory is one of the most influential theories in the study of deviance and crime. It is covered in every textbook on deviance and criminology/delinquency, and is cited in numerous studies. But as most early theories, it has undergone considerable criticism and review, and fortunately it has not been forgotten. Situations like Enron, WorldCom, and Adelphia serve to remind us of the relevance of the learning approach to criminality and deviance: greed and the never-ending search for upward mobility are related to learning the techniques, motives, values and justifications for engaging in white-collar and professional crimes (as examples). Ronald L. Akers is one of those scholars who has taken an early theory and expanded upon it (such as Agnew, Gottfredson and Hirschi, and Braithwaite did). Rather than abandoning differential association theory, Akers added to it (twice) by integrating important notions from other theoretical traditions.

Explaining the Theories

The thought might have crossed your mind when reading about differential association theory that it may be possible to interact on a frequent and even intense basis with deviants or criminals, *and not to become one yourself*. For example, you may have close friends who drank underage and who smoked marijuana, but you never did (or do) either. Likewise, maybe you were raised in youth gang infested neighborhoods where many young people you knew turned to gang life, while you did not. This is reminiscent of the father played by Robert De Niro in the movie *A Bronx Tale*, where he was brought up surrounded by mobsters, while choosing to remain a law-abiding citizen. As a parent he tried desperately to prevent his only son from the lure of the life of a Mafioso, and struggled to do so with limited success. In the Bronx where De Niro spent his entire life, knowing and interacting with salty characters was common and difficult to avoid, but De Niro stayed on the straight and narrow: interaction and learning in-and-of-themselves may not be enough to turn the corner to deviance. There could be more, and this as addressed by Ronald L. Akers.

Social Learning Theory (SLT)

Four hypotheses developed by Akers are identified, and will help to clarify his addition to the learning tradition in criminology/deviance. Akers hypothesized the individual is more likely to commit violations when (1977, 1985):

1. He or she differentially associates with others who commit, model, and support violations of social and legal norms.
2. The violative behavior is differentially reinforced over behavior in conformity to the norm.
3. He or she is more exposed to and observes more deviant than conforming models.
4. His or her own learned definitions are favorable toward committing deviant acts.

Four critical elements surface from the hypotheses that distinguish social learning theory (SLT) from its *differential association* counterpart. The first is differential association. In his theory, Akers did not circumvent the idea deviance and criminality can be learned, instead he couched it within the

broader context of behavioral psychology and traditional criminology. Second is *differential reinforcement*, a notion derived from behaviorism in psychology, and an outgrowth of the works of Albert Bandura's work on learning and human aggression (1973, 1977), and the earlier formulation proposed by Burgess and Akers (1966). Third is *imitation*, or modeling that too stems from the tradition of behavioral psychology, and last is *definitions*, a direct descendant of "techniques of neutralization" by David Matza and Gresham Sykes (1961). In this respect social learning theory is an *integrated theory*, comprised of ideas and concepts from other leading theories.

To better illustrate the theory, let's return to one of the examples used above, drinking underage. According to SLT, having close peers is not sufficient in-and-of-itself to result in underage drinking. However, it, *differential association* is the starting point, and the more we interact with others, the more they may just begin to have influence over us. *Reinforcing* the idea about drinking underage becomes the second step, and combined with extensive interaction with peers increases the probability teen drinking will occur. Add to this exposure to and observing our close peers drinking via *modeling* or *imitation*, the risks become even greater violative behavior will take place. Last, learning the *definitions* in support of teen drinking interacts with the first three processes, with the end result teen drinking is now a reality. It is the *combined effects* of the four variables that strengthen nonconformity over conforming behavior. As Akers stated:

> The probability that individuals will engage in criminal and deviant behavior is increased and the probability of their conforming to the norm is decreased when they differentially associate with others who commit criminal behavior and espouse definitions favorable to it,

are relatively exposed in-person or symbolically to salient criminal/deviant models, define it as desirable or justified in a situation discriminate for the behavior, and have received in the past and anticipate in the current or future situation relatively greater reward than punishment for the behavior. (1985, 60)

The four elements of the theory represent a *progression* into deviance or criminal behavior.

Returning to definitions, Akers identified two types of definitions that favor deviant or criminal behavior. *Positive definitions* involve attitudes and values that raise the antisocial behavior to a higher moral status. Using an example from *The Sopranos* television program, it can be argued *Tony Soprano* and his crew of mobsters believed their criminal actions were morally proper and defensible. This is quite similar to the notion of "ethnocentrism," where groups perceive themselves to be superior to other groups or organizations. *Neutralizing definitions* are mere excuses or justifications for violative behavior. The fictitious mobster Tony Soprano may justify or otherwise rationalize mob criminal activities on the grounds all types of legitimate people such as police officers, judges, and high ranking corporate officials commit crimes, so why shouldn't they? It is important to state neutralizing definitions define antisocial acts as undesirable, but excusable or justified given the circumstances.

Analysis and Empirical Support

Ronald Aker's social learning theory has been tested on numerous occasions, and has received considerable support. For example, a meta-analysis of over 140 studies undertaken by Sellers, Pratt, Winfree, and Cullen (2000) reported strong support for the theo-

ry, as did the meta-analysis undertaken by Andrews and Bonta (1998). A number of studies have reported differential association, differential reinforcement, imitation, and learning are strong predictors of deviant behavior, taken individually and collectively (Akers, 2000; Akers and Jensen, 2003; Gordon, Lahey, Kawai, Loeber, Stouthamer-Loeber, and Farrington, 2004; Hwang and Akers, 2003; Warr, 1993, 2002). Other studies found that when compared with alternative theories of deviance and criminality, social learning theory tends to have greater explanatory power (Benda, 1994; Hwang and Akers, 2003; Kandel and Davies, 1991; White, Johnson, and Horowitz, 1986), and this even holds true when social learning theory is combined with other theories, with results indicating that it's major elements (i.e., differential reinforcement; imitation) surface as the strongest predictors of antisocial behavior (Catalana and Hawkins, 1996; Thornberry, Lizotte, Krohn, Farnworth, and Joon Jang, 1994). Two studies, both undertaken by Ronald Akers and Gang Lee will serve as examples of empirical tests of social learning theory (SLT).

Ronald Akers and Gang Lee (1996) tested SLT in relationship to adolescent smoking, and sampled 454 seventh through twelfth graders from Muscatine, Iowa. The objective of the research was to ascertain the major social learning influences on teenage smoking (of cigarettes) over a five-year period, thus a longitudinal research design was employed. The major variables in the research were frequency of cigarette smoking, differential reinforcement, differential association, and definitions of smoking behavior. Frequency of smoking was measured on a six-point scale, ranging from never smoking, to smoke every day or almost every day. Differential reinforcement was a measure of parent and peer negative and positive reactions to teen smoking, and differential association was determined by asking respondents questions such as "How many of your friends smoke" and "What is the general attitude of each of the following toward teenagers smoking (i.e., peers; parents)?" The measure of definitions of smoking included Likert-type items that asked about attitudes toward smoking such as "smoking is all right if you do not get the habit," and "is all right with parental permission" (1996, 326–327). Imitation was left out of the research because "the measures of differential association and modeling are highly intercorrelated" (1996, 326).

Akers and Lee used several models to test their hypotheses. The first was an overall model that included differential association, differential reinforcement, and definitions, *combined together* to test for its effects on adolescent smoking. The major finding was teenage early smoking predicted smoking in later teen years (1996, 329). The effects of the three independent variables were then examined *individually*, with the results echoing the findings from the combined or overall model. Differential reinforcement, differential association, and definitions all predicted smoking in the later teen years, leading the authors to conclude there is strong support for SLT (1996, 330–331).

Akers and Lee (1999) undertook a test of SLT and social bonding theory (SBT) as they apply to adolescent smoking of marijuana, using a final sample of 3,065 teenagers from the Midwest (1999, 9). The study sought to ascertain which of the two theories was the best predictor of adolescent use of marijuana. The *SLT variables* were differential peer association, which was measured by asking respondents about the proportion of their friends and associates who used marijuana, and definitions, which included items that asked respondents to state favorable or unfavorable attitudes toward using marijuana. Differential reinforcement was measured by

asking respondents their perceptions (good or bad) about the effects of using marijuana. Imitation was left out of this study since preliminary analysis of the data showed that it had a weak effect on the use of marijuana (1999, 10).

SBT variables were attachment, commitment, and belief. Attachment was measured by using a scale that tapped into the closeness of relationships among peers, and commitment was determined by asking respondents about the degree of their commitment to school, work, athletics, church, community, and so forth. Belief was measured by using a Likert-type scale asking respondents about their degree of support for the law, education, and parental moral beliefs and rules. Involvement was included in the measure of commitment (1999, 10–11).

The findings offer more support for SLT then SBT, and a clear indicator is the SBT variables accounted for a *mere 6 percent* of the influence or effect on marijuana smoking, but when the SLT variables were included in the statistical model, the percentage increased, *tenfold to 67 percent* (1999, 13). In addition, the three SLT variables had far more powerful *individual effects* on smoking marijuana, and Akers and Lee also found social learning mediated the effects of age on the use of marijuana (1999, 17, 20).

Social Structure and Social Learning Theory

In 1998, Akers offered a reformulation of and expansion on social learning theory which he titled "Social Structure and Social Learning Theory" (SSSL). SSSL places focus on variables within society, such as race, gender, age, population density, and social disorganization that interact with and affect learning mechanisms (i.e., reinforcement, imitation), and are theorized to be causes of deviance and criminality. Earlier conceptualizations of learning theory are void of structural variables as possible correlates of deviance and crime, *in conjunction* with learning itself. Therefore, SSSL is an *integrated theory* that encompasses factors from other theoretical traditions in sociology, such as anomie and social disorganization.

Akers identified four structural factors that impact behavior (1998). The first is *differential social organization* which includes variables long theorized to affect criminality in communities, such as age composition and population density. The second variable, *differential location in the social structure* refers to social and demographic factors that identify one's place in the social system, such as age, class, gender, marital status, and race. *Theoretically defined structural variables*, the third set of factors SSSL says affects antisocial conduct include anomie, social disorganization, and patriarchy. Fourth is *differential social location*, and it entails groups individuals belong to, and their place in and relationships to these groups. Considered here are family, peer groups, leisure groups, and work groups. Accordingly, it is postulated deviant and criminal behavior occur as a result of learning, couched within and integrated with the four structural factors.

Analysis and Empirical Support

To date there has been little empirical testing of SSSL, therefore a brief overview of the findings is summarized here. The few studies that have tested SSSL report social learning variables exert stronger influences on teenage antisocial conduct (i.e., substance abuse; delinquency) than do structural variables (Lanza-Kaduce and Capece, 2003). For example, in their study of binge drinking among minors, Lanza-Kaduce and Capece reported social learning variables, such as differential association and differential rein-

forcement were better predictors of binge drinking than structural factors, such as age, race and socioeconomic status. Bell- air et al. (2003) research also found stronger support for SLT variables over structural factors, adding family well-being, and learning prosocial behavior have mediating effects on youthful deviance and delinquency. Although the few studies reported show encouraging support for SSSL, much more research is needed to verify their findings, including studies undertaken on older populations.

In Recognition: Howard S. Becker

Howard S. Becker is one of the most influential figures in American sociology, not just in the study of deviance, *but in all of sociology*. As a student, Becker studied under some of the giants and legends at the University of Chicago, including Herbert Blumer, Ernie Burgess, Everett Hughes, and W. Lloyd Warner. Other influences on his writing were philosophers and social thinkers including Bruno Latour, Leonard Meyer, Charles Ragin, and psychologist Donald Campbell. Amazingly, Becker received the doctorate at the tender age of 23, unheard of today, and his background included teaching and research stints at The University of Chicago, the University of Illinois, The University of Washington, The University of California at Santa Barbara, the Visual Studies Workshop, the University of Kansas, and Northwestern University where he spent the majority of his career (Plummer, 2002).

Although Howard S. Becker is recognized by many students and sociologists for his work with labeling theory, the study of deviance actually consumed a fraction of his research interests and publications. To those who know his work well, Becker is an established methodologist, and he spent a good portion of his career developing "The Sociology of Art," a field that appeared to have potential vitality during the 1970s and 1980s, but today is limited in the number of sociology departments that include it as part of their curriculum. Becker described his interests in art in terms of a collage, in which "little bits . . . emerge," and then he then puts the pieces together over time. This is characteristic of his career, since his interests shifted frequently, and it was over time that he would create coherence in his writing and research agenda (2002, 25).

Becker's classic book, *Outsiders: Study in the Sociology of Deviance* (1963), was an outgrowth of his early 1950s interest in the study of marijuana use among jazz musicians. Based on this research Becker wrote about 90 pages on the topic of deviance, which materialized into the 1961 renowned publication. But his career would prove to be anything but stagnating, or of single purpose, which brings us back to his interest in methodology. Howard Becker was a field researcher, a student of participant observation, and perhaps the most important figure in qualitative research of his time. But would he fit into sociology today, with its heavy emphasis on quantitative research-based designs? The answer lies with Becker himself. In reference to the state of contemporary sociology Becker wrote "You see, what I think is wrong these days, why despair, is that everything has become so formulaic and so ritualized. You only have to look at the journals. You're a journal editor and you know that the papers you get are written to a template. . . . It was just like filling out a form" (2002, 33). How Beckerish!

During the fall of 1971, the author of this text had the opportunity to meet Howard S. Becker. Becker made a visit to the Department of Sociology at the University of Nebraska at Omaha, and met with the faculty and graduate students. In the style of

Howard S. Becker, Becker asked one question, and offered one observation: "Why did it take graduate students in the program so long to receive their masters degrees," and he thought all students coming into graduate programs in sociology should be awarded their masters degrees and/or doctorates on the spot, but then given three years to complete their degree objective. This later statement defines the career of Howard S. Becker. Becker "thought out of the box," and led with his scholarship: he allowed his writing and ideas to do his talking. Howard S. Becker is a giant among sociologists of the last 50 years.

SUMMARY

Societal reaction and social processes theories represent yet another major perceptive in the study of deviance and criminality. They are a combination of theories that explain antisocial behaviors as a result of reactions to them, and of learning. The latter have been among the most dominant theories in deviance in recent years, and societal reaction theories have reemerged with the popularity of shaming and restorative justice. Labeling theory as such has a special place in sociology and deviance/criminology, but for over two decades has offered little in the line of empirical testing. Learning theories will undoubtedly continue to be tested and refined for some years, and have taken their place alongside control theories as the most prominent theories in the study of deviance and crime. The last set of theories to be discussed are also important, and like those already presented, characterize the state of theorizing about deviant and illegal behavior.

Chapter 8

CONFLICT AND FEMINIST THEORIES

The last sets of theories to be discussed are referred to as *conflict* and *feminist* theories of deviance. Both categories of theories have been evolving for years, and hopefully it is apparent that the study of deviance has no one theoretical orientation. Conflict theories have had their place in sociology for over a century, and feminist theories began to move during the 1970s. It was not long ago conflict and feminist theorizing were considered "deviant," now both have arrived and have their place in sociology and the study of deviance. This chapter begins with coverage of conflict theories.

CONFLICT THEORIES

Case Study: The War in Iraq

Conflict theory is known by different monikers. It is referred to as conflict theory; Marxian theory; the New Criminology; Left Realism; political economy; and critical theory, to name a few. Critical theory? Yes, one strain of conflict theory is critical theory. Why? Because critical theorists are critical, meaning they are skeptical about the social order, in particular the establishment, especially as this relates to capitalist economies.

Critical theorists see their role as one where they must "debunk" those in control of the capitalist power structure, in order to get to the truth concerning their real agendas, and to unravel the intricacies and issues involved with capitalism and its effects on the human condition. Enter the war in Iraq.

Critical or Marxist theorists would certainly question *why* the United States is fighting in Iraq, and would argue the war is predominately about American dominance, and the enhancement of its capitalist order. Conflict theorists would use the following type of data to conform their suspicions: (Simon, 2006, 170–173; Simon, 2008, 171–175):

- The United States was warned in 1998 by the Saudi government that Al Qaeda was planning to exact violence in the United States.
- Halliburton, a major defense contractor whose previous Chief Executive Officer is Vice President Richard Cheney, has experienced significant increases in profit since the United States invaded Iraq. The company was also sued for fraud over illegal accounting practices, in which Halliburton was counting as revenues money it had yet to receive from its clients, thus inflating its profit portfo-

lio and enhancing the value of Halliburton stock.

- Prior to the war in Iraq the United States made claims Iraq possessed weapons of mass destruction (WMD), which became the *sole* stated reason by President Bush for going to war with Iraq. However, WMD's were never found, *either prior* to or since spring 2003, when the war commenced.
- In 2001, the United States government gave the oppressive Taliban regime of Afghanistan $43 million dollars in economic aid for its farmers, and in July of that same year Osama Bin Laden was treated at an American hospital in Dubai, *and* he was interviewed by officials of the Central Intelligence Agency.
- In March 2001, information from the Freedom of Information Act (FOIA) revealed a task force chaired by Vice President Cheney contained intelligence on critical oil assets in Iraq, leading to suspicions concerning the real motives for going to war with that country.
- Since the war in Iraq began, several major American corporations have experienced significant gains in sales and profits. From the first quarter in fall 2003, to one exactly year later, Halliburton revenues increased over 80 percent, and at that time was awarded $18 billion dollars in construction projects; *all in Iraq.* In the first year of America's most recent war with Iraq, both the Bechtel Group of San Francisco and the oil conglomerate Chevron-Texaco had major gains in profit. Bechtel revenues increased 158% in just one year as a result of water and sewage construction contracts in Iraq, and Chevron-Texaco's profits soared by over 90%, or by three billion dollars from 2003–2004. *What is essential here is the massive increase in profits*

occurred in just one year, dating to the beginning of the war in Iraq. Halliburton, Bechtel, and Chevron-Texaco funneled most of its political contributions to Republican candidates running for office in 2004.

- Exxon Mobil, the world's largest publicly traded company recorded over $10 billion dollars in profit during the second quarter 2007, a 36% increase over second quarter profits from 2006. The $10 billion dollars is the second largest profit recorded by a United States company in American history, second only to the $10.7 billion dollars reported in the fourth quarter 2005.

Conflict theorists would use information such as that from above to support their assumptions that capitalism is all about greed and profit, even at the expense of the lives and safety of others. As suggested previously, they would use this type of data to question and debunk those in power, in the tradition of Richard Quinney who wrote the purpose of the state is to carry out the agendas of the rich and powerful, and Willem Bonger who saw the relationships among humans as being distorted and corrupted by the forces and oppressive nature of the capitalist social structure (both Quinney and Bonger are discussed in this section).

To recognize that conflict theory owes its origins to the nineteenth century philosopher Karl Marx is an understatement. Marx's writings set into motion scores of ideas in sociology, with the major similarity among them being Karl Marx himself. Since the mid-1800s, Marxian thought has slowly but surely enveloped theorizing about the nature of society, and deviance and criminality. For the first half of last century, conflict theory took a back seat to functionalism and symbolic interaction theory. But during the 1960s and since then, conflict theory

grew in popularity, and has become a dominant paradigm in sociology and the study of
deviance and crime. There is no one conflict
theory; instead there are conflict theories. In
the next section some of these theories are
addressed, with an eye on their relevancy to
the study of deviance. *It is to be noted that no
effort on the behalf of the author will come close to
doing justice to Karl Marx and his legion of fol-
lowers/theorists. What follows represents sum-
maries of Marxian thought.*

Explaining the Theories

Make no pretensions about it, Karl Marx
loathed capitalism. Think about that for a
moment. The United States of America is
the world's most influential and dominant
capitalistic society, yet we are about to
embark on an attempt to summarize the
thoughts of Karl Marx and several of his
intellectual descendants on capitalism, a
mode of economic existence they argued is
responsible for many of society's worst ills
and evils. The following paragraph by
Freidrich Engels, whom Marx collaborated
with on several major writings, will help in
clarifying Marx's (and Engels) position on
capitalism and crime (1975, 248–249):

> Present day society, which breeds hostil-
> ity between the individual man and
> everyone else, thus produces a social war
> of all against all which inevitably in indi-
> vidual cases, notably among uneducated
> people, assumes a brutal, barbarously
> violent form–that of crime. In order to
> protect itself against crime, against direct
> acts of violence, society requires an
> extensive, complicated system of admin-
> istrative and judicial bodies which
> requires an immense labor force. . . .
> Crimes against property cease of their
> own accord where everyone receives
> what he needs to satisfy his natural and
> spiritual urges, where social gradations

and distinctions cease to exist. Justice
concerned with criminal cases ceases of
itself, that dealing with civil cases, which
are almost all rooted in property relations or at least in such relations arise
from the situation of social war likewise
disappears; conflicts can then only be
rare exceptions, whereas they are now
the natural result of general hostility, and
will be easily settled by arbitrators.
(Marx and Engels, 1975).

That in a nutshell spells out the Marxian
view of crime and social evils. Individuals
are pitted against one another, with a consequence being that of crime. The cause?
Capitalism. In the same paragraph, Engels
indicated why socialism is a better system
than capitalism: "In communist society . . .
we eliminate the contradiction between the
individual man and all others, we counter-
pose social peace to social war, we put the
axe to the root of crime–and thereby render
the greatest, by far the greatest, part of the
present activity of the administrative and
judicial bodies, superfluous" (1975, 248–
249). In addition to this brief introduction to
Marxian analysis of crime, listed are several
tenets of Marx's thinking about society. Once
again, this is not an attempt to exhaust the
many and great writings offered by Marx. It
is simply an overview of key ideas.

1. **The history of all societies is a history of class struggles.** Marx saw the
   history of humanity as representing
   ages of conflicts between social strata,
   or classes. For Marx, these conflicts
   occurred over the *private ownership of
   property.*
2. **The rich get richer and the poor get
   poorer.** Marx theorized the masses
   (proletariat) suffer at the hands and
   greed of the most fortunate. As the
   wealthy and powerful *(bourgeois)* pros-
   per, the poor lose ground steadily.

3. **The masses in capitalist society suffer from alienation.** So what then is *alienation*? Alienation is a condition that is closely associated with work. In capitalist societies it stems from the lack of meaning and purpose that humans find in the rote, mundane, and noncreative work environment of the factory system. Humans find little of any value or intrinsic worth in what they do. They become detached from their work, and this impacts their notion of self-worth.

4. **Mode of production.** Marx identified two aspects of the mode of production, both related to the above tenets. The *means of production* represent the essential elements needed for economic production such as technology, land, tools, capital, machinery, and monetary systems. *Social relations of production* entail the relationships individuals hold to the means of production, meaning if they *own* the means of production, or are *subjugated to working* within systems, such as the factory structure. Thus, the social relations of production includes but is not limited to slaves, bankers, landed gentry, and industrialists.

5. **False consciousness and class consciousness.** Marx argued the alienation individuals encounter in capitalist societies results in the inability of people to know their own social class position, or *false consciousness*. *Class consciousness* is the polar opposite idea. Individuals do understand their place within the social structure, and for Marx, a critical element to the demise of capitalism was a *class conscious political revolution* that would involve the masses in the destruction of capitalist systems. But the masses would have to be united with a clear understanding of their regimented and subjugated position in society.

In summary, Marx denounced capitalism and advocated its elimination on the assumption that it caused an abundance of miseries and discontent in society. He saw it as the cause of crime, poverty, sexism, and other major social problems. It is from this tradition many of the contemporary theories of crime and deviance have emerged, and it is to several of these theories attention is now directed.

The Works of Willem Bonger, Richard Quinney and Austin Turk

Willem Bonger

Willem Bonger, a Dutchman, is a direct intellectual disciple of Karl Marx who extended and added to Marx's (and Engels) assumptions about capitalism and crime. In *Criminality and Economic Conditions*, first published in 1905, Bonger argued the masses are under the control of a few powerful and wealthy individuals, and as a result they (the proletariat) struggle on a daily basis to survive. Critical to Bonger's theory is how he posits the relationship between the haves and the have-nots. The haves control the means of production, while the great majority of individuals are powerless relative to economic self-determination. Bonger wrote "Little by little, one class of men has become accustomed to think that the others are destined to amass wealth for them and to be subservient to them in every way" (1969a, 44).

Bonger believed crime permeated every social class, but it was the poor who suffered the most as a result of crime. The subjugation of the poor relegated them to no more than the status of beggars, and their crimes reflected their social conditions. The poor committed the crimes of vagrancy, theft, robbery, embezzlement, crimes of violence, including infanticide and rape, and prostitution (1969a, 93). The crimes committed by the bourgeois were a different thing, however, engaging in crimes related to downturns in the economy, as well as crimes occuring as a result of business failures. These crimes include fraudulent bankruptcy, adulteration of food, and fraud (similar to the corporate scandals of the last decade) and were frequently based on greed and corruption (1969a, 134). It is in Bonger's key term, *egoism* that his theory becomes more comprehensible and relevant. *Egoism* is the insensitivity demonstrated by the rich and powerful to the less fortunate. Insensitivity translates into crimes committed by lower class individuals, since the bourgeois turn their backs on them, leaving them in the position of needing to resort to criminal activity just in order to meet survival needs. Additionally, the powerless use crime as revenge against those controlling the means of production.

Bonger is a Marxian in every sense of the word, and his work on race, sex, and crime demonstrates his strong orientation to Marxist philosophy, as well as writing in ways that are relevant in contemporary criminology. In *Race and Crime* (1969b) Bonger wrote "Crimes committed by Negroes are more frequently prosecuted than those committed by whites. Negroes are less well able to defend themselves legally, they are less often in a position to secure a good lawyer, and they are more promptly sentenced to prison" (1969b, 43). In reference to race Bonger continued "No person comes into the world a criminal" (1969b, 105). When referring to sex and crimes, Bonger noted crime rates vary little across nations, and when women commit crimes it is due to economic reasons, such as prostitution (1969a, 60). Bonger wrote women engage in crime less than men, as a result of their disadvantaged social position that affords them less opportunity to engage in criminality.

Richard Quinney

Richard Quinney is one of the most distinguished scholars of deviance and crime in American sociology, and for a portion of his career he was also one of the most prominent students of Marx and crime. For our purposes, Quinney's writings represent some of the most "hard core" Marxian-based statements made about crime and deviance in sociology and criminology (1970, 1973; 1977). *The Social Reality of Crime* (1970) is a highly regarded conflict theory treatise on crime, in which Quinney outlined *six propositions*. The first proposition is Quinney's definition of crime, with propositions two through five his explanatory units. The sixth proposition is a composite of the previous five propositions and describes the social reality of crime (1970, 15–21). The propositions are listed below (in italics), with brief explanations of each provided:

1. **Proposition 1 (Definition of Crime):** *Crime is a definition of human conduct that is created by authorized agents in a politically organized society.* Quinney argues that crime is a social construction created and formulated by agents of the law such as legislators, police, prosecutors and judges. Quinney wrote "Having constructed social reality, man finds a world of meanings and events that is real to him as a conscious human being" (1970, 15), and he also states "Crime is seen as a result of a process which culminates in the defining of persons and behaviors as criminal. It follows, then, that *the greater the number of criminal definitions formulated and applied, the greater the amount of crime*" (1970, 16).

2. **Proposition 2 (Formulation of Criminal Definitions):** *Criminal definitions describe behavior that conflict with*

the interests of the segments of society that have the power to shape public policy. Quinney wrote "By formulating criminal definitions these segments are able to control the behaviors of persons in other segments. It follows that *the greater the conflict in interests between the segments of society, the greater the probability that have the power segments will formulate criminal definitions* "(1970, 17). In addition Quinney addressed why laws change, and suggested that changing social conditions, emerging interests, the need for the overall interests of the powerful to be protected, and changes in the conceptions of what is important to the public, all contribute to the reality of altering criminal definitions. "The social history of law reflects changes in the interest structure of society" (1970, 18).

3. **Proposition 3 (Application of Criminal Definitions):** *Criminal definitions are applied by the segments of society that have the power to shape the enforcement and administration of criminal law.* Quinney is arguing behaviors become criminal when they are in opposition to the interests of the powerful, and that criminals actually represent minority groups who have engaged in political activity. Quinney used two tenets to support this proposition.

The probability that criminal definitions will be applied varies according to the extent to which the behaviors of the powerless conflict with the interests of the power segments (1970, 18), and ". . . the probability that criminal definitions will be applied is influenced by community and organizational factors such as (1) community expectations of law enforcement and administration (2) the visibility of

public reporting of offenses, and (3) the occupational organization, ideology, and actions of the legal agents to whom the authority to enforce and administer criminal law is delegated. (1970, 19–20).

4. **Proposition 4 (Development of Behavior Patterns in Relation to Criminal Definitions):** *Behavior patterns are structured in segmentally organized society in relation to criminal definitions, and within this context persons engage in actions that have relative probabilities of being defined as criminal.* Quinney is arguing individuals who lack the power to shape criminal definitions are more likely to be in the position of having criminal definitions applied against them. Thus Quinney observed that issues such as opportunity, self-concept, and learning all contribute to the probability the less fortunate will be singled out for behaviors defined by the powerful as criminal (and against their interests). The result is those defined as criminal adopt a *self-fulfilling prophecy*: they act out criminal behavior and become the criminal in self-concept (1970, 21–22).

5. **Proposition 5 (Construction of Criminal Definitions):** *Conceptions of crime are constructed and diffused in the segments of society by various means of communication.* Quinney is reiterating that the powerful create social definitions of crime, and then use a tool to transmit these constructions—mass communication. ". . . *the construction of criminal conceptions depends on the portrayal of crime in all personal and mass communication*" (1970, 23). By using mass communication, social constructions of crime and deviance are spread, reinforced, and stabilized over time.

6. **Proposition 6 (The Social Reality of**

Crime): *The social reality of crime is constructed by the formulation and application of criminal definitions, the development of behavior patterns related to criminal definitions, and the construction of criminal conceptions.* The theory is integrative in nature, with all six propositions connecting to one another, creating a "theoretical system" (1970, 23). According to Quinney, "The theory, accordingly, describes and explains phenomena that increase the probability of crime in society, resulting in the social reality of crime" (1970, 23).

Whereas the six propositions laid out in *The Social Reality of Crime* are a significant contribution of Quinney to conflict theory, it is the following six statements that more clearly specify Quinney's adaptation of Marxism to the study of crime and deviance (1974, 16):

1. American Society is based on an advanced capitalist economy.
2. The state is organized to serve the interests of the dominant economic class, the capitalist ruling class.
3. Criminal law is an instrument of the state and ruling class to maintain and perpetuate the existing social and economic order.
4. Crime control in capitalist society is accomplished through a variety of institutions and agencies established and administered by a government elite, representing ruling class interests, for the purposes of establishing domestic order.
5. The contradictions of advanced capitalism–the disjunction between existence and essence–require the subordinate classes remain oppressed by whatever means necessary, especially through the coercion and violence of the legal

system.
6. Only with the collapse of capitalist society and the creation of a new society, based on socialist principles, will there be a solution to the crime problem.

The works of Richard Quinney cannot be given justice in a few pages (as is the case with the great majority of theorists addressed in this book). Quinney, along with Harold Pepinsky introduced *Peacemaking Criminology*, which focuses on resolutions to crime, and over the years has gathered a number of followers (1991, 1997). Peacemaking criminology is an integration of ideas from feminism, humanism, religion, and critical criminology. Perhaps the essence of this perspective is best captured in a statement from *Criminology as Peacemaking* (1991): "In recent years there have been proposals and programs that foster mediation, conflict resolution, reconciliation, and community. They are part of an emerging criminology of peacemaking, a criminology that seeks to alleviate suffering and thereby reduce crime"(1991, ix). It still remains to be seen how major peacemaking criminology becomes in the study of deviance and criminality.

Austin Turk

The conflict/Marxist theorists to cover in this section is a tough call. Bonger is a natural, but after him the field is wide open. Richard Quinney was instrumental in helping to advance conflict theory in criminology and sociology, and the names of Ralf Dahrendorf, Steven Spitzer, and George B. Vold are also prominent in Marxian thought. From the mid 1960s on, the floodgates of conflict theorists slowly opened, and by the mid-1980s it had gained significance as a paradigm to be taken seriously. Another of those scholars is Austin Turk, whose classic

Criminality and the Legal Order (1969) represented an important step in the development and application of Marxism to the study of criminology and deviance.

Once again, ask yourself some questions: "What does it take to have the label of criminal slapped on an individual?" and "In society, who has the power to criminalize others, and under what circumstances?" Turk builds his rather complicated theory around both questions. Much of his focus centers on authority relationships between the powerful and subjects, who Turk labels *resistors*. An essential concern for Turk is who becomes criminal and under what circumstances, and it was not enough for Turk just to conclude that authorities are free to criminalize subjects whenever they so desire.

Turk proposed several conditions under which *criminalization*, or the "assignment of criminal status to individuals" (1969, xi), could occur. But in order to proceed, an important distinction must be understood between two types of norms: *social norms* and *cultural norms*. *Cultural norms* are verbal formulations of values, and are associated with the law as it is written, and *social norms* represent actual patterns of behavior, or the actual enforcement of legal norms. Turk observed the *most important* factor in criminalization was the degree to which legal norms were in congruence with cultural and social norms. For example, the more authorities (most saliently the police) agreed with the legal norms, the greater was the probability that norm resistors would be criminalized. Second, Turk suggested that power differences between the authorities and resistors effected the process of criminalization, but not necessarily because authorities may have greater power than resistors. What mattered most is how much authorities feel threatened by resistors (1969, 67). Third is what Turk refers to as the *realism of conflict moves*, or actions taken by resistors that could

increase the probability of their criminalization. Included are the visibility of the actions; how offensive the actions were to authorities; consensus among the authorities concerning the actions of norm resistors; and the relative power differences of authorities over resistors, that would allow the former to acquire greater resources, such as financial or budget incentives (1969, 64–75). So where does this leave us? Turk conceptualized modern societies as characterized by conflict between authorities and subjects (resistors), and the attempts by those in power to dominate subjects (1969, 32–34). Conflicts between the two segments occur over social and cultural norms, with the power to make and enforce laws resting in the hands of authorities. But unlike other Marxian/conflict theorists, Turk did not conclude conflict was inevitable just as a result of power differentials in society. On the contrary, he argued that the nature of the relationships and bonds between subjects and authorities played heavily into the degree, if any of conflict between the two. When subjects were in agreement and aligned themselves with authorities, conflict was unlikely (1969, 62).

Analysis and Empirical Support

In sociology and criminology/deviance, tests of conflict theory often center around the issues of social class, race and gender. This makes perfect sense given that Karl Marx addressed all three as part of his argument that powerless people are treated differently by individuals who own the means of production and control wealth. This section will depart from the pattern of discussing studies that are tests of theories presented. Instead, it will focus on a major concern of Marxian-based thinkers, and that is evidence of oppression within the American system of criminal justice. No one study is examined specifically, rather a list of findings relative to conflict theory *(and some do not necessarily support it in whole)* are addressed. Empirical studies have revealed:

1. African American defendants are less likely to receive bail than white defendants, and they receive more harsh sentences (Spohn, 2000).
2. Social class has a minor relationship to crime for white adults, but is correlated with crime for nonwhite adults (Dunaway, Cullen, Burton, and Evans, 2000).
3. Individuals from impoverished backgrounds have a higher probability of receiving severe sentences for violent crimes than persons from more advantaged statuses (D'Alession and Stolzenberg, 1993).
4. In a study of over 42,000 cars in New Jersey, African Americans were found to have a far greater probability of being victims of racial profiling than were white drivers on the same turnpike (Harris, 1999).
5. African Americans who kill whites are twice as likely to receive the death penalty as whites who kill whites, and African Americans who kill whites are four times more likely to get the death sentence as African Americans who kill African Americans (Levine and Montgomery, 2003).
6. Social class, rather than race, may very well be the deciding factor in sentencing, and this is often camouflaged in data as a result of poor and inconsistent measures of social class (Zatz, 2000).
7. The police are more likely to search, arrest, and detain African American and Hispanic youth than they are white teenagers (*Harvard Law Review*, 1988).
8. Nearly 70 percent of males and females incarcerated in prisons in the United States are either of Hispanic or African

American heritage, and nearly 50 percent of individuals on death row in the United States are either Hispanic or African American, with the latter comprising approximately 46 percent of Americans in prisons, and 43 percent of those on death row. African Americans comprise 12 percent and Latinos/Hispanci Americans 16 percent of the population of the United States. (www.deathpenaltyinfo.org April 1, 2008)

Data such as that just addressed may be interpreted as support for conflict theory, as do the findings from the next type of theory to be discussed, feminist theories.

FEMINIST THEORIES

Feminist theories of deviance and crime have been evolving for over 30 years, and similar to other theories, represent a myriad of explanations about deviance and crime. Just like there is no one Marxism, or no one strain theory, or a singular learning approach, there is no one feminist paradigm. Feminist theories offer a variety of slants on crime and deviance, including contributions from both females and males, *and they focus both on female victimization, and actual criminality of* women. The question is "what are feminist theories," and it is to this issue attention is now directed.

Kathleen Daly and Meda Chesney-Lind, two leading feminist criminologists, have shed insight into this question, and have identified five key elements of feminist thought (1988, 497):

1. Gender is not a natural fact, but a complex social, historical, and cultural product; it is related to, but not simply derived from, biological sex difference and reproductive capacities.
2. Gender and gender relations order

social life and social institutions in fundamental ways.

3. Gender relations and constructs of masculinity and femininity are not symmetrical, but are based on an organizing principle of men's superiority, and social and political-economic dominance over women.

4. Systems of knowledge reflect men's views of the natural and social world; the production of knowledge is gendered.

5. Women should be at the center of intellectual inquiry, not peripheral, or appendages to men.

This latter point is at the heart of feminist theorizing about crime and deviance. Often in the past, the study of women and crime has taken a back seat to studies of male criminality. When it comes to studying women and crime, or women and men and crime, a feminist position is that gender should not be the determining factor of what gets the attention of social science. Instead, significant interest must be devoted to understanding female criminality *in its own right*. This last point is important. Daly and Chesney-Lind have argued the study of female crime should focus on context, and involves greater use of observational research and interviews, rather than total reliance on statistical techniques, as advocated by male researchers for decades. As Daly and Chesney-Lind write "This gender difference is not related to '"math anxiety" but rather to a felt need to comprehend women's crime on its own terms, just as criminologists in the past did for men's crime" (1988, 502).

Earlier it was stated that there is no one feminist criminology. Five types of it have been identified, and are now briefly discussed (Barkan, 2005; Bierne and Messerschmidt, 2000; Simpson and Elis, 1995).

Liberal feminism argues that variations in male and female crime rates are due to gender differences in socialization, and gender differences in discrimination in the criminal justice system. Females are socialized to be dependent, passive and nurturing, and males are brought up to be aggressive, competitive, and self-confident, with crime reflecting these differences. The differences in gender role socialization account for the limited opportunities for women in society, and the abundance of opportunities for men. The result is males are more likely to commit crimes due their more aggressive and competitive nature, and greater opportunities expose men to more chances to violate laws.

Marxist feminism traces female criminality to their subordinate position to men in capitalist society. Capitalist societies embrace male power and hegemony, and women are forced to turn to crimes such as shoplifting and prostitution. Males commit crimes of violence, especially against women since they (women) are relegated to low social status. In other words, the capitalist mode of production empowers males and depowers females, directly impacting how the genders perceive one another.

Radical feminism states that *patriarchy*–when men control labor power and the sexuality of women–is directly linked to crimes committed by women, since female crime is a result of crimes committed against them by men. Much of the focus of radical feminism is on violence against women, which it is argued occurs as a result of male physical dominance, and the relative powerlessness of women. Rape is the primary example of crimes committed by males against females.

Socialist feminism is a combination of both radical and Marxist feminism, and views *class and gender* as equally important in understanding both female and male criminality. According to this perspective, males have the greatest opportunities for crime, given the fact that they have the most power, and that crime rates for women are lower since they lack power and opportunity (quite similar to liberal feminism). Critical to this theory is that in societies such as the United States, patriarchy and capitalism interact to grant males far more power than females, since males dominate the professional and managerial-capitalist classes. Male crimes are high powered compared to crimes committed by women, who are are likely to emanate from disadvantaged backgrounds.

Muticultural/Multiracial feminism is feminism advocated by *women of color*, who argue crimes committed by women result from *both* racism and gender, which may account for the higher crime rates among African American and Hispanic women (compared with white females). This is an important contribution, since 50 percent of all incarcerated women in the United States are African American.

There are other feminist theoretical frameworks as well. "Doing gender" (West and Zimmerman, 1987) is a theory of the gendered nature of crime, and postulates males and females go about crime along *gender lines*. In other words, when females commit crimes they tend to do so by acting out feminine roles, while males are more masculine in their criminality. So, they "do gender." For example, female robbers more often target women victims and are unlikely to use a gun, whereas male robbers typically rob men and use a gun in the process. In the rare instance when females rob males they most often use a gun, and they set up their male victims by flirting with them, and by carrying on sexual activities, such as prostitution. As Jody Miller stated, the differences between male and female robbers reflects "a gender-stratified environment in which, on the whole, males are perceived as strong and women are perceived as weak" (Miller, 2000, 42).

Two additional feminist theories about

crime focus on *female victimization* (especially rape) either as a result of their *increasing social equality* (Baron and Straus, 1984, 1987, 1989; Whaley, 2001) or their *relative inequality* (Bogard, 1988; Brownmiller, 1975). Theorists who postulate that rape and assault of females occur as a result of their increasing equality argue that as females gain greater equality with males, some males become intimidated and act out their fears of women's progress by violently attacking them. In addition, males find a need to overexaggerate their masculinity when faced with female equality, and this too leads to violence against women (Schwartz and Dekeseredy, 1997). Feminists who take the other approach—that it is inequality of women that exposes them to violence by males—do so on the grounds that women's lower social status brings with it a degree of disrespect, that in the minds of some males makes them suitable targets for violence, especially rape (Brownmiller, 1975; Dobash and Dobash, 1979; Hester, Kelly and Radford, 1996; Yodannis, 2004).

With the above as a backdrop, attention is turned to empirical tests of feminist theories of deviance and crime.

Analysis and Empirical Support

Feminism examines a number of issues related to women and crime, such as *women and victimization* (Campbell, Webster, Kozial-McClain, Block, Campbell, and Curry, 2003; Chesney-Lind, 2004; Fleury, Sullivan, and Bybee, 2000: Dekeseredy and Joseph, 2006; Finkelhor and Yllo, 1985); *gender ratio* or male/female differences in crime (Daly and Chesney-Lind, 1988; Lanctot and Blanc, 2002); and, *female criminality* (Miller, 2000; Miller and Decker, 2001; Wright and Decker, 1998; West and Zimmerman, 1987). Two studies that employ feminist methodology for studying females and crime are discussed below, and are from the academic journal *Feminist Criminology*. Hopefully, they will shed light on findings as they relate to females and crime, and well as the emphasis placed on *case studies, interviews,* and *context* that feminists argue is critical to the way they examine crime and deviance.

One insightful study was undertaken by Emily Meyer and Lori Post (2006) and entailed interviews with 32 adult women concerning their experiences with violence across their life span. As such, it is a test of older women's fear of violence. Personal semi-structured interviews were used in order to get more in-depth and rich data on the lives of the 32 women, as well as to find out in detail the experiences they had with episodes of violence. Issues examined included child abuse, domestic violence involving the sample when they were older and during their younger years, and the perceptions of how safe the women felt in their communities and neighborhoods. The interviews were tape-recorded with the consent of the sample, and began with the probing question "In general how has violence touched your life" (2006, 214). Over the course of the interviews the women were asked questions concerning their own victimizations as children and adults, and victimization experienced by friends and relatives during both childhood and adult years. Once the interviews were concluded the respondents were provided with a list of services that were available to aid them as a result of their victimization. Meyer and Post then proceeded to transcribe the answers from the interviews, and had independent coders read and analyze the responses. The next step entailed running the answers through a software package designed to analyze qualitative data.

Of course, it is the results or findings that are of paramount importance. The majority of the sample reported generational differ-

ences in crime, meaning they felt their neighborhoods were less safe now then years earlier. In addition, the 32 respondents did not have favorable perceptions concerning the criminal justice system, since they tended to report the system did not care about women, nor did it protect them. Related to this is the finding is today women in general are not safe, and that American society has a long way to go in rectifying this perception. Also reported was women feel far safer in their own homes or residences, and all 32 respondents stated they harbored fears about going out at night (2006, 219–220). The in-depth and personalized nature of the interviews provided Meyer and Post with important, and as mentioned earlier, "rich" information on women and violence, and exemplifies the manner in which feminists undertake research on crime.

Walter Dekeseredy, Martin D. Schwartz, Danielle Fagan, and Mandy Hall (2006) interviewed 43 women who were victims of violence, as they proceeded to end relationships with husbands and partners. Semi-structured interviews were employed, with six occurring over the telephone, five off campus, with the remaining held on campus at Ohio University (2006, 235). Various sources were used to recruit women for the research and included local newspapers, announcements over the radio and television, and domestic violence and other types of agencies also spread word about the study. In addition, a strategy called "preparatory component of qualitative investigation" was used which entailed contacts with social agencies, mental health counselors, and local law enforcement to inform them of the research, and it also included receiving input from service providers on the questions to be asked on the survey.

The results revealed significant incidences of abuse, of all kinds. Thirty-five of the 41 women had experienced rape (81%), and 74 percent (32) had been sexually coerced. Nineteen (44%) and eight (18%) had been victims of nonrape sexual contact and attempted rape, respectively. In addition, many of the women had been victims of nonsexual abuses, such as other forms of physical violence, psychological abuse, economic abuse, stalking, and destruction of prized possessions. Five women reported their pets were abused by either husbands or partners (2006, 236). Dekeseredy, et al. also reported that violence against the 43 women was associated with male partners or husbands who frequently drank with other men; informational support, or when males shared stories with other men about their abuse of their wives or partners; and, male peer support, or having male friends who abused their wives or partners. Combined, the three factors interacted to create a frightening and violent environment for women who were divorcing their husbands and separating from their male partners (2006, 238–242).

In Recognition: Susan S. Sharp

The Department of Sociology at the University of Oklahoma, Norman Campus is a mixture of up and coming young whippersnappers and veterans of higher academia. One of the latter is Professor Susan S. Sharp who has distinguished herself as both a scholar and excellent teacher. Dr. Sharp attended Texas Tech University, obtaining a BA in Sociology in 1980 and an MA in Sociology in 1982. She then worked in the field of alcohol and drug counseling for almost a decade while raising her three children. During that time, she remained interested in the field of criminology, ultimately returning for doctoral studies at the University of Texas in 1993, and completing her doctorate in 1996. While there, she developed the belief that much of what she was learning in her criminology classes did

not apply as well to women. Her dissertation research focused on female injecting drug users (IDUs) and their risk behaviors. She found that life-course theory (Sampson and Laub) was inadequate as formulated for explaining the deviance of these women. Instead of marriage and job acting as protective factors against deviance, she found the presence of children was far more important. This, of course, makes sense when one examines the lives of women offenders and addicts.

After completion of her doctorate, Dr. Sharp became involved in the Division on Women and Crime (DWC) of the American Society of Criminology. As the newsletter editor, she put *Division News*, the official newsletter of the DWC, online and created columns such as "Ask A Tenured Professor" and the "Graduate Student Corner" to facilitate communication between members. She then served as an Executive Counselor for the DWC. From 2003–2005, Professor Sharp served as the chair of the Division on Women and Crime of the American Society of Criminology. In 2006, Professor Sharp launched the journal *Feminist Criminology* as its founding editor. Currently, she is a Deputy Editor for the Journal.

Professor Sharp's research continues to focus on various aspects of female crime and deviance. She is the editor of the text *The Incarcerated Woman: Rehabilitative Programming in Women's Prisons* (Prentice-Hall, 2003) and sole author of a 2005 book on effects of death penalty on families of offenders, *Hidden Victims*. Additionally, she has authored 30 articles and book chapters focusing on gender, crime and the criminal justice system. Her research focuses on gendered test of theories of crime as well as incarcerated women, particularly incarcerated mothers. She is currently working on research gendered comparisons of the crime and deviance of Japanese and American students. Additionally, she is working on an article about operationalizing mainstream theories of crime in a way that is gender sensitive.

Dr. Sharp has conducted several annual studies on incarcerated mothers and their children for the State of Oklahoma, compiling a report to the state legislature each year. This research has resulted in policy changes in the treatment available to women offenders, and the establishment of a state-wide task force. She has received numerous awards, including the 2005 Good Teaching Award for the University of Oklahoma, the Rufus G. Hall Faculty Award, the Most Inspiring Faculty Award, and the UOSA President's Faculty Award. It is most important to recognize Susan S. Sharp for her enduring interests and contributions to understanding women and crime from a feminist perspective.

SUMMARY

There is no one conflict theory and there is no one feminist theory of deviance and crime. Conflict theories owe their heritage to Karl Marx, who wrote little about crime but whose critique of capitalism inspired genera-tions of scholars to take up his calling and to apply his thinking to criminal behavior. There are a variety of conflict theorists who approach conflict from a number of directions, with capitalism the undergirding factor in all of their analyses. Regardless of their brand of Marxism, the great conflict theorists trace the problems of modern societies to the capitalist economic mode of production. Feminist theories are often an extension of Marxism as well. Just as Marx saw societies as structured along gender lines, so do modern feminists who, when it is all said and done, arrive at basically the same conclusions, which include viewing the victimization of and crime committed by women as a result of male-structured social systems dominated by capitalism. Although feminists trace the roots of women and crime to different causes such as capitalism, patriarchy, race, gender, inequality, and hegemony, the bottom line for them is that things are seriously distorted in the make-up of society, which forces women into crime and results in their victimization.

With the discussion of theories now completed, attention is turned to substantive areas in the study of deviance, beginning with suicide.

Section 3

SUBSTANTIVE AREAS

Chapter 9

SUICIDE

CASE STUDY: BILL

When the author of this text (for the rest of this story referred to in the fist person) was of college age he had an acquaintance who was involved in restaurant sales (I worked part-time at a restaurant). The salesman's first name was Bill who was married with three children. Bill was a quiet man who would come to the restaurant on a weekly basis to sell paper goods. He would always sit at the same table and drink a cup of coffee while he filled out forms to complete the business transaction. One day the I noticed Bill take out a small black notebook and study it. On successive occasions to the restaurant Bill did the same thing, only each time he would appear more preoccupied with the contents of the notebook. Several months into this process Bill's appearance changed and he clearly had things on his mind. He looked scraggly and his dress had deteriorated to the point that he appeared unprofessional, and he came across as nervous and fidgety. One Sunday I received a phone call at my home from the owner of the restaurant informing him that Bill had committed suicide. I was saddened to receive this news. But it was the means Bill used that was so tragic and frightening. Bill was a hunter and owned rifles and guns, and on Saturday he rigged up a shotgun in his garage in a way that if he even moved it would take off his head. Bill ended his life leaving a wife and three children.

The question became "why?" Was it an extra-marital affair that had gone afoul? Was it marital problems? Was it drugs or alcohol abuse that took him over the edge? Remember the notebook? The notebook contained financial information that apparently had become a serious issue with Bill. It is my understanding Bill had become increasingly desperate and depressed over his finances and saw suicide as his way out of his financial crisis. He left a suicide note detailing his problems and hoped by taking his own life his wife and family would receive enough insurance money to get out of debt. Sadly he may not have given enough consideration to "where there is life there is hope." Perhaps he did and yet determined self-destruction was the best route for all concerned.

Suicide is a painful event that takes lives each year, not to mention it affects many living persons, such as parents, siblings, relatives, friends, and coworkers/students. Completed suicides represent just a portion of the total suicide picture, with many more individuals attempting suicide than those completing it.

DEFINITIONS AND DATA

Definitions

Suicide can mean different things to different people, therefore definitions of it will vary. In his classic work *Suicide* (1951, first published in 1897), Emile Durkheim defined suicide in the following manner: "The term suicide is applied to all cases of death resulting directly or indirectly from a positive or negative act of the victim himself, which he knows will produce the result" (1951, 44). The key words in his definition are ". . . which he knows will produce the result." Durkheim saw suicide as *intentional.* It does not happen by mistake, or mental illness, or as a result of some random event. For Durkheim suicide was simply that: intentional. Also inherent in the definition is the implication suicide can result from some good or heroic situation in which the victim gives up his or her life for others, or perhaps for some cause. Thus, the word *"positive."* Yet Durkheim also recognized that suicide can derive from something *negative*, such as when individuals kill themselves after becoming divorced. Then there is the perplexing word *"indirectly"* perhaps conveying the thought the act of suicide may come some time in the future after positive or negative experiences. Durkheim's theory of suicide is discussed later in this chapter.

The International Statistical Classification of Disease and Related Health Problems defines suicide as "A death resulting from the intentional use of force against oneself with a preponderance of evidence to indicate the force was intentional" (www.health.state.ok.us/program/injury/Summary/OVDRS 2007). This definition is quite concrete and to the point. Suicide is "intentional" and the ICD-10 ends its definition with the word "intentional." Yet, the United States Supreme Court in 1997, in a rare unanimous decision (9–0) upheld state laws prohibiting physician-assisted suicide. Of interest here is not only the Court's decision, but also its interpretation of the act of suicide itself. Associate Justice Sandra Day O'Connor used the words "mentally competent person" in referring to individuals who are experiencing great suffering and who may wish to terminate their lives with the assistant of a doctor (Greenhouse, *New York Times,* June 27, 1997). The words "mentally competent" echo the thoughts of Durkheim and the ICD-10, indicating agreement with the thought that suicide is an act undertaken by rational people who understand its finality. The Court's decision is important since it did leave the door open for states to implement physician-assisted suicide under situations of the greatest patient duress and pain. Associate Justice David H. Souter wrote the court ". . . should stay its hand to allow reasonable legislative consideration" (*New York Times*, June 27, 1997). Scholar Ruth Shonle Cavan recognized suicide as a way out of life's problems by acknowledging it can be a logical solution to issues facing people (1928). As we shall see as the chapter develops, it is very difficult for individuals to understand suicide as anything but an act undertaken by persons with mental illnesses such as depression. Yet, the above definitions state the exact opposite. Sociology has its theories on this matter which are addressed in this chapter.

Data

How prevalent is suicide? How many attempts are made annually? Does suicide vary by age, race, gender, region of the country, nation, and so forth. Attention is now turned to these questions.

United States Data

Overview (Data reported throughout this section, pages 107 to 111, are from the American Association of Suicidology Online, 2004 report)

Annually the United States records approximately *30,000 to 33,000* suicides, with *males comprising 70 percent of suicides and whites 80 percent.* Every year there are over *800,000 official suicide attempts,* or *one attempt every 39 seconds* compared to *one suicide every 16.2 minutes.* Suicide ranks as the *11th leading cause of death* in the United States and it affects at least *six* other individuals. There are *89 suicides a day* with *52 percent committed by firearms, 23 percent by suffocation/hanging, and under 2 percent by cutting or piercing.* The overall suicide rate is *11.1 per 100,000* population and that figure varies depending on the variable under analysis (i.e., age, race, gender). There are over *four million* survivors of suicide, with survivors defined as family members and friends of a victim of suicide.

State Data

Suicide rates vary by state, with *Alaska recording the highest rate,* 23.6 per 100,000 people. The *lowest rate is for the District of Columbia,* 6.0 per 100,000 population. New York has the lowest suicide rate for any *state,* and it is 6.2 per 100,000 people. The top five states with the highest rate of suicide are (actual numbers in 2004 are in parentheses):

- Alaska 23.6 (155)
- Montana 18.9 (175)
- Nevada 18.9 (440)
- New Mexico 18.7 (356)
- Wyoming 17.4 (88)

The five states with the lowest suicide rate are (excluding the District of Columbia):

- New York 6.2 (1,187)
- Massachusetts 6.6 (425)
- New Jersey 6.9 (597)
- Rhode Island 7.9 (85)
- Illinois 8.1 (1,028)

Suicides rates vary by region, and examination of the data for all 50 states would probably lead to that understanding (the numbers in the parentheses by the states is their suicide rate per 100,000 population). The west, with a suicide rate of 12.4 per 100,000 population, has the highest of all regions in the United States and includes states such as Montana (18.9), New Mexico (18.7), Wyoming (17.4), Colorado (17.3) and Arizona (15.3). Next is the south with a rate of 11.8 per 100,000 people and includes states such as Oklahoma (14.4), Arkansas (13.1), Alabama (12.0), and Texas (10.2). The Midwest region has a suicide rate of 10.8 per 100,000 population and includes but is not limited to the states of South Dakota (14.5), Kansas (13.5), Iowa (11.6), Ohio (11.5), and Nebraska (9.5). The northeast has the lowest suicide rate of 8.1 and includes states such as Vermont (15.0), Maine (13.0), Pennsylvania (11.4), New Jersey (6.9) and New York (6.2).

Age Data:

Age: Suicide Among Children 10–14 Years of Age

Very young children commit suicide. Suicide is the *third leading cause of death* for Caucasian children between the ages of 10 and 14. Whereas suicide rates for the next age group to be discussed have decreased in the last decade, the rate has increased over 50 percent for children 10 to 14 years of age. Suffocation is increasingly the method used by these young children to kill themselves, and in recent years has surpassed the use of firearms as the preferred means of self-destruction. Consistent with other data on race and suicide, African American children kill themselves less frequently than do white children, but their rate of suicide increased by over 233 percent from 1980 to 1995. Suicide ranks as the fifth leading cause of death among African American children.

Age: Suicide Among individuals 15–24 Years of Age

Tragically, suicide is the *third leading cause of death* among the nation's young people, behind accidents and homicides. Every day in the United States there are 12 suicides of individuals between the ages of 15–24, with this age cohort accounting for over 12 percent of all suicides annually, while only representing slightly over 14 percent of the total population. After a dramatic increase in suicides among the young from the 1950s to the early 1990s, the suicide rate dropped precipitously, by nearly 29 percent since 1994 (even given this decrease the suicide rate is four times greater for males and twice as great for females than it was during the mid-1940s). In addition, there are up to 200 suicide attempts for every one completed suicide among the young. How do young people choose to terminate their own lives? Firearms. Suicide by gun or rifle accounts for 49 percent of all suicides of individuals between the ages of 15–24.

Suicide for adolescents is most likely to occur after school hours and in the home of the victim. When considering attempts, young females are most likely to attempt self-destruction by ingesting pills, and attempts generally follow conflicts with other teens or parents. What is more, young people who frequently (more than one attempt) attempt to take their lives tend to emanate from families with histories of suicide and drug and alcohol abuse, and they use suicide attempts as a means of coping with stress. When it comes to stress, these youngsters usually exhibit poor coping skills and display signs of suicide, such as depression, drug and alcohol abuse, and poor or ineffective communication.

Age: College Age Suicide

College is supposed to be a time of great enjoyment and growth; intellectually, spiritually, physically, and emotionally. It is not a period in one's life where thoughts of suicide and actual suicides are supposed to take place. Yet, college-age students (18–24) do attempt and complete suicide, according to the American Association of Suicidology (from which most data in this section are derived). The reasons for suicide include:

• Living in a new and unfamiliar environment which includes experiencing new demands and increased workloads
• Pressures from coursework and social stresses
• Believing one has failed or is not performing up to expectations
• Alienation, feelings of hopelessness, and ineffective coping skills
• Family issues such as mental illness
• Depression and sadness

It is difficult to know the actual overall or national rate of suicide among college students, but there are approximately 1,000 suicides on college campuses annually, and it is estimated one in 12 students has made a suicide plan. Additionally, it is believed there are a large number of college students who suffer from depression, but do not receive any type of intervention. Depression has been diagnosed in 10 percent of the college-age population, and depression is correlated with suicide attempts and completions.

Age: The Elderly and Suicide

The college years (and younger) are times for happiness, enjoyment, and achievements, but have their issues such as depression and suicide. The "golden years" are also shrouded with serious mental health-related issues, one of which is suicide. Persons 65 years of age and older comprise just 12.4 percent of the population, but account for over 16 percent of suicides. Whereas the national rate of suicide is *11.1 per 100,000 population*, the rate for the elderly is 29 percent higher, or *14.3 per 100,000 people*. The suicide rate among older white males is staggering; 31 per 100,000 for white males between the ages of 65 and 84, and an unbelievable 48 per 100,000 for white males who are over 85 years of age. Older males of all races and ethnicities have a suicide rate nearly eight times that for females, and 85 percent of all suicides among persons 65 years of age or older are to males. Suicide rates for females decline after age 60 after having peaked between the ages 45–49. Interestingly, the elderly attempt suicide less but have a greater completion rate. It is estimated individuals between the ages 15–24 complete one suicide for every 100–200 attempts, compared with one estimated suicide for every 25 attempts among persons 65 years of age and older.

But the question is why? Why are the elderly at such great risk for self-destruction? Several explanations include the recent death of a loved one, pain, physical illness, and loneliness. Retirement is also associated with attempts and completed suicides, as is perceived poor health. Of course, depression is believed to play into the decisions of older Americans to take their own lives (and overlaps with issues such as loneliness and poor health). Older people used to be young, with all the hopes and dreams that go with youthfulness, and growing old can be a stressful and difficult existence–physically, emotionally, and relationally. For some older people the choice then is to end their lives.

Observations and Generalizations

Race Date:

Race: White American Suicide rates

Caucasian Americans have higher rates of suicide than all other racial and ethnic categories, except *Native Americans*. The rate per 100,000 population for whites is 12.3, and it is 12.9 for Native Americans. For African Americans the suicide rate is 5.2, and for Hispanics it is 5.3 per 100,000 persons. Whites accounted for 29,251 of the 32,439 completed suicides in 2004, or over 90 percent of all reported suicides. This is an interesting fact since whites account for 70 percent of the population of the United States, which means that whites kill themselves in disproportionate numbers to their total percentage of the U. S. population. Caucasian males commit nearly 80 percent of all suicides reported for whites, and their rate is far greater than it is for white females. The suicide rate for white males is 19.6, and for white females it is 5.1 per 100,000 population. What is more, white males account for *71 percent of all total suicides*, and white females comprise a staggering *90 percent of all suicides committed by women*. In 2004 there were 6,170 white female suicides compared to 6,873 total suicides for women.

Race: African American Suicide Rates

On the face of it or on the basis of common sense, people may conclude that as a result of the long-term prejudice and discrimination faced by African Americans, the despair and hardships this brings would translate into high rates of suicide. Nothing could be further from the truth. African Americans have much lower rates of suicide than do white Americans. The suicide rate for whites is 12.3 per 100,000, and for African Americans it is 5.2. Breaking this down further, the suicide rates for Caucasian males and females are 19.6 and 5.1 per 100,000 population, respectively. For African American males and females the rates are 9.0 and 1.8. Consistent with other races and ethnicities, males commit the great majority of suicides among African Americans (82%), and female African Americans attempt suicide far more than their male counterparts. The ratio of African American female to male suicides is 4.54:1, and African American males are far more likely than black females to end their lives by use of firearms, and this really stands out for black males 65 years of age and older where 84 percent of black male suicides occurred via firearms, compared with 29 percent for African American females in the same age category. Approximately 56 percent of suicides committed by African American males under age 65 occur by firearm, and 33 percent for black women under age 65 are tied to firearms.

Like all other racial and ethnic categories African Americans have high suicide rates among their young. The suicide rate per 100,000 for African American males 15–24 years of age is 12.2 per 100,000 persons, compared to 2.16 for African American females in the same age cohort. But like other racial and ethnic youth in the same age range, the suicide rate has fluctuated over the past 30 years. The suicide rate for young blacks was low until the 1980s when it soared upward for over a dozen years, increasing by 78 percent from 1981 to 1994. The rate of suicide for black youth grew more rapidly during this period for black young people than it did for white youth. However, since 1994 the suicide rate among blacks 15–24 years of age has declined by

just under 30 percent, and African American young people complete suicide *twice less often* than white young Americans.

Race: Hispanic American Suicide Rates

The suicides rate among Hispanics is lower than the national average (5.6 per 100,000 population), but the rate of suicide for the Hispanic younger and elderly is high (The American Association of Suicidology defines Latino as including Mexican, Puerto Rican, Cuban, Central and South American, and Hispanic Americans of unknown origins). Suicide is the seventh leading cause of death among Hispanics under 75 years of age, and the third leading cause of death of Hispanics between the ages of 15 and 24. Males commit 85 percent of all suicides completed by Hispanics and their rate of suicide is 5.9 times greater than it is for Hispanic females. The rates, respectively are 10.46 and 1.78 per 100,000 population. The rates of suicide among Hispanics are very high for its elderly males, with the rates 36.5 for males over 85; 31.5 for males between the ages of 80–84; and 21.7 for males 75–79 years of age. The highest rate for Hispanic females is for women 50–54 years of age, and is a quite low, 3.12. After that, the highest rate is for females 45–49 years of age, and it is 2.52 per 100,000 population.

Younger Hispanic males have high suicide rates, with the highest for males between the ages 20–24 (12.49), followed by younger males ages 40–44 (12.42), with the third highest suicide among younger Hispanic males ages 35–39 (12.23). The suicide rates for females in all three age cohorts (just reported) are 1.97, 2.18, and 2.28, respectively. Hispanic females and African American females share one very important attribute: *very low rates of suicide*, a fact also found for white females, although their rate is higher than for either Hispanic or African

American females. Firearms are the primary means by which Hispanic males kill themselves, although the majority of suicides for young Hispanic males between 10 and 14 years of age occurred as a result of suffocation (46 by suffocation; 18 by firearms; and 1 by poisoning). Hispanic females kill themselves fairly evenly among the three methods, and the method used will vary by age. For example, Hispanic females between the ages of 15–19 killed themselves via of suffocation first (N=45), and then by firearms and poisoning (N=32 and 13, respectively). However, for Hispanic females between 40–44 years of the age, the primary means of self-destruction is poisoning, with 27 ending their lives using that method. Twenty women chose suffocation, and 18 women took their own lives by firearms (based on data from 1999–2001).

Observations and Generalizations from the United States

The following observations and generalizations are offered about suicide in the United States:

1. There is consistency in terms of the total annual number of *reported/official* suicides. Each year there are between 30,000 to 33,000 completed suicides, and this number rarely varies.
2. Males *at all ages* complete suicides at greater rates than females, and females *at all ages* attempt suicide at greater rates than do males.
3. Although suicide via suffocation is increasing, self-destruction by use of firearms remains the number one method of suicide for males. Females continue to prefer less violent means, such as suffocation, pills and cutting.
4. The extremes in age–the young and the old–have the highest suicide rates.

Individuals 25 and younger and 65 and older have higher rates of suicide than other age groups.
5. Depression plays a very important role in suicides (attempted and completed) across all ages, races/ethnicities, and genders.
6. People of color, in particular African Americans and Hispanic Americans, have low rates of suicide. However, consistent with other groups, suicide rates among African Americans and Hispanics are the highest for males, the young and old, and attempted suicides are highest for females.
7. High suicide rates cut across all regions of the country, but are high for some of the least populated areas and states, such as the northwest region, and states such as Alaska and Wyoming. The northeast region of the country has relatively low suicide rates and this includes states such as Massachusetts, New York, and Rhode Island.

International Rates of Suicide

As a phenomenon, suicide varies around the world. Listed are suicide rates of males and females of selected countries, reported by the World Health Organization, with the most recent year of data availability in parentheses (www.who.int 2003). Suicide data from the World Health Organization may vary given the report: The rates are per 100,000 population:

Country	Male Rates	Female Rates
Argentina (2003)	14.1	3.5
Australia (2003)	17.1	4.7
Canada (2002)	18.3	5.0
Cuba (2004)	20.3	6.6
Denmark (2001)	19.2	8.1

Finland (2004)	31.7	9.4
France (2003)	27.5	9.1
Germany (2004)	19.7	6.6
Ireland (2005)	16.3	3.2
Israel (2003)	10.4	2.1
Italy (2002)	11.4	3.1
Japan (2004)	35.6	12.8
Netherlands (2004)	12.7	6.0
Romania (2004)	21.5	4.0
Singapore (2003)	12.5	7.6
United Kingdom (2004)	10.8	3.3
United States (2004)	**17.9**	**4.2**

What follows is a more detailed presentation of suicide around the world, with focus on individual nations, beginning with Australia. The World Health Organization reports suicides for the following age group: 5–14; 15–24; 25–34; 35–44; 45–54; 55–64; 65–74; and, 75 and older. *Unless specified otherwise, all information from pages 112 to 115 is taken from the World Health Organization* (www.who.int. 2003 to 2005).

Australia

The land down under, although not immune to suicide has *relatively low suicide rates*. In 2003, there were 2,155 reported suicides in Australia, and similar to the great majority of nations reporting suicide rates, males kill themselves more frequently than females. The rate of suicide for males is 17.1 per 100,000 population, and for females it is 4.7. The *highest rate of suicide* rate for males and females is for men and women between the ages of 25 and 34, 27.4 and 7.3, respectively. The 15–24 year-old age cohort has rates of 17.1 for males and 3.6 for females. The overall rate for this age group in Australia is 10.7, compared with 9.7 in the United States.

Brazil

In 2002, there were 7,719 reported suicides in Brazil, with 6,025 reported for males, representing 78 percent all official suicides. The overall rate of suicide was 7.4 per 100,000 population, with males over 75 years of age having the highest suicide rate, 13.6 per 100,000 persons. Compared with many other nations, Brazil had a *low overall rate* of suicide, and the rate for the 15–24 year-old age group was 6.9, quite low when compared with countries, such as the United States. What is more, females had low suicide rates, with the highest 2.9 for the 45–54-year age range.

China (only includes selected rural and urban areas)

China, with the world's largest population of 1.3 billion people, reported 16,836 suicides in 1999 (the most recent year suicide date available), for an overall rate of 13.9 per 100,000 population. *Of great significance in 1999 there were more suicides reported for women than for men.* Females committed 8,788 suicides and males 8,048, but the data do not represent all of China. The suicide rates for both elderly males and females are extremely high; 84.2 and 61.2 per 100,000 population respectively, with the overall rate for persons 75 years of age and older estimated at 70.7. In 1999, the rate of suicide increased for females throughout all age groups, and for males it increased up to the 35–44 year age range when it dropped, but assumed an upward liner trend afterward.

France

In 2003, there were 10,856 reported suicides in France for an overall average of 18.0 per 100,000 population. Males committed 73 percent of all suicides, and the *age group-specific* suicide rate for elderly French males 75 years of age and older was 75.8, compared to 15.8 for elderly females. In 2003, for both males and females the rate of suicide increased steadily throughout all age groups, dropping for both genders for ages 55–64, but increasing after that. The overall suicide rate for the 15–24 year age cohort is 8.1, and the breakout is 12.5 for males and 3.7 for females.

Germany

In 2004, the *overall* suicide rate in Germany was 13.0, and there were 10,733 reported suicides, with males accounting for 74 percent of them. The suicide rate for males 75 years of age and older was 55.8, and the highest *age group-specific rate* of suicide for females was for women 75 years of age and older, reported to be 29.7 per 100,000. Of interest is the *relatively low rate* of suicide for 15–24-year-old Germans, reported to be 6.7 per 100,000 population. For both males and females, the suicide rate increased as age increased, except for women between the ages of 65–74, when it showed a decrease, but it rose sharply for women 75 and older (from 10.1 to 17.1 per 100,000 population).

Ireland

In 2005, there were 401 official suicides in Ireland, with the *overall rate* reported to be 9.7 per 100,000 people. The suicide rate for the most prone age group worldwide, 75 and older, was low in Ireland, reported to be 5.4 per 100,000 population. The rate was 26.4 for males 45–54 years old, *the highest for any age group and for gender*. The rate for women between the ages 55–64 was 5.6, the highest for women. Fifteen to 24-year-olds had an overall suicide rate of 11.9; 20.4 for males, and 3.2 for females.

Italy

Italy reported 4,069 suicides in 2002, with an overall rate of 15.2 per 100,000 population. The *highest rate of suicide* was 31.9 for

males between 75 years of age and older, with the rate being 15.2 for women in the same age group, the highest reported for women. The suicide rate expanded as age increased for both males and females, and the overall rate for 15–24-year-old Italians was 4.1 per 100,000 population, quite low when compared with other western nations.

Japan

In 2004, Japan recorded 30,247 suicides, with the *highest rate*, 58.8 per 100,000 population for males between the ages 55–64. The highest rate for females was for the age group 75 and older, and it was 22.9. Once again there is an upward linear trend for suicides by age group and gender with one exception; the suicide rate increased steadily by age group for males up to ages 55–64, then dropped precipitously to 41.5 for males between ages 65–74. The suicide rate increased for the last reported cohort of males, 75 years of age and older, to 46.3 per 100,000 population. Males committed 73 percent of all suicides in 2004, and the overall suicides rate for young people ages 15–24 was 12.8.

Mexico

In 2003, there were 4,088 reported suicides in Mexico, with males completing 83 percent of all suicides. Consistent with that reported for most other nations, individuals 75 and older had the highest suicide rate (although lower than most nations), 7.4 per 100,000. For all age groupings, women had low suicide rates, with the highest 2.8 for 15–24-year-olds. The highest rate for males was for the oldest age group, 16.3.

Norway

In 2004, males completed 68 percent (359) of the 529 recorded suicides in Norway. The suicide rate of 23.4 for males between the ages 45–54 was the highest for all age groups. There was an up-and-down pattern for the rate of suicide by age group, with females between the ages 65–74 having the highest rate per 100,000 for women (23.7). The rate for 15–24-year-olds was 14.0, 20.3 for males, and for females it was 7.3.

Sweden

Males committed 73 percent (862) of the 1,180 reported suicides in 2002, and the rate for individuals 75 years and older was 20.3 per 100,000 population, the highest *overall* rate for all age groups. Except for women 65–74, there was an upward linear trend in the data by age group for both genders. The suicide rate for persons 15–24 was 9.7, however it was the *lowest* for all age groups. The highest *age group-specific group rate* was 36.5 for males 75 and older, and the highest rate for females was 12.6 for women between the ages 55–64.

Israel

In 2003, Israel reported 417 suicides, with 23.3 the highest *age group-specific rate*, for males 75 years and older. There was a clear upward linear trend in suicide rate for females by age group, and for males this too was the case up to ages 55–64 when it declined slightly, but increased for the last two age groups, 65–74 and 75 and older. Males committed 83 per cent of all suicides, and the highest overall rate, 12.7 was for persons 75 and older. Individuals 15–24 had the lowest age group-specific rate, 6.0 per 100,000 population, and females 65–74 had the highest for women, 6.4.

Observations and Generalizations from the Selected Countries

Based on that which has just been reviewed, the following observations and generalizations are offered:

1. Elderly people 75 years of age and older are most prone to suicide *worldwide, especially males*. It is possible that conclusions drawn by The American Association of Suicidology about suicide among older Americans applies to other nations. Older people are more socially isolated, have greater issues with physical illnesses, and may be without a spouse or partner whom they were attached to many years.

2. A number of nations show progressive increases in suicide rates by age group. This is not necessarily the case for the United States, where younger age groups display high rates of suicide. America is a nation that places significant expectations and much pressure on its young to succeed, and has an ongoing problem with school violence and bullying, which may account for the differences with other nations relative to suicide by the young. On the other hand, many nations do not offer the same opportunities for advancement and continued personal and professional growth as does the United States, and this may partially explain why rates of suicide go up for many age groups around the world.

3. High rates of completed suicides are a phenomenon of males worldwide, and the one exception to the data above was China. Worldwide, males more than females are more likely to commit suicide by use of violent means such as firearms. Apparently, the socialization of the genders has commonalities

across nations, and surfaces when considering self-destruction. Males are socialized to be more physically aggressive and violent, and this clearly impacts their rates of *completed* suicides.

Explaining Suicide: Theoretical Contributions

It is indeed difficult to understand suicide as anything but some form of psychological or emotional abnormality. After all, why would anyone commit the ultimate act: self destruction? In this section explanations of suicide are presented from a *sociological framework*, or attempting to understand suicide in relationship to social interaction and the social order. The discussion begins with the classic and groundbreaking research and theory undertaken by Emile Durkheim.

Emile Durkeim: Le Suicide

Throughout this book the name of Emile Durkheim has been used. Durkheim is simply one of the most important influences on sociology. His work *Suicide* published in 1897 was essential to the development of sociology on the following grounds. First, Durkheim's research on suicide represented an early attempt to unravel its causes, undertaken from a *social fact* perspective. Previous attempts to understand self-destruction were typically couched in psychology, religion, and philosophy. Durkheim sought to apply *sociological ideations* to the study of suicide that would explain it in terms of its relationship to the social. Second, Durkheim's methodology (to be discussed) helped to pave the way for, and the importance of using secondary data to collect and analyze information, no small thing since secondary analysis is a major and convenient method used by contemporary sociologists when

undertaking research. Third, in addition to employing secondary analysis, Durkheim analyzed data on suicide using statistical-type techniques that would become important to social inquiry (discussed in the next section).

Methodology: Secondary Analysis and Statistical Analysis

Durkheim's study of suicide entailed an extensive analysis of secondary data from multiple European nations including Austria, Bavaria, Belgium, Denmark, England, France, Italy, Norway, Saxony, Sweden, and Wurttemberg, and his analysis of suicide in the military included data from the United States (1951, 228). Throughout *Suicide* Durkheim successively introduced and examined the effects of multiple variables on suicide, an approach used in contemporary sociology and other disciplines, and in advanced form called multivariate analysis. When analyzing data on suicide, Durkheim examined the effects of variables such as the economy, religion, marital status, ethnicity, gender, military rank, and occupation in relationship to suicide. He also cross- tabulated data, such as his analysis of suicide by gender and age, and suicide by age and marital status. Given the years of his research (during the 1890s) and the technology available to him (or the lack thereof), Durkheim undertook an incredibly comprehensive and detailed study of suicide. Most saliently, many of his findings continue to stand the test of time.

Types of Suicide

The most well-known information from *Suicide* involves the identification of three major types of suicide: *altruistic suicide; egoistic suicide; anomic suicide* (Durkheim very briefly discussed *fatalistic suicide*, which is not addressed here). But what is usually not known or is forgotten is a very important discussion from "Book One: Extra-Social Factors," the first section of *Suicide* that considers the relationship of psychopathology, race and heredity, geographical region, and imitation to suicide. This "book" is important since it lays the framework for Durkheim's overriding assumption concerning suicide: it has *social causes*. Durkheim argued that in the final analysis suicide was not a product of insanity or heredity, instead it was steeped in social roots that are strongly affected by the degree of individual *social solidarity* and *social integration* to society. In other words, the strength of individuals belonging to social groups (solidarity) and how deeply people were connected with them (integration) had direct consequences for suicide. Durkheim perceived strong solidarity and integration with social groups as representing a buffer zone to suicide. He also discovered that those same factors (solidarity and integration) were associated with suicide under specific circumstances.

But let's return to a generally unrecognized discussion by Durkheim where he addresses suicide and psychopathology. Durkheim recognized four types of insanity that psychiatrists claim are associated with suicide (1951, 63–67). The first is *maniacal suicide* in which people kill themselves because they are hallucinating or they are delirious. *Melancholy suicide*, a second type of psychopathic suicide, results from extreme depression and sadness. The third type of psychopathic suicide is *obsessive suicide*, or when people engage in self-destruction because they are preoccupied with the idea of death, which they are unable to get out of their minds. The fourth type of suicide is *impulsive* or *automatic suicide*, and as it sounds occurs on the spur-of-the-moment, without warning or premeditation: it has no definitive explanation. These four types of psy-

chopathic suicide discussed by Durkheim are explicated here for the purposes of *comparison* to what Durkheim believed to be the most important reasons for suicide: it has *social causes*, and is predominately a societal and group-driven behavior, *rarely a direct result of insanity or mental instability*. Durkheim wrote "Since the suicide of insane persons do not constitute the entire genus but a variety of it, the psychopathic states constituting mental alienation can give no clue to the collective tendency to suicide in its generality" (1951, 67).

Since Durkheim argued that the etiology of suicide lies predominantly in the social, he identified *three major types* of suicide which represent the most well-known and famous elements of his theory and research on the topic. The first two types of suicide are related to the degree of *social integration* of individuals to social groups, and include *egoistic* and *altruistic suicide*. The next type of suicide is related to the degree of *social regulation* over individuals and includes *anomic suicide*. Each type of suicide is now addressed with examples of each provided.

Egoistic suicide is associated with too little social integration and occurs when individuals lack strong bonds to social groups. A prominent example of egoistic suicide used by Durkheim is *suicide and religious affiliation*, in which he reported that members of Protestant denominations had the highest likelihood of suicide, Roman Catholics the second highest rate, followed by Jews with the lowest suicide rate. Durkheim explained this in terms of the strength of individual relationship (integration) to faith, and observed that due the diversity of Protestant denominations there was more of a free spirit to interpret the bible or religious doctrine, leaving individuals dangling and vulnerable to self-destruction. Durkheim wrote ". . . the proclivity of Protestants for suicide must relate to the spirit of free inquiry that animates this religion . . . the greater the concessions a confessional group makes to individual judgment, the less it dominates lives, the less its cohesion and vitality" (1951, 158–159). Durkheim suggested the presence of more unified doctrine among Roman Catholics shored up a stronger sense of social solidarity among them, and the persecution faced by Jews historically served as a glue to build a strong sense of solidarity and unity (1951, 159–160).

A second type of suicide identified by Durkheim is *altruistic suicide*, or suicide resulting from *too much social integration*. A major example of altruistic suicide discussed by Durkheim was *suicide in the military*. Durkheim compared the suicide rates of military personnel to the general populations of eight European nations, and reported the rates of suicide for the former were much higher than they were for the general population, *for all eight nations* (1951, 228). Using data from France, Durkheim compared the suicide rates of regular enlisted soldiers to officers, and reported the rate of suicide to be 380 per one million population for soldiers compared with 430 per one million population for officers (1951, 229–230). Durkheim offered several explanations for the higher rates of suicide for members of the military, one being that suicide in the military is analogous to suicide in lower (primitive societies) societies, meaning soldiers or officers are characterized by a primitive morality that predispose them to self-destruction. Durkheim wrote "Influenced by this predisposition, the soldier kills himself at the least disappointment, for the most futile reasons, for a refusal of leave, a reprimand, an unjust punishment, a delay in promotion, a question of honor, a flush of momentary jealousy or even simply because other suicides have occurred before his eyes or to his knowledge (1951, 238–239).

The third type of suicide is *anomic suicide*, or suicide resulting from *low social regulation*.

Durkheim uses several prominent examples of anomic suicide, *economic crisis* being one of them. Durkheim analyzed suicides in relationship to economic crashes and depressions, and reported "It is a well-known fact that economic crises have an aggravating effect on the suicidal tendency" (1951, 241). Durkheim noted the rise in suicides in Vienna, Paris, Prussia, and Germany during periods of economic downturn, arguing that hard economic times place strains on individuals that could lead them to self-destruction. Durkheim wrote "In the case of economic disasters, indeed, something like a declassification occurs which suddenly casts certain individuals into a lower state than their previous one. . . . So they are adjusted to the condition forced on them, and its very prospect is intolerable; hence the suffering which detaches them from a reduced existence even before they have made trail of it" (1951, 252). Durkheim also analyzed *marital status* in relationship to anomic suicide, and reported divorced males and females commit suicide three to four times greater than married individuals, and more frequently than the widowed. But the question is "why"? Among other possibilities Durkheim noted that marriage provides a type of immunity from suicide that is lost with divorce; in other words the "glue" that held individuals together in marriage is no longer present. Durkheim explained this in the following manner:

> Briefly, when conjugal society is dissolved by the death of one of the couple, the effects of which it had with reference to suicide continue to be felt in part by the survivor. Then, however, it is not to be supposed that the same thing takes place when the marriage is interrupted, not by death, but by a judicial act, and that the aggravation which inflicts divorced persons is a result not of the divorce but of the marriage ended by divorce? It must be connected with some quality of

the matrimonial society, the influence of which the couple continue to experience even when separated (1951, 263)

Listed are major findings by Durkheim concerning suicide, some of which have already been cited:

1. Suicide is high among single people and lowest among individuals with children.
2. There is an inverse relationship between the number of children married couples have and the rate of suicide: the rate decreases with each additional child.
3. Not only are the rates of suicide high during times of economic depression, they are also high during times of economic prosperity.
4. Suicide is higher among members of the military than it is for the general population, and it is higher for those who volunteer for military service than it is for those who were drafted.
5. Suicide increases with knowledge as result of the attenuating effect knowledge can have on traditional beliefs (such as religious beliefs). Traditional beliefs may be supplanted by increased levels of knowing.

Durkheim in the Contemporary

Several of Emile Durkheim's findings on suicide from over 100 years ago have stood the test of time, yet other findings have been questioned, failing to demonstrate long-term viability. Breault and Barkley (1982), Danigelis and Pope (1979), Gibbs (1982), Gove and Hughes (1980), and Stack (1979) have offered support for key findings reported by Durkheim. For example, Breault and Barkley found in their analysis of suicide in 42

nations that strong ties to family, religion, and nation were associated with low rates of suicide, and Gove and Hughes reported that living alone was associated with high rates of suicide. Gibbs echoed Durkheim's findings on marital status and suicide, reporting that being married is associated with low rates of suicide. Thus some research has found ongoing support for the idea that social integration and social solidarity are related to low rates of self-destruction. Yet other scholars have questioned some of Durkheim's findings. Maris (1969) found little support for Durkheim's observation that elite occupations have higher rates of suicide. To the contrary, Maris' reported that suicide was more prevalent among individuals from lower social strata, a finding supported by Li (1972) in research documenting that suicide was more common among individuals with low levels of education. Since the time of Durkheim's research, Roman Catholics have shown an increase in their rates of suicide. Yang (1992) and Pope (1976) questioned Durkheim's conclusions concerning suicide, religion, and social integration suggesting that he employed less than adequate measures of social integration (a point addressed in the next theory). This is no minor criticism, since the religion/suicide nexus represents one of Durkheim's most famous and important findings. Lester's (1992) examination of preliterate tribes found spotty evidence for the relationship of the degree of social integration and suicide. Based on these studies, it is concluded that Durkheim's research on suicide receives support, and does not in other instances. But for our purposes, *Suicide* represents a strategic and very important step in the direction of sociology becoming an empirical science. The indebtedness of sociologists to Durkheim cannot be understated, or underestimated. The next theory is a direct extension on the seminal study undertaken by Durkheim, putting to the test many of his key findings. The theory is "Status Integration and Suicide" by Jack P. Gibbs and Walter T. Martin.

Jack P. Gibbs and Walter T. Martin: *Status Integration and Suicide*

Let's return to the question exercise. Ask yourselves two basic questions: "How many statuses do you occupy in your life?" "Do you keep these different statuses in line (are they in accord with one another)?" Other questions that have probably entered your mind are what is meant by "status," and what does any of this have to do with suicide? According to Jack P. Gibbs and Walter T. Martin, *the amount of status integration* individuals experience in society has a great deal to do with self-destruction. The statuses they examined include age, gender, race, marital status, and occupational status. Gibbs and Martin hypothesized that individuals who are tightly integrated along all five statuses (or various combinations of them) have a low probability of suicide, and those persons who have weak status integration will experience higher rates of suicide. Several examples of different levels of status integration *and suicide* are: male and being older; female and high occupational status; African American and high occupational status; and, widower and being elderly. Going through each combination individually, it could be argued that being male and older can imply weak status integration (recall older males have high rates of suicide), and becoming older for males often means weaker ties to society, and therefore greater vulnerability for self destruction. This conclusion could be reached for *females* (especially in past years) when it was rare for them to achieve high occupational status, with status inconsistency a potential source of suicide. The same argument applies to *African Americans* with elite careers. Finally, being a *widower* and *old* can

also entail weak status integration and high rates of suicide, since older males who have experienced the deaths of their wives may have lost an important source of status integration. Gibbs and Martin focused their research on suicide around its connection to the degree of status integration found in society, and arrived at the following postulates (1964, 27):

1. Postulate 1: The suicide rate of a population varies inversely with the stability and durability of social relationships within that population.
2. Postulate 2: The stability and durability of social relationships within a population vary directly with the extent to which individuals in that population conform to the patterned and socially sanctioned demands and expectations placed upon them by others.
3. Postulate 3: The extent to which individuals in a population conform to patterned and socially sanctioned demands and expectations placed upon them by others varies inversely with the extent to which individuals in that population are confronted with role conflicts.
4. Postulate 4: The extent to which individuals in a population are confronted with role conflicts varies directly with the extent to which individuals occupy incompatible statuses in that occupation.
5. Postulate 5: The extent to which individuals occupy incompatible statuses in a population varies inversely with the degree of status integration in that population.

Operational Definition of Status Integration and Methodology

In testing their theory of status integration and suicide, Gibbs and Martin were immediately faced with an important challenge, and that was to operationally define status integration, a term neither felt was adequately clarified by Durkheim (1964, 14). The authors arrived at what they called "a weighted total integration measure," which took into account the full and combined impact of multiple statuses such as age, gender, and marital status on rates of suicide. This measure allowed for an observable dispersion of scores that made it possible to separate risks of suicide, depending on the issue under examination (such as suicide differentials by race and sex). Sources of data for this research included the Bureau of the Census, Vital Statistics, and documents including information on occupations in the United States, all from the early 1950s (the study also includes international data). Three findings are covered in this section and they are: *occupational integration by sex and race; measures of the integration of marital status with age, and suicide rates by age; and, the ratio of suicide rate of widowed to married persons.*

One of the findings reported by the authors was a measurement of *occupational integration by sex and race.* The importance of undertaking this analysis early in their research was that it explicated *how* their measure of status integration worked, as well as for the intrinsic value of what this type of information would reveal. Gibbs and Martin reported that males had a stronger measure of status integration for five of eleven occupational categories ("farmers and farm managers"; "managers, officials and proprietors"; "craftsmen and foremen"; "operatives"; and, "laborers") than for females, *but that females had a stronger total-overall weighted measure of status integration.* A similar finding was reported for *race, occupational status, and status integration* where whites had stronger status integration in six of 11 occupational categories ("professional and technical"; "managers, officials and proprietors"; "clerical and kindred"; "sales workers"; "craftsmen

and foremen"; and, "operatives"), *but African Americans had a stronger total-overall measure of status occupation* (1964, 62). Thus the analysis was able to discern numerical differences in status integration by race and gender when examining its relationship to occupational status (one important indicator of status integration).

Gibbs and Martin examined the relationship between *age, marital status,* and status integration and found *the ages with the highest suicide rates (45–75+) had the lowest levels of status integration,* implying although individuals were married, as they grew older they experienced less intensive status integration (1964, 88). In addition, the authors reported the ratio of suicide rate of *widowed to married people* was greatest for widowed persons between the ages of 20–34, when the *ratio of integration of married persons to widowed individuals* was very high, implying strong status integration for married individuals at younger ages, but far less status integration at the same ages for those who lost a spouse through death (1964, 99). Gibbs and Martin's study is quite extensive and detailed, and consistently found support for their leading assumption that *rates of suicide vary by the degree of status integration in society.* Yet there are other explanations of suicide that are not necessarily grounded in the work of Durkheim, and now discussed.

The Substance of Suicide

As an act, and what some persons might define as the ultimate act, suicide can be extremely difficult to comprehend, and as we will see, for the survivors of a loved one who has completed suicide, there are many emotions and trying times. Two important discussions concerning the meanings of suicide shed some light on what may be going on in the minds of persons who are contemplating or who have engaged in self-destruction.

Jerry Jacobs (1967) identified 10 phases individuals pass through and must overcome before they engage in the act of suicide:

1. Problems arise that are overpowering and appear too difficult to overcome.
2. The problems have developed over time and are not mere isolated incidents or necessarily of recent origins.
3. Death becomes a way for these individuals to solve their problems.
4. Individuals become increasingly isolated, since they do not believe they can talk about or share dilemmas with others.
5. In order to move on with their thoughts of suicide, individuals search for ways to resolve very powerful internal and moral prohibitions against committing self-destruction.
6. As a result of their perceptions of increasing isolation from others and the resulting feelings of greater autonomy, individuals contemplating suicide are able to overcome the prohibitions.
7. After resolving their prohibitions against suicide, individuals develop rationalizations to justify the act and to minimize other fears they may harbor concerning suicide. One such justification is that although they are going to kill themselves, they still place a major value on life.
8. Individuals arrive at the conclusion that suicide is the answer to their issues, since the problems they face are not of their doing anyway.
9. In order to alleviate any feelings of guilt or responsibility for their actions, individuals come to the conclusion self-destruction is the only solution to their crisis, and have no other choice but to proceed.
10. Suicidal individuals are concerned with what happens to them in the afterlife, and in order to diffuse the possibility of

punishment (in the afterlife) they pray for themselves, and leave suicide notes asking others to pray for them as well.

Jack Douglas undertook an analysis of suicide notes that offer additional insights into the meaning of suicide for those persons who have attempted or completed it. The six patterns of social meaning are (1967, 284–319):

1. A means of transforming the soul from this world to another. In this instance suicidal persons have a desire to return to God, or to transform their lives to a different world or existence.
2. A means of transforming the substantial self in this world, or another world. Individuals commit suicide in order to draw attention to themselves; to prove their worthiness. It is if the individual was saying "I am important, so please take notice of me."
3. A means of achieving fellow-feeling (self-pity). In this case individuals commit suicide because they feel sorry for themselves, and they envision how they will appear to others in the coffin.
4. A means of obtaining revenge by blaming others for one's death. Suicide is completed to get even with others, perhaps to get even with bullies at school, or a partner who has just ended a romantic relationship. Clearly, blame for the suicide is being placed on other people, possibly to make them feel guilty and terrible over the death.
5. A means of escaping the responsibilities of continued life. In this scenario suicide is an alternative to facing up to problems in life, which can include financial difficulties and marital issues. Rather than continue to confront these problems, the individual opts for self destruction.

6. A means of self-destruction after killing another person. Although rare, this is suicide that occurs after a murder has been committed, such as when a husband murders his wife and then takes his own life.

Warning Signs of Suicide and Depression

In concluding this chapter, attention is directed toward practical and important information concerning suicide: *warning signs of suicide, and depression.* The data for both discussions is derived from *The American Association of Suicidology,* January 2007. **IS PATH WARM** is a mnemonic that can be used to remember *warning signs* of suicide. The letters stand for:

I=Ideation
S=Substance Abuse

P=Purposelessness
A=Anxiety
T=Trapped
H=Hopelessness

W=Withdrawal
A=Anger
R=Recklessness
M=Mood Change

The aforementioned *warning signs* of suicide are frequently associated with depression, which is the most common mental disorder in the United States. The common symptoms of depression that are present almost every day, for a two-week period include:

1. depressed mood, such as feeling sad or empty
2. lack of interest in previously enjoyable activities

3. significant weight loss or gain
4. insomnia or hypersomnia
5. agitation, restlessness, and irritability
6. fatigue or loss of energy
7. feelings of worthlessness, hopelessness, or guilt
8. inability to think or concentrate, or indecisiveness
9. recurrent thoughts of death
10. recurrent thoughts of suicide ideation
11. a suicide attempt or plan for completing suicide

Whereas the above represents the most common symptoms of depression, the next is a list of *symptoms* of individuals who are depressed, and who are at risk of committing suicide:

1. hopelessness
2. rage, uncontrolled anger, and seeking revenge
3. acting reckless, or engaging in risky activities, without necessarily thinking
4. feeling trapped, and there is no way out
5. increasing substance abuse
6. withdrawing from friends, family, and society
7. anxiety, agitation, and inability to sleep, or sleeping all the time
8. dramatic mood changes
9. expressing little reason for living
10. feeling no sense of purpose in life

The American Association of Suicidology has also identified *verbal and behavioral* clues to suicide. *Verbal clues* would include *direct messages* such as "I am going to commit suicide" and "I don't want to live anymore." *Indirect messages* would include "Life isn't worth living" and "Soon it won't matter anymore." *Behavioral clues* include many of the issues addressed when discussing individuals at risk of suicide, and: loss of energy; recent lack of concern for physical appearance; communication difficulties; and, giving away

SummarySuicide123

prized possessions. Other behavioral clues for suicide are: a drop in school grades and work performance; making final arrangements, in particular making a will; and, previous suicide attempts (80% of persons who have completed suicide have attempted it previously). It is noted that great caution is to be exercised in applying the information on clues and symptoms to individuals we fear may be considering self-destruction. One of the clues or symptoms alone may not be sufficient to drive a person to the point of committing suicide. A number of the clues or symptoms combined may be indication that individuals may be in need of intervention.

In Recognition: Jack P. Gibbs

Jack P. Gibbs has one of the most distinguished careers of any sociologist of the last half century. Dr. Gibbs has well over 170 publications, including scholarly articles in refereed academic journals, and books. One-hundred-seventy is incredibly hard to fathom and attests to Dr. Gibbs commitment to sociology, and to the pursuit and expansion of knowledge. The depth and breadth of his publication record is amazing, with articles and books on suicide, status integration, research methods, societal reaction to mental illness, urbanization and technology, sociology of law, criminal deterrence, conceptions of deviant behavior, capital punishment, social control, and terrorism (and this is just the tip of the iceberg). Dr. Gibbs has received many honors and recognitions over the course of his career, as a student and professional. He graduated with honors from Texas Christian University in 1950, and over the course of his graduate studies was a Fulbright Scholar, and was awarded a Carnegie Fellowship. His professional awards and recognitions are too many to mention, but extended across major positions in academic societies and organizations, including the American Society of Criminology, the National Research Council, and editorial boards on several major scholarly journals. Dr. Gibbs held faculty and research positions at the University of California, Berkeley; the University of Texas, Austin; Washington State University; the University of Arizona; and Vanderbilt University. Dr. Gibbs was chair of the Department of Sociology at Washington State University and Chair of the Department of Sociology and Anthropology at Vanderbilt. In addition, Dr. Gibbs held visiting professorships at other American Universities, as well as internationally. But it is his work, his long and distinguished career with so many important contributions to the study of deviance and sociology that will be remembered, honored, and respected for decades. Jack P. Gibbs is a giant of his time.

SUMMARY

Suicide is a worldwide phenomenon that largely affects young persons and the elderly. Across nations, with few exceptions, males complete suicide far more than females, and females attempt it more than males. In the United States, suicide is uncommon among African-Americans and Latinos. Sociological theories of suicide tend to echo the work of Emile Durkheim, and focus on the roles of social integration and social solidarity as explanations of self-destruction. Although sociological theories of suicide place heavy emphasis on social causes and correlates involved in this tragic act, a number of experts trace the roots of suicide to depression, which in the psychological and psychiatric sciences is often considered the powerful force in the decision to end one's life.

Chapter 10

CRIMINAL BEHAVIORS

CASE STUDY:
RICHARD KUKLINSKY

Think about this for a moment. An individual who does not drink alcohol; does not gamble; spends time with his wife and family; owns a home and is living out that part of the American dream; makes a good income; and has been able to achieve much in life on an eighth-grade education. Without knowing a great deal about this individual, it might be easy to conclude he is a person to admire and respect. Take another look. He was Richard Kuklinsky; hired killer. The home, income, and wonderful family, all was supported via killing people for money. The guy next store was no model citizen after all. He killed for five figures, often at the higher end of that dollar amount, and he also trafficked in drugs and pornography, apparently to the total naiveté of his wife, and to those who resided close to him.

The question becomes "why," "why would anyone kill for profit?" A look into the past of Kuklinsky holds keys to that question. As a youngster growing up in New Jersey, he was skinny and quite frequently was bullied, until one day he had enough, and the tables were turned. When attacked by a group of bullies, Kuklisnky returned the favor and physically hurt those who were

once again attempting to injure him. He became the hunter instead of the hunted. In his own words he said "it was better to give then to receive." His parents were also abusive to him: to what would become one cold-blooded and callused human being. By age 18 he committed his first homicide by beating to death another individual with a pool stick after an argument that ensued while playing pool. That murder was just the beginning, and by the time he was arrested in the 1990s he had killed over 100 individuals, only now he wasn't killing out of pure anger; he was killing for money. The means he used to murder people were brutal, and included the use of cyanide, firearms, stabbing, beating, and dismembering people after he had murdered them. He was called the "Iceman" because on occasion he would put a corpse in an industrial freezer until he felt it was time to dispose of it. In one instance he waited two years to remove a corpse from the freezer.

Kuklinsky's reputation in the criminal underworld brought him much business, becoming the "turn-to" guy when someone or an organization wanted another person killed. One such organization was the notorious and violent Gambino crime syndicate out of New York City, a mafia family that needed no help in pulling off murders, but who would turn to Kuklinsky because he was effective and seemingly invincible. But that invincibility would slowly come to an end by the time Kuklinsky was approaching age 50. Kuklinsky murdered several of his business associates, drawing the attention of law enforcement. The state of New Jersey united with, and formed a federal task force, and a federal agent, Dominic Polifrome went undercover and befriended Richard Kuklinsky, wearing a wire and having his conversations with Kuklinsky recorded. Polifrome was posing as a "wise guy" out of New York City, but after some months the task force became concerned that Kuklinsky was aware of Polifrome and was going to kill him, and the decision was made to arrest Kuklinsky on the basis of evidence collected from the electronic surveillance. Kuklinsky was eventually sentenced to life in prison where he died at the age of 70 in March 2006. During his reign of terror he continued to live in New Jersey with his wife and three children, unsuspected by anyone who knew him that he was one of America's most notorious killers.

Criminal Deviance

Richard Kuklinsky is one example, albeit one very violent and media noteworthy example of criminal deviance. The great majority of criminality is anything like the situation involving Kuklinsky, and even the great majority of violent crimes, including homicides, are a far cry from those involving Richard Kuklinsky. So why even discuss Kuklinsky in this chapter? We will return to that question later.

Criminal deviance includes many types of acts in violation of the criminal law, including crimes for which we are most familiar, such as homicide, assault, rape, theft, and drug trafficking. But it also includes the most financially costly and devastating criminal activities, usually subsumed under the labels "white-collar crimes" and organized crime. In this chapter attention is directed at two major types of criminal deviance: *violence* and *property offenses.*

Violent Criminal Deviance

This section will focus on the following violent crimes: homicide; rape; and the "abuses," with emphasis on child abuse. It begins with an overview of violence in the United States.

Violence in America

The good news is that from 1993 to 2003 the rate of violence in the United States decreased. The not-so-good news is the rate of violence *appears* to be on an upswing, and even though the rate of violence decreased for a decade, *America remains the most violent of civilized societies on earth.* Total violent crime decreased from 1993 to 2003, and this means there were decreases in the rates for homicide, rape, assault and robbery. Unless stated otherwise, all graphs on pages 126 to 128 are from the Bureau of Justice Statistics (www.ojp.usdoj.gov 2007)

There are several explanations for the decreases in rates of violence, and some are offered here. First, during most of the 1990s, the *unemployment rate* was around 4 percent, as low as it had been in 30 years. Lower rates of unemployment are believed by some experts to be associated with decreases in violence (Reiman, 2007). Second, there was an apparent *end to turf wars* related to drug trafficking. The argument is that drug dealers killed each other off, and as a result there is now a stable drug trade within areas once characterized by turf wars, fueled by the illegal drug industry (*U.S. News and World Report,* 1996). Third, Alfred Blumstein (2000–2001) cited the importance of the *dis-*

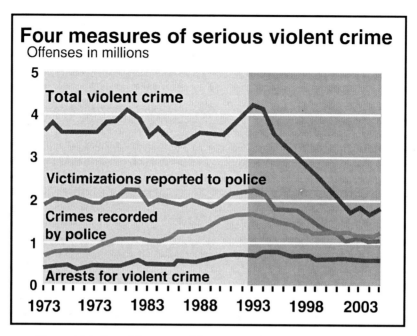

Figure 10:1. Four Measures of Serious Violent Crime 1973–2005.
Adapted from the Bureau of Justice Statistics.

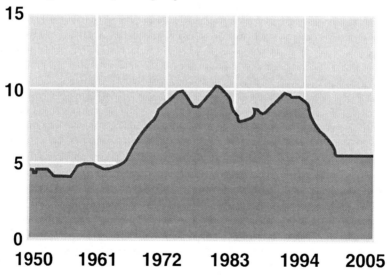

Figure 10:2. Homicide Victimization Rates 1950–2005.
Adapted from the Bureau of Justice Statistics.

Rape rates
**Adjusted victimization rate
per 1,000 persons age 12 and over**

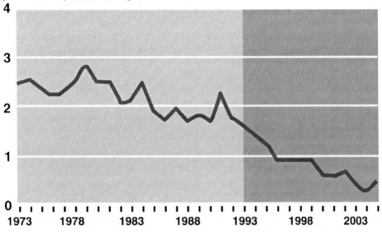

Figure 10:3. Rape Rates 1973–2005.
Adapted from the Bureau of Justice Statistics.

Assault rates
**Adjusted victimization rate
per 1,000 persons age 12 and over**

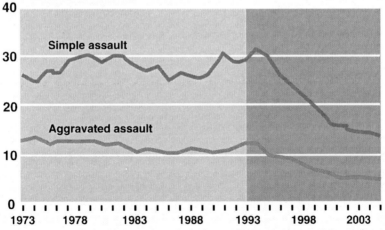

Figure 10:4. Assault Rapes 1973–2005.
Adapted from the Bureau of Justice Statistics.

Robbery rates
**Adjusted victimization rate
per 1,000 persons age 12 and over**

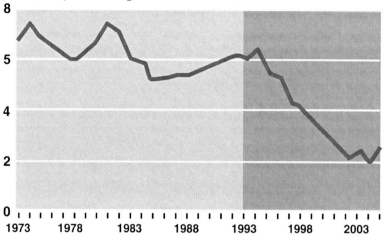

Figure 10:5. Robbery Rates 1973–2005.
Adapted from the Bureau of Justice Statistics.

continued widespread use of crack cocaine because of its dangerous effects, and crack itself was related to abundant inner-city youth gang violence. In addition, Blumstein noted the *reduction in the availability of handguns* occurring as a result of police suppression strategies, and community outcry concerning youth and firearms. Last, Blumstein noted the *improved economy* that created legitimate job opportunities for many young people, employment opportunities that kept many youth from wandering into the destructive life of street gangs.

Homicide: Race

As suggested in Figure 10:2, the rate of homicide decreased sharply from 1993–2003, and has leveled off since then (again unless stated otherwise, all figures are from the Bureau of Justice Statistics). But how does the rate of homicide break out by race,

gender and age? Starting with race, homicide victimization by race shows a discernible difference, for both the rate of *victimization* and the rate of *offending* for whites and African Americans. *In both instances, the rates are greater for African Americans,* but for both categories the rates of victimization and offending decreased during the 1990s and early into this century. The rates of offending and victimization have shown a slight increase in 2005 for African Americans, a trend that will need to be watched over the next few years.It must be emphasized that homicide is an *intraracial act*, in which 86 percent of white victims are killed by whites, and 94 percent of African American victims are killed by African Americans (www.ojp. usdoj.gov 2007). However, the data on homicide by race show that homicide victimization is *six times* greater for African Americans than it is for whites, and African Americans are *seven times* more likely than whites to kill people. Additional data on homicide by race includes:

- African American victims are disproportionately represented in homicides involving drugs.
- African Americans are less likely than other Americans to be murdered at the workplace, to be victims of sex-related crimes, and to be murdered by poison.
- Almost all murder involves either white or African American, with 51 percent of homicide victims being white, and 47 percent African American. Nearly 46 percent of murderers are white, but 52 percent are African American.
- Stranger homicides are more likely to *be interracial* than homicides involving either friends or acquaintances.
- The greatest percentage of multiple mur-

der victims and offenders are whites.

Homicide: Age

One of the tragedies associated with homicide is age. *Younger Americans kill; younger Americans get murdered.* The *18–24-year-old* age group is *most prone* to homicide victimization, and to homicide offending. Next is 25–34, and the 50 and older, and 14 and younger age categories are *the lowest* for both homicide victimization and offending. Homicide victimization by age decreased for all age groups during most of the 1990s, demonstrating the same trends of leveling off and spiking, depending on the age category. Homicide victimization shows similar patterns, although there is slightly more evidence of increases (spiking) for age cate-

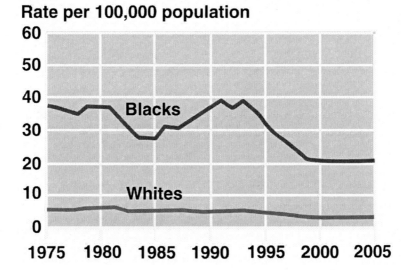

Figure 10:6. Homicide Victimization by Race 1976–2005.
Adapted from the Bureau of Justice Statistics.

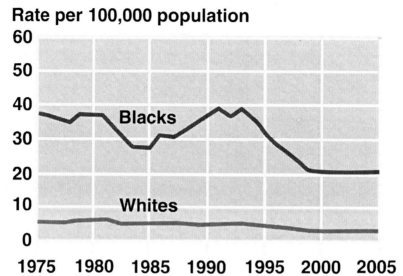

Homicide victimization by race, 1976-2005

Rate per 100,000 population

Figure 10:7. Homicide Offering by Race 1976–2005.
Adapted from the Bureau of Justice Statistics.

gories 18–24 and 25–34.

Other data on age and homicide includes (www.ojp.usdoj.gov 2007):

- The average age of homicide victims is slightly over 30, and the average age of homicide offenders is slightly under 30.
- Young homicide victims are more likely to know their assailants than older victims.
- 25% of the victims of gang-related murders were under the age of 18, and 64% of the victims of gang-related murders were between ages 18–34.
- 29% of gang-related murders were committed by youth under age 18, with 69% the percentage for ages 18–34.
- juveniles accounted for a relatively large number of people killed in sex-related murders, victims of arson or poison,

and being killed by family members.

Homicide: Gender

Whereas homicide tends to be the business of younger individuals, it is also the purview of males. According to the Bureau of Justice Statistics, the homicide breakout by gender is (www.ojp.usdoj.gov 2007):

- Male offender/male victim: 65.3% of all homicides
- Male offender/female victim: 22.7% of all homicides
- Female offender/male victim: 9.6% of all homicides
- Female offender/female victim: 2.4% of all homicides

Homicide victimization by age,1976-2005

Rate per 100,000 population

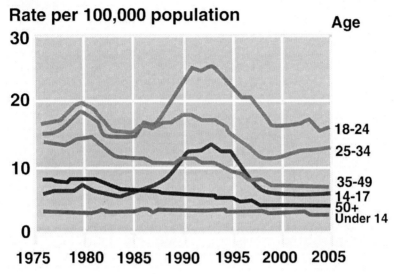

Figure 10:8. Homicide Victimization by Age 1976–2005.
Adapted from the Bureau of Justice Statistics.

Homicide offending by age, 1976-2005
Rate per 100,000 population

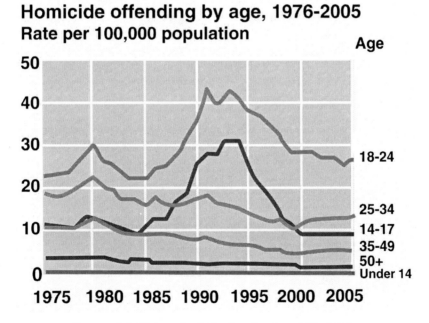

Figure 10:9. Homicide Offending by Age 1976–2005.
Adapted from the Bureau of Justice Statistics.

As Figures 10:10 and 10:11 indicate, *males have higher rates of both homicide offending and victimization*, and consistent with that reported previously, the rates for both victimization and offending decreased for males from 1993–2003, with the leveling-off effect apparent from about 2000–2005 (offending and victimization rates for males appear to have increased slightly from 2004–2005). Both homicide offending and victimization rates for females decreased steadily from the mid-1990s until 2005.

Additionally, homicide data by gender reveals:

- In 2005 males were 10 times more likely than females to commit murder.
- Male victims have a lower probability of being killed by an intimate or family member than female victims (intimates include spouses, ex-spouses, and partners), and 11 percent of murder victims were killed by an intimate.
- In every age group (i.e., 12–17; 18–24; 50–59) females are more likely to be killed by an intimate.
- Male victims are more likely than females victims to be killed by acquaintances or strangers.
- 76.5 percent of all people murdered are males, and 23.5 percent are females. 88.8 percent of murderers are males, and 11.2 percent are females.
- Approximately 54 percent of male murder victims were killed by either strangers (15.5%) or undetermined (37.4%), whereas 36 percent of female murder victims were killed by strangers (8.7%), or undetermined (27.6%).

Serial Killings

John Wayne Gacy, Jeffrey Dahmer, Theodore Kaczynski, Ted Bundy, and Dennis Rader. These are just some names you may recall, or might have heard about. What do they have in common? Mayhem. They are all serial killers who have captured the fancy of Americans and the media. The media jumps on every serial killing, and helps in shaping the perception that serial killings are a dominant form of murder; that they comprise a significant percentage of all murders in any one year. Nothing could be further from the truth. Maybe, at the most, serial killings comprise four percent of total homicides in a year, and it is easy to understand why the media is so enamored with them. One, maybe two or three people kill up to a dozen people or more over an extended period of time, and this becomes call for intensive media scrutiny and reporting, not only of the killers and their victims, but of the police who so often seem to be baffled by who has committed such atrocities. But what exactly is serial killing, and who undertakes such horrible crimes?

It is common to conclude that serial killing is the purview of mentally deranged individuals, and therefore an area to be addressed by the psychological sciences. Two sociologists, James Alan Fox and Jack Levin (2005) have examined serial killers through the twentieth century, and identified patterns and trends that cut across these type of violent offenders. As their first step, Fox and Levin defined serial killing involving " a string of four or more homicides committed by one or a few perpetrators that spans a period of days, weeks, months or even years" (2005, 31). Given this definition, the authors identified 558 serial killers, and understanding that at times serial killing involves multiple murderers, Fox and Levin discovered 494 unique individuals or partnerships existing in the United States during the twentieth century. Their research revealed (2005, 36-41):

Homicide victimization by gender, 1976-2005

Rate per 100,000 population

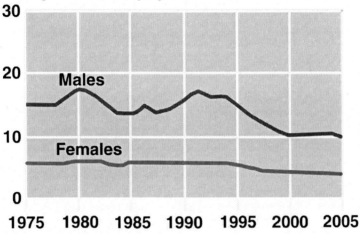

Figure 10:10. Homicide Victimization by Gender 1976–2005.
Adapted from the Bureau of Justice Statistics.

Homicide offending by gender, 1976-2005

Rate per 100,000 population

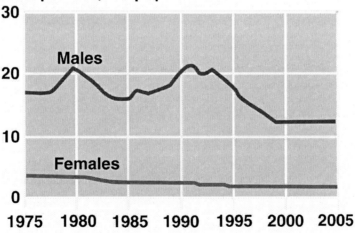

Figure 10:11. Homicide Offending by Gender 1976–2005.
Adapted from the Bureau of Justice Statistics.

• 86% of serial killers were male.

• 82% of serial killers were white.

• 41% of serial killers were between the ages of 20–29, and 29% were between the ages 30–39.

• 81% of serial killers acted alone, and 12% involved multiple offenders.

• the major victim preference for male serial killers was women.

• the major victim preference for female serial killers was family members, or patients in nursing homes or hospital settings.

• there were between 120–180 serial killings in the United States annually, a far cry from the annual estimate of 3,500–5,000 reported by the media.

• 73% of serial killings occurred locally, meaning confined to the same general area, city or state. 16% were regional occurring across contiguous states, and 11% were national, such as in the case of Ted Bundy, who moved across the nation killing college coeds.

• serial killing peaked in the 1980s, and has dramatically decreased since then, following the pattern of homicides in general.

Based on the research by Levin and Fox, this author has arrived at the conclusion that serial killers cannot be pigeonholed or cast typed, and that serial killers look just like you and me: they have jobs; they have families; they are community and church leaders; they are our neighbors; they mow their yards and take out the trash; they are Boy Scout and Girl Scout leaders; they go to church on Sundays; and, they kill on the side.

Rape as Violent Crime

Defining Rape

Rape is defined here as *an act of violence*, be it stranger rape, acquaintance rape (i.e., spouse rape; date rate), and even attempted rape. As the title of the groundbreaking book *Against Our Will: Men, Women, and Rape* (1975) by Susan Brownmiller suggests, rape is an act against the will of victims. Going one step further, rape is conceptualized here as not only including the unwanted sexual penetration of another human being, but also as acts of violence that may fall short of penetration, such as forced petting, touching of the genitals, and physical and emotional dominance and control over others that may result in some type of harm to victims (identified later in this section). So a *broad-based* definition of rape is used knowing that statistics on rape often reflect and include forced sexual penetration. But the point being made cannot be lost, and that is rape is an act of *violence*.

Rape Data

The National Crime Victimization Surveys (NCVS) that are conducted by the United States Department of Justice and the United States Bureau of the Census report there are between 150,000–200,000 rapes annually in America. This is much higher than that documented by the Federal Bureau of Investigation, which typically places the figure between 70,000–80,000 rapes each year. It is important to note that of the average 200,780 rape victims in 2004–2005 13 years of age and older, approximately 64,080 were victims of reported rape, 51,500 were victims of attempted rape, and 85,210 were sexual assault victims (National Crime Victimization Survey, 2007). But how are we to interpret or to comprehend 200,000 or so rapes each year? How can this be placed into words that may better sensitize us to this violent act? According to *Rape in America* (1992) and the Rape Abuse and Incest National Network (RAINN, 2007):

- there are 78 rapes per hour of females 18 and older.
- Every 2.5 minutes someone is sexually assaulted in the United States.
- nearly 20% of females surveyed reported that they were victims of completed or attempted rape. The figure for males is three percent.
- 62% of victims were under age 18 when first assaulted sexually.
- 22% of victims were under age 12 when first sexually assaulted.
- 32% of victims were between the ages 12-17 when first raped.
- Most rapes go unreported, with males the least likely to report being raped.
- 83% of rape victims 12 years age and older are white, and the figure for African-Americans is 13.3% (whites 12 years of age and older comprise 84% of the population, and African-Americans 12.3% of the population, rounded). Other races accounted for 4% of all rapes in the same age category.

One very important question is "who" rapes? The data strongly suggest victims and offenders *frequently know each other.* Approximately *80 percent of rapes are nonstranger rapes* which has an interesting relationship by age. Ninety percent of rapes of children under the age of 12 involve rapes committed by someone who knew the victim, with 65 percent the figure for adults between the ages 18–29 (National Victim Awareness Survey, 1998). Focusing on youth, The National Survey of Adolescents (2000) reported that approximately 75 percent of victims knew their offenders well, and break-

ing this down by nature of relationship, of these 75 percent slightly over 30 percent were friends with the offenders; about 20 percent of offenders were family members; and, just over 20 percent of offenders were strangers.

The Consequences of Rape

It is one thing to banter around numbers and data concerning rape, however, it is another issue to discuss its consequences. Rape victims face physical and health-behavioral, psychological, and social consequences, that can be life-changing and even life-threatening. It is to these issues attention is now directed.

Physical and Health Behavioral Consequences of Rape

Rape is first and foremost an act of *violence.* It entails physical struggles on behalf of victims that often result in increased anger and hostility from assailants. Rapists are violent individuals who brutalize, humiliate, and denigrate their victims. Listed are some of the physical consequences of the act of rape (RAINN, 2006):

- victims of rape are more likely to have sexually transmitted diseases.
- Over 32,000 pregnancies occur annually as a result of rape.
- The long-term consequences of rape include chronic pelvic pain, back pain, and severe headaches. In addition, over time the victims of rape may experience facial pain, disability preventing work, gastrointestinal disorders, and premenstrual syndrome.
- Rape victims run the risk of engaging in unprotected sex, may have earlier initiation into sexual behavior, and often have multiple sexual partners.

• Victims of rape may turn to drug and alcohol abuse as means of coping with and escaping the realities of the event of rape.

Psychological Consequences of Rape

Rape has both *immediate* and *long-term* psychological consequences. It is an act of violence that portends lengthy and serious emotional problems for its victims. Rape is more, much more than an act of physical violence that begins and ends with harms done to the body. Rape can have devastating and life-changing effects on the self-concepts and personalities of its victims, and some victims of rape never fully recover, in the emotional sense. Listed are several *immediate* consequences of rape (RAINN, 2007):

- Shock
- Denial
- Fear
- Confusion
- Guilt
- Withdrawal
- Emotional attachment
- Flashbacks
- Distrust of others
- Anxiety

In addition to the immediate aftermath of rape, there are also *longer-term* psychological consequences, and these can include (RAINN, 2006):

- Depression
- Attempted or completed suicide
- Alienation
- Overeating vomiting

Social Consequences of Rape

Rape carries with it its fair share of *social consequences.* Not only will victims face physi-

cal and emotional trauma, they may also experience life-altering changes in all types of interpersonal relationships that include (RAINN, 2007):

- Strained relationships with family members, friends, and intimate partners.
- Less emotional support from family members, friends, and intimate partners.
- Less frequent contact with family and friends.
- Lower likelihood of marriage.

Abuse as Violence

When the author of this text was in high school he was friends with a rambunctious (some would say rebel) young man who was frequently in trouble with school officials, and even sometimes with law enforcement. This teenager, who is called Slim here, was essentially a good youngster, but one whose wild streaks would seemingly not go away, and an individual who not only liked to get into fistfights, but who was good at them. For this he gained quite a reputation, somewhat like the old west gunslinger who other "slingers" would seek out for the gun battle at the O.K. Corral. Slim rarely lost a fight, and on the face of it appeared to enjoy living on the wild side. But many years later I spoke with Slim, and he told me something I never knew about his earlier years, and that is his father physically abused him as a young boy, and even into his teenage years, until Slim was big enough to fend him off. The abuse was more frequent than not, and my long sought-after question about why Slim could be mean was finally answered: he was abused, and he would take this out on others.

There are several types of abuse, all of which can be further subdivided into additional categories. The types of abuse are *physical, sexual, and, emotional and psychological abuse.* Abuse is also conceptualized as *child abuse; spouse or partner abuse; and elder abuse.* These later types of abuse can involve the aforementioned types, such as physical and sexual abuse, therefore abuse of children (to use an example) can entail sexual and physical abuse, as well as emotional abuse and neglect. This section will cover child and spouse/partner abuse, and begins with a discussion of child abuse data.

Child Abuse

Each semester the author of this text (referred to in the first person for the rest of this brief discussion) will ask his students the following question: "how many of you received *corporal punishment* as a frequent means of discipline from your parents or guardians when you were growing up?" The key to this question is the word *frequent.* I explain what I mean by "frequent" before students raise their hands (of course, answering the question is completely voluntary). My operational definition of frequent is: the majority of the times students violated their parents/guardians rules and got caught, they received some form of corporal punishment. Rather than predetermining what I am referring to as "corporal punishment," I let students first raise their hands to the question, and then I ask them what the punishment entailed. Normally, corporal punishment includes use of the belt or some close facsimile, the use of hands, and in some instances, fists. The great majority of my students, who are between ages 20–22 indicate they received corporal punishment, and frequently. But my next question takes students by surprise and it is: "what would you say if I told you that in some circles the corporal discipline you received, frequent or not, is considered a form of child abuse?" The normal reactions are rolling the eyes, and looks of surprise.

As discussed previously, abuse can be difficult to define, and perhaps this is most true for child abuse. Whereas some people may define corporal punishment as abuse, others may see it as *the way* to keep their kids in line; walking the straight and narrow. Remember in the first chapter when discussing the Hutterites, it was stated that corporal punishment is common, and is said to be proclaimed by the Bible. Yet none of my students are Hutterites, and most did receive physical discipline when they were younger. But consider the following examples of *physical abuse* of children that are encountered by the police, child protective services workers, and other professionals:

- Punching
- Kicking
- Scratching
- Beating with an object (i.e., belt, broom, shovel)
- Burning children with matches, by pacing their hands or feet on a hot stove, or placing parts, or all of their bodies in hot or scalding water
- choking
- Suffocating with pillows or hands over the face
- Drowning, or nearly drowning children
- Murder or attempted murder

But how can child abuse be *defined?* There are differing opinions on what exactly constitutes child abuse, however a standard definition is found in The Child Abuse Prevention and Treatment Act (CAPTA), that includes as *child abuse and neglect the failure to act or a recent act* (Mignon, Larson, and Holmes, 2001):

- that results in serious physical or emotional harm of a child normally under age 18, including sexual abuse, and also involving the exploitation of children.

• by a parent or caretaker and any employee who is responsible for the health and safety of children.

James Garbarino and James Eckenrode (1997) define child abuse as developmentally inappropriate actions against children that include four criteria:

• the intention of the actor
• the act's effect on the child
• an observer's value judgment about the act
• the source of the standard of the judgment

Keeping our focus on physical abuse, Garbarino and Eckenrode proceed to define it as "the inappropriate and developmentally damaging use of force." The authors conceptualize child abuse of any kind as *maltreatment*, including actions, or the lack thereof, that impede normal human growth and development. We will return to Garbarino, Eckenrode, and other scholars after addressing the issue of child abuse data.

Child Abuse Data

An important question is "how much child abuse is there?" In 2005, there were just under 900,000 official cases of child abuse and neglect in the 50 states, the District of Columbia, and Puerto Rico. In order to understand what this number means, it calculates to 12.1 victims per 1,000 children, down from 12.5 per 1,000 children in 2001. However, the rate of child abuse *investigations* increased from 43.2 per 1,000 children in 2001, to 48.3 per 1,000 children in 2005. In addition, there were 1,460 deaths as a result of child abuse and neglect, down from 1,490 in 2004 (*Child Maltreatment,* 2005). Of course, this represents official counts, and official or government-based counts are typically *underestimates*, and significant underestimates (for example, the FBI annual reports on crime underestimate crime by as much as 60 percent, and the federal government reporting on poverty may miss the actual number of poor by as much as half, or more). It is important to note in 2005 there were over 74 million children under age 18 in the United States, the District of Columbia, and Puerto Rico (2005, 35). This does raise a significant fact, and that is if there were approximately 900,000 *official* cases of child abuse in 2005, that means there were over 73 million children who at least *officially were not victims of abuse.* Perhaps the number of officially abused children is much greater, similar to the underestimating of crime and poverty.

Rates of child abuse victimization *vary by age*, with the highest rate 16.5 per 1,000 children, *for ages one through three.* After that, the rate drops for every age category, with the lowest rate 6.2 per 1,000 children, for ages 16–17. Child abuse also *varies by race*, with the highest rate for African Americans, 19.5 per 1,000 children. The rate for white children is 10.8, and the *lowest rate* is for Asian children, 2.5 per 1,000 children in the population (2005, 28).

But what about the perpetrators? Who are these sordid individuals, and what is their relationship to the victims? According to *Child Maltreatment* (2005), mothers constituted over 40 percent of abusers, with fathers occupying second place, slightly over 18 percent of known perpetrators. Mothers and fathers *abusing together* represented 17 percent of perpetrators by relationship, and nonparental (i.e., foster care parent; unmarried partner of parent; child daycare staff) accounted for just under 11 percent of known perpetrators. What is clear is that *parents are by far the greatest source of child abuse,* either acting alone, in concert together, or engaging in child abuse with another individual. This brings us to child abuse *fatalities.*

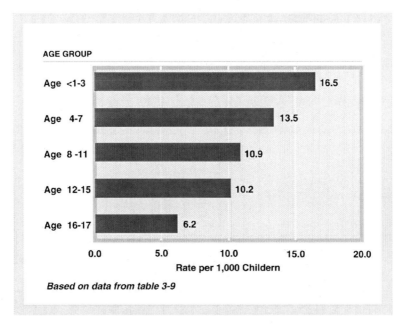

AGE GROUP

Age Group	Rate
Age <1-3	16.5
Age 4-7	13.5
Age 8-11	10.9
Age 12-15	10.2
Age 16-17	6.2

Rate per 1,000 Childern

Based on data from table 3-9

Figure 10:12. Child Abuse Victimization Rates by Age Group 2005.
Adapted from Child Maltreatment, 2005.

It is one thing to abuse and neglect children without this resulting in death; it is another reality when abuse crosses the line, with the consequence being child death. Before examining data on this topic, another experience from the life of the author of this text is reported (again with reference to the first person).

When I was in my mid 30s, I attended a funeral of a child who had been killed by her mother. I had been friends with her husband and had seen him only on occasion since our early 20s, when we were in college together. His first marriage ended in divorce, and my friend who will be called Stu (not his real name) eventually remarried, and had a son through his second wife. One evening while Stu was not at home, the mother of the toddler son was giving him a bath and began drowning him, and while doing so she beat his head up against the bathtub, causing serious brain damage. Apparently, the mother

had become extremely frustrated with her infant son's reluctance to be bathed, and lost all control over her emotions and reasoning. This was an absolutely terrible situation since "Stu" not only lost a son through a horrible crime, but also lost his wife (who killed him) to prison. Fortunately, the death of children from child abuse is relatively infrequent, but in terms of the relationships involved, is quite similar to the tragedy just discussed.

As previously noted, in 2005 there were 1,460 reported deaths as a result of child abuse, and in 28 and 16 percent (rounded) of these deaths, the perpetrators were mothers and fathers, respectively. Mothers and fathers combined, accounted for an *additional* 20 percent of child abuse fatalities, but what is so striking is that mothers, either acting alone or with another person (i.e., husband; boyfriend) were present in *nearly 60 percent* of deaths to children resulting from abuse (the figure for fathers is much lower, approximately 39%). Breaking child abuse fatalities down by age, it is reported that nearly 77 percent of such deaths occur to children one to three years in age, with 59 percent occurring to children *one year of age or younger*. Of interest is while the rates of *nondeath abuse of children decrease with age,* there is a *deviation* in this pattern reported for child abuse fatalities. The percentage of child abuse fatalities is 13 and 4 percent, respectively, for age categories four through seven and eight through 11, but it is 6 percent for children between the ages 12 through 17 (2005, 62). Perhaps this is a function of the greater number of years included in the latter age category (six years for ages 12 to 17, compared with four years for ages four through seven and eight through 11), but it is hard to overlook the fact that deaths to older children do occur, and this is especially important in the light of what was reported for very young children.

Emotional Abuse of Children

James Garbarino has studied child abuse for three decades, and has examined all types of child abuse, including the emotional abuse of children, which is the focus of this discussion. Garbarino has identified five types of emotional abuse which can occur individually, or in combination with each other (1978). The first type of emotional abuse of children is *rejecting,* which involves denying the child's self-worth. Rejecting is when parents or guardians convey to their children that they are no good, or they are failures. Remember Robert Hanssen? His father did this to him throughout his life, even as an adult, but the damage to Robert was apparently sufficient by the time he had graduated from high school. *Isolating* is the second type of emotional abuse, and it entails cutting the child off from the social

world, or preventing children from developing and engaging in productive and positive social relationships with other children. Garbarino's third type of emotional abuse of children is *terrorizing,* or verbally abusing children. When parents or guardians engage in this type of abuse, they create a climate of fear and total intimidation. Terrorizing may take the form of screaming or verbal manipulation and control of children, via use of words beyond their stage of cognitive development, or both. *Ignoring* is the fourth type of emotional abuse of children, and entails being psychologically unavailable to children. When "ignoring," parents or guardians simply act as if the child does not exist, and like the previous three types of emotional abuse, it is done on a frequent basis. The effects of ignoring children can be devastating, since it conveys to children that they have little worth or value to their parents or guardians, in addition to sending them the message they are unloved. The last of Garbarino's five types of emotional abuse of children is *corrupting,* or missocializing children by giving them immoral and inappropriate upbringing and values. This is similar to Gottfredson and Hirschi's social control theory, where they lay the blame for criminal and delinquent children on the doorsteps of irresponsible parents or guardians. Missosocialized children can become destructive and antisocial, such as in the case when parents frequently abuse drugs and alcohol in their presence, or even engage in prostitution or other forms of illicit sex in plain view of, or in close proximity to their children.

Child Sexual Abuse

In 2005, there were an estimated 84,000 official cases of child sexual abuse, representing an apparent decline since the mid-1990s (Finkelhor, 1998; Jones and Finkelhor,

2004; Mignon et al., 2002). But what exactly is sexual abuse of children? Child sexual abuse can take many forms, including the physical, emotional and verbal sexual abuse of children (Mignon et al., 2002).When discussing the physical sexual abuse of children, attempted, or actual sexual penetration comes to mind, but physical sexual abuse can also entail disrobing and being nude in front of children, as well as fondling, kissing and masturbating children. In addition, having children pose for videos, and exposing them to pornographic materials also constitutes examples of child sexual abuse. The list is endless, and includes the use of electronic sexual devices to penetrate the vagina or rectum of a child (2002, 53). Similar to all forms of child abuse, the perpetrators tend to be family members, with girls representing the overwhelming majority of victims. In the case of incest, stepfathers are five times more likely than the natural father to sexually abuse daughters (2002, 54). Ample child sexual abuse goes unreported, or there may be delays in reporting it because the great majority of the perpetrators of sexual abuse are relatives of their victims. Arata (1998) found that over 70 percent of cases went unreported when the perpetrator was a relative or stepparent, and at least that many were unreported when the perpetrators were acquaintances. But what would bring family members or acquaintances to sexually molest children? David Finkelhor (1984), one of the nation's leading researchers on the subject, has developed a model that is helpful in answering this complex question. Finkelhor has developed what he calls the *four preconditions model of child sexual abuse.* As such it is an integrative explanation, encompassing assumptions from psychology, sociology, and social psychology. In addition to being a model that is intended to explain the processes and stages involved in the sexual abuse of children, it is also useful as a tool for

intervening in, and perhaps even *preventing* it.

Finkelhor argues that four preconditions must be met before child sexual abuse can occur, and they must go in the order as presented. The abuse is not a given, since at any point the potential perpetrators may decide not to proceed with the act. The *first precondition* is *the motivation to sexually abuse,* and itself has *three possible components,* any one of which can be the force behind the decision to molest children. The motivation to sexually abuse may develop from an *emotional congruence or attachment* that develops between the child and the perpetrator. The second source can be *sexual arousal by a child,* and the third motivation to sexually abuse may be that the perpetrator is *unable to get his or her sexual needs met in normal or appropriate ways.*

The *second precondition* is *overcoming internal inhibitors* (of perpetrators), which can include fear (of getting caught), one's socialization, and morals. How does one get around these potentially powerful inhibitions against sexually abusing children? The use of alcohol and drugs may do the job. *Overcoming external inhibitors* is the third precondition, and entails the issue of *supervision. Closely monitored* children represent a major risk to perpetrators, and this in itself may prevent child sexual abuse. On the other hand, lax supervision of children may result in child sexual abuse because the potential pedophile may see this as an opportunity, with minimal risk of getting caught. *Overcoming the resistance of the child* is the last stage, and it is about trust. When the child develops trust in the adult perpetrator, the stage is set for sexual abuse. With the first three stages behind them, pedophiles now can now feel in their convoluted minds that the abuse can occur, again with minimal risks (Finkelhor, 1984, 53–68).

Effects of Child Sexual Abuse

There are numerous effects of sexual abuse of children. Like the effects of rape, the consequences for the victims of child sexual abuse may be both short and long-term. Listed are several *overall* effects of child sexual abuse. The survivors of childhood sexual abuse face an increased risk of (Kilpatrick et al., 1992; Kilpatrick, Rugerrio, Acierno, Saunders, Resnick, Best, and Schnurr, 2003):

- substance abuse as a means of dealing with posttraumatic stress disorder.
- becoming adjudicated juvenile delinquents and convicted adult offenders.
- Becoming child sexual abusers themselves.
- Having a wide array of mental health disorders.
- Being sexually abused again, only later in life as adults, as abused partners or spouses.

Child sexual abuse carries with it serious emotional scars. Several years ago the author of this text attended a national conference on juvenile justice, and one of the major sessions was about incest. A former Miss America was the speaker at this session, and recanted her tragic story to the audience, a story that involved being sexually penetrated by her father from early childhood into her teenage years. After she finished speaking, the male emcee went to hug her, and she pulled away from him with a vengeance. I could not help but assume that this was due to her horrible past experiences with what was supposed to be a leading male figure in her life: her father.

There are initial/short and long-term emotional effects of child sexual abuse, and some are identified below (Saunders, 1999, 7).

Short-Term or Initial Emotional Effects of Child Sexual Abuse

- Fear and anxiety
- Low self-esteem
- Depression
- Anger and hostility
- Sexual behavior problems
- Delinquency
- Substance abuse
- Impaired affective and social processing

The Longer-Term Effects May Include (Saunders, 1999):

- Sexual disorders
- Posttraumatic stress disorder
- Depression, anxiety disorders, and personality disorders
- Attempted and completed suicide
- Impaired social relationships
- Substance abuse
- High risk of future victimizations

Spouse and Partner Abuse (Intimate Partner Violence)

One might think that when people come together in romantic relationships, the last thing that may occur is violence: violence between those involved romantically. But partner abuse, or abuse between married and unmarried partners occurs with some frequency, and it can entail danger and even death. In addition, intimate partner abuse occurs in both heterosexual and in homosexual relationships.

Partner Abuse Data

The majority of data from pages 143 to 147 is from The Bureau of Justice Statistics

(2007), which reports information collected from the National Crime Victimization Surveys that are undertaken annually.

Nonfatal Intimate Partner Victimization

Nonfatal intimate partner victimization (NFIPV) declined from 1993–2005, a trend reported for much crime, including violent offenses (Figure 10:13). NFIPV includes simple assault, aggravated assault, robbery, and rape/sexual assault. Consistent with other data on abuse, *women are by far the greatest number of victims* of NFIPV. The rate for females in 2005 was four per 1,000 females age 12 and older, and for males it was barely one per 1,000 males, age 12 and older. What is more, when nonfatal violent victimization and relationships are taken into

account, those including victimization by intimates, other relatives, friends/acquaintances, and strangers, an interesting pattern emerges: females and males have higher rates of victimization undertaken against them by strangers and other friends/acquaintances (Figure 10:14).

NFIPV by *age* also has some interesting patterns and trends. From 2001 to 2005, females 50 years of age and older, and those between ages 12–15 had the *lowest rates* of NFIPV for females (both under 3.0 per 1,000 females), and females between ages 20–24 were reported to have the *highest rates* for their gender (12 per 1,000 females). The information is quite similar for males, with the *lowest* NFIPV rates for ages 12–15, and 65 and older. The highest rate for males was for ages 20–24, and it was just under 2.0 per

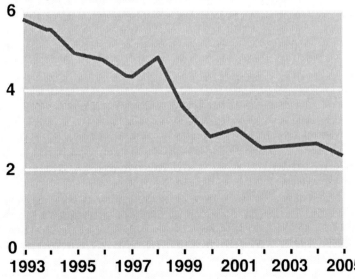

Figure 10:13. Nonfatal Intimate Partner Victimization Rate 1993–2005. Adapted from the Bureau of Justice Statistics.

Nonfatal violent victimization rate by victim offender relationship and victim gender, 1993-2005

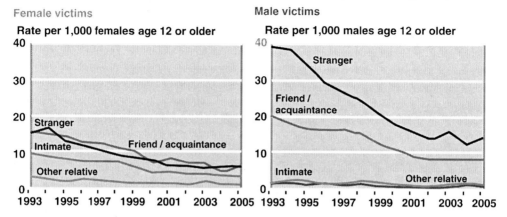

Figure 10:14. Non-fatal Violent Victimization Rate by Victim/Offender Relationship
and Victim Gender 1993–2005.
Adapted from the Bureau of Justice Statistics.

Average annual nonfatal intimate partner victimization rate, by gender and age, 2001-2005

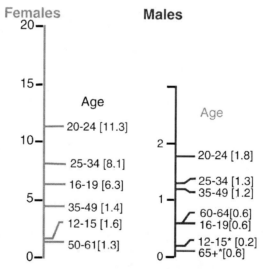

Rate per 1,000 persons in age group
*Based on 10 or fewer sample cases.

Figure 10:15. Average Annual Nonfatal Partner Victimization Rate
by Gender and Age 2001–2005.
Adapted from the Bureau of Justice Statistics.

1,000 males (Figure 10:15).

NFIPV by *gender* and *race* shows the following patterns. From 1993–2005, white females and males experienced a decrease in the rate of NFIPV (all under 5.0 per 1,000 persons, 12 and older by 2005), while the rate for African American females increased from 2002 to 2004, then dropping, but still higher than for white females (Figure 10:16). Interestingly, from 1993–2005 the rates of NFIPV for Hispanic females showed a steady and sharp decline (Figure 10:17).

But what about marital status? Of the following marital statuses, which ones have the *highest* and *lowest* rates of NFIPV: divorced; married; never married; separated? The answer for females is "separated" (highest) and "widowed" (lowest). For males the average annual nonfatal intimate partner victimization rate is highest for "separated" and lowest for "married" and "widowed" (Figure 10:18).

Homicides of Intimates

In general, the data are similar for homicides of intimates when compared with NFIPV. The rate for males *decreased* through most of the years from 1976–2005, but for females the slope was different, only starting its descent in 1993, and continuing downward until 2005 (Figure 10:19). The Bureau of Justice Statistics reported that from 1976–2005, homicides of intimates accounted for 11 percent of all murders, and approximately one third of female murder victims were killed by an intimate, compared with 3 percent for males. According to the Bureau, from 1976–2005, 54 percent of homicides were classified as nonintimate, and 35 percent as undetermined.

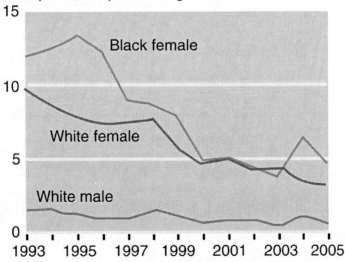

Figure 10:16. Nonfatal Intimate Partner Victimization by Gender and Race, 1993–2005. Adapted from the Bureau of Justice Statistics.

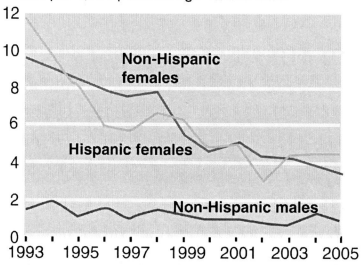

Nonfatal intimate partner victimization rate, by gender and Hispanic origin, 1993 - 2005

Rate per 1,000 persons age 12 and older

Figure 10:17. Nonfatal Intimate Partner Victimization Rate by Gender and Hispanic Origin 1993–2005. Adapted from the Bureau of Justice Statistics.

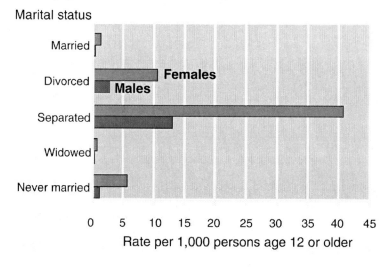

Average annual nonfatal intimate partner victimization rate, by gender and marital status, 2001-2005

Figure 10:18. Average Annual Nonfatal Intimate Partner Victimization Rate by Gender and Marital Status 2001–2005. Adapted from the Bureau of Justice Statistics.

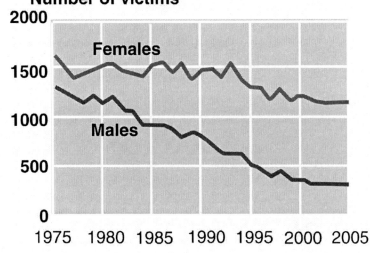

Figure 10:19. Homicides of Intimates by Gender of Victim 1976–2005.
Adapted from the Bureau of Justice Statistics.

The majority of homicides of intimates involved spouses, with boyfriend/girlfriend ranking second (drawing just about even with spouses in 2005), and ex spouse a distant third (Figure 10:20). When considering gender and race of victims, the rates of homicide dropped for black females and for white and black males. However, homicides of intimates for white females increased for a portion of the years shown on Figure 10:21, with a slight decrease and leveling off the past few years.

Listed is additional information on homicides involving intimates (Bureau of Justice Statistics, 2005):

• Children killed by their parents is the second leading type of intimate homicide.
• Siblings are the least likely members of families to experience intimate homicide.

• Fathers are more likely to be killed by their children than are mothers.
• Adolescent sons represent the greatest number of offenders in parental killings.
• Brothers are more likely than sisters to kill siblings.
• There has been a decline in murders involving all family relationships for both African Americans and whites.

Property Offenses

The trend in property offenses followed a similar path as that for violence. From 1993-2005, the *overall* rate *dropped significantly*, and the rates for *all three* major types of property offenses also decreased (the rate actually started to decline during the 1970s). The explanations for this decrease are the same as provided for crimes of violence. The

1990s saw a decrease in the unemployment rate, as well as improved job opportunities, meaning fewer individuals resorted to property offenses to survive. Tough law enforcement practices aimed at putting a major dent in the crack cocaine trade also resulted in a decrease in property offenses, since fewer individuals turned to crimes such as theft in order to support their crack habits.

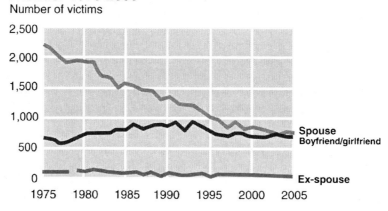

Figure 10:20. Homicides of Inmates by Relationship of Victim to the Offender 1976–2005. Adapted from the Bureau of Justice Statistics.

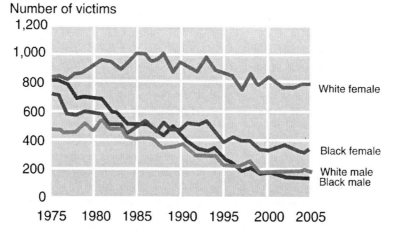

Figure 10:21. Homicides of Inmates by Gender and Race of Victim 1976–2005. Adapted from the Bureau of Justice Statistics.

Property crime rates

Adjusted victimization rate
per 1,000 households

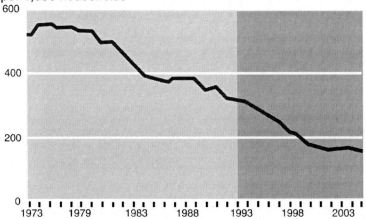

Figure 10:22. Property Crime Rates 1973–2005. Adapted from the Bureau of Justice Statistics.

Burglary rates

Adjusted victimization rate
per 1,000 households

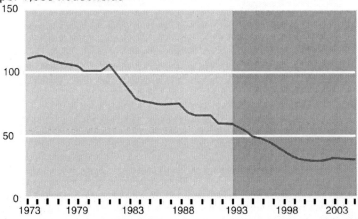

Figure 10:23. Burglary Rates 1973–2005. Adapted from the Bureau of Justice Statistics.

An examination of the figures shows the trends by type of property offense. Burglary, which entails the unlawful entry or attempted entry into a business or residence, saw its rate start to decrease in the early 1970s (with a spike by 1980), with a continued downward slope from that point on. Theft, by far the most voluminous of all property offenses, experienced a drop-off from about 1980 to 2005, and motor vehicle theft had its sharpest period of decline from 1993 to 2000.

Theft rates

Adjusted victimization rate
per 1,000 households

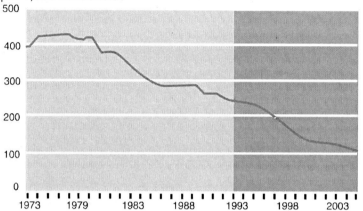

Figure 10:24. Theft Rates 1973–2005. Adapted from the Bureau of Justice Statistics.

Motor vehicle theft rates

Adjusted victimization rate
per 1,000 households

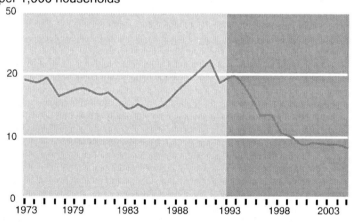

Figure 10:25. Motor Vehicle Theft Rates 1973–2005.
Adapted from the Bureau of Justice Statistics.

A detailed examination of property crime rates from 1973–2005 show America getting more safe, basically every year for over 30 years.

Understanding Property Offenses

The Professional Thief: Edwin H. Sutherland

In this section types of property offenders are considered, beginning with the classic work of Edwin H. Sutherland, *The Professional Thief* (1937).

There are thieves, and there are thieves. Thieves come in all sizes, shapes, and forms, with most being unskilled, and because of this a number of them are sent to prison. But is there such a thing as a professional thief, one who makes a living via stealing? The answer is yes, and it was ages ago that one of the most important scholarly contributions to understanding thieves was made by renowned criminologist Edwin H. Sutherland. Sutherland used the accounts of an excellent thief–a professional thief among thieves–to illustrate the characteristics of one who is at the top of his trade. The thief's name was Broadway Jones, aka Chic Conwell. Sutherland sought to accomplish more than just a cursory look at that which makes a thief operate. His reliance on the career of Conwell allowed him to analyze the behavior characteristics, attitudes, organizational features, subcultural patterns and views of the world held by Chic Conwell, and professional thieves in general. In this respect Sutherland determined that professional thieves are much like all of us, who go about their business like nonthieves perform their business activities. As Conwell noted "It (stealing) is no more thrilling than the work of the factory slave" (1937, 140). Chic Conwell made a career out of stealing.

Simply, it was his raison d'etre. Compare this with the 16-year-old teenager who steals a car for a joyride, or the heroin addict who breaks into a residence, in hope of finding money needed to support his or her addiction. However, Conwell, and for that matter any professional thief, just doesn't manage on the ambition to make a living from theft: *they are taught their trade by already established professionals.* There is tutelage taking place, and over time the Chic Conwell's of the world become quite adept at what they do for a living. For example, the author of this text is aware of a professional thief who would break into homes (after casing them over a period of time) containing major gun collections, steal one of the guns and replace it in the cabinet, where it was on display with a bogus, look-alike model. Usually, these were treasured handguns with considerable monetary value on the market. It may be days, weeks, months, even years until the unsuspecting owner realized that the look-alike gun was a fraud, and by then the real gun had probably been fenced, bringing quite a cash reward to the thief. Good, really good, top-of-the-line professional thieves do the same with jewelry, stamps, and artwork. Sutherland noted that professional thieves rarely specialize in just one type of criminal activity, with the one exception being pickpockets (1937, 197–228).

Professional thieves such as Chic Conwell are highly skilled at what they do, as talented at their trade as the cardiologist who is performing the risky angioplasty on a patient, or the surgeon who is repairing the damaged knee of a star athlete. But it is not only technical skill that is involved, it is also and most saliently the ability to manipulate and to take advantage of people. Professional thieves can have charisma and are frequently likeable, very likeable, and it is their charm that advances them in their scams, and or it is their ability to intimidate others that can lead to success with their criminal modus operandi. Take the case of one of America's greatest thieves, a con artist by name of Eddie Pace. Pace, as his friends in the world of thievery would call him, was a professional criminal who made a significant amount of money stealing from the inno- cent. One of his scams was extorting large sums of money from gay men who had not "come out." Through his contacts he would learn who was gay and wealthy around America, and he would travel to those places and extort up to $50,000 from them (he did this during the 1960s and 1970s when $50,000 was more like $100,000). Pace would use charm, intimidation, and threats, whatever it took to rip off his mark (victim). His approach was simple, but effective. Pace would meet face-to-face with his victims, at first smooching them over, winning their trust, and then he would lay it on them: give me money, or everybody will know you are gay (some of his victims were married men with children who would never want their families knowing they were gay, and some were prominent members of their communi- ties who stood to lose everything if their sex- ual preference was revealed). Over his career Eddie Pace made a lot of money harming others, but like even some of the most sophisticated thieves Pace's luck would on occasion run out, and he would spend time in federal prisons for his crimes (per- sonal interview with Eddie Pace, circa 1980). Manipulating and burning others is a trade- mark of some thieves, as is their ability to carefully *plan* their crimes, down to the nuts and bolts: they dot every "i", and cross every "t". As a matter of fact, it can be argued it is just exactly this, planning, that is the rush for the professional thief. The end result–the actual criminal act–may be like a post mortem for the Chic Conwells out there, after all they may have spent weeks, if not months planning their crime, and then in a matter of hours–if that–it's over with. The crime has been committed, and the thrill has started to dissipate.

But what other extant characteristics of the professional thief did Sutherland unveil? Professional thieves clearly view themselves as *superior* to amateurs at their trade, and they especially consider themselves in a much different ballpark than people who commit sex crimes (1937, 197–228). More- over, Chic Conwell, and others like him have a code *of ethics* that is probably more binding then that in legitimate business and industry, and this entails professional thieves being sympathetic and congenial to one another. In this respect, professional thieves usually operate in gangs or partnerships, and they share a criminal slang or vocabulary that creates a "we feeling," and acts to pro- mote ease of intra-professional communica- tion.

A Continuum of Types of Property Offenders

Property offenders vary in terms of skill, training, cerebral power (CP) and, probabil- ity for arrest (PFA). Drawing and inferring from the works of Marshall B. Clinard and Richard Quinney (1973), Marshall B. Clinard, Richard Quinney, and John Wildeman (1994), and Marshall B. Clinard and Robert F. Meier (2008), it is possible to evaluate property offenders along a continu- um, ranging from the least sophisticated to the most sophisticated and talented crimi- nals. Point "A" represents *occasional property offenders*, or the least skilled of the three areas on the line, and point "C" represents the most advanced thieves, or *professional crimi- nals*. Point "B" is the in-between and would include talented but not top-of-the-line prop- erty offenders, referred to here as c*onvention- al criminals*. Please remember what was stat- ed earlier: "there are thieves, and there are thieves."

A_____B_____C

The characteristics of the three types of offenders are now presented. This is not intended to be an exhaustive classification of property offenders. Instead, it is used simply as a typology that may shed light on variations that operate in the criminal world.

Characteristics of Occasional Property Offenders:

- Often are teenagers who commit crimes for thrills.
- Crime is not a way of life or *the* means to earning a living, and few will continue in a life of crime.
- May not have a prior criminal record or any prior criminal involvement.
- Low criminal skill level.
- No self-concept of themselves as criminal.
- High probability for arrest (PFA) since they lack talent and criminal savvy.
- Little if any planning of the crimes (spontaneity may be the rule).
- The crimes they frequently commit include car theft, check forgery, shoplifting, employee theft, and vandalism.
- Low cerebral power (CP), meaning their crimes involve little insight, and almost no sophistication of thought.

Characteristics of Conventional Criminals:

- Began their criminal paths as teenagers, often in youth street gangs, that frequently committed violent crimes.
- Emanate from poverty stricken areas, especially inner-city slums.
- Progress in their criminal careers by becoming better at committing crimes and then justifying their actions.

- Hold legitimate jobs, but still commit crimes.
- May or may not perceive themselves as criminals, although as many continue in a life of crime they become the secondary deviant.
- Have substance abuse issues.
- Commit a variety of crimes such as robbery, burglary, and drug trafficking which may entail planning.
- Have a relatively high PFA, and their crimes usually call for low CP.

Characteristic of Professional Criminals include:

- High skill and talent level, usually developed through differential association.
- Heavy emphasis on planning their crimes.
- High status and respect in the criminal underworld.
- Looking down on persons who earn their money legitimately as saps and losers.
- Development of a criminal self-concept and identity, and the values and attitudes that support, verify, and justify a life of crime.
- Low probability for arrest, and high CP.
- Commit a variety of crimes, including pickpocketing, professional shoplifting, running confidence games and telephone scams, identity theft, and extortion (i.e., extorting large sums of money from gay men who have not "come out" on the threat that their gay identities will be revealed).

In Recognition: Scott Menard

Dr. Scott Menard joined the faculty of the College of Criminal Justice at Sam Houston State University in 2006, after spending 12 years as one of the most distinguished researchers in criminology at the Institute of Behavioral Science, the University of Colorado, in Boulder. Dr. Menard is recognized here not only because of his contributions to the areas to be identified, but also because his work has enhanced the sophistication of research in criminology through use of advanced statistical techniques. Dr. Menard's areas of academic interest include: Statistics (Longitudinal Research; Logistic Regression Analysis; Multilevel Analysis), Research Methods (Survey Research; Evaluation Research), Juvenile Delinquency, and Life Course Criminology (Victimization; Substance Use; Theory Testing).

An experienced researcher, Dr. Menard has served as the Principal Investigator on over $3 million in federally-funded research projects. He has recently completed data collection for the tenth, eleventh, and twelfth waves of data for the National Youth Survey/Family Study (NYSFS), a longitudinal, multigenerational, national probability sample whose focal respondents were 11–17 years old in 1976–77. In waves 10–12, 2002–2004, the sample has been expanded to include data on the spouses and children of the focal respondents, as well as reinterviewing the focal respondents' parents, who were last interviewed in the first wave of the survey. The survey includes data on criminal victimization and perpetration, licit and illicit substance use, marital and employment status, academic attainment, mental health, and attitudes toward crime and delinquency, and has most recently been augmented by the collection of DNA data on the respondents. Currently funded projects include "Evaluation of the Bully-Proofing Your School Program," an evaluation of a school-based, curriculum-driven program for reducing bullying and other forms of school violence, funded by the National Institute of Justice; and "Inhalant Abuse Across Generations in a National Sample," a project which

examines inhalant abuse and related behaviors in the NYSFS developmentally and intergenerationally, and is funded by the National Institute on Drug Abuse.

Dr. Menard has published in the areas of both statistics and criminology, including articles on logistic regression analysis, and monographs on logistic regression and longitudinal research, and he is presently writing a book on logistic regression analysis. His publications in the area of criminology include papers on theory testing in crime and delinquency, the relationship of substance use to crime and delinquency, and papers on repeat victimization and the consequences of violent victimization. Recent publications include a coauthored book on youth gangs, a coauthored book on the impact of neighborhood characteristics on family, school, peer groups, problem behavior, and prosocial development, and an edited volume on longitudinal research.

SUMMARY

In this chapter emphasis is on two broad types of criminal deviance: violent offenses and property crimes. The United States witnessed a decrease in violent crimes from the early 1990s to about 2004. There is some evidence violence may be on an increase, and this remains to be seen. The violent crimes addressed are homicide, rape and abuse, all of which did decline for about 10 years, and are at their lowest levels since the 1970s. However, every year in the United States anywhere from 14,000–16,000 people are murdered, and approximately 200,000 are raped and sexually assaulted. In addition, there are typically around 900,000 cases of child abuse, and thousands of cases of partner and spouse abuse, with the majority of all types of abuse perpetrated by family members, friends and acquaintances. The rate of property offenses has also decreased, but there are still millions of thefts, including car theft, and burglaries. Property offenders will vary on a number of issues including skill and talent, planning of their crimes, and their probability for arrest.

Chapter 11

ADDICTIONS AND THE USE AND ABUSE
OF SUBSTANCES

CASE STUDY: RINGO STARR

Some people seem to have it all: fame, friends, and wealth. On the surface, these individuals can make us a little envious, but beneath it all there can be despair and pain, quite frequently emanating from the abuse of drugs and alcohol. Such is the situation involving one of the world's most famous personalities, former Beatle drummer Ringo Starr. Ringo lucked into the phenomenal rock group, the Beatles, in 1962 when he was hired to replace drummer Pete Best. From that point until the present, the world changed for Ringo, going from a popular musician on the Liverpool, England rock scene to a member of a musical group that stormed America in February 1964, and that remains prominent today. Like so many rock-and-roll stars, Ringo was born of humble beginnings in Liverpool, on July 7, 1940. His health was frail as a child, and his formal education was duly impacted by this to the point Ringo dropped out of school at age 15. But it was at that time Ringo took up the drums, and the rest is history. Ringo played the Liverpool beat until joining the Beatles–John Lennon, Paul McCartney and George Harrison in 1962. Many of the aspiring rock-and-rollers in Liverpool knew each other,

and it was through this route, the good old network, that Ringo found his way into fame and fortune.

The story of the early Beatles with Ringo as the drummer are legendary, but one thing is quite clear, and that is all four enjoyed partaking in drinking alcohol, a practice not uncommon to rockers around the globe, then and now. Ringo began drinking as a teenager and his drinking became progressively worse, and was eventually joined by the use of other drugs, including marijuana and cocaine. Ringo married Maureen Cox in 1965, and ten years later they divorced, with alcohol and drug abuse playing a role in the failed marriage. In April 1981, Ringo married actress Barbara Bach, and not only did his substance abuse continue and worsen, so did Barbara's, largely as a result of being married to the famed drummer. In 1988, Ringo Starr did the unexpected: he entered substance abuse treatment with his wife Barbara, and neither has used since then, a turnaround that is rare, since the majority of patients going through treatment relapse a short time after completing treatment. Ringo once said the following: "I'm not a violent man . . . but I was getting violent. And it was painful getting up in the morning and starting drinking again" (*Daily Mail,* December

2007). Perhaps it is in Ringo's "No, No" song that the truth about his addiction is truly revealed. In that song Ringo sings of his becoming so inebriated from drugs and alcohol that he could no longer pick himself up from the floor, in apparent reference to his passing out cold, and then waking up in a stupor so strong that he lacked the psychological and physical ability to start a new day. But hats off to Ringo and his wife Barbara for battling back from alcohol and drug abuse. Their strength and courage is a role model for the millions who are addicted, and who would greatly benefit from treatment.

Data

This chapter will address *three types of addiction and use* issues: heroin and cocaine use and abuse; alcohol use and abuse, and; gambling addictions. Reference to other drugs such as marijuana and the party drugs will be made when discussing their prevalence in American culture.

The question posed here is "what is going on with drug and alcohol use in American society?" (Gambling is covered later.) Each year the Department of Health and Human Services (DHHS) undertakes an extensive survey of drug use among Americans. In this section results from the 2005 National Survey on Drug Use and Health are covered (NSDUH), and unless indicated otherwise, all data are from this research. The survey is a representative sample of the civilian, non-institutional population of the United States 12 years of age and older. In 2005, 68,308 respondents completed the survey, which is accomplished through face-to-face interviews, and use of self-administered computer-assisted questioning. What follows is coverage of the findings by selected categories (i.e., age, gender, geographical region), *with emphasis on the use of illicit drugs by younger Americans, easily the biggest and most frequent users of illicit drugs.* The issue of race and eth-

nicity and illicit drug use is covered in its own section.

Illicit Drug Use: 2002–2005

There is an up-and-down pattern in the use of illegal drugs by *age* (percent using in the last month), from 2002 to 2005. Ages 12 to 17 show a steady *downward slope* over the four-year period, but age categories 18 to 25 and 26 and older indicate a slight *curvilinear* pattern in the use of illicit drug. For example, the percent using for the 26-year-old and older category from 2002 to 2005 is 5.8, 5.6, 5.5, and 5.8. It is important to recognize the variations in the use of illicit drugs across the cage categories. *Eighteen to 25-year-olds report the largest percent of those who have used illegal drugs in the one month prior to being interviewed.* The drugs under consideration are marijuana, psychotherapeutics (pain relievers, stimulants, sedatives, and tranquilizers), cocaine, hallucinogens, and inhalants.

Reported use of *marijuana* shows a steady decrease from *ages* 12 to 17 from 2002 to 2005, no matter if the issue involves lifetime, past year, or past month use of the drug. Marijuana use by *gender among youths* aged 12 to 17 also entails a decrease over the four-year span for both males and females, although the drop is more obvious for males. The patterns of use of marijuana for young people aged 12 to 17 will vary by *region* of the country, with both the northeast and midwest parts of the United States indicative of a decrease in use from 2002 to 2005. However, the south has a curvilinear trend, and the west an upward one for three years, with a dramatic decrease from 2004 to 2005. Interestingly, there is an increase in the percentage of adults fifty to fifty-nine years old who reported using illicit drugs in the month prior to being surveyed, making one wonder if the "flower power" children of the 1960s weren't starting to resort to some old behavior patterns.

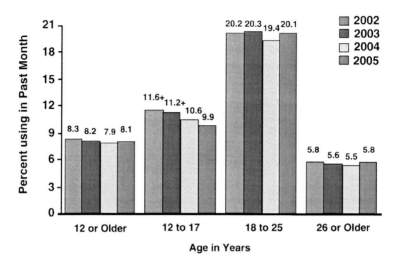

Figure 11:1. Illicit Drug Use, by Age: 2002–2005. Adapted from NSDUH 2005.

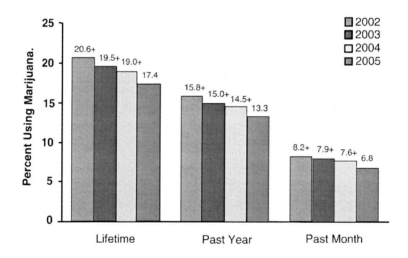

Figure 11:2. Lifetime, Past Year, and Past Month Marijuana Use Among Youth 12-7, 2002–2005.
Adapted from NSDUH 2005.

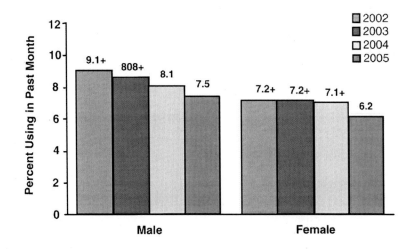

Figure 11:3. Marijuana Use by Gender, Among Youths Ages 12–17: 2002–2005.
Adapted from NSDUH 2005.

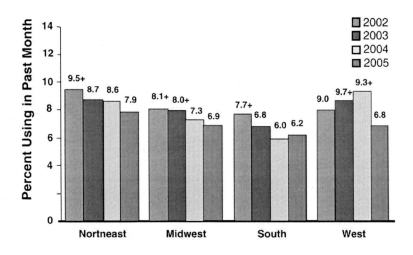

Figure 11:4. Marijuana Use by Geographic Region, Ages 12–17: 2002–2005.
Adapted from NSDUH 2005.

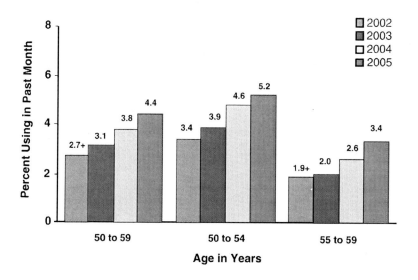

Figure 11:5. Illicit Drug Use Among Adults 50–59: 2002–2005.
Adapted from NSDUH 2005.

According to the NSDUH, 52 percent of the population 12 years of age and older used *alcohol* in the month prior to being interviewed, translating to 126 million Americans. Of these 126 million individuals, 55 million were reported to be binge drinkers (defined as consuming five or more drinks on the same occasion on at least one day in the past 30 days), and 7 percent, or 16 million Americans as heavy drinkers (operationalized as drinking five or more drinks on the same occasion on five or more days in the past 30 days). As reported in Figure 11:6 nearly 30 percent of persons aged 12 to 20 have consumed alcohol in the month prior to being interviewed, and the percentages across the four years are similar for males and females. Figure 11.7 corresponds with the data on heavy drinking among young people, confirming that binge drinking is a major issue among older young adults.

There has been a decrease in the percent of Americans using tobacco. In 2002, 30.4 percent of those surveyed reported using tobacco in the month prior to being inter-viewed. In 2005, the percentage was 29.4 percent. Although this appears trivial, any decrease in smoking by Americans represents a major victory in the fight to reduce smoking-related health hazards. The data for younger Americans aged 12 to 17 is most encouraging, since it indicates that use of tobacco products is down, with smoking of cigarettes the major contributor to the decrease. Cigarette use by gender for young people also portends encouraging trends, with decreases reported for both males and females (Figure 11:9). Most saliently, the use of cigarettes among women who are pregnant is lower than women who are not pregnant, except for women ages 15 to 17 (Figure 11:10).

Race and Ethnicity Data

The issue of race/ethnicity and illicit drug use is not as easily verified as may seem upfront. America is a heterogeneous society that is not only comprised of individuals

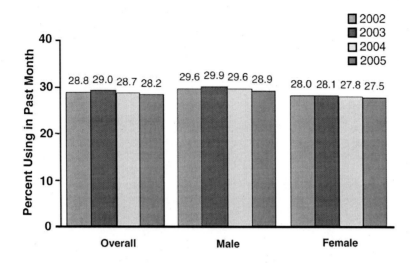

Figure 11:6. Current Alcohol Use Among Persons 12–20, by Gender: 2002–2005. Adapted from NSDUH 2005.

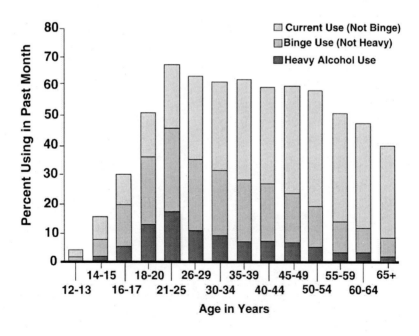

Figure 11:7 Current, Binge, and Heavy Alcohol Use Among Persons Aged 12 or Older by Age 2005. Adapted from NSDUH 2005.

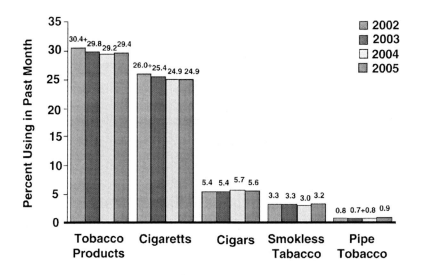

Figure 11:8. Past Month Tobacco Use Among Persons Aged 12 or Older: 2002–2005.
Adapted from NSDUH 2005.

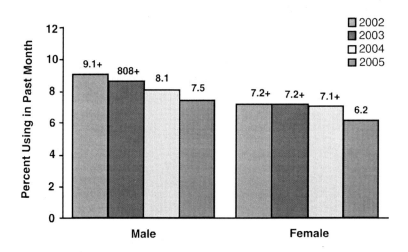

Figure 11:9. Cigarette Use by Gender, Youth Aged 12–17: 2002–2005.
Adapted from NSDUH 2005.

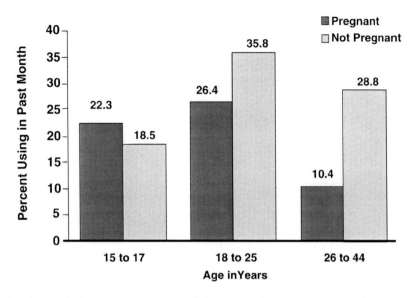

Figure 11:10. Cigarette Use Among Women aged 15–44, by age and Pregnancy Status Combined: 2004–2005. Adapted from 2005.

from many diverse ethnicities and nationalities, but it is also a nation of the "Heinz 57" variety, in which numerous Americans come from *multiple ethnic and racial identities.* Having said that, the NSDUH does classify drug use by racial and ethnic background, and reported in 2005 the highest rates of illicit drug use for individuals 12 years of age and older occurred among persons from *two or more races/ethnicities,* with 12.7 per cent of respondents from this category reporting use of illegal drugs in the month prior to being surveyed. An examination of the *major* racial and ethnic distinctions found that *9.2 percent of African Americans, 8.1 percent of whites, 7.4 percent of Hispanics, and 3.1 percent of Asian Americans used illegal drugs.* When it comes to *marijuana* the data show an identical pattern, with 10.1 percent of individuals reporting two or more races having used the drug in the previous month (the percentages are 7.3, 6.2, 5.0, and 1.8 for African Americans, whites, Hispanics and Asian Americans, respectively). The use of alcohol also reflects

the above. Thirty-four percent of persons reporting two or more races used alcohol in the month prior to being surveyed, and the percentage for whites was 41 percent, followed by African Americans (28%), Hispanics (24%), and Asians (15%). The data for *cigarettes* is quite interesting and appears more affected by age than it does race/ethnicity. Cigarette smoking for the ages 12 to 17 and 18 to 25 years of age was more common among whites than African Americans, with 13 percent of whites compared to 6.5 percent for African Americans 12 to 17 years of age reporting smoking cigarettes in the month before being interviewed. For ages 18–25, the percentages are 44 and 29 for whites and blacks, respectively. However, for adults 26 and older, between 24 and 27 percent of white and African Americans respectively smoked cigarettes just prior to the survey, indicating little difference for both categories as they age. The data for Hispanic Americans also varied by age, with 9 percent of the 12 to 17 year age group reporting smoking cigarettes, and the percentages for the 17–25 and 26 and older categories were 32 percent and 22 percent, respectively. The NSDUH did not report figures on Asian American cigarette smoking. It should be noted that the percentages of illicit drug use for American Indian/Alaska Native and Native Hawaiian/Other Pacific Islander are generally second and third to "two or more races," meaning they are higher than that reported for the other races and ethnicities just addressed (their percentages of the total population are quite small by comparison, with American Indian/Alaska Native representing just under one percent of the population of the United States, and Native Hawaiian/Other Pacific Islander comprising one-tenth of America's population). Whites, Hispanics, and African Americans constitute 74, 15, and 12 percent of the population, respectively. The issue of race and drug use will also be analyzed in the next sections when discussing heroin and cocaine.

Heroin

"H"; junk; scag; smack; horse; stuff: with slang names like these for heroin it is hard to fathom that many of the most illegal drugs would have spectacular medical value. The synthetic opioids are marvelous for relieving pain, and chemically-produced derivatives of the coca plant (from which cocaine is derived in its natural form) have significant value for reducing bleeding, and as a topical anesthetic. When used as legally intended and prescribed, the opiates and cocaine are beneficial to millions of people around the world. When used for illegal purposes, they can be destructive to millions of persons worldwide, and nowhere is this more the case than with heroin. It should be noted that drugs such as heroin and cocaine can be used naturally, and their derivatives are produced chemically in the laboratory.

Heroin is a derivative from opium, which itself is a product of the milky fluid found in flowering poppy plants that have been growing in the Mediterranean region since 3,000 B.C., and now are produced across the globe. The opiates, which are opium and its derivatives, include *opium, morphine, heroin* and *codeine.* The synthetic narcotics–the opioids–include well-known legal drugs such as *methadone, oxycodone (OxyContin), Darvon, Percodan, fentanyl, Dilaudid,* and *Demerol* (Goode, 2005). Heroin was initially derived from morphine in the later 1800s (morphine is a direct product of opium), and in the early 1900s in the United States preparations of heroin were used as a painkiller to provide relief for headaches and menstrual cramps. In the early part of the twentieth century these heroin-based medications became so widely used that they created a class of heroin addicts that would shock most contemporary Americans: *white, middle-class, rural females* who relied on over-the-counter medicines that included heroin to cope with menstrual cycle discomforts (Goode, 2005, 88). As a result of the growing number of Americans addicted to heroin (especially women), in 1914 the United States Congress passed what is now popularly known as the Heroin Narcotics Act, which outlawed the sale of over-the-counter medicines that included heroin and cocaine. Portions of this major drug legislation are presented below:

> Be it enacted by the Senate and the House of Representatives of the United States of America In Congress assembled, That on and after the first day of March, Nineteen Hundred and Fifteen, every person who produces, imports, manufactures, compounds, deals in, dispenses, sells, distributes, or gives away opium or coca leaves or any compound, manufacture, salt, derivative, or preparation thereof, shall register with the col-

lector of internal revenue of the district his name or style, place of business, and place or places where such business is to be carried on. . . . It shall be unlawful for any person required to register under the terms of the Act to produce, import, manufacture, compound, deal in, dispense, sell, distribute, or give away any of the aforesaid drugs without having registered and paid the special tax provided for in this section. . . . That it shall be unlawful for any person to sell, barter, exchange, or give away any of the aforesaid drugs except in pursuance of a written order of the person to whom such article is sold, bartered, exchanged or given, on a form to be issued in blank for that purpose by the Commissioner of Internal revenue." (*Public Acts of the Sixty-Third Congress of the United States*, 1914.)

A rather interesting side-effect of the Act occurred between 1919 and 1922, when the United States Supreme Court decided in several cases that *maintenance* of addicts was outside the scope of legitimate medical practice. As a result of ambiguity in the legislation, some doctors continued to prescribe opiates to addicts, resulting in the arrests of a few physicians. The confusion centered around whether or not physicians had the right to prescribed opiates to addicts for the purpose of *maintenance*, and in 1925 the high court decided in the Linder case that addiction per se was not a crime, paving the way for legality of maintenance (Goode, 2005). Over time a decrease occurred in the number of individuals, in particular *white women* addicted to opiates, but the landscape of those addicted to opiates, especially heroin would dramatically change by the 1960s. In the earlier part of the twentieth century it was *whites* who represented a large percentage of opiate addicts. Sixty years later, and continuing until the present, the largest share of those addicted to heroin are *urban, poor, young, African American, males*. Trafficking in heroin

became a lucrative venture, and poor inner-city African Americans became a target, especially by organized criminals who assumed given the overpowering addictive effects of heroin, African Americans would turn to crime to fund their addictions.

But why use heroin if there exists the dangers of ruining lives? There is no one answer, but two issues immediately arise. One is the incredibly powerful *euphoric* effects of the drug. As one former heroin addict once told the author of this text, take the best sex you've ever had and multiply it by 1,000, and you do not even get close to a heroin high (paraphrased). So initially, for many users the reason for taking heroin is the high, and this remains the case for other individuals who use it recreationally. The second answer is more gruesome and it involves *withdrawal symptoms*, or what is known as *abstinence syndrome* (AS). For some addicts, coming off a heroin high can result in a powerful sickness that can last up to 72 hours. The former heroin addict mentioned earlier described AS in this manner: take your worse flu and multiply it by 1,000 and you then know what withdrawal is like (paraphrased). Therefore, some heroin addicts continue to inject the drug to prevent the onset of AS, which at various points of the illness can include diarrhea; excessive tears; restless sleep (the "Yen"); tremors; dilated pupils; gooseflesh; severe low back pain; and high blood pressure. At this juncture it should be mentioned that common methods of using heroin include *injection* and *smoking*. *Inhaling* occurs with some younger users of the drug.

AIDS represents another danger from using heroin, and how it is contacted differs across gender and race. For males, the *primary source* of AIDS is *homosexual contact;* for females it is *heterosexual contact.* Breaking this down by race, it is reported homosexual contact is the primary source of AIDS for whites, African Americans, and Hispanics, although the percentage for contacting AIDS through homosexual contact is far greater for whites than it is for African Americans and Hispanics (77%, 43%, and 47%, respectively). Turning attention to the heroin/AIDS nexus, it is reported about one-fourth of males and nearly 40 percent of females contacted AIDS by injecting drugs, primarily heroin. Approximately 10 percent of white, and 33 percent of African American and Hispanics cases of AIDS are traced to intravenous drug use (Goode, 318–319).

An important issue concerns the extent of use of illegal heroin in the United States, and its origins-routes into the country? The Office of National Drug Control Policy-ONDCP (2007) estimates there are 500,000 addicts in the United States and over three million occasional users of the drug, with most of these addicts residing in three cities: *Chicago, Los Angeles,* and *New York City,* the latter housing the largest number of individuals addicted to heroin. Heroin is *the least used of the illegal drugs,* but its addictive effects engender significant concern. One percent of heroin addicts die each year, but it is to be noted their deaths have as much to do with auxiliary factors as they do the direct consequences associated with the use of heroin. The use of dirty (unsterilized) needles is associated with two conditions that lead to death for heroin addicts; hepatitis and tetanus, and other diseases such as pneumonia result in death for some abusers of heroin, as a result of their unhealthy life styles (Goode, 2005, 308). The origins of heroin to the United States may be surprising to some individuals. The ONDCP reports that 65 percent of heroin coming into the United States is from South America, with Southwest Asia (Pakistan, Afghanistan, and Iran), Southeast Asia (Burma, Laos, and Thailand), and Mexico supplying the remainder of heroin sold in the country.

Before leaving the discussion of heroin, mention should be made of its (and drugs in general) connection to criminal behavior. Needless to say, there are many stereotypes about heroin users and crime; few are accurate. One of the leading stereotypes is heroin addicts are nonviolent offenders who commit theft in order to maintain their habit. This is clearly inaccurate, and study after study over the past 30 years has confirmed the exact opposite, that being heroin addicts are often violent offenders who commit crimes such as assault and robbery *while under the influence of the drug* (Goode, 2005, 340). But not to muddy the waters, the argument exists that it is difficult to establish a *cause and effect relationship* between not only heroin and crime, but drugs and crime in general. The argument goes something like this: Joe is a drug abuser who is also a criminal, but Joe commits a lot of crime, and also happens to use drugs. There is a strong correlation between drug use and crime, but not necessarily a causal one (Harrell, Ojmaarh, Hirst, Marlowe, and Merrill, 2002). It is accurate that people who use drugs do commit more crimes than nonusers, *but many of these individuals were committing crimes before they began using drugs.* Such is the case of teenagers where delinquency is found to have *preceded* the use of drugs, and to no one's surprise there is evidence of peer influence on the decision to use drugs, with or without engaging in criminal behavior (Kappeler, Blumberg, and Potter, 2000; Menard, Mihalic, and Huizinga, 2001). In addition, there is little systematic evidence that any of the so-called dangerous drugs lead to criminality, and this includes PCP, crack cocaine, and the hallucinogens (Roth, 1994). Alfred Blumstein (2000–2001, 17–18) has shed light on this issue by identifying *three potential connections* between drug use and crime. The first involves *pharmacological/ psychological* effects, or the belief drugs cause crime. The second is *economic-compulsive*, which is the argument that drug users commit crimes to support their addictions. Finally, there is the *systemic* link, which involves violent crimes that occur in the dirty and dangerous business of drug trafficking. Blumstein's research on 414 mostly crack-related homicides in New York City found that *74 percent of drug related homicides were systemic in nature*, 14 percent pharmacological/psychological, and four percent were economic-compulsive.

There are other models of the drug/crime relationship. The *enslavement model* posits that some individuals become trapped into a life of using addicting drugs, in particular heroin. These are usually law-abiding people, who because of bad luck or issues such as poverty and mental illness, turn to crime to support their heroin habits. Accordingly, it is argued if heroin and other drugs were legal, then these individuals would not have to commit crimes (Lindesmith, 1965; Schur, 1962). The position of the *predisposition model* is distinctly different from the enslavement approach, since the argument is that some people are predisposed to committing crimes, and *also* to using heroin. These persons were not forced into using drugs, nor were they law-abiding citizens before they started using heroin. This is a "birds of a feather flock together" approach, since the predisposition model explains much crime and drug use as occurring among people who share similar deviant backgrounds and interests (Gottfredson and Hirschi, 1990). Another approach, *the intensification model*, is a reformulation of the previous two models, and its proponents argue there is no consistent relationship between the use of drugs and crime. In some instances individuals engage in crime before becoming addicted, in others, addiction precedes criminality (Anglin and Speckart, 1988.) But what about alcohol and crime? This will be addressed later in this chapter.

Cocaine

"The Champagne of the Rich" or "The Champagne of Drugs." These are just two of the labels given to cocaine. In past decades cocaine was considered to be a drug used by the more affluent, out of sight from the public and the law enforcement community. It is said to be a drug used by entertainers and during the 1980s, and it was a drug of choice of some professional athletes. The issue of who uses cocaine will be addressed later, but for now attention is directed on its origins, and why it is preferred by some people.

Cocaine is a natural stimulant that is derived from the leaves of the *coca plant*. The people of Peru have crushed the leaves of the plant and then chewed them for centuries, mostly to overcome altitude sickness, and to sustain high levels of energy needed for strenuous mountain farming. In other words, cocaine in its natural or chemically produced states gives one a big boost. It is a powerful central nervous system stimulant that is used today for many of the same reasons it has been used over time, and that is the kick or rush that is reported to occur with some forms of cocaine, after initial administration. However, similar to other drugs, cocaine has legitimate medical value, and as an alkaloid derivative of the coca plant. It is used today as a topical anesthetic applied on sensitive tissues, such as the eyes and the mucous membranes. For years it has also been used to constrict blood vessels, and to reduce bleeding. This brings us back to a point made when discussing heroin, and that is like heroin and other drugs, cocaine has been used via its natural state (chewing crushed leaves), and it is also synthetically produced in the laboratory. The methods used to produce cocaine, and its valuable synthetic derivatives have two different markets: one legal; the other illegal.

Cocaine has an interesting history, and an important pharmacological fact. Not only was its use condoned by the Inca Indians of the Andes Mountains in South America, but it was also tolerated by the Spanish crown since the Andes people would refuse to work in the silver mines unless they were paid in coca leaves. The Roman Catholic Church attempted to eradicate the use of natural cocaine because of the worship value it had to the Andes population, and because the Church was just plain flat opposed to its use. Its efforts failed since mining silver was profitable to the Spanish crown. After cocaine was first isolated by scientist Albert Nieman of Germany in 1860 it was hailed as a medical breakthrough that could be used to relieve fatigue and depression. In addition, psychoanalyst Sigmund Freud prescribed it to his friends, patients, and even used it himself. Cocaine even found its way into beverages and in 1886 pharmacist John Styth Pemberton included it in Coca-Cola to act as a "brain tonic". Twenty years later with the passage of the Pure Food and Drug Act cocaine was removed from the popular drink because it was found to be addictive. Coca leaves were also used as an ingredient in wine, and some of its connoisseurs included President William McKinley, Thomas Edison, Popes Leo XIII and Pius X, Jules Verne and H.G. Wells-to name a few (Goode 2005, 279). The pharmacological fact about cocaine? *It is not physically addicting,* and before continuing with coverage of cocaine additional street names are identified and include: *coke, snow* (because illegally it is produced in the form of white powder), *candy, flake, cholly, girl, Charlie, Big "C" or just "C", and gold dust.*

Cocaine is a powerful *central nervous system stimulant.* But for the illegal use of the drug just what does this entail, and are there dangers involved in using cocaine? Cocaine *produces intense psychological effects* that normally do not last longer than 30 minutes. Some of the effects are a sense of exhilaration, feel-ings of superabundant energy, hyperactivity, extended periods of wakefulness, and confidence, or the belief that under the influence of cocaine the user can accomplish and master anything (2005, 283). A cocaine high can equal or exceed the pleasure of sex, thus the use of the term "girl." As a party drug cocaine has the quality of keeping people up long hours so they can imbibe on drugs and alcohol until the wee hours of the morning. The *method of administration* as well as the purity of the drug does impact the nature of the high experienced by users. Cocaine is *usually snorted, injected intravenously or smoked.* Snorting appears to be the least potent means of acquiring the high, since its effects will generally take longer to reach the bloodstream than either smoking or injection. It takes about six to eight seconds to get the high when smoking, and 12 to 15 seconds when injecting cocaine. So the nature of the effects of using cocaine will vary according to the route of administration (2005, 282).

This brings us to *freebase* and *crack* cocaine which are frequently confused as being one and the same. Freebase was popular from the early 1970s until about 1985 when it was replaced by crack cocaine. Like crack, freebase is smoked and the vapors are inhaled, but what distinguishes it from crack is that during the process of producing freebase *the hydrochloride salt is removed* (what is sold on the streets is cocaine hydrochloride), thus producing about 90 percent pure cocaine (far greater than the five to 15 percent pure cocaine than is typically purchased on the streets, and far greater than for crack). The production method used to make freebase is volatile, combustible, and unstable, and the dangerous and unpredictable manner in which it is made and associated accidents (such as explosions) helped to give way to the emergence of the use of crack (2005, 282). By contrast, crack contains between 30 and 40 percent cocaine, and cocaine hydrochloride is involved in its production. Crack is considered "impure" because it includes adulterants such as baking soda, powdered laxatives, and sodium bicarbonate, returning us to the discussion of method of administration (2005, 287–288). As a refresher please recall that cocaine can be snorted, smoked (inhaled) or taken intravenously, and the effects–both immediate and longer term–are impacted by how it is administered. So with powder cocaine on the streets why is there the existence of freebase or crack? If powder cocaine can give one a super high, why is there need for anything else? The answer is someone can always make a better widget and this is so true of the illegal drug market. The illegal drug profiteers are always looking for the "new" powerful money-making drug and/or an innovative way to use an already existing substance. So powder cocaine may not be king of the hill after all, as far as cocaine is concerned. Because they are smoked, both freebase and crack produce an almost immediate rush with a high that can last up to 20 minutes. When cocaine is snorted the initial effects may take several minutes to occur, without necessarily a rush, and its longer pleasurable effects may last up to 30 minutes. But with crack and freebase the overall effects are *far more intense and powerful*, and because of this its users will frequently crave and use them more so than is the case for powder cocaine administered by snorting. This is even true for injecting cocaine, meaning smoking crack and freebase produces greater euphoria by comparison (2005, 288).

Any drug abuse can have adverse effects on its users. The Drug Abuse Warning Network (DAWN) has reported that there are *more deaths from cocaine* than any other illegal drug, and that it is the number one drug when dependency is the issue (DAWN, 2002). However, sociologist Eric Goode has argued the dangers of cocaine have been overexaggerated, but at the same time it is not wise to assume there are few if any real dangers associated with using it (Goode, 2005, 287). There are a number of variables involved in whether or not cocaine (or many drugs for that matter) is harmful, and some of these include the frequency of its use and how it is administered (needles can pose serious issues for drug users). But for the very heavy and less cautious users of cocaine the problems can include irritability, apprehensiveness, seizures and even death. In addition, snorting can produce permanent damage to the mucous membranes, and psychological crisis (the author of this text has personally known people whose lining in their nostrils has been deteriorated because of heavy snorting of cocaine). There are no givens and for some users the big issue becomes cost, and for the abusers of illegal drugs it is frequently the minority of individuals who have serious problems from abusing drugs, and then their "dangers" are projected onto others who use them (2005, 286). But what about crack? The crack scare was prominent in the 1990s and in some instances the concern was justified, especially reports of "crack babies" born to women who were pregnant while using it. But this fear and others concerning crack were overblown and the majority of those using crack did so only occasionally. But crack, like other illegal drugs can be destructive, and again this has much to do with the frequency of its use. Compulsive use of the drug can lead to paranoia, violence, heart problems, male impotency, tremors, convulsions and depression (2005, 290).

The majority of cocaine used in the United States comes from Peru, Bolivia, and Columbia, and each year these three countries produce nearly 600 tons of pure cocaine, with approximately 150–200 tons of it seized annually by federal and state law enforcement agencies. In addition, each year there are 100,000 hospital emergencies resulting from the abuse of cocaine, however it is important to reiterate that the majority of those who use cocaine do so only on occasion, for so-called recreational purposes. Those who use cocaine can be classified as following: *younger persons, mostly members of minority groups who are using crack; the older injector who is "speedballing" (mixing cocaine with heroin); and, the older, more affluent user who snorts the drug* (Office of National Drug Control Policy-ONDCP).

Methamphetamine

Drugs can get one up; drugs can get one down. Some drugs do both. Drugs can be stimulants that are used to give people a boost (adrenaline). This category includes drugs such as cocaine and the amphetamines. Some drugs have the purpose of taking people down; to sedate them. This category of drugs includes alcohol and the barbiturates. Examples of legal amphetamines are Adderall, Benzedrine, and Dexedrine, and examples of legal barbiturates are Nembutal, Seconal and Phenobarbital. Please notice the word "legal" in the previous sentences. Once again, many drugs have important medical value and if not abused can be used to help people in important ways. There are antidepressant drugs such as Prozac and Paxil, and there are antipsychotic agents that include Thorazine and Haldol. Then there is *methamphetamine*, a type of amphetamine that is considered one of the most dangerous drugs used illegally in the United States. Why slip this in here? Because it is important to understand that many legal drugs spurn the use of illegal drugs when placed in the hands of the wrong people. The legal painkilling narcotic opiates such as morphine and codeine have their illegal counterpart in heroin, and the legal sedative/depressants such as the barbiturates and the Benzodiazepines (i.e., Librium, Valium, Xanax) have their illegal derivative in GHB (gamma-hydroxybutyrate). Methamphetamine (meth) is a very powerful stimulant that not only provides a rush described by some persons to be second-to-none, but it also has staying power that can result in an orgasmic-type euphoric state that can last hours. Remember the "better widget"? Meth is an example of a drug that has been used increasingly over the past 10 years, and is either the most popular illegal drug or close to it in states such as Arkansas, Oklahoma, and Texas, although its origins were in Hawaii and California (Goode, 2005, 278). Put simply, meth is king of the hill with some drug users, and can be very dangerous if used frequently. It gives a big-time high and for those seeking such thrills it is easy to comprehend its popularity. Depending on its form meth can be smoked, snorted, injected or taken orally, and its *street or slang names include meth, poor man's cocaine, crystal meth, ice, glass, speed, crank, and white tablets.* Its forms are white powder which dissolves easily in water; clear, chunky crystals called crystal meth or ice; and pills that are sometimes called by their Thai name, Yaba. The illegal drug scene is characterized by much misled intelligence and this is evident in the various ways meth is made, ways that invoke danger and in some instances even death (discussion will follow concerning meth labs). The retail level of meth will vary, but $400 per ounce is common as is $3,500–$21,000 per pound, on a regional basis. The average purity of methamphetamine (d-methamphetamine) is 40 percent which is down from 72 per cent in the mid-1990s. The potency of the drug becomes clearer when it is stated that 40 percent purity is the norm for most users (West Slope Methamphetamine Symposium, 2004).

A recent trend in the United States, most meth is produced in Mexico, and is trafficked into the country, *primarily as a result of both federal and state laws* curtailing the sale of over-the-counter cold medications that include ephedrine and *pseudoephedrine, the primary ingredient required to make meth.* Previously, in states such as Arkansas, Oklahoma, and Texas the common denominator in producing meth was the *"mom and pop" shops,* or homemade "laboratories" that like freebase are dangerous and unpredictable. One of the reasons for such danger and unpredictability is the *producers* themselves. "Cooks" as they are called may know little about the chemicals and gases they are using to make meth, and what is more they may have little if any knowledge of chemistry, therefore making themselves high-risk candidates for explosions, burns, and even death. So making meth is not necessarily a simple process, instead it requires a number of steps and ingredients that "cooks" must understand if they not only want a powerful product, but also if they desire to avoid the dangers inherent in producing the drug. So what goes into making meth? Common ingredients include starting fluid; phosphene gas; drain cleaner; two-layered liquids; lighter fluid; ether; acetone; hydrogen peroxide; acids such as sulphuric acid; iodine; anhydrous ammonia; and denatured alcohol (and this is just a partial list). Of course, equipment is required to make meth and can include a basic chemistry glassware set; propane tanks to siphon out the ammonia; coffee pots and coffee filters; matches; empty blister caps; lithium batteries; tubing; trash bags; and, stoves–again a partial listing (West Slope Methamphetamine Symposium, 2004). So when using things like starting fluid, phosphene gas, andryhous ammonia, matches, and stoves, one best know what they are up against.

Remember the comment about misled intelligence? There are *three common methods* of making meth and they are the *Cold Cook,* the *"Nazi"* or *Birch,* and the *Red Phospherous*

or *"Mexican"* methods. What the three methods have in common is the use of over-the-counter cold medications that include ephedrine and pseudoephedrine that are essential in producing the powerful d-*methamphetamine.* With the *Cold Cook* method ephedrine, iodine and red phosphorous are mixed in a plastic container, then methamphetamine oil precipitates into another plastic container through a connecting tube. The oil is heated, typically through sunlight or by burying the containers in hot sand in order to produce the highly desired end result: pure d-methamphetamine, in small quantities. The *nazi* or *Birch* method typically entails the use of sodium or lithium metal, anhydrous ammonia, and ephedrine and usually produces up to one ounce quantities of highly pure d-methamphetamine. This method is frequently employed by independent Caucasian meth cookers (mom and pop shops). The *Red Phosphorous* or *Mexican* method, also known as the ephedrine reduction technique, usually requires ephedrine or pseudoephedrine, hydrolic acid, and red phosphorous. As suggested by its name, this method is frequently used by Mexican criminal organizations, or by cooks trained by Mexicans, and its end result is also pure d-methamphetamine, *only in large quantities.* Of course the "mom and pop" shops will vary in terms of how they make meth, and a number of these "shops" use production techniques that are spinoffs of the three methods just discussed, or are the results of the creative imaginations of the so-called cooks (West Slope Methamphetamine Symposium, 2004). Since ephedrine or pseudoephedrine are required to make meth, huge quantities of cold tablets have to be purchased, so much so that in many instances businesses selling them would have their stock of such medicines reduced to nothing. Thus the passage of the laws controlling how these medications can be sold.

The National Survey on Drug Use and Health reported that in 2005 there were 512,000 persons who used meth in the past month, representing a downward trend from 2003 when the figure was 607,000 (2005, 16). The number of new users of the drug was 300,000, which is consistent with recent years, although in 2004 there were 318,000 initiates into meth use, and in 2005 the average age of the new user was 18.6. Meth use is greatest for individuals between the ages of 19 and 40, and it appears males and females are equally likely to use the drug. Of major concern is the finding that men who have sex with other men are more likely to use meth than other men, which increases the chances of becoming infected with HIV/AIDS. The number of persons addicted to meth declined, and rather dramatically. In 2005, 257,000 people indicated addiction to meth, down from 346,000 in 2004 (2005, 13), which brings us to the dangers of using methamphetamine. Again, the answer to this issue depends on frequency of use, since data indicate the majority of people who use meth do so only on occasion. But meth is a powerful drug and its users must exercise considerable caution if they do not want to become addicted. So addiction is one danger, and there are other dangers associated with abuse, including brain damage similar to Alzheimer's disease, stroke, and epilepsy. Psychotic and violent behavior are also reported to stem from abuse of meth, as well as depression, anxiety, fatigue, and paranoia. Meth is highly toxic, and when entering environments housing meth labs, the police often wear protective suits. There is also the danger of "death bags" or bags containing chemicals and residuals from making methamphetamine. Just picking one of these bags up may create health issues as result of toxicity (West Slope Methamphetamine Symposium, 2004).

Alcohol

Marijuana, cocaine, heroin, methamphetamine, the hallucinogens: When discussing illegal drugs or drug abuse it is frequently these substances that dominate the concerns of Americans. But what about alcohol? It is not that alcohol gets a pass. On the contrary, the abuse of alcohol is of concern to Americans, but when placed in the same sentence as illicit drugs such as marijuana or cocaine, it is not unusual to hear people raise greater opposition to them than to alcohol. Why? Alcohol is legal (at age 21), and in the minds of some individuals this makes alcohol more acceptable and maybe even less dangerous (a foolish assumption, indeed). The National Survey on Drug Use and Health (2005) reported that *126 million Americans* 12 years of age and older are current users of alcohol. *No illegal drug comes close to that* and it is possible to add up the current users of marijuana, heroin, methamphetamine, and cocaine, and combined the number of users falls far short of 126 million people (less than 20 million users). Of course, there are clear dangers associated with the abuse of alcohol and these will be addressed later. But for whatever reasons alcohol use carries with it far less stigma than using illegal drugs such as marijuana, that are not known to cause nearly as much damage to society.

One-hundred twenty-six million people? This represents 52 percent of the population 12 years of age and older. But it is not moderate use that is addressed in this section since over *70 percent of Americans who drink do so in moderation, and drink infrequently.* The concern here will be the abuse of alcohol, or the *7 percent* of the adult population of Americans that consumes *50 percent of all alcohol.* That's correct. Fifty percent of all alcohol consumed in the United States is ingested by 7 percent of the adult population, which means that the other 50 percent of all alcohol consumed is imbibed by the remaining 93 percent of the adult population. In both instances we are talking about truly disproportionate representations.

Alcohol abuse and alcoholism are difficult to define, and when one considers there is a *cultural nuance* relevant to such definitions, it becomes even more difficult to clarify. In the United States, especially in the south, if one is seen drinking any alcoholic beverage at noon (or even earlier) it may be immediately assumed alcohol is a problem for that individual. But what about lunch time in France, Germany, Greece, Italy, Ireland, and so forth? It is common for the natives of those and other European countries to drink wine or beer at lunch, and to repeat that at supper. It is not uncommon for Europeans to drink alcohol in between those meals, or even in the morning. This does not imply that citizens of other nations do not have problems with alcohol. The point made here is that in the eyes of some Americans viewing drinking at times of the day when we are not used to it may be misconstrued as abuse of alcohol. Once again culture is an issue, even within the United States where people from the south drink the least, but ironically have the most serious problems with alcohol. *Context* is important when analyzing drug use in general.

The National Institute on Alcohol Abuse and Alcoholism (NIAAA) provides the following definitions.

Alcoholism is characterized by compulsive drinking, preoccupation with drinking, and tolerance to alcohol.
Alcohol Abuse is drinking-related failure to fulfill major obligations at work, school or home; interpersonal, social or legal problems, and drinking in hazardous situations.

The NIAAA has also broken down alcoholism into the following three categories:

Loss of control: This involves people drinking when they do not intend to drink, and it entails drinking more than people planned.
Presence of functional or structural damage: This includes physiological, psychological, domestic, economic, and social damage as a result of alcohol abuse.
Use of alcohol as a kind of universal therapy: This refers to the abuse of alcohol in order to keep one's life from coming apart.

Let's return to the issue of damage momentarily, and focus on economic damage. Over the years the author of this text ("I" for the rest of this discussion) has asked students in his "Sociology of Deviance" classes how many are or have been bartenders. I usually have a few in each class, but it is the discussion that ensues from there that grabs the attention of the other students. After asking the question, I then tell a story about the owner of a popular pub in the midwest who once told me he paid the lease on his bar on the basis of one or maybe two heavy drinkers who frequented his establishment. The owner astounded me with a fact I did not know, there is always at least one customer who will spend up to $50 a day, every day of a month drinking in his place. Assuming 30 days in a *month*, this adds up to *$1,500 dollars spent in the pub*, enough to pay the lease. *Over one year this is $18,000.* Unfathomable? Yes, to the moderate or nondrinker, but to bar owners and bar tenders everywhere this is matter of fact. Now take two such customers, and the figure is *$36,000* a year; three customers, *$54,000* a year, and so on. When I asked the pub owner why he would allow such obvious individual consumption of alcohol in his premise he responded: "if they don't drink here they will elsewhere. Besides if they get too drunk I call a cab for them" (paraphrased). Back to the bartender students. Every one of them over my many years of teaching "Deviance" has echoed the same fact, and that is in every bar there are at least several patrons who pay the bills. I also tell the students that as people enter this pub they may notice three plaques on the wall, close to the door. These are plaques in the memory of three patrons who killed themselves drinking, mostly at the pub. On cold winter days customers will come into the place and hang coats on hooks that covers the plaques. What a legacy?

Physician E. M. Jellinek, one of America's leading authorities on alcohol abuse classified alcoholism into three stages, or patterns of symptoms: *early symptoms; middle symptoms;* and *late symptoms.* Problems inherent within each stage or symptom are repeated below (1946):

Early Symptoms (Incipient alcoholism that lasts 10 years in duration):

• Breaking promises
• Lying about drinking
• Gulping drinks
• Drinking before a party
• Drinking at regular times
• Rationalization
• Irregular eating
• Blackouts

Middle Symptoms (Mostly a continuation of early symptoms, lasting from two to five years):

• Minimizing drinking
• Carrying a secret supply
• Extravagant behavior
• Irregular eating
• Weekend bouts
• Frequent intoxication
• Nervousness
• Missing work

Late Symptoms (Advanced stages of alcoholism that last until death, psychosis, or recovery):

• Morning drinking
• Solitary drinking
• Benders
• Irritability
• Substitution of alcohol for food
• Loss of jobs
• Broken homes
• Delirium tremors (DTs)
• Deficiency diseases

Some decades ago, another physician, Dr. Robert V. Seliger developed an alcoholism evaluation instrument used as a preliminary tool to ascertain if people are addicted to alcohol. Answering "yes" to six of the 39 items on the scale may indicate addiction to alcohol. Several of these questions are repeated below (1950):

Do you need a drink at a definite time every day?
Do you prefer drinking alone?
Do you sneak your drinks?
Do you lose time from class work while drinking?
Do you desire food while drinking?
Have you lost any friends as a result of drinking?
Has your life become alcohol centered?
Have you ever felt a religious need?
Have you lost any job as a result of drinking?

Answering yes to the six of the 39 items does not automatically imply that one is an alcoholic, instead this and other evaluation instruments are used by treatment specialists as tools to *start the process* of determining the nature and the extent of alcohol abuse issues. Two other evaluation tools, The Addiction Severity Instrument (ASI) and the Substance Abuse Subtle Screening Inventory (SASSI) are discussed later in this section.

Now more definitively to the question of *who drinks?* Earlier in this chapter preliminary data on the use of alcohol by race was presented. When it comes to heavy use of alcohol it is *white males* who dominate the scene. White males between the ages of 18 and 29 are the *heaviest drinkers* in the United States, and Latino males and African American males remain relatively alcohol abuse-free until their early 30s, when it is reported their heavy use of alcohol ensues (NIAAA). The rates of alcohol abuse for females present an interesting picture. In 2005, 58 percent of males and 46 percent of females were reported to be current drinkers, but when breaking this down by age the data show that for 12 to 17-year-olds, 17 percent of females as opposed to 16 percent of males were current drinkers. What is more, over 55 percent of females and 66 percent of males 18 to 25 were reported to be current drinkers, making one wonder if this pattern will be reversed in the future, should younger age females continue to out drink their male 12 to 17-year-old male counterparts? (NSDUH, 2005, 25.) As noted earlier, young people (under age 30) represent the highest percentage of current users of alcohol and this also translates into the serious legal issue of driving under the influence of alcohol. Twenty-eight percent of respondents between the ages 21 and 25 reported driving under the influence of alcohol, and the percentages steadily decreased from there (with the exception of 40 to 44-year-olds) to 65 and older where 3 percent reported driving while intoxicated. Of course, sociologists will also ask the question about the relationship of social class or socioeconomic status (SES) to drinking, and one of the indicators on SES is education. It may appear on the grounds of common sense that the least educated Americans are more likely to consume alcohol (the old "Joe Six-Pack" stereotype). This assumption is clearly incorrect, except in one very important instance. Goode (2005) reports that among respondents 26 years of age and older, 77 percent of college graduates reported drinking on at least one occasion in the previous year, compared with 64 percent of people with some college, 54 percent of high school graduates, and 46 percent of respondents who had not completed high school. According to Goode: "The higher the income, education, and socioeconomic status of the respondent, the greater the likelihood that he or she drinks alcohol" (2005, 212). The one exception: *college educated African-American males who drink less as SES increases* (Herd, 1991; Peralta, 2005).

What are some other data concerning the use of alcohol in the United States (NIAAA; Goode, 2005, 207–208):

- The era of prohibition (1919–1932) saw a 50 percent reduction in alcohol related deaths.
- Americans consume 2.18 gallons of absolute alcohol per person each year which is the equivalent of 2.5 beers each day, three drinks of hard liquor each containing one ounce of alcohol, and one eight ounce glass of wine.
- It may take years before heavy users of alcohol develop an addiction to the drug.
- When considering Euro Americans, the abuse of alcohol is a problem for Irish Americans, but not a serious issue with Asian, Italian or Jews of European origins.
- The total cost of alcohol abuse in the United Sates is $185 billion annually.

Earlier cocaine, heroin, the hallucinogens, marijuana, and methamphetamine were discussed. There is the belief, and in some instances it may be correct that using any of these drugs will lead to criminality and to violence. Well to begin with, just by possessing these substances the law is broken, and the use of some drugs such as meth may result in violence. Enough said? Not even close. *Alcohol is the number one drug*–the kingpin–when violence is considered. Up to *60 percent of murderers* were under the influence of alcohol when they committed their crimes (2005, 341), and a *quarter of all* violence has a relationship to alcohol, adding up to nearly three million acts of violence each year (2005, 207). The alcohol/violence connection has long been established, but is it a given? The answer is no–it is not a given that just by drinking people are destined to become violent. First of all, the great majority of people who drink do not become violent, and second, it may not be drinking alone that leads to violent acts. Quite frequently drinkers mix drugs, meaning they will consume alcohol and use other drugs such as meth or ecstasy, and the symbiotic effects of poly drug use may increase the likelihood of violence. Then there are the issues of context and culture. Drinking is considered a macho thing to do, and when co-joined with drinking in an environment such as a bar where things can get a little rough or out of control, even without the presence of drunkenness, the *overall context* may lead to violence, not just the drinking alone. Plus as Barkan argues (2005, 444), there is a *self-fulfilling prophecy* that is present, meaning alcohol is presumed to lead to violence, and at times it does. Clearly, the use of alcohol precedes the commission of at *least 50 percent of violent acts such as homicides and rape*, and research confirms its use *does increase* the chances for assaults, murder, and that rape will occur (Nielson and Martinez, 2003; White, Tick, Loeber and Stouthamer-Loeber, 2002). There is ongoing theory and research as to the "why" of the alcohol/violence relationship, but the findings are inconclusive. The idea the use of alcohol

reduces inhibitions is offset by theory and research that finds little support for the alleged connection. The first notion is referred to as the *drunken component* perspective and the second is the *cognitive/guidedness* approach. But as Barkan writes, *norms*, the standards for conduct that structure the social context, are in operation when alcohol is used, and cannot be overlooked. People learn what is expected of them when drinking, and if the norms lean toward relaxation and just having a good time, violence may not occur. If the norms are more "macho," violent behavior may transpire (2005, 343). This is an important issue that is frequently ignored or bypassed when discussing the effects of alcohol, and drugs in general. *Norms impact a wide range of behaviors*, and with drug use this can include when one feels "high," how to use drugs, and other than the pharmacological effects of drugs, norms can impact behaviors before, during and after using substances.

Alcohol clearly portends risks for health and automobile fatalities. Beginning with the latter, each year between 35 and 40 percent of all fatal car crashes involve alcohol. Why is this? The national legal limit for driving drunk is .08, far higher than what is required to increase the risk of being involved in a car wreck. For persons with a Blood Alcohol Content (BAC) between .02 and .04, there is a 1.4 times greater chance of getting into an automobile accident. Consider what happens as the BAC gets higher. BAC levels of .05 and .09 and .10 and .14 increase the risk of car crashes 11 and 48 fold respectively, and the chances of a fatal car wreck increase 385 times with a BAC of over .15 (Goode 2005, 206). Of course these data reflect fatalities, and do not cover the many thousands of nonfatal injuries resulting from drunk drivers. In addition, the abuse of alcohol has definitive consequences for *health* including the 900,000 Americans diagnosed with cirrhosis of the liver, a disease which kills 26,000 people annually. Alcohol abuse is also associated with immune deficiencies that can lead to tuberculosis, pneumonia, HIV/AIDS, and hepatitis. If this is not enough, abusers of alcohol are twice as likely to have mental disorders (2005, 208).

Gambling

Ask yourself the following questions:

"Did you ever lose time from work or school due to gambling?"
"Has gambling ever made your home life unhappy?"
"After a win did you have a strong urge to return and win more?"
"Did you ever borrow money to finance your gambling?"
"Did you ever gamble longer than you had planned?"
"Have you ever considered self-destruction or suicide as a result of your gambling?"

These are six of 20 questions included on a scale used by Gamblers Anonymous (GA) to evaluate the possibility of problem gambling and addiction to gambling. But you may be asking yourself "what does gambling have to do with addiction and why discuss it in the same breath as heroin, cocaine and alcohol?" Gambling is a behavior and enterprise that is largely ignored by sociologists—but it should not be. Millions of Americans gamble; most recreationally. Millions of Americans drink alcohol; most are modest drinkers. Millions of Americans smoke marijuana; most just on occasions. Yet sociologists have undertaken extensive research on drinking alcohol and smoking pot. However, few sociologists are interested in or write about one of America's biggest addiction issues: gambling. *If abused, gambling can be as destructive to individuals and society as alco-*

holism or addiction to heroin and cocaine. Gambling and its other name–*gaming*–is a multibillion dollar a year industry. In 2005, the gross revenues from gaming exceeded 84 billion dollars, and this only represents revenues from legal gambling. Breaking this down, the GRR-gross gambling revenue (the amount wagered minus the winnings returned to players) is derived from the following sources (American Gaming Association, 2006):

- card rooms–1.12 billion dollars
- commercial casinos–31.85 billion dollars
- charitable games and bingo–2.33 billion dollars
- Indian casinos–22.62 billion dollars
- legal bookmaking–130.5 billion dollars
- lotteries–22.89 billion dollars
- pari-mutuel wagering–3.68 billion dollars

Total gaming revenues have consistently increased over the years, and from 1995 to 2005 the revenues increased by 86 percent, or from 45.1 billion to 83.7 billion dollars (American Gaming Association, 2006). Put simply, Americans like to gamble and there is enough variety or different forms of it to satisfy their gaming desires. In recent years, *lotteries and casinos have become the most prominent types of gaming* in the United States. Communities and states supporters of lotteries and casinos usually argue that these forms of gambling will boost local and state economies because they will create jobs and provide for major additional sources of tax revenues. Proponents of gaming proceed to argue that when jobs are created there is an economic multiplier effect, meaning people will have more money or more people will have dollars to spend, thus benefiting local and state economies. A few examples may help to explicate this point. In 2006, the annual revenues produced by casinos in the

cities listed below were:
- Tunica/Lula, Mississippi–1.252 billion dollars
- Shreveport, Louisiana–847 million dollars
- Biloxi, Mississippi–845 million dollars
- Black Hawk, Colorado–554 million dollars
- Council Bluffs, Iowa–477 million dollars

The author of this text (again referred to in the first person for the remainder of this specific coverage) worked in Council Bluffs, Iowa, located across the Missouri River from Omaha, Nebraska. In the mid 1990s, the city of Council Bluffs, Iowa voted to have river boat casinos largely on the auspices that they would jump-start the economy of the city by creating jobs, and also by infusing large sums of dollars into the local communities. Part of the approval process mandated that the casinos give a certain percentage of their profits back to the local communities to meet their various needs. One example (and there are many) of this was the building of a new library in the center of Council Bluffs. What followed is rather amazing since not only were the casinos built, but so were hotels and a number of major businesses–right in the vicinity of and in juxtaposition to the casinos. The casino area also includes a convention center that houses many events, such as sporting activities and concerts. The case of Council Bluffs represents an example of what can occur when gaming begins to operate in cities and states, but of course the question becomes "what is the cost/benefit analysis associated with casinos and other forms of gambling?" Some people argue that all types of social problems are created or worsened by the existence of gaming; others argue the positive benefits outweigh any negative results from gambling. It is to this discussion attention is now directed.

In order to address the question of the effects of gaming, two sources are used. The first is a major study conducted by the *National Gambling Impact Study Commission* and the second represents data from the *American Gaming Association* (AGA). The former research does not necessarily represent any particular side of the debate over the benefits/consequences of gambling. The later data is collected to support the positions of the AGA, although this does not imply the data are inaccurate.

The National Gambling Impact Study Commission was established during the latter 1990s and its resulting document is known as *The Gambling Impact and Behavior Study* (herein identified as GIBS). The research was conducted by the world renowned National Opinion Research Center (NORC) in conjunction with Gemini Research, The Lewin Group, and Christian/Cummings Associates. The data collection period was from 1998-1999, and its purpose was to investigate "the gambling behavior and attitudes of adults and youth in America and also estimates the effects of gambling facilities on a variety of economic and social indicators" (National Gambling Impact Study, 2002). Respondents for the study were selected through the use of probability sampling techniques, in which samples were drawn from the adult and younger populations of the United States via random-digit dialing (RDD), and random selection of patrons who gambled at casinos in eight states. The sampling process yielded 2,714 adults through RDD, 530 adults who were interviewed in the gaming facilities, and 534 youth ages 16 to 17 who were selected by RDD. Data were collected through the use of telephone interviews, personal interviews, self administered questionnaires, and data reported in sources such as Regional Economic Indicator Series, City and County data Book, FBI Uniform Crime Reports, and the NCHS Vital and Health Statistics series. The study sought to collect information on and about the following issues related to gaming and gamblers:

- demographic information about gamblers
- geographic regional information where the gaming facilities are located
- gambling behavior and attitudes of gamblers
- motivations for gambling
- gambling history of gamblers
- problem-gambling diagnostic assessment
- gambling treatment experience
- family/marital status and issues
- income and financial information of gamblers
- mental and general health of gamblers
- substance use of gamblers

A major focus of the study was to differentiate among the *types of difficulties* experienced by several *categories of gamblers.* A major question was: "do *pathological gamblers* have greater issues with problems such as bankruptcy and loss of employment than *other types* of gamblers?" *Proponents* of gambling typically argue that gaming opportunities have limited association with various social ills, meaning that these problems would exist anyway. *Opponents* of legalized gambling assume the opposite, and argue strongly that legal gambling can destroy lives and even ruin communities as a result of bankruptcy and marital failure which they purport are directly linked to gaming.

Before discussing the results from this study, several operational definitions are in order. The study classified gamblers as *low-risk, at-risk, problem and pathological gamblers,* based on *nine criteria* established in the *Diagnostic and Statistical Manual-IV.* *Pathological gambling* is defined as "persistent and recurrent maladaptive gambling behav-

ior" as indicated by *five or more* of the nine criteria including *preoccupation* with gambling, *tolerance,* or needing to gamble in increasing amounts of money, and *lying,* or lying to family members, therapists, and others about the extent of their gambling (2002, 16). *Problem gamblers* are characterized by *three or more* of the criteria, and *at-risk* and *low-risk gamblers* are defined as having *one or more criteria* as established by the DSM-IV, and never having lost more than $100 in a single day, respectively (2002, 21). The other criteria from the DSM-IV are (2002, 16):

- **withdrawal**–becoming restless and irritable when attempting to stop or cut back on gambling.
- **escape**–gambling becomes a way to escape from or to avoid problems.
- **chasing**–means chasing one's losses whereby gamblers resume gambling the next day in hopes of winning money.
- **loss of control**–gamblers are unable to control their gambling.
- **illegal acts**–gamblers steal, embezzle, and forge checks in order to finance their gambling addiction.
- **risked significant relationship bailout**–gamblers become dependent on other people to support their gambling and they lose relationships and jobs as a result of their addiction.

When comparing problem and pathological gamblers to the other three categories, the results from the study lend support to the negative side of gambling. A greater percentage of both problem and pathological gamblers had *lost their jobs* in the past year, and were more likely to have been *arrested and incarcerated.* In addition, problem and pathological gamblers had *higher rates of divorce and mental health issues,* and problem gamblers were far more likely to have *filed for bankruptcy,* and along with at-risk gamblers had *higher percentages of receiving unemployment benefits and welfare* (2002, 43–53). It is to be noted that in most cases problem and pathological gamblers were far more likely to have experienced social problems as a result of their gambling, and at-risk gamblers shared many of the same problems as problem and pathological gamblers, only in lower percentages.

So, case closed? Not quite easy to state. *The American Gaming Association* (AGA) utilizes research on the effects of gaming undertaken by various organizations and arrives at a much different picture. Reporting on a study commissioned by the Department of the Treasury in 1999, the AGA noted a finding of *little association* between casino gambling and bankruptcies in the United States. The study found that bankruptcies were a function of changes in bankruptcy law as well as a reduction in the stigma associated with filing for bankruptcy, the enormous growth in the use of credit cards, and indebtedness from overspending. In addition, the AGA reported that Utah, which is the only state without legalized gambling had the highest rate of bankruptcies per household in the United States, and that of the 15 states with the highest bankruptcy rates only one, New Jersey has casinos. What is more, Colorado which entered into the casino business in 1991, was the only state to experience a decline in bankruptcies during the 1990s (American Gaming Association, 2003). What about crime and gaming? Relying on the F.B.I. Uniform Crime Report and locally undertaken research from Detroit, the AGA reported that in 2005 Las Vegas, Nevada, the kingpin of gaming cities in America, had one of the lowest rates of crime of any major tourist community in the states, and that Detroit, a city with a large casino presence also had a relatively low crime rate. Additionally, the AGA reported that based on data from the National Institute of Justice and the Public Sector Gaming Study Commission, there is little evidence that gambling causes or is linked to crime (American Gaming Association, 2003). This brings us to pathological gambling. Earlier it was stated that gaming revenues have soared over the past decade and that the number of casinos has dramatically increased during the same time period. Given this, one might expect to find a large percentage of Americans hooked on gaming. Not so according to the AGA. Employing research from the Harvard University Medical School's Division on Addictions, the National Research Council of the National Academy of Sciences, the *Journal of Clinical Psychiatry* and the General Accounting Office (GAO), the AGA reported a pathological gambling prevalence rate of no greater than 1.5 percent. Keeping in line with its other findings, the AGA also reported that in Connecticut, a state with one of the world's largest casinos, pathological gambling rates may have actually declined, and the results appear to be the same in Louisiana, South Dakota, Michigan, Minnesota, Oregon, Texas, and Washington (American Gaming Association, 2003).

So whom does one believe? It is important to keep in mind that different data collection methods may result in varying and contradictory results. The Gambling Impact and Behavior Study based its conclusions on actual interviews with people who gamble. The AGA bases most of its findings on data collected by other organizations that may not be derived from surveys, but instead are often studies done using secondary analysis involving economic, social and crime variables that are documented in major publications such as the F.B.I. Uniform Crime Reports and United States Bureau of the Census.

Evaluating Addictions

There are a number of instruments used to evaluate addictive behaviors and two examples of these instruments have been discussed in this chapter. The "Twenty Questions" tool and the screening device developed by Dr. Robert V. Siegler are *basic tests* used as preliminary means to ascertaining the nature and degree of addiction to gambling, and drugs and alcohol. But there are two other instruments that are widely used, primarily to evaluate drug and alcohol abuse and addiction. The instruments are *The Addiction Severity Index* (ASI) and *The Substance Abuse Subtle Screening Inventory* (SASSI).

The ASI is a standardized tool for evaluating alcohol and drug addiction, and it is comprised of the following six scales or areas used in assessing the degree of addiction to substances (some instruments include a spiritual category). The areas include: *(1) medical status; (2) employment/support status; (3) alcohol and drug use; (4) legal status; (5) family status and social relationships; and (6) psychiatric status.* The instrument is designed to determine the types and frequency of use of drugs and alcohol, and as a result of using substances if the respondents (patients) have had marital and family problems, have been arrested or incarcerated, and if they have missed work or lost jobs as a result of drug and alcohol abuse. It also asks patients to identify their health issues (such as ulcers) as well as including items concerning depression and anxiety. Of course, this is just an overview, and the ASI includes *many more detailed items* in each of the areas/scales, as well as asking basic demographic information such as race, gender and age of patients. When implementing the ASI, two individuals are involved: the *interviewer* and the *respondent.* Each gives a rating to the items on the instrument, and at the conclusion of the questioning the interviewer derives a *severity profile.* The interviewer uses a scale ranging from "no problem" (0) to "extreme problem" (9), and the respondent uses a scale that ranges

from "not at all" (0) to "extremely" (4). Obviously the higher the *composite scores* determined by both the respondent and the interviewer, the more likely it is that the latter will conclude the patient has drug and/or alcohol problems. It is not uncommon to have a disconnect between the respondent and interviewer composite scores. This may be due to dishonest answers provided by respondents and/or misreads on behalf of the interviewer. Interviewers are not necessarily social scientists trained in the art of asking questions and coding responses, so at times they may be off the mark in their assessments of respondents. What is more, respondents may be filling out the ASI because they have legal problems associated with drug and alcohol abuse (such as DUIs or MIPs), and they may be lying about a wide variety of issues covered on the ASI. The questioning will take about 30 minutes to one hour, depending on the respondent, and especially if the interviewer feels a need to probe in more detail if he or she suspects respondents are giving false answers. As questions are posed the interviewer may take notes, and this can add time to the interview.

The Substance Abuse Subtle Screening Inventory (SASSI)

Brief Description

The SASSI is a brief one-page, two-side self-report questionnaire that helps identify individuals who have a high probability of having a substance dependence or a substance use disorder. It is an easily administered psychological screening measure that is available in separate versions for adults and adolescents. The Adult SASSI-3 and Adolescent SASSI-A2 have an overall empirically tested accuracy of 93 and 94 percent, respectively (Lazowski, Miller, Boye, and Miller, 1998; Miller and Lazowski, 1999, 2001, 2005), while validation research on the Spanish SASSI demonstrates an overall accuracy rate of 84 percent (Lazowski, Boye, Miller, and Miller, 2002). Each questionnaire can be administered, scored, and interpreted in approximately 15 to 20 minutes. The SASSI includes both face valid questions and subtle items that have no apparent relationship to substance use. Subtle items are included to identify individuals who are unwilling or unable to acknowledge substance misuse/abuse or the related symptoms.

The adult version (ages 18 and up) consists of 93 items and 10 subscales, and the adolescent version (ages 12–18) consists of 100 items and 12 subscales. Products published by the SASSI Institute are available in paper-pencil, web-based, optical scanning, and computerized formats. Free clinical and technical assistance is available Monday through Friday via a toll free number.

Face Valid and Subtle Scales

The Adult SASSI-3 contains three face valid scales *Face Valid Alcohol* (FVA), *Face Valid Other Drugs* (FVOD), and *Symptoms* (SYM). The Adolescent SASSI-A2 contains five face valid scales FVA, FVOD, SYM, *Family-Friends Risk Scale* (FRISK), and *Attitudes* (ATT). Examples of some face valid questions are: "Became depressed after having sobered up?" "Taken drugs to improve your thinking and feeling?" "Taken drugs to forget school, work, or family pressures?" (Adult SASSI-3 and Adolescent SASSI-A2 questionnaires.)

Subtle items on the Adult SASSI-3 and the Adolescent SASSI-A2 do not have an apparent relationship to substance misuse and related behavioral characteristics. The subtle scales are: *Obvious Attributes* (OAT) (adult and adolescent instruments) reflect an

individual's tendency to endorse statements of personal limitations that were shown to be endorsed by those diagnosed with substance use disorders in validation research; *Subtle Attributes* (SAT) (adult & adolescent instruments) endorsements reflect the extent to which clients recognize the impact of their substance abuse problems on their lives; *Defensiveness* (DEF) (adult & adolescent instruments) item responses identify clients who are willing or unwilling to acknowledge evidence of personal problems and limitations; *Supplemental Addiction Measure* (SAM) (adult & adolescent instruments) is an additional measure that increases the accuracy of the SASSI, but is not intended for interpretation; *Family vs. Controls* (FAM) (adult SASSI-3 only) distinguishes individuals who were known to be family members of substance abusers from control subjects; *Correctional* (COR) (adult & adolescent instruments) measures the extent to which an individual's responses on the SASSI are similar to people with relatively extensive histories of problems with the legal/judicial system; *Secondary Classification Scale* (SCS) (adolescent SASSI-A2 only) helps differentiate substance dependent from substance abusing adolescents; *Validity Scale* (VAL) (adolescent SASSI-A2 only) flags low probability profiles with an elevated VAL score for further evaluation for substance use disorder (Miller & Lazowski, 1999, 2001).

Examples of some true/false subtle items are: "Most people would lie to get what they want." "I know who is to blame for most of my troubles." or "I think carefully about all my actions." (Adult SASSI-3). *For additional information about the subscales go to www.sassi. com*

The *purpose* of the SASSI is to help identify people with substance use disorders so that they may be referred for treatment. Its brevity, ease of administration and scoring makes it a useful clinical instrument for clinicians, researchers and substance abuse professionals.

In Recognition: William Ricketts

William "Bill" Ricketts, M.S., L.M.H.P. joined the faculty at Iowa Western Community College in 1991 and serves as the department chair for the Human Services Addictive Studies program. Bill has been recognized by the National Institute for Staff and Organizational Development as a master teacher and was voted "most outstanding teacher" at the Great Iowa Teachers Workshop. Bill currently serves as a teaching consultant for the faculty at Iowa Western and is also a training mentor for the Iowa Community College Online Consortium (ICC OC).

Mr. Ricketts is a nationally certified SASSI trainer, joining the SASSI Institute in 1990 and has completed over 300 trainings for mental health and substance abuse counselors throughout the United States. He has been recognized by the SASSI Institute as their top training consultant. Bill currently conducts SASSI trainings in Kansas, Missouri, Nebraska, Iowa, North and South Dakota, Wyoming, and Montana.

Mr. Ricketts is a clinical member of the American Association for Marriage and Family Therapist (AAMFT), and a licensed mental health practitioner. He trained under Dr. Laura Perls at the New York Institute for Gestalt Therapy. An experienced clinician, Bill has over 25 years in the mental health and substance abuse fields as a clinical family therapist specializing in working with chemically dependent families and running groups for adult children of alcoholics.

As a consultant, he helps area agencies develop programs for recovering families. In 2007, Bill helped designed a program called Families Also Serve Time (FAST) for the Regional Correctional Facility in Council Bluffs, IA, a program for family members of inmates. He has also served on boards of directors including Youth Emergency Services and YES Youth Street Outreach program, which he initiated as president of the board in 2001.

Bill resides in Omaha, Nebraska with his wife Susan. Together they enjoy the classical arts, remote camping, 4-wheel jeeping, and golf.

SUMMARY

Millions of Americans use drugs and alcohol. The patterns of use of illegal drugs will vary by age, race, and gender, and most individuals who use illegal drugs do so recreationally, and many cease illegal drug-taking behavior by their 30s. Heroin is the least used of the illegal drugs, and it is potent. The abuse of heroin can lead to addiction and some addicts experience serious withdrawal symptoms or illness within hours of injecting it. Cocaine is used more frequently than heroin but far less so than marijuana or alcohol, and it is not known to be physically addicting. Cocaine can be a party drug and like heroin it can be snorted, smoked or injected. Powder cocaine is the most commonly used type of the drug, but over the years cocaine has taken the form of freebase and crack, both more dangerous and physically addicting. Methamphetamine (meth) has been around for years but it has been in the past decade that it has hit the streets in some parts of the country with a vengeance. Like freebase and crack, meth is a dangerously addicting drug that can produce deleterious effects for the individual. The major source of meth is Mexico and not even tough laws curbing its production in the United States has slowed down its use. Alcohol is used by nearly 130 million Americans, but mostly in moderation. It is only a small percentage of drinkers who become problem drinkers and alcoholics, but this small percentage contributes vastly to the crime scene in the United States. If abused, alcohol has numerous mental and health consequences, including death (as do other drugs such as heroin and methamphetamine). One does not become an alcoholic overnight, instead it may take years before alcoholism sets in, and by then alcoholics may have done substantial *overall* harm to themselves. Millions of Americans gamble, most just for enjoyment, but some individuals become problem or pathological gamblers and this can be costly to themselves, their families and their communities. Persons with gambling issues may turn to crime to support their habits, and like those addicted to drugs they may need to enter treatment. The need for treatment for addiction may depend on evaluation and for drug and alcohol abuse. The Addiction Severity Instrument and The Substance Abuse Subtle Screening Inventory are tools used to assess the nature and extent of problems with substances.

Chapter 12

SOCIETAL REACTION AND STIGMATIZATION: MENTAL DISORDERS AND PHYSICAL DISABILITIES

CASE STUDY: JOE

Joe was born on August 6, 1946 and was diagnosed with diabetes at age three. By the time he was age 10 Joe had become legally blind. His adult height was four feet eight inches, and he weighed no more than 80 pounds. From his earliest years on Joe was faced with numerous physical issues and challenges that would eventually lead to his being dropped from formal K-12 education, long before passage of the Americans With Disabilities legislation. During his first 10 years of life Joe attended school and was a top student, and during this time he became proficient at reading Braille. Until he lost nearly all sight by age 10 Joe would read with books placed closely to his face, and he would sit in the front row in his classroom so that he could see the teacher and the blackboard. At times he would be moved just in front of the blackboard in order to see what was written on it. By the time he was in the fifth grade the school systems had decided Joe was too much trouble for them to educate, and he was summarily prevented from receiving either public or parochial education. This was a crushing blow to Joe since he was a top student and

was more than capable of continuing his formal education with a little help and flexibility from teachers and administrators, after all he was no behavioral problem and only required minimal assistance. Joe never asked for special treatment and always wanted to be seen like the other kids: he did not want to stand out. But to society Joe had physical *stigmas* at a time when such characteristics were looked down upon, and during an era when little was done to accommodate the "Joes" of the world. Joe was independent and could walk the streets comfortably and he loved to play sports, especially baseball. He would stand at the plate and take pitches, and had an amazing knack for being able to hit the ball. He could also catch the ball and had an equally impressive sense of where the ball was in the air. By the time Joe was denied his formal education he was more than capable, physically and emotionally of carrying on his life like that of a healthy child, and he loved life. But shortly after being removed from his education, which also meant his friends (Joe was popular and loved by his peers), Joe's health started to deteriorate to the point that he became weaker with each year, but his spirits were good and his courage admirable; most admirable. It was also at this time when Joe quit growing and his younger brother would eventually surpass his height. So here was a youngster on the verge of his teenage years who was now only four foot, eight inches tall, visually impaired, and without access to one of the most crucial aspects of adolescence in the United States, a formal education, and all that goes with it: learning: friendships; sports; a future; and, girls. As he watched his brother age and have the advantage of all the good and not so good things that happen to children as they grow older, Joe was increasingly the victim of being left in the dust, having few friends and basically little social life, except that which he had with his family and the friends of his brother who were kind to Joe. From about age 10 to just before his death at 20, Joe's diabetes worsened and he experienced numerous diabetic comas and shocks. He was frequently bedridden and the occasional target of comments made about his slight stature and eyesight. Some of these comments were directed at his parents. For example, once Joe's father was chided by another individual about "sitting in the first row in church just so the family could be seen." Of course the explanation was that the family sat in the first pew to make it easier for Joe to see the altar and for him to receive communion (Joe was most likely 95% visually impaired but his parents at least wanted him to see the little he could at church). As Joe's physical health became worse, so did his mental health. Joe simply was not "Joe." He was not his usual happy self, and he appeared to be losing his confidence and zest for life. During his last few years Joe became incontinent, frequently wetting the bed, and he became so weak he was almost an invalid. He required constant care and was often rushed to the hospital because of shocks or comas. Just three months before his 21st

birthday Joe's health was so bad that he could no longer fight the good fight, and he passed away on May 8th, 1967, just three weeks before his younger brother, the author of this text, graduated from high school. But it must be mentioned that even given his enormous pain, pain emanating not only from his physical condition but also from the stigmas he faced in our society, Joe was courageous and loving to his family, even to the end. He was and is an incredible role model, and his example is used in this chapter.

MENTAL DISORDER AND PHYSICAL DISABILITY: AN OVERVIEW

Just because some individuals have mental disorders and physical disabilities, does this mean they are deviant? How could it be that Joe was a deviant? Part of the answer lies in the term used when discussing Joe: *stigma.* Throughout history persons with both physical disabilities and mental disorders have been *stigmatized* by society, often on the basis of such primitive thinking that they were demonized. After all, they would not have these issues if it wasn't for the insertion of the devil into their very beings and souls, right? But stigmas are about social reactions, and history is replete with examples of the way that people have defined, constructed, and reacted to the mentally ill, and those with physical disabilities. So when sociologists study mental disorders and physical disabilities they often examine *the role of society in constructing worldviews* of the mentally and physically disabled, and what the consequences are for the people they are stigmatizing. Sociologists also study the ways that the *stigmatized react* to their own stigmatization, in other words how they *cope with and manage* their societal effected self identities. Of course, sociologists are interested in mental disorders and physical disabilities, per se, meaning they study such issues as being visually and hearing impaired, physical handicaps, depression, and anxiety disorders *in and of themselves.* Mental disorders are covered first.

Mental Disorders

The Diagnostic and Statistical Manual of Mental Disorders-IV (DSM-IV): The Professional Construction of Mental Disorders

In order to understand mental disorders it is important to comprehend how mental disorders are *"created," refined,* and *agreed* upon by psychiatrists and other mental health professionals. In 1952, The American Psychiatric Association on Nomenclature and Statistics published the first edition of *The Diagnostic and Statistical Manual of Mental Disorders,* or DSM-I. Since then there have been three additional editions of this manual, with DSM-IV published in 1994 (1994, xxvii). The DSM manuals are a thorough and comprehensive coverage of known mental disorders (MD), but attention here is how these disorders are *agreed upon* and *constructed.* But first the definition of mental disorder is presented as defined in the DSM-IV. Mental disorder is (1994, xxxi):

> a clinically significant behavioral or psychological syndrome or pattern that occurs in an individual and that is associated with present distress (e.g., a painful symptom) or disability (i.e., impairment in one or more areas of functioning) or with a significantly increased risk of suffering death, pain, disability, or an important loss of freedom. In addition,

this syndrome or pattern must not be merely an expectable or culturally sanctioned response to a particular event, for example, the death of a loved one. Whatever its original cause, it must currently be considered a manifestation of a behavioral, psychological, or biological dysfunction in the individual. Neither deviant behavior (e.g., political, religious, or sexual) nor conflicts that are primarily between the individual and society are mental disorders unless the deviance or conflict is a symptom of a dysfunction in the individual, as described above.

Working from this definition the professional psychiatric community proceeds to update its knowledge of mental disorders. For version IV, thirteen work groups were established to update and to refine previous knowledge of the mental disorders. These work groups consisted of five or more experts within their respective fields (i.e., mood disorders) with assistance from any where between 50 to 100 additional advisers whose task was to critique the efforts of the work groups. Examples of the work groups are the schizophrenia and other psychotic disorders work group; the substance abuse-related disorder work group; the personality disorders work group; and, the anxiety disorders work group (1994, 13–26). In development of the DSM-IV a number of other organizations had input into the process of updating knowledge about MD, and some of these are the American Nurses Association, the Occupational Therapy Association, the National Association of Social Workers, and international experts. Therefore, the final product is representative of contributions from a number of individuals and organizations (1994, xxiv).

The production of the DSM-IV entailed three extensive efforts on behalf of the 13 work groups. All groups undertook *literature reviews* on the different disorders since the

DSM-III was published in 1987. The literature reviews included numerous empirical studies of the different mental disorders, and are a major source in the development of the fourth manual. The second stage was *data reanalysis* that were undertaken when the review of the literature revealed a lack of or conflicting evidence concerning the resolution of an issue. *Field trials*, the third task undertaken by each work group, were also undertaken for the same reasons (i.e., conflicting evidence) and included 12 field trials in more than 70 sites involving more than 6,000 subjects (1994, xxvi-xxviii). The DSM-IV disorders are characterized into 16 major diagnostic classes such as sexual and gender identity disorders, dissociative disorders, and anxiety disorders. It does not work from any assumption the disorders are mutually exclusive, "with absolute boundaries dividing it from other mental disorders, or from no mental disorder" (1994, xxxi). The disorders are also divided into different types within a specific disorder, such as those listed below for *anxiety disorders*:

- panic disorder without agoraphobia (fear of open spaces)
- panic disorder with agoraphobia
- agoraphobia without history of panic disorder
- specific phobia
- social phobia
- obsessive-compulsive disorder
- posttraumatic stress disorder
- acute stress disorder
- generalized anxiety disorder
- anxiety disorder due to the general medical condition
- substance-induced anxiety disorder
- anxiety disorder (NOS)

What is more, the types as just described can be further subdivided into specific types such as that for "specific phobia," which

includes animal type, natural environment type, blood-injection-injury type, situational type, and other type (1994, 21). Therefore, the 16 diagnostic categories include *dozens of subtypes* that are grouped together for the purposes of planning treatment and predicting outcomes. This classification process is referred to as the "multiaxial assessment" and includes the following axes (1994, 27):

- Axis I: Clinical Disorders and Other Conditions That May Be a Focus of Clinical Attention
- Axis II: Personality Disorders and Mental Retardation
- Axis III: General Medical Conditions
- Axis IV: Psychosocial and Environmental Problems
- Axis V: Global Assessment of Functioning

In addition, an individual's current diagnosis can be specified as mild, moderate, severe, in partial remission, and in full remission, with the first three (mild, moderate, severe) differentiated in terms of the degree of impairment in social or occupational functioning. "In partial remission" signifies that few of the symptoms or signs of a disorder are still present, and in "full remission" specifies there are no longer any symptoms or signs of a disorder (1994, 2). Publication of *The Diagnostic and Statistical Manual-IV* is a major undertaking that entails the efforts of numerous mental health professionals, whose task is to improve knowledge of the various mental disorders so that they can be more effectively diagnosed and treated. Listed below are the mental disorders included in the DSM-IV. Some of the specific types of mental disorders subsumed within each category are identified for the purposes of clarification (1994, 13–25):

- Disorders Usually First Considered in

Infancy, Childhood and Adolescence (i.e., mental retardation; learning disorders; attention-deficit and disruptive behavior disorders)

- Delerium, Dementia, and Amnestic and Other Cognitive Disorders
- Mental Disorders Due to a Medical Condition Not Elsewhere Classified
- Substance-Related Disorders (i.e., alcohol-related disorders; caffeine-related disorders; opioid-induced disorders; polysubstance-related disorder)
- Schizophrenia and Other Psychotic Disorders (i.e., delusional disorder; shared psychotic disorder)
- Mood Disorders (i.e., depressive disorders; bipolar disorders)
- Anxiety Disorders (i.e., panic disorders; obsessive-compulsive disorder)
- Somatoform Disorders (i.e., pain disorder; hypochondriasis).
- Factitious Disorders
- Dissociative Disorders (i.e., dissociative amnesia; depersonalization disorder)
- Sexual and Identity Disorders (i.e., sexual arousal disorders; sexual pain disorders; gender identity disorders)
- Eating Disorders (anorexia nervosa; bulimia nervosa)
- Sleep Disorders
- Impulse-Control Disorders Not Elsewhere Classified
- Adjustment Disorders
- Personality Disorders (i.e., paranoid personality disorder; antisocial personality disorder; avoidant personality disorder)

Two very important question are: "what is the prevalence of mental disorders in the United States?", "and do mental disorders vary by demographic factors such as age, race, gender and social class?"

Definitions of Mental Disorders

Listed below are definitions of several of the major and most common mental disorders, adapted from the DSM-IV (only some of the types of disorders within each category are mentioned).

Disorders Usually First Diagnosed in Infancy, Childhood, or Adolescence: These are disorders that begin before adulthood, and in addition to those listed above (i.e., mental retardation) include stuttering, sleepwalking, and bedwetting.

Schizophrenia: Is characterized by delusions or hallucinations, and includes deterioration from previous levels of functioning. Normally symptoms exist for more than six months, and include classic psychosis and brief psychotic disorder.

Mood Disorders: This disorder includes major depression and the bipolar disorders, and is also known as affective disorders, involving extremes in the emotional state of individuals.

Anxiety Disorders: Includes the phobias, acute stress disorder, panic attacks, and obsessive-compulsive disorder, all which share the same common symptom; anxiety.

Psychosexual Disorders: These are mental disorders that involve sexual arousal, usually by some objects or situations, and it also includes disorders involving sexual dysfunctioning. This is a large category which also encompasses exhibitionism, pedophilia, and sexual masochism.

Personality Disorders: This is a category for a variety of abnormal or deviant behaviors that usually cannot be diagnosed as psychotic or neurotic. Personality disorders are also referred to as character disorder or sociopathic/psychopathic disorder, with disregard for society's rules as its most extant characteristic. Its cause is thought to be a lack of moral development and includes con men, serial killers, and pimps.

Psychophysiologic Disorders: These are disorders that involve problems for which there is no physical explanation such as the inability to walk, paralysis, and headaches. Often known as psychosomatic illness, the symptoms can range from relatively minor to severe.

Data on Mental Disorders in the United States

Overview

Millions of Americans suffer from or have experienced a mental disorder. One in four adults, or *26 percent* of the adult population of the United States have some kind of mental disorder in any given year, translating to nearly *58 million* Americans. When it comes to serious mental disorders (those impairing social and occupational functioning), one in 17 persons are affected, and mental disorders are the number one cause of disability in the United States and Canada. In addition, many individuals are believed to meet the criteria for two or more mental disorders, nearly *29 million* Americans. Breaking this down further it can be said that *one in five Americans* experience a mental disorder during one year's period, and *one in five children and adolescents* also experience a mental health disorder in any given year. These numbers are just the tip of the iceberg. At least *15 percent* of the adult population of the United States uses a mental health service in a year, and the costs for treating mental disorders exceeds *$100 billion* annually (www.nimh.gov/health/statistics/index/shtml 2004).

In terms of the disorders Americans are most likely to experience in a given year, *anxiety disorders* are number one. Eighteen percent of Americans 18 years of age and older suffer from some form of anxiety dis-

order which includes but is not limited to phobias, panic disorders, posttraumatic stress disorder, and obsessive-compulsive disorder. Specific disorders (i.e., animal type; natural environment type) account for just under half of all anxiety disorders with social phobias (fear of people) a close second. As a matter of fact, the two combined comprise over 85 percent of all anxiety disorders. Approximately 9.5 percent of Americans 18 years and older have a *mood disorder*, with "major depressive disorder" by far the most common. Just under 9 percent of adult Americans suffer from *impulse-control disorder*, which includes oppositional-defiant disorder, conduct disorder, attention-deficit/hyperactivity disorder, and intermittent-control disorder, and nearly 4 percent of adults in the United States have a *substance abuse disorder*, including alcohol abuse, alcohol dependence, drug abuse and drug dependence. If the percentages for the types of disorders are summed they will exceed 40 percent, well beyond the 26 percent figure for Americans suffering in a year from mental disorders, but please remember that nearly half of the individuals *have two or more* mental disorders (www.mentalhealth.samhsa.gov/publications/allpubs/SMA06-4195/chp15table1.asp 2004). It is also worthy to note that of the four major types of disorders just discussed and the subtypes within each (anxiety, mood, impulse-control, and substance) that many individuals are given a *severe rating* for their disorder, and the severe guideline tends to be greater than the ratings for "moderate" and "mild," for all four types and their subtypes. For example, for panic disorder (anxiety disorder) the percentages are (rounded) 45, 27, and 27 for severe, moderate and mild respectively, and for posttraumatic stress disorder the percentages are 36, 32, and 30 (anxiety disorder). For any *mood disorder* which includes depression and bipolar disorders, the percentages are 45, 40, and 15. This pattern exists for the impulse-control disorders and substance disorders.

Demographic Data for Adults: Age, Gender, Race/Ethnicity, Community, and SES: Any 12-Month Disorder

Based on a scientifically selected sample of approximately 9,200 adults 18 years of age and over studied during a 12-month period, it is reported there are *statistically significant differences* among adults by *age* for the prevalence of mental disorders. The 18–29 year age cohort has the highest percentage of Americans 18 and older reporting some type of mental disorder (4.4%), and *the percentages decline by age after that.* The percentages for individuals 30–44, 45–59 and 60 and over are 3.6, 2.6, and 1.0, respectively. There are also statistically significant differences by *gender* with 1.4 percent of adult women reporting a mental disorder (12-month period) compared with 1.0 percent for males (clarified later). There are no statistically significant differences in 12-month reporting of mental illness among Hispanic, African American, White and "other" Americans. Therefore, when looking at the *general* picture (any 12-month disorder), mental disorders are not reported to vary by *racial* or *ethnic* background. Breaking down SES into its component parts, it is reported there is a statistically significant difference in mental disorders by level of *educational achievement,* with college-educated individuals experiencing a lower probability of suffering from mental disorders, and lower *income* persons more likely to suffer from MD than individuals in upper income categories. Mental disorder also varies by *marital status* with never married, divorced, and separated individuals experiencing higher rates of MD than married people. Finally, MD is not found to vary by type of *community* or community size, i.e.

urban, suburban, rural (www.mentalhealth.samhsa.gov/publications/allpubs/SMA06-4195/chp1table2.asp 2004). So where does this leave us? The rate of mental disorder in the adult population of the United States, *as measured over a 12-month period,* will differ dependent on the variable under consideration. Mental disorder varies by age, gender, education, marital status, and income, but it does not vary by race/ethnicity and community size. A further look at *two* of these issues, gender and social class is now addressed.

In *general,* there isn't much difference between males and females when it comes to mental disorders, however the statistically significant difference reported above reflects differences in a limited number of mental disorders *that impact the overall picture by gender.* For example, *women* have higher rates of *depression, anxiety attacks, and posttraumatic stress disorder. Men* are more likely to suffer from *antisocial personalities, paranoia, and substance abuse disorders* (Norris et al., 2002; Younkers and Gurguis, 1995) Why is this the case? According to Sharon Schwartz (1999) the differences have to do with social roles. Schwartz argues that the role of women in American society is *more restrictive and oppressive,* and as a result women are more likely to experience depression and anxiety attacks, and as a result to hurt themselves. Men on the other hand have *more open and liberating roles* and are socialized to be more assertive and aggressive, and this can result in antisocial personalities where they take their emotions out on others.

The data above report variations in mental disorders by education and income status, two important indicators of socioeconomic status and social class. For years sociologists have been able to confirm the relationship between lower SES and mental illness (Barker, Manderscheid, Gendershot, 1992; Farris and Dunham, 1938; Hollingshead and Redlich, 1958; Horwitz and Scheid, 1999;

Leighton, Harding, Macklin, Macmillan, Leighton, 1963; Srole, Langer, Michael, Kirkpatrick, Oppler, and Rennie, 1978), and as a matter of fact this is one of the most consistent findings reported in the sociology of mental health. People from the lower social strata are both more likely to be mentally ill and to be labeled as such (Littlejohn, 2004). There are two explanations for this phenomenon. The first called *social causation* purports that being in the lower class causes mental illnesses because of the stress that accompanies factors such as poverty and unemployment. In addition, the poor are more likely to experience infectious diseases, neurological impairments, and the lack of quality mental health treatment. The second explanation is what is called *social selection or drift*, where individuals with mental disorders *fall down into-drift-into* lower-class life (Link, Lennon, and Dohrenwend, 1993; Rogers and Mann, 1993). This explanation is the reverse of the first, since its position is mental illness forces some persons into a spiral of downward social mobility.

Children and Adolescent Mental Disorders in the United States

Please consider the following data (*MMWR Weekly* 2008; Ohio State University Medical Center 2008; SAMHSA's National Health Information Center):

- One in five children and adolescents have a mental disorder.
- Three percent of children and 8 percent of adolescents suffer from depression, and the recurrence rate of children and adolescents with depression is quite high, with up to 40 percent surfacing within two years, and 70 percent by adulthood.
- The most common mental health disorders in children and adolescents are anxiety disorders.

- Attention Deficit and Hyperactivity Disorder (ADHD) is one of the most common mental disorders among children and adolescents, with estimates ranging from two to 18 percent of children and adolescents suffering from ADHD.
- Two major eating disorders, anorexia nervosa and bulimia nervosa are common among American children and adolescents.
- Two-thirds of children and adolescents with major depressive disorder suffer from an additional MD such as dysthymia (severe depressive disorder), an anxiety disorder, a substance abuse disorder, or a disruptive or antisocial disorder.
- As noted in Chapter 9, children and adolescents are at risk for suicide.

A major question becomes why is it that children experience mental disorders? There is no easy answer to this question, but it appears a combination of *social, environmental and biological* factors contribute to MD in younger people. This includes being exposed to environmental toxins; stresses related to the hardships of life such as poverty and discrimination; the loss of people one is close to through death, divorce and broken relationships; being the victims of violence, such as physical or sexual abuse; and, witnessing violence such as drive-by shootings and assaults. The *signs* involved in mental disorders reveal much about their substance and include when a child is troubled by feeling sad, hopeless, very angry and worthless. Signs also include when children and adolescents go through *major changes* such as experiencing suicidal thoughts, decline in school performance, and persistent nightmares and poor concentration. In addition, there are some major *behavioral indicators or clues* and these include substance abuse, killing animals, and committing criminal acts without regard for the well-being of others

(SAMHSA's National Health Information Center).

Depression is a major health problem in children and adolescents, and its explanations are now briefly addressed. The exact causes of depression in the very young are not known precisely, but appear to include *family and genetic factors, gender differences, biology, and cognitive factors.* Based on data from mental health clinics and patients it is estimated the children of parents who are depressed are up to *three times more likely* to experience depression, thus giving some credence to the position that depression has roots in *genetics and the family.* It is also believed that between 20 and 50 percent of depressed children and adolescents emanate from families where there is a history of the mental disorder. As previously noted there are also *gender differences* in the types of mental disorders and these show up in children and adolescents, with girls more likely to suffer from depression. Once again it is reported the greater vulnerability to losses of social relationships for girls, and the emphasis they place on positive relationships apparently exposes them to higher rates of depression than is the case for boys. *Biological* explanations, such as abnormalities in the pituitary function, although more heavily researched with adults, may contribute to childhood and adolescent depression. Greater attention has been placed on the neuroendocrine area and depression in children and adolescents, where research has examined the connections between neuroendocrine cells and factors such as stress. One additional explanation for depression in children and adolescents is *cognitive factors,* or interest in a "mindset," or a way of perceiving external events. This involves taking a *pessimistic view* of the world and entails blaming oneself for negative events, and just generally being down about most things. Individuals with this type of mindset often will see the successes of oth-

ers as being the works of someone else, and they tend to interpret positive events in a negative vein. This mindset is referred to as a *pessimistic attribution* bias, and debate ensues over whether or not it precedes or is a result of being depressed. It does not appear in children until after age five which may account for the very low suicide rate in early childhood (www.surgeongeneral.gov/librarymentalhealth/chapter3/sec5.html).

A Sociological Approach to Mental Illness: The Work of Thomas J. Scheff

Much of what was stated above as causes or explanations of mental disorder tend toward a medical model, or biologically-based set of explanations for MD. The exception is when gender differences in MD were addressed, with the emphasis slanting more toward a social scientific perspective on causation. In 1966, Thomas J. Scheff offered what has been a major sociological paradigm on mental disorders, one that places strong emphasis on *social context* in understanding MD. Scheff contends that much of what psychiatry labels as mental disorder is really nothing more than rule-breaking, or "a class of acts, violations of social norms, and deviance to particular acts which have been publicly and officially labeled as norm violations" (1966, 33). In arguing this point Scheff observed that societies have a plethora of terms for categorizing the violation of rules, but there are times cultures lack any identifiers for such violations, resulting in a residue of acts (the leftovers) which have yet to be labeled or classified. For example, societies have rules or norms relevant to crimes such as theft and murder, but they may not take into account such things as witchcraft, spirit possession, or even mental illness, leading Scheff to write "the diverse kinds of rule-breaking for which our society provides no explicit label, and which therefore, sometimes lead to the labeling of the violator as mentally ill, will be considered to be technically residual rule-breaking (1966, 34). This is what Scheff means by the term *residual deviance*, or those acts that fall outside the boundaries of what society knows of and has already labeled as rule violations, *but may result in the convenient label of mental illness*. Scheff, reflecting on the work of Erving Goffman writes of "away" or a time when individuals are momentarily disengaged from the social world around them, and are in a "play-like world" that can be characterized as day-dreaming. Individuals are adrift, so to speak, out there in their own thoughts, and this may be grounds for labeling them as being in an hallucinogenic state, or being mentally ill, when indeed they are just "away" for awhile. A subset of the "away" is occults, where at times people may communicate with spirits, and for doing so they may be labeled as mentally ill (1966, 35–36).

Scheff identified the origins of residual rule-breaking (RRB) as arising from fundamentally diverse sources such as organic, psychological, external stress, and volitional acts of innovation or defiance. Since Scheff devoted much of his criticism to the first two, our attention is directed at external stress and volitional acts of innovation or defiance. External stress can result from the use of drugs such as LSD and psychotic symptoms that may be derived from sleeplessness and starvation. Acts of defiance may be found in certain social movements that do things in unconventional ways, such as when 14 members of the Dada movement were engaged in a poetry-reading contest and all read their poetry at the same time. This may seem harmless except their behavior resulted in a riot among the audience who attended the event, which was held during the Weimar Republic. So what is the point? None of the situations mentioned above entailed mental illness, instead it all involved residual deviance: out-of-the-ordinary acts for which previously held notions of what is normative and acceptable behavior is lacking, *but for which the label mental illness can be attached* (1966, 39–47). In support of the argument the majority of what is called mental illness is RRB, Scheff cited a number of studies that reported conflicting data on the prevalence of MD among the less fortunate and he wrote there are many individuals in society who do such things as "fly off the handle, who imagine fantastic events, or who hear voices or see visions" but are not labeled as mentally ill by themselves or by others (1966, 47). One of Scheff's observations is most RRB is of a *temporary nature*, lasting maybe only days, and therefore should not be recognized as symptomatic of mental illness. In this latter respect he discussed head-banging, temper tantrums, biting, and fantasy playmates or pets by children that do not acquire stable behavior patterns over time (1966, 52). If what Scheff has theorized is correct then a great deal of what is contained in the DSM-IV should be eliminated.

From Thomas J. Scheff to Thomas S. Szasz: The Myth of Mental Illness

Scheff and Szasz—now that can be confusing, not only in name but in substance. Six years before Thomas J. Scheff published his theory of mental illness, Thomas S. Szasz rocked the world of psychiatry and psychology with his conception of *mental illness as a myth*, that mental disorders were really *problems with living* (1960, 113–115). In posing the question "Is there such a thing as mental illness?", Szasz responded "there is not," noting that in the psychiatric sciences mental illnesses are treated like any other disease, which to Szasz is a major fatal flaw in thinking (1960, 113). For Szasz, mental illness refers to the undesirable behaviors, feelings, and thoughts of individuals, whereas the term disease conjures up notions of biological defects in animals, plants, and humans. With that in mind there can be no such thing as mental illness, since illness connotes disease that could be treated like cancer or diabetes. Szasz wrote "Since medical action is designed to correct only medical deviations, it seems logically absurd to expect that it will help solve problems whose very existence had been defined and established on nonmedical grounds" (1960, 115). Therefore, what is meant by the word "illness?" Szasz argued that illness simply suggests "deviation from some clearly defined norms," be they deviations from bodily or mental illnesses (1960, 114). When referring to the deviation from bodily illnesses, Szasz stated the norm is the "structural and functional integrity of the human body," but when referring to deviation from mental illness the norm is psycho-social-and ethical in context (1960, 113–114). This leads to the question of *who* defines the norms and deviation, and Szasz observed it is the *patient* who comes to the conclusion that he or she has deviated from some important norm, and a *psychotherapist* whose job is to treat the patient. Szasz used artists as an example who are facing a work inhibition and conclude they need to get a jump-start therapy from a mental health professional in order to get motivated once again. So, *one source* of the deviation is "us," who arrive at the conclusion that something is not right in our lives, and help is needed. The *second source* of the deviation from norms is *other people*, including physicians, relatives, friends, and legal authorities, who have decided the patient is some type of deviant. But rather than write-off the above as obvious examples of mental illness, Szasz argued it is problems with living, coping, that we all face at some time or another: "The notion of mental illness thus serves mainly to obscure the everyday fact that life for most people is a continuous struggle, not

for biological survival, but for a 'place in the sun,' 'peace of mind,' or some other human value" (1960, 118). Thus to reflect on the work of Szasz, it is observed that life has its ups and downs, and our behaviors and emotional states will both coincide with and reflect the daily challenges posed by living. Just like the example of artists who lose their inhibition to be creative and productive, all of us go through periods where how we act and think could be interpreted as requiring help from the mental health community, *when indeed this is no more than problems with living.*

Disabilities

Are people with disabilities deviants? Social perceptions of groups of people, whether accurate or not, shape human behavior, attitudes, and relationships. Historically, for people with disabilities, their disabilities became their master statuses. They were labeled as deaf, blind, crippled, or handicapped forgetting that they were human beings. These master statuses became more important than any other qualities or characteristics they possessed. Societies could not get past the disability to see the person. Their disability became their social persona, regardless of what kind of person they really were. Without question, the social perceptions of people having disabilities have influenced the parameters in which they have lived throughout time. Some of these social perceptions or if you will stereotypes have been favorable, such as the belief that people who are blind have greater insight and wisdom than those who can see. Other social perceptions have had negative social consequences for people with disabilities, such as people who are deaf are uneducable and less intelligent. Obviously, neither positive nor negative stereotypes are based on fact.

Historically, societies have been very

good at separating and limiting people with disabilities from participating in the mainstream. For centuries, western societies warehoused people with mental illness, developmental disabilities, or those with other challenges in institutions, hospitals, special schools, jails, or prisons. Historically, there also have been periods when people with disabilities were relatively invisible to mainstream society. They existed below the social radar screen and as long as they were not perceived as a threat, they were essentially ignored or in some cases hidden from society. Whether the intention was to help them or rid society of them, the net result was the same. Their rights, freedom, and participation were all restricted. By defining them as a distinct group, we separate them from mainstream society. The more separated they are from mainstream society, they less familiar they become and the more likely society is to stereotype them. Societies have treated them as social deviants. Even in societies where people with disabilities were or are free to move about the mainstream and had rights, they remained socially isolated and viewed as different. Being different sets them aside from full participation, consequently for those defined as having disabilities, much of their lives is spent diminishing and overcoming these perceived differences.

The disability rights movement in recent decades has been very much a struggle fought on several dimensions. One dimension has been the struggle of people with disabilities for inclusion or participation in mainstream society. People with disabilities have found it necessary to fight to be included in the societies in which they have lived. They seek a voice in how they live their lives. Ironically, it is the same societies that stereotype and limit them, that they seek acceptable and full membership.

Overcoming prejudice and discrimination has been another struggle. Similar to

the struggles characteristic of the American Civil Rights, Women's Equality Opportunity, or other movements, people with disabilities have fought prejudice and discrimination. A major milestone for the disability rights movement was the enactment of the Americans with Disabilities Act (ADA) of 1990. The ADA provides for equal access of people with disabilities to employment, public and private services, and other aspects of society. It also calls for reasonable accommodation for those needing adaptive devices or other considerations in the workplace or other settings.

Another dimension has been the debate over what constitutes a disability. It is debatable whether true disability rests with the individual or group or in the social perceptions of society at large. For example, today many members of the deaf community would argue that the absence of hearing is really not a disability at all and that they have effective and meaningful ways to communicate. They would further suggest that the hearing society is really the disabling force because it is the hearing society that forces individuals who are deaf into unnatural ways of communicating, such as lip reading and oral communication.

The odds are (if we do not have one already), we all will develop some degree of disability during our life spans. Our abilities to hear, see, think, move, and so forth become more challenging as we age. Thus, the social issue of disability becomes important to us all at the personal level. We should all take an interest in the civil rights of those having disabilities or challenges. Are people with disabilities deviants? Most in modern society would not hesitate to say no but some of their perceptions and behaviors would indicate otherwise. American society has made much progress in its perceptions and acceptance of people with disabilities but more needs to be done starting with the acknowledgement that people with disabilities are first and foremost members of society and deserve to be recognized as such. They need to be recognized as individuals who have and will continue to be contributing members to society.

The above thoughts are those of Herbert C. Covey whose *Social Perceptions of People with Disabilities in History* (1998) is one of the most inspiring and scholarly treatises to date on disabilities, and serves to inform the structure and organization of what is to be covered in this section. *When discussing disabilities the emphasis is to be placed on the societal reaction to persons who are disabled rather than on explaining the medical or biological nature of disabilities themselves.* As Dr. Covey so aptly stated "Social perceptions of people, whether accurate or not, shape human behavior, attitudes, and relationships. Historically, for people with disabilities, their disabilities became their master statuses. They were labeled as deaf, blind, crippled, or handicapped forgetting they were human beings. Their master statuses became more important than any other qualities or characteristics they possessed. Societies could not get past the disability to see the person. Their disability became their social persona, regardless of what kind of person they really were." Take for instance, Joe was judged and perceived largely on the basis of being visually impaired, short, and ill. Most people could not get beyond his disabilities to see and get to know the person inside; the real Joe; the true Joe. It was not uncommon for the ignorant to come up to Joe and to ask him how many fingers they were holding up, which was humiliating to him. Instead of engaging him in talk such as asking him about his interests, or his opinions on issues, he was seen and treated as a blind, short man. However, he could rattle off baseball statistics until the cows came home and he could discuss the great books, but few people ever sought to view him in any other light

than that of a disabled individual. It is these types of experiences that are addressed in this section, with *emphasis placed on the role society plays in stigmatizing the disabled.* Terms critical to understanding the subject at hand are presented next.

Definitions and Overview

Disabled; handicapped; impaired. What do they mean? It can become quickly obvious that many people run these terms together, using then interchangeably as if by doing so it doesn't matter, or others will not care or mind. But think about this for a moment. Calling someone handicapped? Doesn't that word imply something negative, such as the inability to do something? Joe was often referred to as being handicapped, and what usually followed was a self-fulfilling prophecy. Joe was socially constructed as being handicapped, and then society proceeded to treat him as such by cutting him off from gaining a formal education. But there are clear distinctions among the words disabled, handicapped and impaired, and a starting point is first to define what is meant by *ability*. *Ability* "refers to the individual's capacity both to learn new skills and behaviors and to perform previously learned skills and behavior. Individual differences in abilities may or may not be limited by disabling conditions. . . . Depending on the context in which it is used, the concept of ability may be defined narrowly or broadly. In the narrow sense ability refers to intellectual functioning, which is composed primarily of general intelligence (g) and other constructs such as verbal, numerical, spatial, and perceptual abilities. In the field of rehabilitation, ability is used in a broader sense to refer to those capabilities required to function in both living and vocational roles" (*Encyclopedia of Disability and Rehabilitation 1*, 1995). *Disability*, on the other hand "is a condition that impairs and imposes restrictions on a person's ability to function at normal or expected levels of mental or physical activity," and to be labeled *handicapped*, (which does not mean the same as being disabled) "refers to the presence of physical and social barriers constructed by individuals, institutions and societies that prevent people with disabilities from participating equally or fully in their environments" (1995, 257). What about *impairment?* According to Braddock and Parish (2001), "disability exists as it is situated within the larger social context, while *impairment* is a biological condition. The authors cite the important contribution by Leonard Davis that adds to the clarification between the two terms: "Disability is not so much the lack of a sense or the presence of a physical or mental impairment as it is the reception and construction of that difference. . . . An impairment is a physical fact, but a disability is a social construction. For example, lack of mobility is an impairment, but an environment without ramps turns that impairment into a disability . . . a disability must be socially constructed; there must be an analysis of what it means to have or lack certain functions, appearance and so on" (2001, 12). For many disabled individuals the result of the social constructions that impact and permeate their lives is *ableism*, or perhaps the most unknown of and unrecognized of the "isms" (i.e., racism, sexism, ageism). *Ableism* involves prejudice and discrimination against people with disabilities and emanates from individuals, communities, social institutions, and society at hand. There are a number of individuals who believe it is prejudice and discrimination directed against the disabled that is the primary obstacle preventing them from full participation in the social and economic environments in which they reside, rather than their physical impairments (*Encyclopedia of Disability 1*, 2006). Joe clearly had impairments: he was a diabetic

(not necessarily known on sight), visually impaired, and his adult height was four feet eight inches. He occasionally used a cane (which he hated to do since it furthered his stigmatization), read Braille in public, and toward the end of his life required significant assistance in order to get around. But, he was intelligent, articulate, funny, and if people could look beyond his noticeable impairments they might have been able to get lost in the other side of Joe, which as already stated was "the real Joe." *But this is the essence of the sociological interest in disabilities, and that is the way society reacts to those people with impairments, and the social constructions that can and have served to negatively affect them.* Think about this for a moment, some individuals without legs can downhill ski as can some people who are visually impaired. Hearing impaired individuals go to concerts, and theoretical physicist Stephen Hawking, one of the world's greatest geniuses suffers from Amyotrophic Lateral Sclerosis, a life-threatening degenerative illness. Hawking continues to marvel the scientific community with his research on unifying General Relativity with Quantum Mechanics, is mobile through a high technology wheelchair, and speaks with the support of a portable computer and voice synthesizer (Humphrey, 2006, 309). The list of the successfully disabled is endless, including the magnificent accomplishments of Erik Weihenmayer who has climbed Mount Everest, the world's highest mountain and seven other of the world's highest summits (*Weihenmayer is blind*). Unfortunately, history is replete with examples of the unfair and cruel treatment of the disabled that has not only stood in the way of their full integration into the social fabric, but also destroyed that possibility for many.

Disabilities can be either hidden, such as having diabetes or learning disabilities, or they can stand out such as in the case of Dr. Stephen Hawking or Joe, and the origins of disabilities will vary. *Congenital disabilities* are hereditary in origin, such as cystic fibrosis; *developmental disabilities*, which can become more serious with time, include conditions such as epilepsy and cerebral palsy that normally develop in individuals before age 22; and, *acquired disabilities* in which full mental and physical functioning are prevented, have their origins in accident, disease, or injury, and include paraplegia, quadriplegia, and severe brain damage. There are many different types of disabilities and from a *broad* perspective some of the most common include: Alzheimer's disease; autism; blindness and vision disorders; burns; childhood disabilities; communication disabilities; deafness and hearing impairment; eating disorders; head injuries; learning disorders; mental retardation; musculoskeletal disorders; neurological disorders; neuromuscular disorders; spinal cord injury; and stroke (*Encyclopedia of Disability and Rehabilitation 257*, 1995). There are three dominant perspectives on disabilities: the *medical and rehabilitative perspective; the legal perspective; and the social perspective*. The *medical and rehabilitative* perspective focuses on the role of the medical community in reversing, eliminating, or controlling disability through treatment, habilitation, and rehabilitation. This perspective recognizes functional limitations resulting from physical (e.g., mobility), sensory (e.g., vision, auditory), organic (e.g., diabetes, epilepsy, cerebral palsy), intellectual (e.g., learning), or psychiatric (e.g., schizophrenia, depression) impairment. The *legal perspective* whose most important recent example is the Americans with Disabilities Act (discussed later) entails legislation protecting the rights of individuals with disabilities, and ensuring justice through full participation in society for the disabled. The *social perspective* addresses the issues of prejudice, discrimination, and stigma that emanate from culture and society toward the disabled, and it also focuses on the myths and stereotypes concerning persons with disabilities and that they are victims, and all disabilities have their etiology in biological conditions. In addition, the social perspective also examines the effects of sociocultural-based stigmas on the self-perceptions of the disabled, and how the disabled react to these perceptions (1995, 259–260).

Disabilities in History

The societal reaction to persons with disabilities has been varied through history, and has differed within and between cultures and civilizations. *The Old Testament* offers contradictory notions concerning disabilities. Leviticus 9:14 states "Thou shalt not curse the deaf nor put a stumbling block before the blind, not maketh the blind to wander out of the path." Yet, in Deuteronomy 28: 15, 28–29 one finds . . . "if you do not carefully follow his commands and decrees . . . all these curses will come upon you: the Lord will afflict you with madness, blindness, and confusion of mind. At midday you will grope around like a blind man in the dark." Braddock and Parish write the disabled were believed to be unclean and were placed in the same category as prostitutes and menstruating women. Ironically at times persons with disabilities were allowed to participate in religious observances, while another strange twist came in the early Christian church, based on Romans 10:17 which states "So then faith cometh by hearing, and hearing by the word of God" rendering the hearing impaired as being without faith in the eyes of God (Braddock and Parrish, 2001, 14).

The back-and-forth societal reactions to and stigmatization of the disabled is also found among the *ancient Greeks and Romans*. Both civilizations harbored contradictory attitudes toward disability. For example, the ancient Greeks and Romans believed that babies born with congenital deformities was interpreted as a sign that the Gods were displeased with the parents, yet the Roman Emperor Claudius had severe congenital deformities, and the Spartans elected a near-dwarf as their king. On occasion and not nearly as widespread as once believed, infanticide was practiced among the Greeks for children with disabilities, but children *in general* were often put to death for economic reasons when there were too many of them for the culture to support. Among the Spartans infanticide was practiced with children born with serious physical deformities, *but* in Athens there is limited evidence that they were actually cared for and raised. In Sparta some children with disabilities did survive largely out of the fact that their deformities may not have become noticeable until early adulthood, and older adults with congenital disabilities were apparently present in Greece. Greeks wounded in war were expected to keep fighting since being mobile was not always necessary in combat, and there is evidence that prosthetic devices were used by individuals who were injured during combat (2001, 15–16). There were interesting developments among the Romans concerning disabilities. The property rights of the disabled were protected under early Roman law, and individuals who would today likely be classified as suffering from mental retardations were provided with guardians who would manage their affairs. The deaf who could speak were permitted to marry and own property, however hearing impaired persons incapable of speaking were denied many rights, and they were placed in the same categories with the mentally ill, infants, and individuals labeled as intellectually deficient. Later Roman law actually awarded rights to the disabled, and during the Roman Empire slaves who were short and who had intellectual disabilities were used by wealthy men as entertainment, normally as court jesters (2001, 16–17).

The vast span in time that ran from about the fourth through the fourteenth centuries, often referred to as the *medieval period and the middle ages*, also reflects the ambivalent nature of societies toward the disabled. The fourth through the sixth centuries saw hospices for the blind established in what is now called Turkey, Syria and France, and individuals with intellectual disabilities were housed and cared for in southern Turkey by Bishop Nicholas. Institutions for persons afflicted with Hansen's disease (leprosy) were sprinkled across parts of Europe, with Italy and Germany constructing hundreds of them by the Early Middle Ages, and in the thirteenth century persons with mental disabilities received care in family settings in the Belgian village of Gheel. But these rather positive developments speak only to limited progress during this 1000-year period since demonology also played a role in how the disabled were perceived and treated. Deafness, epilepsy, and mental illness among other disabilities were said to be caused by demons and to have their origins in the supernatural. For example, epilepsy was believed to be caused by the devil, exorcism was used with persons with mental disabilities, and by the early eleventh century the persecution and execution of thousands of witches occurred. These executions were generally undertaken by the Catholic Church but they also involved Protestant countries, and witch hunts were reported in colonial New England and were most likely directed at the mentally ill. The squalid conditions during the medieval period resulted in high levels of malnutrition and infectious diseases which no doubt contributed to many types of impairment, and the disabled, largely as a result of poverty were forced to the streets to beg, a practice some scholars have mistakenly said resulted from the disabilities themselves. Benevolence towards the disabled beggars was found in places like

France where their family and friends would carry them to spots to beg, and in England between the thirteenth and seventeenth centuries the Crown had differentiated between intellectual disability which included natural fools and idiots, and mental illness. The mentally ill and their property were protected by the Crown through Prerogativa Regis, but "idiots" and "lunatics" were not as fortunate since the Crown seized their land and any profits generated from it. The middle ages were also known for the rise in residential institutions for the poor, those with mental illnesses, and individuals who were separated from the general population as a result of leprosy (2001, 17–21). To say that the medieval period and the middle ages were ripe with contradictory beliefs about and treatment of the disabled would be an understatement.

The eras of the *Renaissance and the Enlightenment* brought with them a combination of continued stimatization of those with disabilities and gradual progress toward more humane care of the disabled. During these eras disabled persons deemed mentally ill, those suffering from intellectual deficiencies, and the hearing and visually impaired received significant attention. The Renaissance covered the fourteenth through the sixteenth centuries and was a hodgepodge of reactions to the disabled, including beating the heads of the mentally ill and the intellectually disabled as a method of treatment, and physicians would bore holes in the heads of the mentally ill in order to release the black bile or stones believed to be the cause of mental illness and conditions such as idiocy. What is more, other "treatments" included the use of earthworms that were fried with goose grease creating a solution that was dropped into the ears of the deaf, and at the start of seizures epileptics would ingest the warm gall of a dog or the brain of a mountain goat. All of this occurred

during the period of "rebirth," the Renaissance, which is said to have been an era of advances in science and in the study of anatomy and physiology. However, the day and age of the belief in demon possession as cause of some disabilities was still much alive, so it is no wonder that such primitive methods of treatment were used. Major figures from the Protestant Reformation such as Martin Luther and John Calvin reinforced the beliefs in demonism by arguing that mental illness was caused by Satan, and the mentally disabled were possessed. There were other developments as the Renaissance progressed, such as the education of deaf children of the rich in Spain and the Turkish Ottoman court. England applied the Poor Law of 1601 to the needy and disabled that placed support of these individuals into the hands of the local communities when families were unable to provide relief. The disabilities at hand included being lame, impotent, elderly, visually impaired, and intellectual deficiencies. Persons with mental illnesses did not fair as well, with many having a greater likelihood than the intellectually disabled of being incarcerated in houses of corrections, and in gaols. Workhouses were also established with the first opening in Bristol, England in 1697 and then spreading across Europe over the next two centuries. Even given the emergence and growth in workhouses the majority of care of the disabled and poor was still in the hands of families. Meanwhile, the United States experienced the rise of almshouses, starting in Boston in 1662 which served persons who were poor, visually impaired, hearing impaired, mentally ill, elderly, and orphaned (2001, 21–23). Like the historical eras before it, the Renaissance represented a combination of old and new ways of reacting to the disabled, and how they were perceived and treated was spotty and varied across Europe and the emerging nation to be called the United

States.

The Enlightenment or Age of Reason also represented a combination of humane yet archaic ways of reacting to the disabled. Schools for the visually and hearing impaired became common in Europe by the eighteenth century, especially in England and in France, and actually had their origins in Spain during the early sixteenth century under the guidance of the monk Pedro Ponce de Leon, who opened a school for the hearing impaired for the children of wealthy Spanish parents. Although he only taught 20 students, de Leon is credited with beginning a movement toward humane education of those with hearing disabilities. His teaching methods included a manual alphabet and conventional signing and helped to pave the way for more modern techniques for educating the hearing impaired, as is seen in the use of signs for educating the hearing disabled in France in the mid-eighteenth century. Although signing was emerging as a major technique for communication and education, the founder of the French school for the hearing impaired, Michael de L'Epee worked under more ancient assumptions concerning the causes of hearing impairment, advocating the hearing disabled were the ancestors or more primitive species, and the sign language that he helped to advance was considered by de L'Epee as a primitive form of communication, but nonetheless suited for those whom could not hear. During the seventeenth and eighteenth centuries similar schools were opened in Germany and Italy, and in 1784 the first residential school for the visually impaired opened in Paris, and schools would follow in England, Germany, Ireland, Spain, and a number of other European nations. Valentin Hauy, who pioneered the school in Paris introduced a first model of what would become Braille, and in the United States schools for the visually impaired opened in

Boston and New York City in 1832, in Pennsylvania in 1833, and Ohio in 1887 (2001, 28).

Whereas the above is evidence of more positive care of some disabled, distinctions still existed relative to mental illnesses and intellectual disabilities. The words "idiots" and "madmen" dominated the thinking of the times, and hospitals for" idiots," "cripples," and the visually impaired surfaced in England during the eighteenth centuries. John Locke was instrumental in fostering leading views of those with intellectual and mental disabilities, arguing the former had lost their ability to reason, and that the mentally disabled suffered less from this deficiency and more from forming wrong or bad ideas together. In Germany madhouses were combined with penal institutions that required inmates to work, and in Holland and Germany the wealthy had their mentally disabled family members placed in private facilities, in order to circumvent the embarrassment and dishonor they would face as a result of having loved ones who were classified as mentally sick. Colonial America experienced several different themes through the seventeenth and eighteenth centuries, circumventing the English Poor Law by forcing the poor and the mentally ill from residing and begging in their communities, but in Delaware houses existed for providing relief for mentally disabled individuals, thus showing the type of ambivalence and inconsistency in the treatment of disabled persons that had existed for centuries, especially in Europe. Benjamin Rush, a famous America psychiatrist implemented "modern" strategies for caring for the mentally ill that included bloodletting, low diet, purges, emetics (agents that cause vomiting), and cold baths and showers. However, two of his most noted treatments were the *gyrator machine* used with "torpid madness," employed to increase the heartbeat to 120 beats per minute and to spin the body, and the *tranquilizing chair* that was used to reduce sensory-motor activity (obviously a step up from drilling holes in heads as previously discussed). In some places *"bidding-out"* was used for persons with mental disorders and intellectual deficiencies, and it entailed auctioning off such persons to the lowest bidder who would care for them while paid the amount of the bid. This practice was common across the country but was curtailed in the 1820s because it became too costly. Yet in 1793 Kentucky passed legislation that authorized payment of $75 to families to care for their mentally or intellectually disabled loved ones, and this continued into the late 1920s. However, probably as a result of ignorance, labeling and stigmatization were a part of this system, with the mentally ill or intellectually impaired dichotomized as either "lunatics" or "idiots." Progress seemed always to be countered by old ways of societal reaction (2001, 23–27).

The *nineteenth century* was characterized by progress and threats toward the disabled. Institutions for the mentally and intellectually disabled, visually and hearing impaired, and physically disabled were found in Europe and in the United States, and words such as "idiot," "lunatic," and "deaf and dumb" became or remained part of the vernacular when referring to individuals with disabilities. Although much transpired during this period, two negative issues deserve attention: *freak shows and eugenics. Freak shows* existed in Europe and the United States and speak loudly of the way that disabled persons were perceived. Physically and mentally disabled persons were sold to circuses and fairs, put on display, and wild tales of their origins were told that only accentuated and fueled the belief in the inferiority of the disabled. By attending freak shows people could gain comfort in their own perceptions of what is normal, and fortunately freak

shows began to dissipate by the late 1800s, with a few circuses and fairs still exhibiting them in the 1940s in the United States. The *eugenics* movement coincided with Mendelian genetics and the rise of Social Darwinism, and saw itself played out by associating crime and deviance with physical and mental characteristics of people that were theorized to be the etiology of criminal behaviors and mental deficiencies. What is more, in the United States many physicians refused to treat infants with disabilities and birth defects, and in England in 1886 the "Idiots Act" was passed making the incarceration of persons with "mental defects" more plausible, and the passage of the Education Act of 1899 resulted in the growth of institutions for the mentally ill and intellectually disabled (2001, 37–39).

Advocacy for the hearing impaired was a landmark part of the 1800's in the United States and in England with the development of the British Deaf and Dumb Association (now the British Association of the Deaf), formed largely to oppose a ban placed on sign language in educating hearing impaired children, as well as to fight for broader rights, especially as they related to greater overall autonomy for the hearing disabled. In Boston, Alexander Graham Bell had championed *speech-based education* and the elimination of sign language so that the hearing impaired could "pass" as persons who could hear, and the ban on the use of sign language was a result of a resolution passed in 1880 at the International Congress on Education of the Deaf that was held in Italy. One of the world's most premier institutions for the hearing impaired, Gallaudet University, was made possible in 1864 when President Abraham Lincoln signed legislation authorizing the Columbia Institution for the Instruction of the Deaf and the Dumb and the Blind to confer college degrees (2001, 35–36). The eugenics movement and

Social Darwinism played no small part in the lives of the hearing impaired, and this was apparent in the debate between the "manualists" and the "oralists," the latter claiming that the hearing disabled were less evolved-inferior-to those who could hear. Ironically, the advocacy of Bell for oralism gave rise to greater solidarity among the hearing disabled, and one manifestation of this was the publication of newspapers for and by those unable to hear, and their circulation across residential schools for the hearing disabled. In 1893, 29 of these schools had at least 35 newspapers. Bell did not stop at trying to eradicate manualism, since he was also a strong proponent of preventing marriages among the hearing impaired (2001, 39).

Reflecting the dramatic increase in the population of the United States, in a 45-year period from 1850–1895, 55 psychiatric institutions were opened and soon afterward faced serious problems with overcrowding. One reason for this was that in 1840 the census began enumerating individuals as either "idiotic" and "insane," and just 10 years earlier it began counting the number of hearing and visually impaired in the American population. A good portion of the increase in persons labeled mentally ill was due to the fact that census enumerators were paid more for each person they counted as mentally ill or intellectually disabled. The result was a massive increase in the population counted as insane and intellectually deficient. From 1870 to 1880 the proportion of the population enumerated as insane rose from 97 to 183 per 100,000 population, while the proportion counted as intellectually disabled experienced an increase of 64 to 153 per 100,000 population. Perhaps the most tragic aspect of the role of the census in impacting the count of the mentally ill was that in some communities *all African Americans* were counted as insane (2001, 35).

The *twentieth century* represents the best and the worst treatment of the disabled. Sterilizations, shock therapy, electroshock therapy, physical abuse, and incarceration and institutionalization of the disabled are examples of the worst practices. Legislation, court decisions, the formation of organizations such as the Red Cross and Goodwill Industries, and deinstitutionalization are manifestations of more humane developments relative to the disabled. Focus here is placed on events in the United States.

Between 1907 and 1949 there were over 47,000 *sterilizations* of persons with disabilities in the United States, and this occurred in only *30 states*. Physicians removed ovaries and Fallopian tubes from women diagnosed with depression, hysteria, epilepsy, insanity related to childbirth, and nymphomania in light of overwhelmingly documentation that these practices were completely ineffective, not to mention dangerous and inhumane. The United States Supreme Court even got into the act of supporting sterilization, and in *1929 in Buck v. Bell* it affirmed the right of the states to conduct sterilizations on persons with intellectual disabilities, and the sterilization program that would eventually go into effect in *Nazi Germany* was modeled after that developed in *California* in 1933. It is estimated that up to 275,000 people with mental and physical disabilities were murdered by euthanasia by the Nazis, and between 300,000 and 400,000 were forcibly sterilized in the state of California as a result of the passage of the 1933 legislation (2001, 40).

Sterilizations were not the only questionable practices in use during the early to mid-part of the twentieth century. *Shock therapy* was undertaken on thousands of people using drugs such as insulin and metrazol to induce shock, under the assumption shock therapy would cure mental illness. In addition, malaria was also part of shock therapy treatment. *Electroshock therapy*, invented by the Italian Ugo Cerletti, was not widely used until the 1930s, and its strategy was to apply electricity to help persons with psychiatric conditions. Much of this was done in mental institutions or insane asylums which experienced significant increases in populations during the first 50 years of the 1900s, and many of these facilities were immense in size with 10 housing over 5,000 patients, 22 with a census of at least 4,000, 40 with populations of 3,000 persons, and an additional 475 hospitals housed at least 2,000 patients. The treatment of individuals in these institutions was often harsh, and their purposes frequently served no more than warehouse individuals that society otherwise had no clue how to help (2001, 41).

But all was not lost, and during the twentieth century a number of positive developments would occur in the perception and treatment and of the disabled. The *social model of disability* had part of its impetus among persons who were visually impaired as found in the writings of visually disabled Americans who exploited the view that it is not the condition of being without sight that is the only issue, instead it is the *societal reaction* to those with limited vision that is a major problem. The publication in 1966 of the classic sociological work *The Social Construction of Reality; A Treatise in the Sociology of Knowledge* greatly influenced the way that the disabled would be perceived and treated. Its authors, Peter L. Berger and Thomas Luckman offered insights into how the world around us is socially constructed, and the meanings that people attach to that world in everyday life. From this arose a more powerful understanding among the disabled and others that would lead to the recognition that much of the manner in which persons with disabilities were dealt with was based on *social constructions*, not scientific facts. During the 1950s and continuing until the present, *deinstitutionalization*

became more common and involved releasing mentally ill persons from institutions, largely as a result of improvements in antipsychotic drugs, and the growing awareness that because of labeling and stigmatization some of those patients never needed to be hospitalized in the first place. Of course, there were other factors that led to the decline in the census of mental facilities, including the use of penicillin to cure syphilis, and the passage of the 1935 Social Security Act that resulted in many patients being removed to nursing homes (2001, 45).

Social legislation and court decisions also played an important role in the changing attitudes toward, understanding, and treatment of the disabled. *President John F. Kennedy* commissioned the President's Panel on Mental Retardation that proposed 95 recommendations. These recommendations included the need for civil rights for the disabled, a call for a major decrease in the census of mental institutions, and a greater emphasis on community services. A number of these recommendations became part of the Maternal and Child Health and Mental Retardation Planning Amendments of 1963, and in the same year Kennedy signed into law the Community Mental Health Centers Act that improved and expanded on residential, community and preventive services for the mentally impaired. By 1971 Congress passed additional legislation, including Intermediate Care Facilities/Mental Retardation (ICF/MR) program which was part of Title XIX of the Social Security Act which included increased funding for institutional services for the intellectually disabled. A major piece of legislation was passage of the Education for All Handicapped Children's Act of 1975, which guaranteed children with disabilities the right to a free and meaningful education, and many Americans have heard of and may be familiar with the Americans with Disabilities Act (ADA) passed in 1990 that bars discrimination against individuals with disabilities in a number of sectors (ADA is discussed in more detail later in this chapter). Two United States Supreme Court decisions, *Wyatt v. Stickney* (1972) and *Pennsylvania Ass'n. Retarded Child. v. Commonwealth of PA* (1971) affirmed the right to treatment for persons with disabilities, and are further examples of the changing tide in attitudes, perception, and treatment of the disabled that developed in the last several decades of the twentieth century (2001, 45–51).

Language, Stigmatization, and Adjustment to Disabilities

The history of disabilities is immersed in *language, stigma,* and issues of *adjustment* to disability status. As we have seen, words such as idiot and idiocy, insane, crippled, and freak have often been used in reference to the disabled. But there is more to this story of words that helps to shed further light on understanding disabilities.

Davis (2006) has discussed the emergence and significance of the word "normal" in reference to disabilities, noting the importance of the growth in statistics and how it impacted the use and understanding of the word normal. The conceptualization of the bell curve in early nineteenth century England influenced thinking about what is normal and not normal, and was used heavily in biological research, in particular Social Darwinism and eugenics and the latter's emphasis on the normal body or individual, and those persons who deviated from that standard. Writes Davis "... eugenics became obsessed with the elimination of 'defectives' a category which included the 'feebleminded,' the deaf, the blind, the physically defective, and so on" (2006, 7). The development and spread of the bell curve enhanced historically long-standing references to the "normal" as it applied to the disabled. In a

sense it gave more power to the distinctions between those with and without disabilities, and it would feed directly into some of the offshoots of the eugenics movement, such as sterilizations and exterminations of the disabled. This is also seen in the *medicalization* of disability, in which the disabled are cast into different and specialized categories, a practice common to the medical profession for the purposes of diagnosis and treatment (Linton, 2006). However, when a very powerful social institution such as medicine itself is involved in segregating the "normal" from "not normal," the results can be tragic since those who do not meet the standards of "acceptability" are made to stand out, making them a *political category*. This is precisely what those involved in the disabilities study and disabilities movement oppose and fight against, since both argue the medicalization of disability becomes a stumbling block to efforts at bringing about positive changes relative to the disabled (2006 162). Linton also addresses *nice words* such as "physically challenged," the "able disabled," "handicapable," and "special people and children," and *nasty words* including "cripple," "vegetable," "dumb," "deformed," "retard," and "gimp" as damaging labels that only serve to reinforce the power of the medicalization of disability (2006, 163–164). What is more, Charlton (2006) has addressed the perception of the disabled from the paradigm of *political economy*, meaning that many disabled persons, especially those who live in or near poverty and numbering up to 400 million worldwide, are no more than mere *outcasts*, individuals who become part of an *underclass* because they are forced to reside on the periphery of economic life. Charlton argues persons with disabilities become *dehumanized* through the political economy, and through such policies as Special Education which strengthens the stigmatization of children with disabilities, increasing "the probability that students with disabilities will get some kind of education into a badge of inferiority and a rule-bound, bureaucratic process of separating and warehousing millions of young people that the dominant culture has no need for" (2006, 224). Charlton refers to policies and programs such as this as *disability oppression*, a "complex and multifaceted" issue that is laden with harmful language, stigma, and negative practices toward and about the disabled" (Charlton, 2006, 217).

A major impetus in the sociological study of disabilities is *Stigma* (1963) by Erving Goffman, who was quite influential in the concern for any type of stigmatizing process directed at the disabled. Goffman distinguished between two types of stigmatized individuals: the *discredited* and the *discreditable*. *Discredited* individuals assume that their differentness or disability is *known* to others, while the *discreditable* individual is one who thinks otherwise, operating under the belief that his or her uniqueness is either *unknown* or *not immediately recognized* or perceived by others (1963, 4). An important contribution of Goffman's was the ways the stigmatized dealt with or *adjusted* to their differences. *First*, he identified attempts by the stigmatized to *correct* what is different about them and used as examples individuals who undergo plastic surgery; visually impaired individuals who receive eye treatment; homosexuals who undergo therapy; and, illiterate persons who receive remedial education. A *second* strategy involves *mastery* of some skill or area to overcome disabilities and includes physically disabled individuals who learn or relearn how to swim, ride, play tennis, or pilot an airplane, and visually impaired individuals who gain expertise in mountain climbing and skiing. Another strategy is *reassessing the limitations of the "normal,"* such as a physically disabled individual who helps persons without disabilities to appreciate the small things in life, including being able to shake hands or to listen to music. In essence, through their disabilities

the disabled are able to teach others about the blessings of life (1963, 9–11).

Goffman's work was instrumental in energizing and in helping to grow the study of disabilities, and this is seen in the area of *disability experience*, or the examination of how the disabled react and adjust to their circumstances. Goffman built on the earlier work of Beatrice Wright and others who advanced the importance of understanding disabilities in the light of *social context*. From the early 1960s to the decade of the 1990s an emphasis on understanding the experiences of the disabled was on the *value transformations* involving the disabled, such as those discussed above by Goffman. To explicate this point, studies specified how the disabled would engage in *disavowing* their disabilities, and theories evolved that identified *stages* the disabled go through that entail disavowing of disability status by disabled and nondisabled individuals. Based on interviews with visually impaired persons and those with orthopedic and cosmetic facial conditions, Davis identified three stages which those with and without disabilities travel through as they interact with each other. The first stage, *fictional acceptance* is when nondisabled persons treat the disabled as adults, but superficially. The relationships in this stage are surface at best and lack substance. The second stage is *breaking through* and occurs if relationships were smooth and positive in stage one. In this stage disabled persons engage in disclosing their disabilities in order to get beyond the superficial nature of the original relationship, and they seek to find common ground along the lines of similar interests. If breaking through is successful then stage three, *institutionalization of the normal relationship* occurs in which nondisabled individuals interact with disabled persons as if the latter were "normal." In this stage, nondisabled individuals play a prominent role in helping the disabled in adapting to different scenarios, such as navigating buildings that are not accessible to those with impairments, and relating to individuals who offer them unsolicited help (Gill, 2001, 353–355).

By the 1990s and largely as a result of the lack of empirical evidence to support stage paradigms involved in the disability experience, attention was refocused on *intrapersonal psychological adjustment* to disabilities that involve study of *self-concept, interactions between the disabled and their environments, body image, and changes in the body.* According to Gill (2001) the research on stages failed for the most part to demonstrate an orderly sequence or a consistent pattern of characteristics that describe adaptations to disabilities by either the disabled or nondisabled. Much of the research the past two decades has examined the impact of disabilities on the *emotional status* of those with disabilities, and how they function in various capacities such as student, employee, and family member. Also of interest is how the disabled compensate for functional losses, and the effects disabilities have on the well-being of those close to the disabled (2001, 357). One such direction is discussed by Robert Murphy where he uses the anthropological concept *liminality*, meaning the disabled live in a state of limbo where they are marginalized and only partially accepted by society. In a sense the disabled are caught in a "Catch-22." The door is shut on them until society deems the disabled as ready for greater participation and integration into the social fabric, yet it is society itself that closed the door initially, leaving the disabled to wonder if and when they will ever experience social acceptance. Gill suggests that unlike the term "stigmatization" that implies a static reaction to the disabled, liminality is a more diffuse process that results in less predictability of how society will respond to disabled persons, thus placing greater intrapsychological pressure on them and resulting in feelings of ostracism and dehumanization (2001,

358–359).

The Americans with Disabilities Act

The Americans With Disabilities Act (ADA) of 1990 is the culmination of many previous pieces of legislation passed to protect disabled individuals. On July 26, 1990 President George Herbert Walker Bush signed ADA into law, which *prohibits* disability discrimination in employment, public services and public accommodations operated by private entities, and requiring that telecommunication services be made accessible to the disabled. The three main sections of ADA are Title I: Employment; Title II: Public Entities; and, Title III: Public Accommodations. Elements of each title are briefly discussed (*Encyclopedia of Disability*, 2006).

Title I states "no covered entity shall discriminate against a qualified individual with a disability of such individual in regard to job application procedures, the hiring, advancement, or discharge of employees, employee compensation, job training, and other terms, conditions, and privileges of employment" (2006, 453). An important part of Title I is *reasonable accommodation*, in which an employer must make appropriate adjustments to the workplace in order to make it possible for disabled individuals to perform essential job functions. However, if the request for reasonable accommodation poses *undue hardship* on the employer, such as requiring a major financial investment or a direct threat to the safety of the employer or others in the workplace, the employer then may not be required to implement the accommodation. In addition, Title I prohibits screening of applicants based on disability status, meaning as a general rule individuals with disabilities are to be evaluated for employment solely on the basis of their qualifications. Employers are prohibited from requiring preemployment medical examinations, and it is in violation ADA for an employer to attempt to learn if individuals have disabilities, unless knowing this information is critical to performing the position (2006, 454).

Title II states "no qualified individual with a disability shall, by reason of such disability, be excluded from participation in or be denied the benefits of the services, programs, or activities of a public entity, or be subjected to discrimination by such entity" (2006, 454). Much of Title II is applicable to a public entity's *physical structure* and includes city buildings, city sidewalks, publicly owned sporting arenas, stadiums, theatres, and botanical gardens on the premises of state universities. "Program access" is a critical component of Title II and will vary on whether the facility in question has been previously altered, or is a new or existing facility. A facility may not have to comply with a request for alteration if it can be shown that to do so would place a burden on it (2006, 456).

Title III states "No individual will be discriminated against on the basis of disability in the full and equal employment of the goods, services, facilities, privileges, advantages, or accommodations of any place of public accommodation by any private entity who owns, leases, (or leases to) or operates a place of public accommodation" (2006, 457). Discrimination under Title III is defined as *general and specific discrimination*. *General discrimination* includes, but is not limited to denial of participation and participation of unequal benefit, providing a separate benefit when a separate benefit is not essential, employing contracts or administrative methods that are discriminatory in nature, and discrimination against an individual on the grounds that he or she associates with an individual with a known disability. *Specific discrimination* entails but is not limited to failure to make reasonable modifications that would benefit a disabled person, failure to

remove architectural barriers that impede access when this can be accomplished, and failure to guarantee effective communication by providing auxiliary aids. Title III allows for consideration of a direct threat that poses danger to the health or safety of others that cannot be eliminated by compliance with the mandates of Title III (2006, 457).

In Recognition: Herb Covey

Dr. Herb Covey may be the most published sociologist never to have spent one moment of his career as a full-time academician. Dr. Covey's interests are eclectic and anything he touches (writes about) is fully covered and thoroughly researched. Over the years Dr. Covey has studied education, criminology, gerontology, methamphetamine abuse, youth gangs, perceptions of the aged in history, herbal medicines used by American slaves, and the disabled, to name a few of his interests. He is published in academic journals and he has written eleven books on various topics. One of Dr. Covey's strengths is his creative imagination. His 1991 *Images of Older People in Western Art and Society* should be a classic. It is a moving, inspirational and sensitive treatise on how older persons have been perceived and stigmatized in the arts. The book is in a class of its own, after all who else with an interest in the aged has undertaken a study of them from the angle of their identity in the arts (books, paintings, etc.). In 1998, Dr. Covey's *Social Perceptions of People with Disabilities in History* was published, and similar to his work on the aged is sensitively and carefully researched, including chapters on physical disabilities, lepers, the mentally ill, the hearing and visually impaired, and individuals with developmental disabilities. The book is beautifully illustrated with pictures that are convicting and convincing of the manners in which the disabled have been treated in societies. This work exemplifies the creative directions that Dr. Covey has taken throughout his career. It is to be noted that Dr. Covey has done more than write about the disabled and less fortunate–the stigmatized–he has volunteered to give downhill skiing lessons to persons with disabilities. Not only is Dr. Covey a scholar, but he is also a humanitarian.

SUMMARY

Throughout history individuals with mental disorders and disabilities have been stigmatized and labeled, and as a consequence have faced many types of discrimination and hardships, including physical abuse, sterilizations, murder, and infanticide. Millions of Americans have some form of mental disorder, and this involves persons of all ages. The Diagnostic and Statistical Manual is the primary source of information on mental disorders, and the diagnosis and treatment of individuals with mental disorders is derived from this document. Sociologists and others approach mental disorder from the direction of societal reaction, and the manner in which these types of conditions are socially con-

structed and defined. Disabilities, including mental disorders have been greeted both harshly and in a humane way through the centuries, and the reactions to persons with disabilities has varied within and across societies. From the earliest times to the twentieth century, the disabled have been both protected and humiliated, and for a great period of time disabilities were believed to be a result of demons and the supernatural, thus justifying in the minds of societies a right to treat them in whatever manner they deemed was necessary. The United States was involved in sterilizations largely as a result of the eugenics movement, and one common denominator through history concerning the disabled has been the inconsistent and often ambivalent societal reaction to and treatment of the disabled. The second half of the twentieth century has seen improvements in attitudes toward and the care for the disabled, and legislation such as ADA has been a major source of more humane and positive concern for persons with disabilities. As for Joe, unfortunately, laws that could have protected his right to an education, therefore perhaps contributing to a happier and more prolonged life, were several years into the future after his death.

Chapter 13

SEXUAL BEHAVIORS AND DIFFERENCES

CASE STUDY: PORNOGRAPHY

Pornography, prostitutes, and escort services. At first glance this may not sound all that unusual to you, until it is explained that it involved a wonderful young married couple whose husband was extensively involved with all three, and then some. This is the case of Martha and Sam (aliases to protect their actual identities), graduates of major and prestigious universities, who fell madly in love during their early twenties and who no one in their wildest dreams would ever have suspected of facing a crisis in their marriage as a result of major sexual issues. Sam graduated from one of the nation's military academies, and Martha is a graduate of a top flight state university in the east. Early in their married years Sam became involved with pornography over the internet, and graduated to using the internet to contact prostitutes. Sam eventually became involved with an escort service and was spending significant amounts of money on call girls, typically the most expensive of prostitutes. Martha was unaware of Sam's activities until she encountered his credit card that had items blacked out on it. Later a flyer was mailed to their residence advertising sex parties. Martha obviously became more concerned and depressed, and when she con-

fronted Sam he always denied any wrongdoing, and would laugh at her. But the problems continued. Martha encountered pornography sites on the Internet Sam was viewing, and she grew increasingly suspicious about Sam's involvement with prostitutes. So here are two young persons from solid homes and with outstanding educations whose marriage was on the brink of disaster as a result of Sam's behaviors. To make matters worse, Sam became so entrenched with pornography and prostitutes that he started to visit public parks where gay men would have sex. Sam would go to public bathrooms and insert his penis in a hole in a bathroom wall where oral sex was performed on him, anonymously. Only after leaving Sam and with eventual counseling were Sam and Martha able to save their marriage. According to Sam and Martha and based on the counseling they experienced, their circumstances are far from unusual. Many individuals from the most "solid" upbringing and "respectable" people have engaged in similar behaviors.

OVERVIEW

Four types of sexual deviance are considered in this chapter: the sexual behaviors of Americans; prostitution; homosexuality; and pornography. All four can be controversial in nature. Take pornography as an example and try to define it. The old expression "one man's wine is another man's vinegar" applies to defining pornography. For some people any kind of sexual-based material represents pornography, for others the sky is the limit in considering any definition of the subject. The Internet has become a major player in what some declare as pornography, and there are movies, magazines, newspapers, and the use of the telephone as methods of delivering pornography. Perhaps United States Supreme Court Justice Potter Stuart said it best when he stated (paraphrased) "I cannot define pornography, but I know it when I see it." Homosexuality is also a divisive issue. In recent years some states have had same-sex marriages on the ballot with every one voting against making them legal. Yet what seems to get lost when undertaking such referenda is it wasn't that long ago that voting on this topic not only would not have occurred, but would never have been mentioned to begin with. Of course there is the debate over the so-called "homosexual agenda" which begs the question of the representation of gays in the total population, an issue to be addressed in this chapter. Prostitution is probably the least controversial of the four areas to be explored, but for some there is still the question of whether it is a "victimless crime," meaning the prostitute-client relationship is a matter of choice and free will for both, and therefore does not constitute any criminal action. The sexual behaviors of Americans, which includes a diversity of issues also conjures up debates and disagreements. It is to this topic the attention is now directed.

Sexual Behaviors of Americans

The research on the sexual behaviors of Americans undertaken by Alfred Kinsey (1948, 1953) had a major influence on the development of the study of human sexuality. By the 1960s more research was being conducted on this subject and has escalated since then. Many different individuals and organizations study the sexual behaviors of Americans, including the Centers for Disease Control and Prevention which recently published the results of a national survey that examined such behaviors (Drug Use and Sexual Behaviors Reported by Adults: United States, 1999–2002, 2007). The Centers for Disease Control and Prevention (CDCP) undertook the National Health and Nutrition Examination Survey (NHANES) from 1999–2002 which asked questions about the drug use and sexual behaviors of a scientifically selected sample of Americans. Over 21,000 Americans were interviewed in their homes and just under 20,000 had medical examinations at Mobile Exam Centers (MEC). Respondents were asked if they had ever had sex; age at initiation of sex; and their number of sexual partners (sex here includes intercourse and oral sex). Basic demographic information on respondents was also collected. Ninety-six percent of the sample reported ever having sex, and range in age from 91 percent for persons 20–29 years old to 98 percent for individuals 50–59 (most percentages are rounded). Non-Hispanic whites had the *highest* percentage ever having sex (97%), followed by 96 percent for non-Hispanic blacks and 88 percent for Mexican Americans. The question also showed slight variations by education with 92 percent of respondents who had less than a high school education reporting ever having sex, and 96 percent with a high school education and 97 percent with more than high school indicating they ever had sex. An important question was "age at first sex" which takes on greater significance given the national concern for HIV/AIDS and sexual activity among youth. The percentage of age at first sex for individuals less than 15 years of age was 16, and for ages 15–17, 18–20, and 21 and older the percentages were 41, 28, and 15, respectively. *It becomes clear given this data that young Americans are active in sexual behavior with nearly 60 percent having sex by age 17.* Age and first sex showed variations by gender with 19 percent of males and 12 percent of females reporting having engaged in sex before age 15. After that (15–17, 18–20, 21 and older) the percentages of males and females reporting age at first sex were quite similar. The number of sexual partners also showed variation by gender with males nearly twice as likely to have reported 15 or more sexual partners in their lifetime. Of interest is the breakdown by race and ethnicity with 46 percent of non-Hispanic black males reporting the *highest* number of lifetime sexual partners (15 or more), followed by non-Hispanic white males (27%), and Mexican American males (20%) reporting 15 or more sexual partners. This is sharply contrasted with females where 12 percent of non-Hispanic black females, 10 percent of non-Hispanic white females, and 5 percent of Mexican American females reporting 15 or more sexual partners during their lifetime. The most common number of sexual partners by race and gender was between two and six which was also reported for levels of education (2007, 5–12).

A nonscientific poll taken by ABC News *Primetime Live* in October 2004 sheds light on the sexual behaviors and perceptions of Americans *who were surveyed,* and although not generalizeable to the population of the United States does present some rather interesting results that can serve as talking points, especially between males and females (ABC News *Primetime Live* Poll: The American Sex Survey 2004). Thirty percent of those surveyed reported that they had *fantasized* about cheating on their partners, while 16 percent said *they had cheated* on their partners. When it came to threesome sex, 21 percent of respondents said they had fantasized about it

and 14 percent reported they had done it. The workplace isn't necessarily immune from sexual activity since 12 percent of respondents indicated they had sex at their place of work and an additional 10 percent had fantasized about it. Speaking of thinking about sex, or sex on the mind, 70 percent of males surveyed as opposed to 30 percent of females reported they think about sex *every day,* and 83 percent of male respondents compared to 59 percent of females said they enjoyed sex a great deal. The war of the roses doesn't end there. Men reported having 20 sexual partners on average compared to six for women, while 21 percent of males surveyed said they had cheated on their partners, double that for females. Over 30 percent of males reported they had visited a sex web site, three times greater than that for women, and 42 percent of women compared to 25 percent of men felt that visiting a sex web site was cheating. However, the majority of both males (72%) and females (54%) surveyed had visited a sex chat room. Men and women also differed on the issue of orgasm, with 74 percent of males and 30 percent of females reporting they always experienced orgasms, and 48 percent of women compared to 11 percent of men had *faked* orgasm (2004, 1–15). Other findings from the poll include (2004, 8–15):

- 70 percent of those surveyed reported they enjoy sex a great deal, 50 percent said they were very satisfied with their sex lives, and 36 percent stated their sex lives were very exciting.
- 55 percent of respondents indicated they were sexually traditional, while 42 percent reported being sexually adventurous.
- Discussing fantasies declined steadily by age, with 71 percent of respondents 18-29 reporting they discussed fantasies, but for respondents age 65 and over that figure dropped to 22 percent.

- 72 percent of couples married less than three years had sex at least several times a week, but for those married for more than 10 years the percentage was 32 percent. Eighty-seven percent of respondents married less than three years and 70 percent of those married for over 10 years reported they enjoyed sex a great deal.
- 70 percent of respondents who rarely if ever attended church reported homosexuality is ok, compared to 57 percent and 31 percent who attend a few times each month and who attend church on a regular basis, respectively. Ten percent of regular church attendees reported visiting a sex web site, and 19 percent of the occasional attendees and 29 percent of those who rarely attended said they had visited porn sites.
- Thirty-seven percent of respondents who rarely if ever attended church reported having sex on the first date. The percentages for the occasional attendees and those who go to church regularly were 35 and 14 percent, respectively.
- Last but not least: 57 percent of those surveyed reported they had sex outdoors, in a public place.

One of the least understood aspects of sexuality is the sexual lives of *older Americans,* however between March and July 2006 3,005 Americans ages of 57 to 85 were interviewed in their homes concerning a number of issues, including their sexuality (Lindau, Schumm, Laumann, Levinson, O'Muirch Eartaigh, and Waite, 2007). The data from the National Social Life, Health and Aging Project (NSHAP) indicate older Americans are interested in and do engage in sex, but for many older Americans sexual activity declines after age 70 as a result of *health-related problems.* When older Americans experi-

enced a decrease in sexual activity this was likely to be due to the declining health of male partners. Sexual activity among the respondents included intercourse, oral sex, and masturbation with 50 percent of sexually active couples under age 75 stating they engaged in oral sex, and 50 percent of males and 25 percent of females indicating they masturbate. NSHAP also stated that women who were not in a current relationship were more likely than men to report lack of interest in sex, and when women between ages of 75–85 reported little sexual activity this was due predominately to *outliving their male partners.* Not unexpectedly, sexual activity was found to decline with age, although 73 percent of respondents ages 57 to 64 who reported they had sex with at least one partner in the previous year. The percentages for ages 65 to 74 and 75 to 85 were 53 and 26 percent, respectively. The NSHAP represents the most comprehensive and in-depth study to date on the sexual behaviors of older Americans, and it is important in helping to debunk the myths and stereotypes that older persons are not sexually active.

A major concern of Americans is *teen sex.* Today's teens are *two to three* times more likely to engage in sex (intercourse and oral sex) than were their counterparts of previous generations. *Contemporary American adolescents initiate sex younger, have more sexual partners, are more likely to contact sexually transmitted diseases, and have the highest rate of premarital pregnancy in the world* (Bearman, Moody and Stovel, 2004; Mosher, 2005). A major study of youth risk undertaken by Grunbaum, Kann, Kinchen, Ross, Hawkins, Lowry, Harris, McManus, Chyen, and Collins (2003) echoes the above, reporting 46 percent of high school students and nearly 80 percent of college-aged students 18–24 years old have had sex. The onset of sexual activity was reported to increase with age, with 34 and 41 percent of ninth and tenth grade high school students indicating sexual activity, respectively, compared with 52 percent of eleventh graders and 61 percent of twelfth graders who reported engaging in sexual behaviors (intercourse and oral sex). The study also revealed significant differences by race and ethnicity for teenagers engaging in sex. Sixty-nine percent of African American male high students, 53 percent of Latino male high school students, and 45 percent of white male high school students had engaged in sexual intercourse. The pattern-trend was similar for female high school students with 53 percent of African American, 44 percent of Latino, and 41 percent of whites reporting they had sexual intercourse, respectively. Regardless of race or ethnicity, males were much more likely than females to report engaging in sexual intercourse before age 13. Spencer, Zimet, Aalsma, and Orr (2002) reported *self-esteem* affects the sexual activity of teenagers, but it varies by gender. Boys between the ages of 12–14 with *high self-esteem* are more likely to engage in sexual intercourse, but girls the same ages with high self-esteem were more likely to *postpone* onset of sexual coitus. What about "just saying no to sex"? It appears saying no *delays* entrance into sexual intercourse, however it does not necessarily mean that teenagers refrain from sexual activity altogether, since a growing number of them engage in *"technical virginity,"* or oral sex which is now more common among teenagers than sexual intercourse. Additionally, teens who "say no" delay entrance into sexual intercourse for *18 months*, but when they start engaging in it they are *less likely* to use condoms (McGinn, 2004; Mosher, 2005; Mulrine, 2002).

Prostitution

At first glance prostitution may seem a rather simple and mundane topic; not much to think or write about. But take for example the following observation by Rachel West (Miller, Romenesko, and Wondolkowski, 1993, 300): "Given the economic status of women, how many of us are forced to rent our bodies, stay in marriages we want to get out of, make deals with the landlord, shop keeper, put up with sexual harassment on the job, smile when we don't want to, put out or get fired, and so forth? How many wives make a greater effort at being sexy when they need extra money from their husbands? How many women choose the man who has greater career prospects over the man who is a heartthrob? How much do we all have to prostitute ourselves because women intentionally have so little to show for the tremendous amount of work we do?" Now compare this to a standard definition of prostitution *"as exchange of money for sex"* (1993, 303). The statement by West offers a broader interpretation by what is understood to be prostitution. In other words, women are prostituting themselves in a number of common walks of life (i.e., marriages; jobs). Exchange of sex for money? That reflects a traditional understanding of prostitution.

Prostitution, or the exchange of sex for money, is an ancient practice, but the focus here is on prostitution in the United States. In Massachusetts, nightwalking was considered an offense and laws against it were enacted in 1699 and reenacted in 1787. But it was not until 1917 that the actual punishment of prostitutes occurred in the state. In 1871 and 1875 the state of New York attempted to pass legislation to regulate prostitution but failed, largely due to the work of women's organizations such as the Women's Educational Society that opposed such legislation on the grounds that it had been unsuccessful in Europe. The interpretations of prostitution varied with the times, with nineteenth century feminists oscillating between *econom-*

ic and moralistic-based explanations of the behavior. *Economic views* of prostitution encompassed the notion prostitutes were forced into their trade because of *economic discrimination* which entailed both low wages and inferior jobs. As a result of the fact that some women were forced to engage in prostitution, earlier feminists argued the prostitutes should be free from police harassment and prosecution. But another position on prostitution also prevailed during this period, one that viewed it as *morally wrong* and degrading to both women and society. These women, sometimes labeled *purity crusaders* believed that young women were forced into prostitution by evil men, and argued for a repressive stance against it, one that would *backfire.* A number of prostitutes during the nineteenth century worked for madams who would offer them protection from violence and economic abuse, but the hardened reactions against them forced many prostitutes to work for pimps and organized crime, exposing them to continuous acts of violence and increasing economic insecurity. In addition, and as a result of increasing immigration, industrialization, commercialization and urbanization, a growth in social control agencies occurred including special courts, social workers, and vice squads that resulted in long-term, frequent incarceration and rigid treatment of prostitutes (1993, 302–303). Characteristic of the societal response toward prostitution is a laissez faire attitude whereby the police are unlikely to arrests prostitutes if they are operating in lower class, minority-based neighborhoods. However, when prostitutes, especially streetwalkers employ their trade in middle class to higher communities, their risks of arrest increase, and this is not only evident along social class lines but is also apparent when the prostitutes are *women of color.* To this day in the United States there is only one state that legalizes prostitution and it is Nevada

where prostitution is closely regulated in 13 largely rural counties (1993, 303, 312). In Nevada, brothel prostitutes are fingerprinted and carry prostitution identification cards that are issued by district attorneys and the police.

Types of Prostitutes

As you will see there is no one type of prostitute and prostitution as a trade is a reflection of the broader system of social stratification, since there are what can be categorized as "lower class to higher class" prostitutes.

Streetwalkers are at the bottom rung of prostitutes who walk the streets and solicit customers, and contrary to popular belief they render their service in vehicles (cars, semi-trucks, and pick-ups) and by doing so they open themselves up to a variety of risks and dangers. Needless to say they are not earning their meager pay in the "Beacon Hills" of the world, instead they go about their business in lower-class neighborhoods where they encounter less problems from the police, whom as already noted tend to "look the other way" just as long as prostitution is not occurring in more affluent areas. Motel rooms, of course are also used with the service lasting between 15–30 minutes. In vehicles the prostitute and client will spend no more than four to 15 minutes engaged in sexual activity, which for both cases (vehicles and rooms) suggest the anonymity and emotional detachment involved in acts of selling sex for money. Streetwalkers are *prone to violence* for a number of reasons, including *where* they have sex and the fact they are often lower class women who are not respected. Demands for "kinky sex" are frequent, and the police may assault them in order to get sexual favors, with assault a major issue for young prostitutes under 16 years of age. If this is not bad enough, streetwalkers earn low pay which they must often share with pimps (Thio, 2006: 215–216).

Child and adolescent prostitutes are a second type of prostitute, and perhaps the least known of and most tragic example of selling sex for money. *Child prostitutes* are frequently referred to as *baby pros* and range in age from eight to 12. *Baby pros* are normally from dysfunctional families who learn their trade by observing or being in the presence of mothers and older sisters who engage in prostitution, pornography, or sex with boyfriends and pick-ups (but not sex for money). These young girls are frequently the victims of all types of abuse, especially physical and sexual, and they tend to be involved with prostitution on a part-time basis, with some attending school like other children. *Adolescent prostitutes* range in age from 13 to 17, and like child prostitutes are also likely to emanate from maladjusted environments where abuse and heavy drug use are common, thus adolescent prostitutes themselves are often victims of abuse and are addicted to substances. These young women, many who come from rural America, enter into prostitution to earn money to survive as well as to support their drug addictions, and frequently fall under the control of pimps who promise them security and comfort. Child and adolescent prostitution is a worldwide issue, occurring in places like the Himalayan regions of Nepal where up to 7,000 girls annually are sold to brothels in Bombay, India, and in Brazil where 25,000 young women and girls are forced into prostitution in remote Amazon area mining camps. In Thailand, young girls are sold by their impoverished parents to local brothels, or to German tourists who take the girls back to Germany to perform their trade as house prostitutes. In many instances, it is poverty that leads to these young women and girls being sold by *parents* who are destitute and willing to engage in destroying the lives of their own children in order to survive. On a worldwide basis the demand for sex with children has grown leaps and bounds and often under the misled perception that young children are less likely to have AIDS. It is usually tourists from rich, Western nations and Japan who go in droves to poorer countries seeking sex with children, largely as a result of the less likelihood of being arrested (2006, 216). It is not uncommon for police in the poor countries to look the other way, since they are either bribed or work under the assumption that the problem is so widespread there is little that can be done about it anyway.

A third type of prostitute is *house prostitutes* who work at places otherwise known as the *cathouse, whorehouse, parlor house, bordello, joint or simply house, and of course, brothel.* As noted previously, brothels are only legal in some counties in Nevada, and their legal status not only carries with it the requirement for being fingerprinted and possessing prostitute identification cards, but prostitutes are also required to receive weekly medical checkups as well. Working at a brothel can mean better pay then being a streetwalker, and it may even result in a safer and secure environment. Not all is rosy with brothel work since prostitutes are not necessarily free to set their own hours, and they must give one-half of their earnings to the house. It appears that house prostitutes who work as escorts (escort services) have the most lucrative arrangements, since in addition to the fee for their services they will often receive handsome tips, but they may also face danger since they ply their trade away from the house, and sometimes clients can become violent and demand rough sex (2006, 217).

Call girls represent the upper end of the prostitute echelon and are often known as the "aristocrats" of prostitution, and they can have salaries that parallel those of physicians and lawyers. Some call girls reside in affluent neighborhoods and are the most educated among prostitutes, and as a result of harboring a much different self-concept and image than is the case for other prostitutes, they are insulted if they are seen in the same light as or treated like streetwalkers or house prostitutes. The tool of the trade for call girls is the *telephone*, however, it is common for them not to use their personal telephones, relying instead on answering machines or an answering service, thus avoiding detection by the police and maximizing business. Call girls will listen to their answering machines or use the answering service which allows them to move from one customer to another. Veteran call girls get much of their business from referrals, or satisfied customers, and the novices get their start by getting names from other call girls and through advertising. Call girls are among the most attractive and well-dressed prostitutes, and in addition they respect their clients and work under the informal code of ethics in which names of customers are never mentioned.

Formal Reponses to Prostitution: Law Enforcement and Attempts at Decriminalization

Prostitution is *unevenly enforced* across the United States, and reiterating a point, police efforts against it have much to do with the "where" (impoverished v. more affluent areas) and the "who" (people of color v. whites). The great majority of prostitutes are females who comprise at least 70 percent of persons arrested for prostitution. Male customers are rarely arrested, and streetwalkers who make up about 20 percent of all prostitutes account for 90 percent of all arrests of prostitutes. What is more, 40 percent of all street prostitutes are women of color who comprise nearly 60 percent of arrests for prostitution, and 85 percent of those jailed

for practicing their trade (Miller et al. 1993, 313). On occasion the law enforcement response includes *police sweeps*, crackdowns on prostitution usually for political purposes. A number of what typically are street prostitutes are arrested and jailed, leading members of the community to perceive they are now more safe and secure from crime and perversion. However, the sweeps frequently backfire since these prostitutes will eventually get released from jail and head straight back to the streets, and it usually women of color who wind up paying a double price since they not only have been jailed (and probably have been numerous times before), but their primary source of income has been briefly halted. It is not uncommon for street prostitutes to have limited legal job opportunities therefore jailing them can have serious implications for their economic well-being. When police crackdowns transcend the streets and also involve arresting prostitutes in their apartments, felony charges can be brought against them, and if these women have been sending money to relatives in other states they can then be charged with violating federal racketeering statutes. Ironically, laws such as that just discussed are allegedly passed to protect prostitutes (there are dangers involved in selling sex from an apartment or house) and to hold their male clients culpable for their actions, but often result in further legal stigmatizing of prostitutes. In addition, policies such as urban renewal and urban revitalization that result in tearing down blighted areas where prostitutes often work, can actually force them into practicing their trade in fringe areas including alleys, the back of cars, and doorways, thus escalating the chances of becoming victims of violence. Since prostitution is encompassed in what is called *deviant street networks*, prostitutes open themselves up for greater risks of arrests. *Deviant street networks* include many types of predatory crimes including prostitution, petty larceny, forgery, credit card fraud, embezzlement, auto theft, burglary and robbery, exactly the types of crimes the public demands the police take action against. The police who may want little to do with enforcing laws against prostitution may find themselves doing so since it is carried out within a framework of other visible criminal activities (1993, 314–316).

This section will conclude with a discussion of pimps, but additional mention of the social structure involved in street prostitution is now addressed. In some communities such as Milwaukee, Wisconsin prostitution occurs within *pseudo families* comprised of the pimp and two or three women who referred to each other as *wives in law*. The longest serving women are known as the *bottom woman*, who because of her longevity with her male lover/pimp works less and enjoys higher status among the wives in law. Pseudo families form to meet the needs of both the prostitute and the male, the latter who often has just been released from prison. Both are in need of emotional support, and turning to the streets for prostitution and other activities within the deviant street network offers an immediate and stable source of income. Rather interestingly, the pimp and the "wives in law" both exert social control over each other, with the pimp in control of his women as they ply their trade, but the prostitutes themselves exert control over the man since they know what other crimes he has committed, a fact of interest to law enforcement. When the prostitutes leave the pimp it is usually because he did not meet their total needs, meaning they were seeking out caring relationships which he did not provide for them. Thus women leave the relationships realizing he was doing little more than taking advantage of them, and that he was no more than a pimp anyway (1993, 318).

Prostitutes themselves have organized in order to secure greater rights and protection. Three organizations, Call off Your Old Tired Ethics (COYOTE), Women Hurt in Systems of Prostitution Engaged in Revolt (WHISPER), and the *U.S. Prostitutes Collective* address the issues of decriminalization and the control of prostitution by men. The three organizations oppose legalization of prostitution since they argue it would do no more than enhance male domination over the trade, and result in further stigmatization and oppression of prostitutes. Of the three organizations it is COYOTE that is the most well known and active, and here will get the lions share of attention. Although its name changed to the National Task Force on Prostitution in 1979 (NTFP), the organization is still more widely known as COYOTE, fighting against discrimination against prostitutes and taking a firm stance on decriminalizing prostitution, and the elimination at the federal level of all legal restrictions placed on the profession. Founded in 1973 by ex-prostitute Margo St. James, COYOTE advocates educating the public concerning the costs involved in controlling prostitution, strengthening prostitution through legal rights, and as noted previously, decriminalizing prostitution. It also wants prostitution to be perceived as legitimate work, and it assumes the position that women have the right to control their own bodies, meaning they have the right to sell sex for profit. Women's organizations such as NOW (the National Organization for Women) generally view prostitution as degrading and sexist, and therefore stand at a distance from movements such as COYOTE and WHISPER. In addition, there can be political fallout for organizations such as NOW that fear stigmatization themselves as a result of being associated with pro-prostitution advocacy. COYOTE has met with little effectiveness and success due to a lack of both financial resources and staff to carry out its objectives. In addition, the public has not been enthusiastic in supporting its aims and those of similar organizations on the grounds it opposes decriminalization and is more likely (if interested at all) to support legalization of prostitution (1993, 323–324).

Pimps and Johns

When discussing prostitution and especially when enforcing laws against it, it is usually prostitutes who are the center of attention. Pimps often are the subject of jokes when alluding to prostitution, and clients, the customers, better known as *johns* seem rarely to get much focus from the general public or the police. Kathleen Barry (1979) has authored one of the more insightful and important accounts of prostitution to date, identifying pimping as the oldest profession, while focusing on the methods pimps use to lure women, in particular young teenage girls into the trade. Her book, *Female Sexual Slavery* (1979), is a provocative look at sexual abuses of women undertaken and controlled by male dominance and hegemony in societies. Barry defines *female sexual slavery* as the "international traffic in women and forced street prostitution taken together" (1979, 7), and uses the term *procuring* to accentuate the manner in which women are brought into prostitution. Barry writes: "pimping and procuring are perhaps the most ruthless displays of male power and sexual dominance" (1979 86). Five types of procuring by pimps are identified: befriending or loving; actions of gangs, syndicates, and organized crime; employment agencies; purchase; and, kidnapping.

Befriending or *loving* is typically the first step in procuring a prostitute, entailing the use of love or romance to lure a woman into the ranks of prostitution, and receives the *greatest amount of attention* of the five methods

of procuring discussed by Barry. To understand procuring is to understand the definition of a pimp which is *one who lives off the earnings of a prostitute* (1979, 87). After luring a young woman into his life, the pimp offers her protection and will take care of her overall needs, including bailing her out of jail if necessary. What is important is these young women can be quite naïve, often from small rural towns who have come to larger cities in search of a better way of life, and get hooked into prostitution by streetwise and deceitful males who take advantage of their naivety. Be the pimps white or African American they have some common underlying features, one of which is their view of the *tick* or the customer as a sap who is easily ripped off and for whom the pimps have no respect. In addition, there is learning the rules of pimping, known as *whorology* that is learned either on the streets or in prison. These so-called rules encompass more than just learning how to pimp, meaning more than just how to work the streets, con customers, and control prostitutes. It also entails putting a steel lid on the emotions of prostitutes since it is money that the pimp seeks first and foremost, and getting too emotionally entangled with one of his "wives-in-law" could affect the profits to be made in hustling. Pimps also are aware that many of the women they procure are bored, and seek excitement that the pimp can provide via the hedonistic lifestyle associated with being a prostitute. Yet there are other attractions for young women entering into prostitution such as extravagant clothes, new cars, and more money than they have ever seen in their young lives. On this note there is a major stereotype about pimps, especially African American pimps and that deals with the Lincoln or Cadillac they are perceived as owning and forever cruising the streets in. The big, expensive car is often a reward for successful pimping that has taken years to establish, and owning one of these flashy vehicles only enhances the procuring possibilities available to pimps (imagine being one of these unsuspecting young women who encounters a pimp in an expensive Lincoln, with all of his street smarts and conning personality, and how that can quicken the pace of luring her into what can be a devastating life of selling her body for money). But there are questions such as "what is the first step in getting a young, naïve woman to begin selling sex for money," and "how/where does this all begin?" One answer is the pimp will tell the woman if she really loves him she will need to have sex for money with someone she does not know. If she refuses the pimp may turn on his charm and charisma (perhaps even anger), and when she finally agrees he has her hooked. *This one sex episode leads to what can be thousands of other such encounters over a number of years*, and is known as *seasoning*, or breaking the women's will and separating her from her previous life. Seasoning results in new identities for prostitutes since they will adopt street names used when hustling "johns," and can be a process of getting women to remain in prostitution, with the pimp using violence and intimidation against them. *Obedience* is critical within the pimping social structure and the demands for conformity, coupled with brutality and positive rewards such as money and clothes are keys to keeping women working the streets (1979, 89–96).

The role of *gangs, syndicates,* and *organized crime* is also a method of procuring, however the majority of procuring appears to involve the *free-lance style of the street pimp*. When it moves from this into the realm of prostitution centering around organized criminal interests, the nature of the role in prostitution shifts to behind the scenes, with organized crime involved in massage parlors, prostitution hotels, and pornography, which Barry considers as a form of prostitution since it is a major procurer of children for sexual slavery. *Employment agencies* represent a third type of procuring, and similar to the flashy, con-artist street pimp, possess an enormous power of lure. Frequently, the employment agencies are false covers for female sexual slavery, with young women going to them seeking jobs and being told the positions exist in foreign countries, only to discover upon arriving in these nations the jobs they thought they were hired to perform do not exist. Hard pressed for money, these women are then informed of ways to earn income, including prostitution. They are not only far away from home, but they are in a foreign land without resources or family, and being desperate they agree to begin their careers as prostitutes.

The two remaining forms of procuring are *purchase* and *kidnapping*, with *purchasing* girls accomplished by buying them from impoverished parents (worldwide and in the United States) and, *kidnapping* usually entails stealing young girls, frequently from third world countries. Race plays into the latter two types of procuring with blue eyed, blond haired girls from mid-America, and darker-skinned girls from third world countries in Central and South America, Africa, and Asia desirable in sexual slavery markets (1979, 96–113).

"Johns," or "tricks," are a frequently ignored element of prostitution, both from law enforcement and research perspectives. Remembering that "it takes two to Tango" tricks make up a major part of the sex for money enterprise but are rarely arrested or studied by behavioral and social scientists. Years ago Winick and Kinsie (1971) provided insights into the reasons men purchase the services of prostitutes which include *avoiding competition*, meaning some men feel they cannot compete for women and turn to prostitutes in order to meet their sexual needs. Some men prefer *impersonal* sex in which no love is expected or involved, while other males seek *sexual variations* their wives refuse to engage in, or they feel are inappropriate with their wives. Winick and Kinsie also discussed *sexual peculiarities* that entail sadistic sex with prostitutes, and/or because they have fetishes, while there are males who go to prostitutes because they want *uncomplicated sex*, meaning they show up, have sex, and go their separate ways without having to be concerned or worry about their partner. Not all johns are made from the same stock, with some of them *occasional johns* who are normal psychologically and who only occasionally purchase the services of prostitutes. Yet there are *habitual* or *compulsive johns* who may be less normal, desiring long-term relationships with prostitutes while seeking to help them in a number of ways. However, there is another side to habitual or compulsive johns, and that is they view some sex as dirty and go to prostitutes as a result. These "tricks" do not want to degrade nonprostitutes or their wives with their sexual ambitions, and may even go to prostitutes because they cannot reach erection with their wives or partners, but are able to do so with prostitutes because of the excitement they achieve when having sex with them (Thio, 2006, 224).

Pornography

Some years ago the author of this text was asked to participate in viewing a movie starring Marilyn Chambers, with the goal being to discern if there was any redeeming social or cultural value to the production. I knew little about Marilyn Chambers and even less about the movie, since I was asked last minute to do this by a supervisor who had decided not to partake in watching the film. There were five individuals in the viewing room that included members of the community, one of whom was a minister. We were told by a facilitator we were to evaluate the

movie on its cultural and social merits, and upon watching it we would vote on if it should be shown in local theatres (please keep in mind I was largely in the dark concerning the nature of what we were doing). The movie began with little fanfare, but it soon became apparent to me I was watching a "skin flick" with Ms. Chambers engaging in one sexual act after another. I cannot remember the length of the movie but I do recall two things: first, that I was furious with my boss, and second, I was mortified by what I saw on the screen. I was put to one very important test, and that was to vote to show or not to show the film in the community, and since I had not previously viewed anything remotely close to the movie I was predisposed to vote against it. In my eyes the movie was pornographic since it entailed sex scene after sex scene, and in my opinion had nothing to offer of cultural and social value. However, the vote was 3-2 in favor of allowing the movie to be shown in local theaters that I later learned was restricted to places that only presented sex-dominated films. The question at hand was one that had for asked for sometime: "what is pornography?" For three people in the room the movie was not pornography; for two it was.

Definitions and Legal Decisions

Defining pornography is no easy task. Let us revisit United States Supreme Court Associate Justice Potter Stuart's observation that he was unable to define pornography but he knew it when he saw it. This is the heart of the debate over pornography: some people will see a Marilyn Chambers type movie and identify it as pornographic; others will conclude differently. Much is the same with alternative methods of expressing sexual behaviors, such as sex on the internet and in magazines. Slade (2000) offers insight into the issue of definition by distinguishing between *pornography* and *obscenity*, writing *pornography is legal* in the United States while *obscenity is illegal*, but reminding the reader that pornography still is "in the mind of the beholder" (2000, 315). According to Slade, *pornography* is a term invented in the mid-nineteenth century and historically means *writing about prostitutes*, and over the years has been defined by numerous legal efforts to regulate sexual expression. *Obscenity* on the other hand is *offensive* and is defined as such by legislative action as appealing to the prurient interest (lasciviousness in nature) of the average citizen, based on the application of *contemporary community standards*. In addition, obscenity lacks serious merit, meaning it offers little to communities in the form of artistic, literary, political, or scientific value (2000, 314). However, a reality still remains and that is the line between what some persons identify as offensive or obscene and what is considered pornography remain blurred, not to mention that the United States has experienced significant changes in attitudes, beliefs and values that affect how people define pornography and obscenity.

Over the years court decisions have represented the landmark for gauging the definitions and control of pornography and obscenity. *Regina v. Hicklin* (1868) was the judicial basis for deciding cases concerning obscenity until the mid-twentieth century, forbidding the distribution and sale of obscene materials on the grounds they would corrupt the minds of persons exposed to them. The Hicklin ruling was consistently upheld in cases such as *People v. Doris* (1897) and *Mutual Film Corp. v. Industrial Commission of Ohio* (1915). The substance of both cases was quite compatible with Hicklin, with their arguments based on the dangers still and moving pictures presented to society's morals. However, operating in an era of *smut hunting*, a New York judge decided in *Halsey v. New York Society for the Suppression of Vice*

(1920) that printed materials were to be considered in their entirety (in reference to obscenity) as opposed to judging them on the basis of limited or selected passages. Other court rulings were made prior to the famous *Roth* decision (to be discussed), with *United States v. One Book Called "Ulysses"* (1933) and *United States v. One Book Entitled Ulysses by James Joyce* (Random House Inc. (1934) in support of Halsey. In the 1933 case New York District Court Judge John M. Woosley ruled that although "Ulysses" may cause one to vomit, it was not sexually arousing or excitable, and in "Joyce" appellate court judge Augustus Hand decided "Ulysses" did not aggravate or accentuate prurient interests (2000, 203–208).

Many other rulings have been made relative to pornography and obscenity, but it is *Roth v. United States* (1957) that is recognized as one of the most influential court decisions concerning pornography of the last half century. Depending upon who is asked, the Roth decision either clouded or clarified the pornography/obscenity issue. On the one hand the United States Supreme Court ruled the materials under consideration were obscene and without any redeeming social value, and therefore not were entitled to protection under the First Amendment (Roth was a major publisher of pornography). On the other hand the ruling also declared materials with such value were not obscene. But the issue rested with the expression "prurient interests" with the Court deciding the materials under consideration appealed to the lewd or lustful feelings within humans. To exacerbate issues further, from 1957 to 1967 the United States Supreme Court ruled on thirteen obscenity cases, but reported *55 different concurring or dissenting opinions* (2000, 216–217). The evolving decision making of the high court vis-à-vis pornography and obscenity is found in the 1973 case *Miller v. California* that changed Roth by rejecting the test "utterly without redeeming social value" and replaced it with "whether the work, taken as a whole, lacks serious literary, artistic, political or scientific value" (2000, 217). Removal of the word "redeeming" weakened the original statement decided in Roth and held future tests of obscenity were to be determined by applying *contemporary community standards*. Also in 1973 the high court ruled in the case of *Paris Adult Theatre v. Slaton* that states have the right to close adult theatres when obscene material or commerce in such ". . . has a tendency to injure the community as a whole, to endanger the public safety, or to jeopardize . . . the state's right . . . to maintain a decent society" (2000, 217–218). More recently the courts have addressed the role of the Internet as a resource of pornography, and in two major decisions the courts ruled the Internet is protected under the first amendment. In *American Civil Liberties Union v. Janet Reno, Attorney General of the United States* (1996) the Court of Appeals for the 3rd Circuit ruled the provisions passed by Congress in the Communications Decency Act (CDA) of 1996 were unconstitutional. The CDA was passed to prohibit pornography on the internet, mostly to protect children. One year later in *Janet Reno v. ACLU*, the United States Supreme Court upheld the decision in "Reno" with Justice John Paul Stevens writing "The internet in encouraging freedom of expression in a democratic society outweighs any theoretical but unproven *benefit of censorship*" (2000, 228).

All of the above decisions were made in light of the *first amendment* to the Constitution of the United States that guarantees freedom of speech:

> Congress shall make no law respecting an establishment of religion, or prohibiting the free exercise thereof; or abridging the freedom of speech, or the press, or the right peaceably to assemble, and to petition the Government for a redress of grievances. (2000, 228–229)

Court decisions concerning pornography and obscenity have posed major and interesting challenges to the first amendment, and phrases such as "utterly without redeeming social value," "lacks serious literary, artistic, political or scientific value" and "freedom of expression" demonstrate both the vagueness and difficulties faced in defining and legislating laws concerning pornography.

Court decisions have been one modality in attempts to control pornography and obscenity; *commissions* have represented another. When government commissions are established, it is usually because communities perceive they have a problem they need to address, if not resolve. Two major commissions were created to deal with pornography. In 1970, the Commission on Obscenity and Pornography offered its findings which included America needed to have a more open atmosphere concerning the discussion of *sex in general*, and that there was *little correlation* between pornography and social problems, including violence. The Commission also recommended government should *not interfere* with the right of adults to read, view, or to purchase sexually explicit materials. However, it did recommend legislation to control the sale of such materials to youth who did not have the consent of parents. One of the strongest recommendations was that pornography not be pushed onto the public through the mail or through public display (1970, 64–65). In addressing its position concerning a greater need for open discussion concerning sex in general the Commission stated ". . . it believes that much of the "problem" regarding materials which depict sexual activity stems from the inability or reluctance of people in our society to be open and direct in dealing with sexual matters. This most often manifests itself in the inhibition of talking openly and directly about sex. Professionals use highly technical language when they discuss sex; others escape by using euphemisms, or by not talking about sex at all. Direct and open conversation about sex between parent and child is too rare in our society. Failure to talk openly and directly about sex has several consequences. It overemphasizes sex, gives it a magical, nonnatural quality, making it more attractive and fascinating. It diverts the expression of sexual interest out of more legitimate channels. Such failure makes teaching children and adolescents to become channels for transmitting sexual information and forces people to use clandestine and unreliable sources" (1970, 53).

The second commission in 1986, The Report of the Attorney General's Commission on Pornography, reached different conclusions, especially as these related to women. Its findings reported *exposure to sexually violent materials* which led to an increase in aggression, particularly toward females, and that pornography reduced women to subordinate roles, resulting in their humiliation. By 1986 America had become more concerned about child pornography, and the Commission felt predisposed to address it with a degree of severity, *thus 49 of its 92 recommendations dealt with child pornography*. The Commission made recommendations for changes in both federal and state laws, for the United States Department of Justice, and the Federal Communications Commission as these related to pornography. At the *federal level* the recommendations ranged from granting states the power to seize profits made from obscene materials to prohibiting the transmission of such material via wire. A more complex recommendation dealt with the distribution of obscene material through interstate commerce requiring that states needed to prove these types of materials

interfered with interstate commerce. One of the strongest recommendations at the federal level was that hiring individuals to participate in commercial sexual performances would constitute unfair labor and business practices. Recommendations directed at the *states* were quite similar to those involving the federal level, but also included that states should update their obscenity statues to conform with *Miller v. California* by dropping "utterly without redeeming social value" and replacing it with the standards established in Miller. In addition, the Commission recommended that all second offenses for obscenity be made felonies. Recommendations for the United States Department of Justice included the establishment of an Obscenity Task Force, and the creation of an Obscenity Law Enforcement Data Base that could be used by authorities across the nation in pursuit of interdiction into and prosecution of violators of obscenity legislation. The recommendations proposed for the Federal Communications Commission included using its full regulatory powers in preventing dial-a-porn telephone activities, and in sanctioning cable and television networks for transmitting obscene materials. The Commission also demonstrated its concern for the victims of pornography by recommending that resources be provided for persons *harmed* by obscenity, either as a result of working in pornography or from exposure to it (Slade, 2000, 232–234).

The Effects of Pornography

One of the major questions concerns the effects of pornography on both the user and other persons. These effects can be *direct* or *indirect*, with direct effects focused on the immediate results or reactions to viewing or reading pornography. Direct effects also examine the "arousal-based" nature of pornography, as well as the stimulus results in behavior and attitude changes. Indirect effects are concerned with the longer-term, slow to develop, and subtle reactions to exposure to pornography. So much of what is said about the effects of pornography is political in nature, with some persons advocating pornography as having deleterious effects on users and other people, while there is also the camp that argues pornography has little if any bad or dangerous consequences for anyone. In other words, some individuals and groups claim pornography is a monster that is devouring the consumers of it, turning them into sexually violent predators; yet there are those who argue the exact opposite and even go as far as to state pornography has beneficial consequences for individuals and society. It is to empirical research findings on the effects of pornography attention is now directed.

The results of empirical research on the effects of pornography reflect the broader positions exclaimed in society, meaning they are *mixed.* There are studies that report pornography is not harmful, and there is research that purports the opposite. Studies supporting no harm from pornography date back some years (Ben-Veniste, 1970; Fischer and Grenier, 1994; Kimmel and Linders, 1996; Kuperstein and Wilson, 1970; Kutchinsky, 1991; Russel, 1974; Scott and Culvier, 1993; Winick, 1985). Of course an important question is "what are the effects under consideration?" Few researchers appear to be concerned about immediate sexual arousal that may result in masturbation and enhanced fantasizing. *Most of the serious research has questioned the effects of pornography on violent behavior, such as rape.* In a study of the Uniform Crime Reports published annually by the Federal Bureau of Investigation, Kuperstein and Wilson (1970) reported a *decrease* in overall sex offenses during a period when there was a sharp *increase in the availability of pornography.* Cross-national comparisons between the

United States and European nations have been made, and have also shown a dramatic *decrease in arrests for sex offenses* at a time when there was a corresponding significant *increase* in pornography (Ben-Veniste, 1970; Kutchinsky, 1991). This finding has led some to *distinguish between sexual offenses* that are committed as acts of *violence,* as opposed to being a *direct result of exposure* to sexually explicit material (Russell, 1980; Scott and Curvelier, 1993). Other research has reported arrests for sex crimes were well below the American national average during a period of *expansion in pornography* (Winick and Evans, 1996), and one study went as far as to conclude that rates for rape and aggravated assault *increased* when there was a corresponding *decrease* in the consumption of pornography (Kimmel and Linders, 1996). Fischer and Grenier (1994) undertook experimental research with male subjects, exposing them to sexually explicit materials and treatment conditions, and reported antiwoman fantasies were not caused by or as a result of viewing pornography.

Yet there are strong sentiments in regard to, and research that finds pornography to be correlated with committing sex offenses (Dworkin, 1981; Emmerick and Dutton, 1993; MacKinnon, 1989; Marshall, 1988; Silbert and Pines, 1984; Zillman and Bryant, 1982, 1986). In a major experimental study that exposed both male and female undergraduate students to differing amounts of pornographic videos, male subjects who viewed the greatest amount of pornographic movies gave *shorter* prison sentences to an offender who was accused of committing a rape (the subjects were told to read a newspaper article about the rape), and they were also found to express *greater insensitivity* toward women (Zillman and Bryant, 1986). Emerick and Dutton (1993) studied 76 adolescent boys who had been charged with a number of crimes including rape, bestiality, sexual abuse, child molestation, and making obscene phone calls, reporting 70 percent had been exposed to pornography, and over 60 percent of the young males had been sexually abused as children. Marshall (1988) reported 33 percent of heterosexual child molesters, 33 percent of rapists, and 39 percent of homosexual child molesters *used pornography* during pubescence, compared with 21 percent of nonoffenders exposed to pornography at the same stage of life. So where does this leave us? "One man's wine is another man's vinegar" applies equally to empirical findings reporting the effects of pornography, as well as it does to personal opinions and political agendas concerning the topic.

Alternative Sexual Orientations: Homosexuality

The author of this book graduated with a high school graduating class of 63 peers: 44 women and 19 males. Of the 19 males, three came out as gay (none to my knowledge were lesbians, or female homosexuals). Two of the three have passed away, and one is still living. Three of 19 is just under 16 percent, and by all accounts is much higher than the percentage of gays in the population. One of the three males did marry in his twenties, but was later divorced, apparently after experiencing the coming-out process (he is one of the two who is deceased). Some years ago a male professor acquaintance of the author's was arrested in a park for soliciting sex from an undercover male police officer. This acquaintance, who is married and has adult children exclaimed he is not gay, and said he turned to the illegal sexual activity because he was experiencing depression and frustration. Several years ago I had occasion to speak at social gatherings with a male who had been divorced for some years. One evening a group of friends gathered at a

favorite pub, and as my wife and I approached the table to join them I noticed this rather familiar looking female, and as I came closer I realized that it was this former male acquaintance, who would eventually tell me she was in the earliest stages of changing her sex. She was wearing a dress and make-up. Her new identity is "Venus" (not actually her new name). Many people have encountered similar situations, which does raise the question of the prevalence of alternative sexual orientations in the general population.

Gays in the American Population and the Issue of "Coming Out"

Savin-Williams (2005) sheds light on the question of prevalence by characterizing gays and lesbians into three categories: *same-sex feeling, same-sex behavior,* and, *identifying oneself as gay or lesbian.* When considering same-sex feeling, or being attracted to a person of the same gender, Savin-Williams reports *6 percent of males and four percent of women* fall into this category, with *9 percent of men and 4 percent of women* classified as *same sex behavior,* or engaging in sex with a same-gender person. What about the question of the prevalence of individuals who are *exclusively* gay or lesbian? The author reports *2.8 percent of males and 1.4 percent of females identify themselves as gay or lesbian.* Savin-Williams highlights an important issue, and that is persons who are not exclusively gay or lesbian do engage in homosexual behaviors, and can be attracted to a person of the same gender (2005, 40–44).

One of the most perplexing issues involving homosexuality is *coming out,* which is the process of acknowledging, accepting, and appreciating one's gayness. A number of models describing the process of coming out for gay men and women have been developed, and two are briefly discussed. Richard

Troiden (1979, 1988, 1989) has proposed a four-stage model that includes sensitization; identity and confusion; identity assumption; and, commitment. *Sensitization* occurs when the individual, usually at an early age begins to experience feelings of being different from same sex peers. Confusion often results with sensitization, since the individual is troubled by his feelings and cannot understand them fully. The second stage, *identity confusion* is characterized by the individual feeling inner turmoil and uncertainty about his or her identity. Normally this stage begins during adolescence, and individuals may begin to think they are gay, but not without a price since they may experience feelings of guilt, self-hatred, and isolation. During *identity assumption*, which often occurs in late adolescence, individuals are more certain *they* are gay and may accept this fact. Having developed a more clear understanding of their sexual identity, during this identity assumption individuals may seek out gay friendships, and they begin to find ways to cope with their emerging identity. *Commitment* signifies individuals have become comfortable with their homosexuality, frequently entering into relationships–romantic and nonromantic–with members of the same sex. The comfort zone also permits individuals to acknowledge their gayness when asked about it, with this likely to occur when other people offer them a feeling of safety and acceptance. Eli Coleman (1981) proposed a five-stage model of coming out for gay men and lesbians, beginning with *pre-coming out*. In this stage individuals are not aware of their same-sex feelings, although they may recognize they feel different than other people, especially same-sex peers. During *coming-out*, individuals are aware of their same-sex feelings, and they may begin to tell other people about their sexual identity, which may also entail seek-

ing contact with other individuals who may offer empathy for their emerging sexuality. *Exploration* entails individuals seeking out contact with gay people, and can include initiation into homosexual contact with other gays. *First relationship* is as it sounds and frequently involves a short-lived stable relationship that is romantic in nature. The final stage is *integration* where the private and public lives of individuals begin to merge, without the compartmentalization that characterized the previous stages. Prior to integration it is common for gays to live separate existences in which their sexual orientation is kept largely secret to most people, including family members.

Gay men and women have similar experiences "coming out," and although their sexual activities do not parallel one another, these behaviors do reflect the patterns found among heterosexual males and females. In society in general, males are more sexually active than females, and among homosexuals *gay men are more sexually active than lesbians*. This may be due to the greater expectation in society for males to be more sexually active and aggressive in the first place, and what's more, *gay males are more sexually active than straight males* because when gay men meet they may both be *eager to engage in sex* (similar to heterosexual situations when males are more likely to be seeking sex with women, than the other way around) (Blumstein and Schwartz, 1990). Lesbians are much like heterosexual women since they are less interested in the "one-night stand," *placing relationships above sex*, which develop slowly over time (Nichols, 1990). Lesbians in partnerships exhibit *classic sex role behavior*, and nowhere may this be truer than their desire to be *mothers*. Kantrowitz (1996) reported that lesbians have the *same desire to be mothers* as heterosexual females.

Explaining Homosexuality

There is no one theory or explanation of homosexuality. Over the years a number of *biologically-oriented* theories have been developed, and they are all over the place. One of the most frequently cited of these theories is gay men have *smaller brains* than heterosexual males, more specifically their hypothalamus is less than half the size of straight males (Levay, 1996). There are also *hormone* theories purporting that homosexuality is a result of *lower levels of testosterone in gay* than in straight males, and *lower levels of estrogen in lesbians* compared to heterosexual females (Roper, 1996), claims that have been rejected by others in the scientific community (Burr, 1996; Porter, 1996). Studies have also reported differences in the *size and functions* of areas of the brain between homosexuals and heterosexuals (Allen and Gorski, 1992; Swabb and Hoffman, 1990), and other research has examined the role of *DNA* among gay men, reporting nearly 70 percent of them had male relatives who were gay (Hamer and Copeland, 1994). Quite frequently a major (if not the major) problem with biologically-based theories of homosexuality is *nonrepresentative* or *biased samples.* For example, the Hamer and Copeland study was of 114 males who were not selected using probability sampling techniques, and Simon Levay used the brain tissues of 41 deceased males of which 19 were identified as homosexuals.

Sociological explanations of homosexuality examine the process of socialization in gender and sexual identity. *Gender identity* is the sense of being male or female, and *sexual identity*, which includes sexual orientation, is one's attractiveness to others and feelings of sexual arousal. Based on the data cited earlier, it appears nearly *98 percent* of the population is *heterosexual* which strongly suggests the power of parents/families and social

institutions in producing individuals who will become heterosexual. Although from a sociological perspective the exact processes–the how–in becoming gay have not been clearly identified, some research has pointed to the role of *mothers* in the socialization process to becoming gay. Fleischman (1983) reports that mothers who have *far more physical contact with their toddler sons* than they do with their little girls, may have a higher chance of their sons growing up homosexual. He also cites that a critical period in the socialization process is between *birth and age three*, and mothers who *shower* their little boys with *physical contact* may be setting the stage for their sons leaning toward a gay sexual identity.

The power of socialization cannot be underestimated in searching for explanations for sexual orientation. A *new* explanation *introduced here* is that the major social institutions, including the family, education, religion, government, economy, sport, and the media reinforce each other in a very powerful way to affect the 98 percent prevalence of heterosexuality in the population. In American society, heterosexuality is promoted both directly and subtly through the electronic and printed media, in schools, places of worship and faith, on the athletic fields, and in leadership in government, and business and industry. The *heterosexual look* is accentuated and stressed through every walk of life, and from the time of birth, children are bombarded with and exposed to the idea of heterosexuality: it is all around us, and it is inescapable (for the greatest majority). So this may account for the predominance of "straights" in society, but can it explain the small percentage of individuals who are gay? The answer is boldly "yes." The ever present and *powerful orientation toward heterosexuality* may in itself lead to becoming gay or lesbian. The ominous number of heterosexual messages may actually act as a take-off for

some to try or become attracted to the opposite, or homosexuality. In other words, socialization to the heterosexual choice may not
work for all. It may be a turnoff or even an
enticement to try something different. This
may explain the etiology of homosexuality
for the three or so percent of the population
that is gay.

The groundbreaking research undertaken
by Alfred Kinsey in 1948 and 1953 is still
useful in understanding homosexuality.
Kinsey developed a *heterosexual-homosexual
rating scale* that sheds light on the variations
in human sexual behavior. The scale ranges
from 0 to 6, and is ordered in the following
manner: (0) exclusively heterosexual; (1)
predominantly heterosexual, only incidental
homosexual; (2) predominantly heterosexual, but more than incidentally homosexual;
(3) equally heterosexual and homosexual; (4)
predominantly homosexual, but more than
incidentally heterosexual; (5) predominantly
homosexual, only incidentally heterosexual;
(6) exclusively homosexual. Of interest is the
percentage variation within each category.
For example, Kinsey reported *50 percent of
males* were exclusively heterosexual over
their life course (rating # 1), and *4 percent*
were exclusively homosexual during their
lifetimes (rating # 6). But Kinsey reported
much more, since *18 to 42 percent of males* and
between *11 and 20 percent of females* were predominantly heterosexual, but engaged in
incidental homosexual behavior (rating # 1),
and *13 to 38 percent of males and between six
and 14 percent of females* were predominantly
heterosexual, but more than incidentally
homosexual (rating # 2). Between *9 and 32
percent of males* were equally heterosexual
and homosexual, with the range *4 to 11 percent* for females (rating # 3). Between *7 and
26 percent of males and 3 to 8 percent of females*
were predominantly homosexual, but more
than incidentally heterosexual (rating # 4),
and *5 to 22 percent of males and 2 to 6 percent of*

females were predominantly homosexual, but
incidentally heterosexual (rating # 5).
Although Kinsey failed to employ scientific
sampling techniques in his studies of male
and female sexual behavior, the above data
do suggest that some individuals *cross the line*
between heterosexuality and homosexuality,
and therefore may not be labeled as strictly
homosexual (or heterosexual for that matter).

AIDS and Homophobia: Threats to the Homosexual Lifestyle

Acquired Immune Deficiency Syndrome
(AIDS) poses a real threat to the homosexual community, especially for gay males. In
2005, The U.S. Centers for Disease Control
reported over 60 percent AIDS *for males* was
transmitted through *male-to-male sexual contact*, while over 80 percent of AIDS for
women was transmitted via *heterosexual contact*. Approximately 14 percent of AIDS for
males is a result of *injecting drugs*, with the figure just under 20 percent for females. The
Henry J. Kaiser Foundation (2006) reported
the number of new AIDS cases in the United
States has dropped precipitously, down from
150,000 per year during the 1980s to about
40,000 new infections annually, indeed
encouraging news, but the threat of AIDS to
the homosexual population and to Americans in general can never be underestimated. The *African American community* is at great
risk for AIDS, accounting for over 50 percent of new AIDS cases in 2005, and *over 60
percent of American children* with AIDS are
African American. Among women under
25, African-American women comprised
nearly 70 percent of new AIDS cases in
2005. But a very important fact remains for
men who have sex with men (MSM), and
that is over 60 percent of new AIDS cases in
males occur as a result of male-to-male sexual contact.

Homophobia, or anti-gay prejudice and discrimination also poses a threat to the homosexual community. Also referred to as *heterosexism* since it has comparisons and similarities to other "isms" (racism, ageism, sexism, abelism) homophobia is still a recognized danger to some gays. In 2006, the Federal Bureau of Investigation reported nearly 16 percent of "bias-motivated offenses" (hate crimes) were against gays, and some of these included acts of violence (Summary of the Uniform Crime Reporting Program, 2006). Wilkinson (2004) has identified *homophobics* as individuals who are less educated, more conservative politically, religiously, and sexually. They are also more negative toward racial and ethnic minorities, while supporting traditional gender roles. Wilkinson also states homophobics are men who see themselves as *masculine*, and they are women whose self-perception is that of *feminine*. In addition, homophobic persons are *less likely* to know gays, and they are more given to using *stereotypes* about homosexuals, such as seeing gay men as "feminine" and lesbians as "masculine" women.

Alternative Sexual Orientations: Transgenderism and Bisexuality

Transgenderism is a term of recent origins, first appearing on the scene during the 1990s, and refers to individuals who see themselves as *both* male and female (as opposed to bisexuals, to be discussed shortly). There are basically three types of transgendered people: *transsexuals; intersexuals; and transvestites* (Thio, 2006). Transsexuals, who are typically males, identify with and assume a gender identity of the opposite sex. Transsexuals move through stages before they adopt a complete redefinition of themselves as the *opposite sex*, and some transsexuals will undergo hormone therapy and/or sex change operations. But for the purposes

of distinction, transsexuals assume a more permanent view of themselves as persons of the opposite sex as opposed to transvestites who cross-dress, usually for the purposes of *sexual gratification*. It is important to note that *transvestites are heterosexuals*, again usually males who see themselves as predominantly heterosexual but who enjoy dressing as females, while *not adopting* a more permanent self-concept as a woman (or in the case of female cross-dressers, as a man). Intersexuals are individuals *born* with male and female organs who may undergo surgery during infancy, with most of these surgeries changing infant girls into boys (2006, 255–256).

Bisexuals are heterosexuals who engage in sex with members of their own sex as well as persons of the opposite sex, and according to Weinberg, Williams and Pryor (2002) move through *four stages* in the process of becoming bisexual: initial confusion; finding and applying the label; settling into the identity; and, continued uncertainty. *Initial confusion* is as it sounds, and that is many bisexuals experience *serious doubts* about their sexual identities before developing a self-definition of bisexual. *Finding and applying the label* entails becoming more aware of their bisexuality and receiving encouragement from other persons who have moved through the four stages. *Settling into the identity* involves *secondary deviance*, meaning adopting a more deep and thorough self-labeling as bisexual, a process that may take years. *Continued uncertainty* means that even after inculcating the self-definition of being bisexual, many bisexuals encounter periods of *doubt, even resentment* about their sexual identity.

In Recognition: Shere Hite

When it comes to groundbreaking research in the study of human sexuality, many names come to mind. One name is

Shere Hite who helped to extend the limits of the study of human sexuality with two major works, one on female sexuality in 1976 (the focus of this recognition), and male sexuality in 1981. *The Hite Report: A Nationwide Study of Female Sexuality* is recognized for both how the study was undertaken and what it revealed. It was still only the 1970s and tolerance for such research was not nearly what it is today. Add to this, the study was about how females feel about, enjoy, and engage in sex. Was America ready for this? Shere Hite has two doctorates, one which is in clinical sexology from Maimonides University, North Miami Beach. Dr. Hite originally pursued the Ph.D. at Columbia University, but left because she felt it to be too conservative. Her 1976 study of female sexuality was undertaken in a manner that raised eyebrows in the scientific community that demands probability statistics as the means of acquiring samples that will meet the requirement of generalizability. Hite circumvented this pillar of social science methodology and used women's groups, the National Organization for Women, abortion rights organizations, and magazines to distribute her questionnaire. Over 100,000 questionnaires were distributed, and 3,000 were completed, adding to the skepticism that would follow the publication of her findings. So what were some of the results? Hite reported that most women masturbate, but have guilt feelings about it. She also found only 30 percent of women orgasm regularly from intercourse, that many women fake orgasm, and are critical of their husband/partner's lovemaking. Perhaps the most controversial aspect of her study was on lesbians who she stated found more sexual gratification from sex with women than men, and a number of lesbians interviewed were married. Three thousand completed responses out of 100,000 distributed questionnaires left a number of individuals skeptical about the validity of her findings. But in the tradition of Alfred Kinsey her research weathered the storm, and her contributions to the study of sexuality remain significant today.

SUMMARY

Americans are sexually active across all age groups, and this even includes the elderly. Sex among teens is common and remains a concern among American adults. Prostitution continues to receive attention from social institutions, in particular religion and the law, and there are different types of prostitutes, with most being streetwalkers, many who work for pimps who may exact violence against them. Men (johns) seek the services of prostitutes for a variety of reasons, one which is sex without strings or commitment. Over the years a number of laws have been passed concerning pornography, but the major approach has been to leave the distinction between obscenity and pornography to community standards. The research on the effects of pornography remains inconclusive, and may be dependent on political motives and agendas. Approximately 3 percent of the population is homosexual, a number that appears to remain unchanged for many years. Homosexuality may entail a process of "coming-out," or stages along the path to becoming and adapting to being gay. There is no one explanation or theory of homosexuality, however a sociological approach is to focus on the process of socialization in the development of sexual orientation. In addition to heterosexuality and homosexuality there is transgenderism and bisexuality, which normally involve males. Bisexuals are heterosexuals by self-concept who enjoy sex with both men and women, and transgendered persons can be those born with male and female sex organs, cross-dressers, and trans-sexuals who identify with the opposite sex, and who may undergo major biological procedures to more fully become a male or female.

Chapter 14

ELITE AND POWER DEVIANCE

CASE STUDY: ENRON

Many people have heard about the Enron scandal, just one of a number of major examples of corporate corruption that have occurred in the past decade in the United States. In a general sense what people know about the Enron tragedy is that the company, *as was*, no longer exists, and that many people lost their jobs, investments, and lifesavings as a result of the scandal (to the tune of billions of dollars). But what *if* it was said that what occurred at the highest levels at Enron is the epitome of greed, brazenness, arrogance, cold-bloodedness, and elitism? It is one thing to comprehend how the scandal was pulled off, meaning the understanding of the fraudulent and complicated accounting techniques that were employed to hide the corruption—the *technical elements* of the scandal. It is another issue to address the demise of the seventh largest corporation on the Fortune 500 using principles and theoretical notions from sociology and social psychology. What does this imply? Power, or what will be called *power deviance* in this chapter. The age-old expression "power corrupts" applies magnificently to the Enron scandal. Brilliance in accounting and other technical areas of expertise was not the sole requirement for a number of

high-ranking officials within the company to make millions of dollars via theft and deceit. *Power was the number one element* needed to commit the various crimes for which a number of Enron officials have been convicted. With power can come arrogance, and when the two are co-joined, individuals may come to see themselves as untouchable and beyond reproach. From this may stem fear, fear faced by lower-ranking individuals who are hesitant and frightened to do anything about the scandal, even if they are suspicious that things are not right with the company. But *Sharon Watkins*, the Vice President for Corporate Development for Enron did not cave in to the abuses of power and greed engaged in by people above her, and her integrity was instrumental in revealing the depths of the scandal, a point to be addressed later.

The story of Enron is the story of the late Kenneth Lay, who founded it in 1985 by merging InterNorth from Omaha, Nebraska with Houston Natural Gas, Houston Texas, eventually moving corporate headquarters to Houston. So what was Enron? Enron was an *energy trading giant* providing electricity and gas throughout the United States. In addition, Enron was involved in the water utility market, broadband services, and capital and risk management (to name just a few of its other interests). So respected was the company that from 1996–2001 it was named by Fortune Magazine as "America's Most Innovative Company" (Wikipedia, 2007). Make no mistake about it, Enron was not only big; it was gargantuan.

Before identifying the criminal schemes used in the scandal, a listing of major Enron officials, their positions with the company, and the charges and convictions brought against them is presented. This is discussed here to clearly show that the company was not destroyed by mid-managers or other lower level individuals seeking wealth and prestige. Instead, Enron was decimated by its highest ranking employees, *the very people trusted with the health and stability of the corporation.*

Kenneth Lay: Lay, the founder of Enron was its Chief Executive Officer (CEO) and eventually Chairman of the Board of Directors (COB). As founder of the corporation Lay yielded enormous power and influence, not only within Enron but also nationally and internationally, but all of this power was not enough to prevent him from being arrested, indicted, and convicted of serious criminal charges that included conspiracy to commit securities and wire fraud, bank fraud, and giving false statements to federal authorities. He was convicted of multiple counts on each charge, for which he could have received years in federal prison, but he died unexpectedly at the age of 64 in the summer of 2006, several months before he was to be officially sentenced. What is essential to understand is there is no parole in the federal system, and had Lay lived to begin his sentence he may have spent the remainder of his years in prison.

Jeff Skilling: During his tenure with Enron, Jeff Skilling held the titles Chief Operations Officer (COO) and Chief Executive Officer (CEO), and in May 2006, along with Kenneth Lay, Skilling was found guilty on federal charges of committing securities and wire fraud, making false statements to auditors, and insider trading. He also faced multiple counts on the charges levied against him, such as 51 counts of insider trading. Skilling who was 54 years old at the time of his sentencing, received 24 years in federal prison. Since there is no parole in the federal system, Skilling must do 85 percent of his time, which means he is not eligible for release from prison until he is 74. Along with the serious crimes for which he was involved, if Skilling did anything to receive such a lengthy sentence it was his failure to cooperate with authorities, as well as his lack of remorse for destroying the lives of thousands of investors and company employees.

Andrew and Lea Fastow: If there was ever an example of misdirected intelligence (probably better stated as genius) it is Andrew Fastow who is the former Chief Financial Officer (CFO) of Enron. Fastow was one of the masterminds behind the Enron scandal and is currently spending six years in federal prison on charges of conspiracy, wire fraud, insider trading, and obstruction of justice. In addition to prison time Fastow, who earned at least $30 million dollars in the scandal was forced to forfeit $24 million dollars of his assets. At one point he had over 100 charges filed against him and his prison sentence, which was originally 10 years was reduced to six years as a result of his turning state witness for the federal authorities. In other words, Fastow cooperated with the investigation by helping to give up both Jeff Skilling and Kenneth Lay, and Fastow's wife Lea spent one year in prison on charges of income tax evasion (her original sentence was six months but was extended to one year because she attempted to renege on her plea bargain agreement). Part of her husband's plea bargain deal was that Lea would first serve her time, get released, and then he (Andrew Fastow) would begin serving his longer sentence so that at least one of them would be at home to raise their children. If Andrew Fastow fails to cooperate with the authorities concerning any ongoing or new questions relevant to the Enron scandal, he could automatically have some if not all of the remaining 90 plus charges brought against him in new criminal proceedings.

Richard Causey, Michael Kopper and Ben Gilson: Three other major conspirators in the Enron scandal were Richard Causey, the Chief Accounting Officer (CAO), Michael Kopper, Managing Director of Enron Global Finance, and Ben Gilsan, the Treasurer of Enron, all individuals with significant access to Enron's inner workings, *making them prime candidates for being able to pull off such major criminal activities*, not to mention three men who yielded enormous power within the energy trading giant. Think about this: the CAO, the company finance czar, and the company treasurer: who would be in a better position in any major corporation to know the deepest and most detailed information about the company's finances and investments? If dishonest, and they were, who would be more suited to understand how to swindle the company, its employees, and investors out of billions of dollars? The answer: the people with their hands directly and intimately on the economic heartbeat of the company: Causey, Kopper and Gilsan. For their crimes Causey received 66 months, Kopper 37 months, and Gilsan 53 months in prison. All initially made out like bandits, earning millions of dollars from their roles in the crimes, and this was on top of already major salaries, bonuses, and stock options. For example, based on insider information Causey sold nearly 200,000 shares of his company stock, profiting him over $13 million (www.enron.com/corp/pressroom/bios/rickcausey.html 2008). The charges against the three included money laundering, conspiracy, fraud, and

insider trading. In addition to their prison sentences, millions of dollars of assets were seized from Causey, Kopper and Gilsan, and they could have received much longer prison sentences but chose to enter plea bargaining agreements to avoid punishment that could have resulted in at least 15 years each in federal incarceration.

So what did their crimes entail? It would take a book just by itself to explain and to detail all of the criminal shenanigans involved in the Enron disaster. But at the center of the scandal are *special purpose entities (SPE)*, raptors, or offshore partnerships (the SPE's can be thought of as Special Purpose Entities Offshore Partnerships) which involved investments made by Enron and outside parties. The SPE's could either be entered on Enron's balance sheet, or could be treated as off balance sheet investments according to rules of accounting. Enron chose the latter because company officials thought that would make Enron appear more attractive for investors on Wall Street (*United States Securities and Exchange Commission, Plaintiff v. Michael Kopper, Defendant, 2002).* The creation of these SPE's as part of over three thousand of Enron's offshore investments opened the door for deceit and greed in a manner and magnitude rarely seen in American corporate enterprise. The following statements made by former Enron officials relative to these SPE's will help to place focus on the issue. Said one executive, "they (Enron senior officers) would clear a white board and draw a flow chart that would be absolutely incomprehensible." Another former Enron executive stated "they'd be drawing boxes and arrows going in every direction" (*The Oklahoman*, 2005). So what is the point of this? Individuals such as Skilling, Fastow, Causey, Gilsan, and Kopper were involved in blinding company employees and investors about the company's financial status through the use of deceptive accounting and diagram techniques. Very smart individuals such as lawyers, engineers, accountants, and finance experts employed by Enron and hired as consultants would be misled–bamboozled about investments involving SPE's, allowing the culprits to engage in a shell game where money would be moved in and out of the SPE's in such a confusing and complicated manner that no one, except those directly involved with the crimes would have any clue as to what was really taking place, or the exact locations of the investments. So, what was really taking place? The funneling of millions of dollars from these raptors into the pockets of high ranking Enron executives, such as Kopper and Fastow. That is correct. A funneling game that kept numerous smart and highly educated Enron employees in the dark, with only a small but very powerful number of individuals knowing about, being involved in, and benefiting from the deceit processes. One individual who became very suspicious about the accounting practices used by the Enron elite was Sharon Watkins, herself an accountant who came to Enron from the giant accounting firm Arthur Andersen. Watkins wrote a letter to Kenneth Lay stating that these accounting techniques would destroy the company, and "blew the whistle" on the scams to the Securities and Exchange Commission (SEC), resulting in the full-blown investigation now known to millions of Americans. Unfortunately, she was correct and equally unfortunate was the demise of Arthur Andersen since it was involved in destroying documents related to the Enron scandal. So what seems to be in a heartbeat, a brief moment in time in the cosmic scheme of things, not one, but *two* of America's most highly touted and respected companies, Enron and Arthur Andersen were decimated and largely dismantled as a result of the greed and arrogance of key figures within the Enron status hierarchy. This returns us to a point made earlier, and that is it was not as much the ability to manipulate and deceive via sophisticated accounting or finance skills that made the Enron situation possible. It was the *use and abuse of power* that frightened and stymied other Enron employees to the point that they would accept anything that was told to them of Enron's overall financial health, by people they believed in and thought they could trust. There was also the factor of "awe," or being in awe of the likes of the Lays, Skillings, Fastows and Koppers, so much so that this alone was enough to blind top flight mid-managers and others to the crimes occurring around them. There is more to the Enron scandal including fraudulent activities involving Kopper, Fastow and others in California with wind farms, and corruption involving that state's public retirement system. The end result? The collapse of a corporate giant: the destruction of "America's most innovative company"; the loss of thousands of jobs and billions of dollars of investor loss; and company bankruptcy in December, 2001.

Elite and Power Deviance Defined

Elite deviance will be defined in light of the work of David Simon (2006) who has authored nine editions of *Elite Deviance* dating back to 1982. Elite deviance is deviance engaged in by the highest corporate, military and political figures in the United States. It can and does include criminal and unethical behavior, with a common denominator being it is done at the expense of the public, for power and profit. Therefore the characteristics of elite deviance are (2006, 12):

- it is undertaken by individuals from the highest social classes.
- acts of elite deviance can be criminal, immoral, and unethical.

- elite deviance can be done for personal gain or to enhance the power and wealth of organizations.
- little risk is involved for those engaging in elite deviance.
- acts of elite deviance can pose serious threats and danger to citizens and to society in general.
- elite deviance can be concealed for many years (thus the issue of little risk).

So if elite deviance entails activities undertaken for power and profit that can damage the best interests of millions of other people, what then is *power deviance*? Power deviance is a term coined by the author of this text that is an *extension of* and *addition to* the meaning of elite deviance. Power deviance is behavior that involves corruption, immorality, callousness, greed, and arrogance. It is the ability to *walk over others* and to do them harm without feelings of remorse or sympathy. Individuals engaged in elite deviance may actually know their activities endanger others, the environment, and plant and animal species, and this may include feelings of remorse or regret on behalf of the culprits. However, *power deviance is cruel*, and those engaged in it simply *do not care* what they do to others. Take the example of Enron. As the company's stock value and profit levels plunged, many of those involved in the scandal continued to rip off the company, not caring what that entailed for thousands of others. As noted, Richard Causey cashed in over $13 million in stocks completely aware that Enron was in deep financial trouble, but he still took the money and ran, contributing immensely to the precarious financial status of the company. What is more, Kenneth Lay and Jeff Skilling continually misled the company and its investors by telling them things were good, when all indications on Wall Street told a much different story. By engaging in

power deviance the two prevented others from knowing in advance that their jobs/careers, lifesavings, and investments were in serious jeopardy (preventing them from taking actions that might have reduced the effects on them of this terrible scandal). At one point in a meeting with investors who were questioning the economic health of Enron, Skilling directed profanity at one stock holder, demonstrating his lack of caring and concern for people who had invested their lives and savings in the energy giant, *exemplifying what is meant by power deviance.*

Types of Elite Deviance and Power Deviance

Elite and power deviance cover much ground. All types of corporate, military, and political deviance serve as examples of the concepts. This can include stock fraud, insider trading, polluting the environment, unethical experiments on humans, bribery, graft, monopolies, padding the payroll, false advertising, unsafe products, embezzlement, wasting resources, war, and assassinations. The list is endless because the examples are endless, *but they all have certain elements in common*, including the abuse of power, unethical conduct, and callused attitudes toward the human condition by individuals holding significant prestige and status. Consider *Watergate* for one moment, perhaps the cat's meow of examples of political corruption, and for the purposes of this discussion prima facie evidence of *both elite and power deviance.* Many people understand Watergate as a burglary involving zealots convicted to the reelection of President Richard Milhous Nixon. On June 17, 1972, five men broke into the Watergate Hotel in Washington D. C. to bug telephones. Why? The area that was burglarized was home to the Democratic National Committee, and with the 1972 election less than six months away, those responsible for the crime believed that any critical information relative to the upcoming election could become known to Republican interests (this is one explanation for the burglary). Those arrested for the burglary were former CIA operative Bernard Barker, who is believed to have been involved in the ill-fated Bay of Pigs evasion in April, 1961, and Virgillio R. Gonzales, a Cuban refuge and a locksmith from Miami, Florida. Others arrested included former F.B.I and C.I.A. agent James W. McCord who was the co-cordinator of the Republican National Committee and the Committee for the Re-election of the President (CREEP), and anti-Fidel Castro Cuban exile Eugenio R. Martinez who had ties to Barker. The arrests included one very interesting person from Miami, who went by the alias Frank A. Sturgis, also with connections to Bernard Barker. Not only was Sturgis himself involved in anti-Castro activities, but it was later discovered that his real name was Frank Fiorini, a bagman for a major Florida-based mafia don, Santo Trafficante *(Ultimate Sacrifice: John and Robert Kennedy, the Plan for a Coup in Cuba, and the Murder of JFK, 2005)*. Why might this be interesting? In-and-of-itself the fact that a member of the mafia was involved in the burglary should immediately raise suspicions since the crime entailed breaking into a leading political party's base of operations. Co-joining this issue with *who* Sturgis/Fiorini was involved with in committing the crime makes his participation in the act even more interesting (to use a light word). Sturgis' partners in the burglary were either former CIA and F.B.I. employees (Barker and McCord), not to mention that McCord held a major position within the Republican Party at the time he committed the felony. In addition, Sturgis participated in the burglary with two Cuban exiles who hated Fidel Castro, and who may have participated in the botched Bay of Pigs invasion.

So what is a made man in the Santo Trafficante crime syndicate doing breaking into the national headquarters of the Democratic Party, with Cuban exiles and former operatives within the CIA and F.B.I.? One other question: what are former members of America's premier law enforcement and foreign intelligence gathering apparatuses doing committing a burglary?

The story of Watergate is much bigger and in-depth then what is covered in this chapter, but a few more names should be mentioned in connection with the burglary. Two other former employees of the CIA and F.B.I. were the "brains" behind the break-in. G. Gordon Liddy, who is a popular radio talking head these days, was a former "G" man, Treasury official, and former CIA case officer who at the time of the crime was a member of Nixon's White House staff. E. Howard Hunt, who passed away in 2007 was former C.I.A, and a consultant to President Nixon, and is believed to have played a role in planning the Bay of Pigs invasion. Also intimately involved in the planning of the burglary were the two most powerful men in the Nixon White House: H. R. Haldeman, Nixon's Chief of Staff, and John Erlichman, domestic affairs advisor to the president. Now for another question: why would two men occupying powerful positions within the most important political office in the world plan what turned about to be not only a two-bit burglary, but a stupid one at that? Before it was all said and done other important officials within the Nixon White House resigned, were fired, indicted, or convicted of their roles in the crime including John Mitchell, the Attorney General (AG) of the United States–the nation' top law man; counsel to the president John Dean who testified before Congress that he had discussed the cover-up of Watergate with Nixon at least 35 different occasions; and Alexander Butterfield who was Nixon's appointments secretary. What is more, Mitchell's replacement as AG, Richard Kleindienst also resigned over the scandal and Charles Colson, counsel to Nixon and today one of America's most well-known Christian writers spent time in prison for his role in the scandal (www.watergateinfo.com 2008). Let's not forget Richard Nixon himself who on August 8, 1974 became the first president to resign from office, and it can be argued that Nixon wanted to be president of the United States more than anything, or perhaps even anybody before or since him. All this pain and controversy over an ill-conceived and misadvised burglary. As this is not enough, Vice President Spiro Agnew was forced to resign from office before Nixon for crimes unrelated to Watergate. Agnew's situation is detailed when discussing political corruption.

Watergate is prime representation of both elite and power deviance. It is an example par excellence of deviance committed by people at the highest levels of government, and it speaks to the meaning of power deviance. Nixon and his most trusted staff members placed the stability and security of the United States at great risk for over two years. At stake was national security and the image of the nation that had already been tarnished by the war in Viet Nam. Cover-up and lies came out of the Nixon White House in mathematically incalculable droves, and all along it was about the men at the top, or "All the President's Men" to echo the book written by Bernstein and Woodward (1974). Nixon, Haldeman, Erlichman, Mitchell, Liddy, et al. were out to protect their hides at the expense of millions of other Americans. Watergate is power deviance at its finest: corruption, deceit, lying, arrogance, and callousness. For two years Nixon and a number of his closest allies expended much of their time trying to bail themselves out of a scandal that became a national nightmare, and while doing so failed to pay heed to their

roles and responsibilities running the most powerful office in the land.

Elite and power deviance cover much ground and include many examples. What follows are major examples of these types of deviance occurring within the corporate, military, and political sectors of the country. The discussion begins with three examples of political corruption, two which have all but faded from the memories of the American people, the Spiro Agnew fiasco and Wedtech, and one that still remains a topic of conversation, Iran-Contra.

Political Elite and Power Deviance

The Case of Spiro Agnew

There are many examples of political elite and power deviance including Watergate, and smack dab in the middle of Watergate was a scandal involving Vice President Spiro Agnew who resigned from office on October 10, 1973. But as previously noted, Agnew's departure from the Vice Presidency had nothing to do with Watergate, instead it had everything to do with political graft, or accepting money illegally to perform favors for others. Although forced out of office by President Richard Nixon who himself would resign from office just 10 months later, Agnew never went to trial and instead pleaded no contest or nolo contendere to charges of income tax evasion and money laundering brought against him by the Attorney General of the State of Maryland. So what is it that got Agnew into trouble? Agnew's political career in Maryland included holding the positions of Baltimore County Executive (BCE) and Governor, and as BCE Agnew took numerous bribes from engineering firms in order to secure contracts for them. In doing so Agnew developed close relationships and consorted with four individuals: I. H. Hammerman, a real estate developer and mortgage banker; Jerome B.

Wolff, an attorney and an engineer who was president of Greiner Environmental Systems; Allen Green, president and co-owner of Green and Associates, Inc.; and, Lester Matz, president of two Maryland-based engineering firms. Most of the illegal contracts were awarded to the four individuals or their close associates, and it is to be noted that the five principles rarely collaborated together on specific contracts, instead the contracts would be made to one, maybe two firms at any given time (Beall, Skolnik, Baker, Liebman, 1978).

Normally there is a bidding process involved in awarding contracts in state and federal government, with the contract awarded to the lowest bidder. The process is supposed to be "blind" in nature meaning that bids are sealed and no one knows the dollar amounts contained in the envelopes until they are opened. But in the 1960s in Maryland, engineering contracts were not awarded on the basis of this type of bidding process, instead who received the contracts was totally up to the discretion of public officials such as the Governor and county executives. Enter *power deviance*. Spiro Agnew was a corrupt individual who learned the ropes of awarding contracts illegally earlier in his career as Baltimore County Executive, procuring his skills with small contracts and then graduating to bigger ones that would hold for him larger sums of money. He was also ruthless, demonstrating complete disregard for law and procedure. By awarding many contracts to the few, a number of engineering businesses were never afforded the opportunity to profit legally from working with state and local government, clearly demonstrating Agnew's lack of concern for fairness, equity, and the common good, not to mention his violation of trust and oath of office.

The procedures involved in awarding the contracts were quite simple, but effective. As Baltimore County Executive and Governor, Agnew had access to information concerning construction projects such as the building of bridges, and relayed this information to the four individuals discussed earlier, proceeding to take money from them so that their firms or interests would get contracts. To enhance the bribery scheme, Agnew appointed Jerome B. Wolff Chairman Director of the Maryland State Roads Commission, and in that capacity Wolff was largely responsible for determining what firms would receive contracts, collecting money from them and giving 50 percent of the take to Agnew. Some firms were implicitly involved in the scandal and were so because they needed the work (1978, 829).

Agnew received cash payments in white envelopes either directly or indirectly from Green, Hammerman, Wolff, and Matz, and his take was normally between three and five percent of the contract amount. The money was usually given to him in his government office, including when he was Vice President, and the payments ranged from $1,000 to $20,000. Depending on the individual, Agnew would receive multiple payments per year, and as one example Allen Green provided Agnew with up to six white envelopes annually, and while Agnew was Governor Green and Associates received ten contracts totaling $4,000,000. At one point during the time he was receiving bribes, Agnew reached into a suit jacket and found an envelope containing $20,000, apparently forgetting that he had placed the envelope in the jacket, an indication of the number of bribes he had taken since he had forgotten this one particular payoff. Be it $1,000, $11,000 or $20,000 Agnew said he took bribes because he needed the money to support his political ambitions, and to maintain a lifestyle of a high-ranking public figure (1978, 833–842).

Iran Contra: Arms for Hostages

Presidential administrations are often muddled in scandals and doubts concerning decisions they make. For instance, the past two presidents, William Jefferson Clinton and George W. Bush have faced scandals and questions, Clinton for the Monica Lewinsky and Whitewater scandals and President George W. Bush for the situation involving the firing of eight federal prosecutors, and serious questions centering around his decision to take the United States to war with Iraq. President Gerald R. Ford may have lost his bid for a second term in office as a result of his pardon of former president Richard Nixon, and Lyndon Johnson's decision to escalate the conflict with Viet Nam based on the so-called Gulf of Tonkin Resolute has raised serious doubt for years. Former president Jimmy Carter, arguably the greatest former president in American history, will always have the image of his administration tarnished as a result of his inability to end the Iranian hostage crisis. Forgotten is his enormous success with the Camp David Accords where he brokered a major peace agreement between the leaders of Israel and Egypt (Menachem Begin and Anwar Sadat, respectively). It is believed that John Kennedy carried on affairs while president, and of course the greatest scandal of them all in the past 50 years is Watergate involving Richard Nixon. But what about President Ronald Reagan, was his administration squeaky clean?

While Jimmy Carter was president of United States 52 diplomats were kidnapped by Iranian militants and held captive for 444 days, from November 4, 1979 until January 20, 1981 the day Reagan was inaugurated, raising suspicions that Ronald Reagan had made a secret deal with the Iranian government for the release of the hostages prior to his taking office (in addition to the 52

American hostages there were 16 other hostages whom were released before January 20, 1981). The hostage crisis was a major embarrassment to the United States since it appeared it was unable reach a settlement with Iran for the release of the captives, and it proved to be a crushing blow to the reelection bid of Carter. But why the release on January 20, 1981? Was it because this new, tough talking conservative president had led the Iranians prior to his inauguration to believe that he would take military action against them, or did it possibly involve other motives?

The answer to the question may very well lie in what is now known as the Iran-Contra Affair or scandal. In October 1980, either Vice President-elect George Walker Herbert Bush or future CIA Director William Casey *allegedly* met secretly in Paris, France or in Washington, D.C. (there has been debate just who met with the Iranians and where the meetings were held) with representatives from the Iranian government and offered them a deal of *arms for hostages*, and the Iranian government would receive armaments (probably missiles) in return for the captives (Simon, 2008). If this seems a bit confusing it should since Iran had become a major adversary of the United States, causing it great embarrassment, and here is a presidential candidate (Reagan) supposedly tough on anything and anyone who is anti-American and it is alleged he was secretly making a deal with the Iranians through some of his closet confidents. At stake for the Reagan bid to become president was the fear of a so-called "October surprise" in which Jimmy Carter would win the release of the hostages just weeks before the 1980 election, bolstering his chances of reelection that had been severely damaged as a result of the Iranian crisis (2008, 313). If there was such a deal made by Reagan interests with Iran it apparently was with the understanding that the hostages would not be released until after the election, and Iranian agreement with this would spell sure defeat for Carter. What may have begun as a win-win involving both governments whereby Iran would receive sorely needed military armaments and the United States would get back its hostages is believed have evolved into bigger theatre early in the Reagan presidency.

The country of Nicaragua was involved in civil turmoil during the Reagan presidency that involved the *Sandinistas,* said to be sympathetic to Communism and a CIA-created organization known as the *Contras.* The Reagan administration along with the CIA, now directed by William Casey feared that without substantial military and economic support provided to the Contras, the Communist-backed Sandinistas would take control of the country, a thought totally unacceptable to the big time anti-Communist Ronald Reagan. During the first two years of his presidency Reagan was able to authorize funds for the Contras by working with Congress, but then from 1982–1984 Congress passed what have become known as the *Boland Amendments* which cut off funding to the anti-Communist Contras (2008, 312). Reagan, Bush, Casey and others then sought ways to keep military aid alive to the Contras, and once again enter Iran which itself was engaged in a brutal and lengthy war with neighboring Iraq. Iran was in need of armaments and it is alleged entered into an agreement to buy these arms from the United States who then would divert the proceeds from the illegal sale to the Contras. Why illegal? The sales were in contradiction to the Boland Amendments which were forbidden by law.

The Iran-Contra issue gets even more interesting from here. Take for example the following monikers: *Operation Polecat,* the *Enterprise,* and, *Operation Black Eagle* (2008, 314–316). The sales of arms for cash scheme

was called "Operation Polecat" by those with knowledge of it within the State Department because it stank so much, and carrying out the illegal arms sales was placed in the hands of what would be called the "Enterprise," which was comprised of retired military and intelligence personnel, arms dealers, and drug smugglers, and was allegedly created by Marine Lieutenant Oliver North, who eventually stood trial for his role in "Irangate." But it is "Operation Black Eagle" that raises the greatest eyebrows, since it entailed making a deal with Panamanian dictator Manuel Noriega who enjoyed a profitable relationship with the United States during the 1980s, but in 1992 began serving a 30-year prison sentence on a number of charges including cocaine trafficking. The deal struck with Noriega involved the use of Panamanian airfields by the Black Eagle operatives to support the efforts of the Contras in neighboring Nicaragua. The illegal operations were run from these airstrips in exchange for the use of the cargo planes, but for what purposes and why did Noriega need the cargo planes? The answer is to smuggle cocaine and marijuana into the United States in collaboration with one of the world's most violent and dangerous drug trafficking organizations, the Medellin drug cartel from Columbia, South America. One route taken by these planes was to Costa Rica where they would land in farm area owned by a CIA and National Security Council (NSC) liaison officer to the Contras, John Hull. From Hull's ranch area the drugs would be smuggled into the United States by air and land, and for his efforts with the drug smuggling scheme Hull was receiving up to $1,000 a month, courtesy of the NSC. It is worthy to note that 80 percent of the cocaine smuggled into the United States each year came directly from the Medellin operation which was controlled by two of the most notorious drug traffickers in world history, Pablo Escobar and Jorge Ochoa (Geiss, 1988; Simon, 2008, 313–314).

What about the trial of Marine officer Oliver North, who has become a popular television personality since the Iran-Contra affair? In 1989 North was convicted on the charge that while serving as an aide to the National Security Council under Ronald Reagan he destroyed classified documents related to "Contragate," a conviction that was overturned by a federal appeals court in 1990 (*The New York Times*, 1990). For many Americans Oliver North is a hero who served his country with dignity, who should never have faced criminal charges for his role in the Iran-Contra scandal since he was acting as a patriot carrying out orders given by the highest powers in the land.

Wedtech

Mention Wedtech to the majority of Americans and they would probably say "Wed what? Yet the scandal involving Wedtech is *one of the worst in American history*, one so bad that Fred J. Crook, writing for *The Nation* said it was more severe than one of America's worst political nightmares, the Teapot Dome scandal of the 1920s (1988, 458). Earlier in the text the theory "Institutional Anomie" by Messner and Rosenfield was discussed. A major premise of this theory is everyone wants a part of the American dream and will do anything to get their share of the pie, thinking that applies to a once small-time tool and die company in the poverty stricken south Bronx of New York City, the Welbeit Electronic Die Corporation, later known as Wedtech. Wedtech is an example of the American dream founded in 1965 by John Mariotta, the son of Puerto Rican immigrants. For some years the company struggled to stay alive, and by the 1980s it was in need of a quick fix, hoping to get its hands on government contracts, espe-

cially since Jimmy Carter when campaigning for president in 1976 visited the south Bronx and gave the impression he would come to the aid of Wedtech. He never did, thus opening the door for the scandal.

There were so many names associated with the Wedtech scandal it would be futile to mention all of them here, however it is believed to have involved lower level players and individuals all the way to the top of the Reagan White House. Enter *Mario Biaggi*, a member of the United States House of Representatives from the south Bronx who was instrumental in winning military contracts for John Mariotta, but illegally. Well aware of Wedtech's precarious financial status and the company's inability to secure loans from the Small Business Administration (SBA), Biaggi went to work contacting individuals within the Reagan administration concerning Wedtech's need to secure financing from the SBA, a move that was neither crooked or unusual since members of the House made these types of requests on a frequent basis (1988, 458). The problem became how the awards from the SBA were actually made. Biaggi was given *kickbacks* for his role in winning SBA money for Wedtech, and he was able to arrange a cover-up by having Wedtech hire the law firm that employed his son (Richard Biaggi) to overview and manage the contracts. The money awarded to Wedtech was substantial and this called for the need for legal counsel to help John Marriata understand the intricacies involved in the contracts with the SBA. Mario Biaggi owned over 100,000 shares of Wedtech stock that he hid by placing his ownership of it in the name of his lawyer son, who was paid $500,000 by Wedtech for his services. This is another example of "scratch my back and I'll scratch yours" since it entailed a company that needed work, a corrupt politician that accepted bribes to secure the needed contracts for Wedtech, and the politician's son who was willing to go along with the scheme for a large sum of money.

But it doesn't end there. Wedtech needed help and through his efforts Biaggi was able to set up a meeting in the basement of the White House that included an Assistant Secretary of the Army, representatives from the SBA and from Wedtech, and Mark Bragg who was a partner in a Public relations firm with Lynn Nofziger, a major political advisor to President Reagan. Out of this meeting came the contracts with the SBA and eventually contracts with the American military that included building 13,000 six-cylinder engines for generators and pumps for the U.S. Army and pontoon boats for the U.S. Navy, none of which would have been built by Wedtech if it wasn't for the bribes accepted by Biaggi, his son, and others. So how well did Wedtech do? The company flourished with annual revenues exceeding $100 million annually, and with military contracts that totaled over $250 million. However, by 1986 the company had gone bankrupt as a result of paying individuals like the Biaggis large sums of kickbacks and bribes. Unfortunately, the victims also included at least 1,500 Wedtech employees who lost their jobs as a result of the bankruptcy (1988, 461). The scandal is said to have involved Edwin Meese, a close personnel friend of President Reagan's and a counselor to him, and a cousin of then Vice President George H. W. Bush, Charles Dickey Dyer III, who was instrumental in getting the Reagan White House to secure the SBA loans and military contracts for Wedtech. Anything else? Here is a sampling of others who benefited from the scam (1988, 460):

• James Jenkins, an aide to Edwin Meese became a Washington representative of Wedtech and received an annual salary of $165,000.
• Four members of the Board of Directors of Wedtech who looted the company of over 2 million dollars.

• Michael Mitchell and his brother Clarence Mitchell, two Maryland State Senators who received $50,000 in bribes from Wedtech, and whose uncle was a member of the House of Representatives and head of the Congressional oversight committee that monitored the SBA.
• South Bronx officials of teamster Local 875 who extorted nearly $500,000 from Wedtech on the threat of invoking labor strife within the company.
• Auditor Richard Bluestine who was paid in excess of $2,000,000 in stocks, favorable loans, and salary to cover-up invoice forgeries.

All of this may sound like only your basic corruption and greed until it is explained that Wedtech may have lacked the capacity and competency to build the armaments requested by the United States military, therefore placing soldiers and sailors in harms way, illustrating further and once again the meanings of elite and power deviance. The Wedtech scandal involved very powerful people at the top in government, and greedy people who apparently could care less about others and who benefited financially from the scam. A number of convictions did follow, including an eight-year prison sentence for Mario Biaggi (French, 1988).

Corporate Elite and Power Deviance

The Enron scandal is just one of numerous examples of corporate crime in American history, and it is just one example, albeit a major example, of fraudulent activities engaged in by corporate America during the last decade. In this section two other examples of corporate elite and power deviance are examined, the *WorldCom* and *Tyco* scandals. The section will end with brief but detailed examples of other corporate crimes.

WorldCom

How would you like to receive a 25-year prison sentence? Many students enrolled in a course in deviance are about 20 years old, and if they received 25 years in prison they would be in their mid-40s when released. Now place yourself at age 63 and given 25 years behind bars, that would mean you would be 88 when you left prison (federal and various state crimes require the convicted to serve 85% of the time, so it is possible to be released in less than 25 years). Thus is the case with *Bernie Ebbers,* a basketball coach turned tycoon CEO of what was one of America's largest telecommunications firms, *WorldCom* (now MCI Inc.). Other top WorldCom executives were also convicted in the scam, including the company's CFO Scott Sullivan who received a five-year prison sentence and David Myers, the former Controller who received a light one year and one day sentence, primarily because he cooperated with authorities investigating the WorldCom scandal. Sullivan's sentence too was relatively light because he testified against Bernie Ebbers, but he played a larger role in the crime than did Myers and received more time in prison.

So what was it Ebbers and others did that was so criminal? A major crime was *fraud* which was accomplished by *lying about inflating company earnings* by nearly four billion dollars, thus misleading stockholders into believing WorldCom was in excellent financial health. Of course by doing so Ebbers, Sullivan, Meyers, and others benefited greatly since WorldCom stock became so hot, when in reality the company's earnings were not anything close to that reported on its financial statements (Lyman and Potter, 2004; Simon, 2008). At stake was a *massive accounting fraud* whereby in January, 2001 WorldCom began labeling some of its routine expenses as capital expenses in order to avoid having to deduct them as a result of doing business. The result was a massive overstatement of the company's net income, a classic example of what is meant by *cooking the books.* Perhaps the most devastating criminal act was *Ebbers looting the company of over $1.5 billion in personal loans,* a move that diluted the company's treasury of money required to maintain itself in a competitive telecommunications industry. The company did agree to pay back investors $500 million, a sizeable amount until one considers that it is just a small percentage returned to investors. Henry J. Bruen Jr. a former executive with Enron said "Where do I get my life savings back from . . . or my career reinvigorated." Exhibiting sympathy for Ebbers long-time employee of WorldCom, Gino Cavalla, who also lost many thousands of dollars stated "The man is 63 . . . He's going to die in jail. How much sterner could you get" (*The Oklahoman,* July 2005). Another example of the ruthlessness and cutthroat mentality of Ebbers and his co-conspirators in the crime is that along the way to becoming a giant in its industry, WorldCom ate up and devoured other companies, including MCI. Part of the reason that Ebbers received such a harsh sentence was his failure to cooperate with authorities practically up to his sentencing, and what appeared to be an ongoing display of arrogance and a failure to elicit any remorse. At his sentencing Ebbers wept as the judge, Barbara Jones read the sentence and afterwards stated "This was not a minor fraud . . . Mr. Ebbers committed a fraud that caused numbers of investors to suffer losses. His statements deprived investors of the truth about WorldCom's financial condition" (2005, 8A).

Tyco International Ltd.

Tyco was a large conglomerate that was chartered in Bermuda to avoid paying U.S.

corporate taxes, and like other American conglomerates and corporations its head-quarters were in the United States, thus giving it access and all rights to government contracts that are so important to the successes enjoyed by American corporations (Reiman, 2003). The two principle conspirators in this crime were *Dennis Kozloski*, the CEO and the CFO, *Mark Swartz*, both who were convicted of charges of looting Tyco of millions of dollars. The charges against the two included grand larceny and conspiracy, falsifying business records, violating business law, and securities fraud. So what is it they did? Kozloski and Swartz looted Tyco of over $600 million. In other words, they just plain stole from the company, never paying back a dime until ordered to do so during their sentencing. Their means of committing the crime included embellishing themselves with unauthorized pay and bonuses (after all they were the bosses), stealing from loans made to Tyco, and cashing in their company stock at inflated prices after lying to investors about the company's financial status (*The Oklahoman*, June 2005).

So what did they use 600 million dollars for? Kozloski and Swartz purchased expensive art, jewelry, and houses, and in addition they were known to throw extravagant parties that would cost millions of dollars. An example is the party thrown by Kozloski for his wife's 40th birthday party on the Italian island of Sardinia that featured waiters dressed in togas and an ice sculpture of David by Michelangelo. So what's so big about that? The ice carving had Vodka flowing from the genitals. What is more, Kozloski's art purchases included paintings by Renoir and Monet valued at over $13 million, for which he evaded over one million dollars in New York sales tax through a scheme that entailed mailing empty boxes to the company in New Hampshire where he purchased the art (Reiman 2003, 128). In

short, it did not take a rocket scientist to steal the $600,000,000. It required *power deviance* (PD), or the brazenness, arrogance, elitism, and bullying that personifies PD. Kozloski, who has the looks of a professional wrestler and Swartz who reminds one of the late John F. Kennedy, Jr. proceeded to rip off Tyco of its very existence, and investors of their life-savings. For their greed or egoism, as coined by Willem Bonger, both received prison sentences of eight and a third to 25 years. At the time of their sentencing Kozloski was 58 and Swartz, 44. Even if they serve the lower end of the range, Kozloski will be 66 and Swartz 52 when released from the penitentiary. Additionally, both were ordered to pay $239 million in restitution and fines (Wong, 2005).

Other Examples of Corporate Elite and Power Deviance

During the past 10 years there have been a number of indictments and convictions of once big-time corporate executives. The following is a list of just some of these:

- James Olis, the former finance executive of Dynegy Inc. is serving 24 years in prison for his role in cooking the books in the Enron scandal (*The Oklahoman*, June 18, 2005).
- John Rigas, founder of Adelphia Communications Corp. is serving 15 years and his son, Timothy Rigas, former company finance director 20 years for their roles in looting millions of dollars from the company, using methods analogous to those employed by Bernie Ebbers, Dennis Kozloski, and Mark Swartz (*The Oklahoman*, June 18, 2005).
- Richard Scrushy, CEO of HealthSouth Corp. and Donald Siegelman, a former Governor of Alabama were convicted of charges of fraud, and Scrushy was ordered by the court to pay the Securities

and Exchange Commission $81 million. Siegelman and Scrushy are serving seven-year prison sentences for collaborating in a bribery scheme to establish a state lottery in Alabama (Whitmire, 2006; Whitmire, 2007).

- Diva Martha Stewart was sentenced to five months in prison, and five months of in-house confinement upon release from prison for lying to federal authorities about her sale of ImClone Systems stock. She was also fined $30,000, pocket change for the billionaire (Crawford, 2004).
- Joseph Nacchio, former CEO of Qwest Communications International was sentenced to a seven-year prison term on charges of insider trading, and he was ordered to forfeit $52 million in stock gains accrued from the insider trading scam, and in addition he was fined 19 million dollars for his role in the crime (Coffman, 2007).

Military Elite and Power Deviance

Deviance can and does occur at the highest levels of every American institution, including the military. As we have seen individuals involved in *corporate elite* and *power deviance* engage in activities such as insider trading, theft, fraud, and deceit, and *political elite* and *power deviance* include much of the same, with bribery and graft added to the mix. *But what about corruption and abuse of power within the military sphere?* Once again, *much of the same.* However, military elite and power deviance can involve the loss of life and may even place the entire nation at risk. The history of the United States is replete with examples of this, including the cases that are now discussed.

The Pentagon's Black Budget: Secret Military Spending

The Pentagon has often enjoyed the luxury of having access to substantial amounts of funding that are unavailable to other major government institutions, such as the Departments of State, Education, and Health and Human Services. It is unclear how much money over time has been allotted to the Pentagon, *unknown to Congress and the general public* (thus the term black budget), but it may very well range into the billions of dollars. One such example is secret military spending involving *MZM Inc.*, a once small and obscure consulting firm that contracted with the Pentagon, that eventually earned $200 million annually in defense industry contracts (Kelly and Drinkard, 2005). So how did this relatively miniscule, "blurt on the radar screen" company go from being out-of-the-loop to making millions of dollars? It is called *bribery*.

MZM supplied computer systems and analysts for use in intelligence gathering and was located in the district of Congressman Randy Cunningham, Republican from California. Cunningham received substantial sums of Political Action Campaign (PAC) funds from MZM employees, and also benefited greatly from a house deal worked out with Mitchell Wade, CEO of MZM Inc. Cunningham was not alone in the scheme since it also involved Representative Virgil Goode, Republican from Virginia. The scam basically went as follows: *MZM needed work, and the two Congressmen were willing to push contract deals for MZM through the House of Representatives, for a price, or better stated, for bribery money.* One way this was accomplished was that Cunningham and Goode would add provisions for spending onto bills, with little or no notice by other Congress persons. Doing such favors for one's district is quite common, and frequently members of the House look the other way when one of their peers engages in such add-ons, since they do it as well. One explanation given for this procedure is that members of Congress are often seeking to strengthen or add jobs in their districts, and defense industry contracts are one way of doing business (2005, 2). When this occurs money is allotted for contracts that can go *unrecorded*, thus becoming part of the *black budgeting process*. An example is *$23 million* added by Representative Goode for a classified project that was awarded to MZM, *ironically money that was not requested by the Pentagon or accounted for in its budget, thus creating 23 million dollars in black budget money.*

Listed are examples of the payoffs made to Cunningham and Goode, beginning with Representative Cunningham whose campaign donations from MZM included (2005, 1–5):

- $1,000 in May 2002, just two days after the General Services Administration approved MZM as an information technology service provider, a huge step in acquiring government contracts.
- $5,000 on September 23, 2003, just one day before Cunningham was instrumental in placing language in a bill favorable to MZM, and an additional $2,000 the day the House passed the Pentagon spending bill, which was on September 24, 2003.
- $2,500 on June 22, 2004, the day the House passed the annual defense budget.

Payoffs from MZM to Representative Goode included (2005, 1–5):

- donating $90,000 to Goode's campaign treasury from 2002–2005, support from not only Mitchell Wade but from 70 MZM employees.

- $1,000 a month in 2002 which resulted in a contract worth *$163 million* for an open-ended computer services contract at the National Ground Intelligence Center in Goode's district, for which Cunningham also received $250 a month.
- $19,000 in March and April 2003 just before Congress awarded MZM with Pentagon contracts.
- Many thousands dollars more to both Cunningham and Goode in and around the times Congress was to award defense industry contracts to MZM and other companies.

The unethical behavior did not begin and end with these types of bribes, which brings this discussion back to the home purchased by Mitchell Wade from Representative Cunningham. Wade via company he controlled paid nearly $1.7 million for the home owned by Cunningham, and then sold it for nearly half that price eight months later, giving the nearly $700,000 back to Cunningham so that he could use the profit to purchase a different home in Rancho Santa Fe, California (2005, 2). On March 3, 2006 Cunningham, 64, received the longest sentence ever by an American Congressman, eight years and four months in federal prison for accepting $2.4 million in bribes, and is not eligible for release in the federal system until age 71 (Archibold, 2006). In addition, Cunningham was ordered to pay nearly $4 million in fines and back taxes and to give up his interest in the Rancho Santa Fe home (talkingpointsmemo.com/grandolddocket.php December, 2007). Mitchell Wade will be sentenced sometime in 2008 (Kramer, 2007), and of this writing Virgil Goode has not been sentenced.

By now you may be asking what makes this different from the other examples of elite and power deviance presented in this chapter? There is much similarity, but we must keep our eye on the ball, meaning here we are addressing secretive funding for the military that is not known to the public. In addition to the typical graft and bribery that has long been used to line the pockets of politicians for their votes and favoritism, the situation involving MZM includes two powerful members of the House of Representatives who used chicanery to get contracts for the company when that funding was not recorded in the Pentagon budget. The add-ons to bills at the last minute were recorded elsewhere, and since this practice was so common in Congress other representatives would turn a blind eye to what people like Goode and Cunningham were doing, knowing that their day for also engaging in similar actions was just around the corner and/or had already transpired. *To accentuate this point it is believed that from September 11, 2001 to 2005 classified Pentagon spending (black budget; secret military spending) had increased by 48 percent to nearly $27 billion.* But is this all: is the case involving MZM Inc. the only concrete example of the Pentagon's black budget? Consider the following (Simon 2008, 171–173):

- Even after the cold war was over following the collapse of the former Soviet Union, the Pentagon continued development of a *$20 billion* top-secret satellite project known as MILSTAR which was designed to coordinate a six-month nuclear war with Moscow. The project has since been dissolved (we think).
- The development of the B2 stealth bomber was laced with corruption and fraud resulting in enormous *costs over-runs,* a reality in the Pentagon *in addition to its black budget.* The project, awarded to Northrop was originally estimated in 1981 at 22 billion dollars but wound up costing three times as much ten years

later. This was due largely to criminal activities such as those involving William Reinke, Northrop's chief engineer on the project who established his own firm, RE Engineering that siphoned off at least $600,000 from Northrop in subcontracts allegedly related to the bomber.

- A practice in awarding defense contract known as *the nickel job* that entails price fixing was also a part of the B2 top secret project. Northrop's top purchasing agent, Ron Brousseau received kickbacks from companies that amounted to 5 percent of a contract's amount in return for the purchase of their products by Northrop. Brousseau allowed competing companies to take turns receiving contacts by using the ago-old practice of awarding contracts to the lowest bidder, of course known to all companies involved in the scam.
- In the end Northrop was indicted for fraud and conspiracy for overcharging the government $400 million for the stealth aircraft, and the so-called overcharge was probably a drop in the bucket relative to the actual amount of the rip-off on the American taxpayer.

Violations of Human Rights and U.S. Establishment of Puppet Governments

Military elite and power deviance include actions *directly related to the military,* in particular decisions and conduct that favor and are engaged in by the Pentagon. But this type of deviance also includes actions that if not directly connected to the military are at least tangentially related to and in support of its *philosophies and culture.* Take for example Guatemala and Iran in 1953, South Viet Nam in 1963, and the Dominican Republic in 1965, when the CIA and the American military were involved in installing leaders sympathetic to the United States and its interests (Simon, 2008, 182–184). Iran is an example of the show of military and clandestine muscle for which the United States and the world community are on edge today. The CIA placed the Shah's family in power in Iran in 1953, and what took place from there laid the seeds for the Iranian Revolution in 1979, and the Iran-hostage crisis. During the 26-year period the Shah was in power the United States gave billions of dollars worth of aid to Iran, most of it for military purposes, while Iran was involved in violations of human rights that included (Baraheni, 1976; Simon, 2008, 185–187):

• the arrests of at least 18,000 people annually by Iran's secret police, the SAVAK.
• the murders of 6,000 Iranian citizens on *just one day,* June 5, 1963.
• in 1975 Amnesty International estimated that between 25,000 and 100,000 Iranians were arrested and imprisoned.
• native languages were forbidden to be learned by minorities, and Iran had a serious problem with poverty that especially affected its minority population.
• the abuses and severe problems within Iran were never reported in Iranian newspapers, because the Shah controlled all media within the country.

Previously it was mentioned the United States gave billions of dollars to Iran, much of it secretly, to support the Shah who in turn used much of what Iran purchased with the money against his own people. Between 1961 and 1973 the United States provided Iran with $1.7 billion in foreign aid which was used to purchases guns, grenades, teargas, computers, and patrol cars which went to the Iranian police force controlled by the Shah. During a 30-year period from 1946 to 1976, Iran received $1.6 billion from United States military assistance programs that was used for arms purchases, and training over 11,000 Iranian military officers (2008, 185). It doesn't end here since between 1971 and 1978 the United States sold Iran $15 billion in military hardware, and it aided the Shah's government in developing a helicopter fleet known as the Sky Calvary Brigade, similar to American helicopter units in Viet Nam. By the time of the revolution, the United States had approximately 40,000 military advisors and a contingent of CIA operatives inside Iran (2008, 185–186). The very powerful Rockefeller family played a significant role in the Shah's rise to power since it was part of the planning of the coup that overthrew Mohammad Mossadegh, the prime minister of Iran who was believed to have leftist leanings. In return for his being placed into power with the assistance of the Rockefellers, the Shah deposited millions of dollars into the Chase Manhattan Bank owned by the Rockefeller family, and in 1979 when the Shah was very ill and as a result of pressure from David Rockefeller and former Secretary of State Henry Kissinger, the Shah was admitted into the United States to receive medical treatment. While in America militants overran the United States Embassy in Iran, taking hostages, and starting the nerve wracking and embarrassing Iran hostage crisis. What is more, in 1973 and 1974 the Shah increased the price of Iranian oil by nearly 500 percent with the blessing of Secretary of State Henry Kissinger who was a close ally of David Rockefeller (2008, 186). It is to be noted that a number of human rights organizations cited the Shah for his inhumane and cruel treatment of Iranian citizens and this included Amnesty International, the International Commission of Jurists, and the United Nations Commission on Human Rights. Individuals such as David Rockefeller and Henry

Kissinger were most likely knowledgeable of the atrocities occurring during the reign of the Shah, but for political and economic motives chose to look the other way (2008, 186).

Additional Examples of Military Elite and Power Deviance

Iran is just one of many cases whereby the military and other wings of the United States government have been involved in aiding and abetting violations of human rights, overthrowing old leaders, and installing new ones around the world. Yet the United States has been a strong proponent of human rights policies for years as exemplified by its participation in the International Bill of Rights passed by the United Nations in 1948, and as a major signatory of the Helsinki Agreement of 1975 which has a strong clause on the protection of and support for human rights. However the United States has done its fair share to circumvent these documents and examples of this include (Simon, 2008, 187–190):

- Millions of dollars of aid to El Salvador for years that was involved in brutalizing its own people through government death squads. It is estimated that from 1979 to 1983 over 40,000 civilians were murdered, and an additional 800,000 people or 20 percent of the country's population were forced to become refugees as they attempted to escape the atrocities occurring in their homeland. In 1993, the UN released an official report on the violence in El Salvador documenting that over 80,000 mostly unarmed people were actually killed, representing one in 70 persons in the population. What is disturbing is that during the 1980s when so much of this violence was taking place, major oil

conglomerates such as Chevron and Texaco poured an estimated $100 million of investments into El Salvador.
- In 1974, General Augusto Jose Ramon Pinochet Ugarte led a coup in Chile against Socialist President Salvador Allende with the assistance of the CIA and U.S. military, immediately implementing a dictator-style government. What was to follow were years of oppression of the Chilean people which included exile status for one out of every 55 Chileans by 1988. During his reign of terror Pinochet resided in a 15,000 square foot home estimated to cost between 10 and 13 million dollars, protected by seven dozen guards and a high-tech infrared security system. In some areas of Chile the unemployment rate was as high as 60 percent, not to mention that the overall economy was a disaster. Meanwhile, Pinochet's government was known to have tortured hundreds of thousands of citizens by use of means such as electrodes on genitals and knees, mock executions, sleep derivation, submersion in water, sexual abuse, and loud music. Police loyal to Pinochet made a practice of going to homes and removing men from them, and then taking them to sports complexes where their names would be checked up against lists of persons suspected of opposing Pinochet. They were either released or further detained.

Theories of Elite and Power Deviance

Two theories related to elite and power deviance are discussed. The first is by David R. Simon and the second is by C. Wright Mills, one of the most time-honored American sociologists. It is to be noted that the term *power deviance* was developed by the author of this text and was not directly addressed by either Simon or Mills. Power deviance is an extension on the term *elite deviance* used for over 25 years by David Simon, and elite deviance itself is an outgrowth of the work of Mills.

Elite Deviance: David Simon

As noted earlier in this chapter, elite deviance is deviance engaged in by the *most privileged* members of our society. It is deviance involving the *highest ranking* members of corporate, military and political America. Simon has identified the key elements of elite deviance, that include (2008, xi):

- "The notion that elite deviance in and of itself is a great social problem in American life. Elite deviance consists of criminal and deviant acts by the largest corporations and the most powerful political organizations."
- "Elite deviance stems from a system of political economy in which power and wealth are increasingly concentrated in the hands of a power elite."
- "Within this power elite there has emerged a series of criminal and deviant acts that have been termed "the higher immorality.""
- "Elite deviance is intimately related to each and every other type of nonelite deviance."
- "The solution of the problem posed by elite deviance involves a serious restructuring of the major institutions of postmodern society; the political, economy, and mass media."

In addition to these elements Simon has identified six characteristics of elite deviance (2008, 9-10):

- "The acts are committed by persons from the highest strata of society: mem-

bers of the upper and upper-middle classes . . . committed by the heads of corporate and governmental organizations; others were committed by their employees on behalf of the employers."
- "Some of the acts are crimes in that they violate criminal statutes and carry penalties such as fines and imprisonment. Other acts violate administrative and civil laws, which may also involve punishment. Included are acts of both commission and omission. Other acts, such as U.S. presidents lying to the public about the Viet Nam War, although not illegal, are regarded by most Americans as unethical or immoral (that is, deviant). Thus, elite deviance may be either criminal or noncriminal in nature."
- "The acts were committed with relatively little risk. When and if the elites were apprehended, the punishments inflicted were in general very lenient compared with those given common criminals."
- "Some of the incidents posed great danger to the public's safety, health, and financial well-being."
- "In many cases, the elites in charge of the organizations mentioned were able to conceal their illegal or unethical actions for years before they became public knowledge (for example, Hooker Chemical's dumping of poisonous chemicals and the presidential misuses of the FBI and CIA). Yet the actions mentioned were seemingly compatible with the goals of such organizations (that is, the maintenance or enhancement of the organization's power and/or profitability)."

According to Simon elite deviance includes criminal, deviant, and unethical behaviors, which strikes up an interesting point. Those engaging in elite deviance *may not be committing crimes*–they may not be violating any laws–but their actions may be *unethical* and injurious to a society, not to mention to the entire planet. These actions can include the polluting of air, land, and water that is permitted under laws of the Environmental Protection Agency, and *known to corporate executives who own and control the polluting companies.* It may include *job-related illnesses and dangers* occuring within the workplace that are may not be covered under the criminal law. Several examples are workplace-associated cancers, carpal tunnel syndrome (repetitive strain disease), black lung disease, and serious accidents and even death that occur on the job (Reiman, 2003, 77–81). In addition, the debate goes on concerning global warming, including data such as that reported by a Public Interest research Group (PIRG) in summer 2006. PIRG documented *over 2,300 daily global temperature records* that were set in *just one month* of that summer; July. In addition, PIRG reported above normal temperatures from 255 major weather stations across the world during the period 2000–2006. A major contributor to global warming is *carbon dioxide emissions* in the atmosphere that stem chiefly from *automobile emissions* and *corporate pollution* (Simon, 2008, 9), which returns us to the term *power deviance.* Again *elite deviance* refers to criminal, deviant, and unethical actions committed by those at the top–individuals who control America's major social institutions. *Power deviance goes one step further* and is defined as behaviors or conduct that have serious consequences for others, *involving knowledge by those in power that their actions are harmful and dangerous.* Adding to this is the elites *could care less, and show no remorse* for the dangers they have posed to society and civilization in general.

Critical to Simon's theory of elite deviance are the *linkages* among the elites, meaning that corporate, military, and political elites do not exist in mutual exclusion from one another, instead they feed into each other, supporting each other's major goals and priorities, which include wealth, power and prestige. Consider the following examples of the linkages (2008, 21–25):

- 656 individuals either serve as trustees or presidents of America's 25 most prestigious universities. Thus there is a *higher education-corporate link* (discussed when covering C. Wright Mills).
- NBC, CBS, and ABC, the nation's three major television networks are either owned by or own other major corporations. For example, General Electric, maker of appliances and weapons systems owns NBC, and all three networks are owned by the following commercial banks: Chase Manhattan, Morgan Guaranty, Bankers Trust, Citibank, and the Bank of New York. The interlocks include *(but are not certainly limited to) ABC/Disney* and corporations such as FedEx, Edison International, Northwest Airlines, and Xerox. *NBC/GE* interlocks include Anheuser-Busch, Dell Computer, Texaco, and Kellogg. *CBS/Viacom* linkages include Amamazon.com, American Express, Electronic Data Systems, and Verizon. Thus there is an *elite media and corporate giant link.*
- The largest 50 financial institutions and 500 manufacturing firms are controlled by *less than 0.5 percent* of the United States population, and they are *interlocked* and control nearly 70 percent of all business income and over half the nations' banks. What is more, the *richest 10 percent* of the population of the United States possesses *70 percent* of the nation's household wealth, and *one-third* of net wealth is possessed by a mere *1 percent* of the population. Thus there is an *elite and corporate elite to total wealth link.*

Examples of the interlocks or linkages are too numerous to present here and would take volumes to identify, but suffice it to say they are for real, and cut across and involve the most influential players from the major institutions of society.

The Power Elite: C. Wright Mills

C. Wright Mills is an influential figure in American sociology and his classic work *The Power Elite* (1956) remains one of the most important books written in sociology since the 1950s. Mills conceived of an American society dominated by a handful of elites, men of enormous power and influence, and it is his writing on this topic that had the most important effect on theorists such as David Simon and G. William Domhoff (1970, 1978, 1983, 1998, 2002). Mills conceptualized American society as a pyramid, with the top comprised of the most important military, political and corporate leaders, representing just a tiny percentage of the entire pyramid (Figure 14:1). The second layer on the pyramid, representing perhaps no more than 20 percent of the total area

includes Congress, other legislators, interest group leaders, and local opinion leaders. Finally, there are the masses who comprise at least 70 percent of the pyramid and who include the unorganized, exploited, and basically those who feel disenfranchised from society's social institutions, especially government, the polity, and the economy. Much of what Mills accomplished in *The Power Elite* was to speculate on the make-up and operation of the power players in American society, and in doing so he offered insights into how they were able to *sustain* their enormous influence over time. One of the avenues for the maintenance of the power elite was *closed society* where the elites would be raised, educated, married, reside, and spend their social lives among themselves. In early life nowhere was this more important than in *education*, where children of the elites would receive K-12 private educations, next attending America's most prestigious universities, colleges, and military academies, assuring for the first 21 or so years of life the social circles of elite children were highly selective and restrictive (1956, 281).

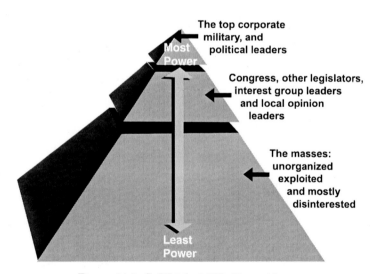

Figure 14:1. C. Wright Mill's Pyramid.

Mills identified the power elite as those whose names would appear in *The Social Register*, referring to them as *The Metropolitan 400*. These were America's aristocrats, the "bluebloods of society" who belonged to *the world of celebrity*, or *café society*. These individuals, few in number but great in wealth, power and prestige, held pedigree unknown to over 99 percent of Americans (1956, 47–70). But Mills was wise to the ever-growing and expanding heterogeneity in America, distinguishing between the "old rich" and the "new rich" (1956, 95–117). The *old rich* were people who came to power *prior to the Civil War* and included names such as the Astors, Cabets, Lodges, and Mellons all who had much in common, most noteworthy they were White, Anglo, Saxon, Protestants (WASP), emanating from the east coast aristocracy, with the emphasis on northeast pedigree. The *new rich* were individuals who made their wealth and acquired power *after the Civil War*, and were basically non-WASPs, and using examples from the last century would include the Kennedys, Vanderbilts, Gates and Buffetts. Critical to understanding the elites, be they "old" or "new," was that they would only meet on *occasion* (within and between the two types) *when it was in their best interests to come together*. Be they of older or new privilege they also shared one other factor in common: *wealth.* Although marriage was to be *within the power structure* (old or new), meaning never between the two types of elites (and certainly to the total exclusion of the rest of us), the power elite of America hoarded their wealth and power, rarely sharing it, except through foundation. One way this was accomplished was through corporate board membership where the power elite held a monopoly on the most important corporate boards in America. The elites would *sit on multiple boards* as also observed by William Domhoff (2002), setting policies that not only affected

specific American corporations, but also the legislative and moral agendas of the United States. In other words they "circled the wagons," controlling the economic, political, and military destinies of the country.

Power in the Hands of the Few: The Business Roundtable

There are a number of influential economy-focused power groups in the United States of which several are The Economic Council, The Council of Economic Advisors, the Business Council, and the Business Roundtable (BRT). Attention here is directed at the BRT, an organization unknown and unheard of by the great majority of Americans, but one of the most powerful institutions not only the in United States, but the world. It is an organization in the tradition of C. Wright Mills in the sense that it is comprised of a tiny, but enormously powerful and influential number of Americans. The BRT is much of what Mills, Simon, Domhoff and others have written about, it is an organization comprised of the elites in corporate America who are interlocked and whose decisions affect every major aspect of American life. The BRT has profound effects on legislation, foreign affairs, elections, the environment, trade, and it permeates every major part of the economy. How could this be? Please consider the following (www.businessroundtable.org 2006):

- the BRT is comprised of the top CEOs of the leading *150* companies in the United States.
- the membership of the BRT accounts for nearly *five trillion* dollars in annual revenues.
- the 150 companies employ over *10 million* people.
- the BRT membership accounts for nearly *a third* of the value of the U.S. stock

market, and returned nearly *$100 billion* in dividends to shareholders and the economy in 2004.

- the BRT contributes *a third* of all corporate income taxes paid to the federal government.
- Members of the BRT donate more than *seven billion* dollars each year to charitable organizations, and this represents *more than 60 percent* of all giving from corporate America.
- the BRT spends *$90 billion* annually on research and development (R&D) which is *one-half* of the total private spending on R&D in the United States.

Is this power? Is this influence? *It is extremely important to state that the BRT is not a deviant, criminal, or unethical organization.* It is devoted to capitalism and to America. To put it mildly, the BRT is patriotic to the core, and makes no bones about it. The BRT home page states "The Roundtable is committed to advocating public policies that ensure vigorous economic growth, a dynamic global economy, and the well-trained and productive U.S. workforce essential for future competitiveness. . . . The Roundtable believes that the basic interests of business closely parallel the interests of the American people . . . the Roundtable focuses on issues it believes will have an effect on the economic well-being of the nation" (www.businessroundtable.org 2006).

The BRT was a major player in the passage of support for trade with China having donated nearly $100 million in campaign contributions to individuals running for the senate in 2000. Both Republicans (R) and Democrats (D) alike received contributions, in effect urging them to vote for China trade. Listed are the top five donations from companies in support of this legislation (most figures are rounded up):

- AT&T–$4.1 million: $1.6 for D and $2.5 for (R)
- Citigroup Inc.–$3 million: $1.7 for D and $1.3 for (R)
- Verizon Communications–$2.6 million: $1 million for D and $1.6 million for (R)
- United Parcel Service–$2.5 million: $580,000 for D and $1.9 million for (R)
- Phillip Morris–$2.4 million: $511,000 for D and $1.9 million for (R)

There are many powerful corporations on the BRT and the list includes: Lockheed Martin; Merrill Lynch; Boeing Co.; General Electric; Union Pacific Corp.; American Airlines; Anheuser-Busch; Exxon Mobil Corp.; Chevron Corp.; Eli Lilly & Co.; General Motors; Dupont Co.; Texaco; Halliburton Co.; Kellogg Co.; Union Carbide; and Black & Decker. The BRT is a *prima facie* example of the type of power, wealth, and influence that people like C. Wright Mills have addressed: power that can shape and change a nation, if not the world.

The Assassination of President John F. Kennedy

Wedtech, Iran-Contra, Watergate, Enron; Tyco, Worldcom, MZM, the black budget, Chile, El Salvador, and the list goes on and on. These are examples of elite and power deviance, par excellence. They are at the top of the pinnacle of the abuse of wealth, power, and prestige. They all involved individuals from the highest levels of their respective entities (i.e., government; corporate America), and they were also characterized by power deviance, or actions that hurt others for which there was little expressed remorse or sorrow. However, within the past 50 years in the United States there is perhaps no greater example of crime against the American people and crime against government than the assassination of the 35th president of the United States, John F. Kennedy (JFK). The murder of the president is addressed since he himself came from the elites, and it has been claimed for years that much information concerning the assassination has been covered-up, destroyed, or just plain buried in lies and deceit, actions common to those engaged in elite and power deviance. The coverage of the assassination will begin with a brief overview of JFK, and then it will consider two major arguments concerning who killed the president: *nonconspiracy* and *conspiracy*.

Overview of John F. Kennedy

John Fitzgerald Kennedy was the 35th president of the United States, at age 43 the youngest ever to be elected to that office. His rise to power was made largely possible as a result of the wealth and power of his father, Joseph P. Kennedy who acquired much of his riches in the stock market, the movie and oil industries, and bootlegging. The elder Kennedy was one of America's wealthiest and most powerful Americans who was more than capable of swinging the political winds in the favor of his children when they ran for political office. John Kennedy was elected to the House of Representatives in 1946 and the United States Senate in 1952, both on the heels of enormous financial and networking support provided by Joseph P. Kennedy. It was not all the work of the father, since JFK was a World War II hero, and a man who had to overcome serious childhood illnesses and health problems that also carried over to his adult years (Perret, 2001). In addition, it is often overlooked or forgotten that JFK spent 14 years in Congress before becoming president, so his was not necessarily a meteoric or overnight rise to that office. Winning the presidency was no walk in the park either. JFK made an unsuccessful bid for vice president for the

Democratic Party in 1956, with the eventual nomination for president going to Adlai E. Stevenson. But the stage was set, for JFK gained exposure in 1956 that would pay off in 1960 when he won the party's nomination *for president*, entering into a contentious and very tight race for the presidency against Vice President Richard M. Nixon. Kennedy carried the election by a mere 118,574 popular votes out of over 68 million casted. In the end he had 303 electoral votes to Nixon's 219, and it was the state of Illinois that carried JFK over the top in the electoral count (www.potus.com 2004). For years it has been argued it was the influence and contacts of Joseph P. Kennedy that won Illinois. The elder Kennedy was acquainted with one of America's most notorious Mafioso, Sam Giancana from Chicago, who it is alleged Joseph Kennedy turned to in order to get more votes for his son. It is believed that Giancana used his influence in Chicago to get out the votes on behalf of JFK, which was a deciding point in the final vote tally. What is more, it is alleged that Joseph P. Kennedy also used his wealth, power, and prestige in the Democratic Primary in West Virginia, a state which at that time was crucial to winning the nomination for president from the Democratic Party. It has been asserted that the father of the president turned to Frank Sinatra, one of the world's most renowned entertainers to acquire the support for his son in West Virginia. It is argued that Sinatra had mafia ties and used these to influence how unions would vote in the primary, since mobsters like Johnny Rosselli were involved in corrupting unions nationally. Sinatra was friends with Rosselli and was able to convince him to carry out the wishes of the elder Kennedy with West Virginia unions, contributing to JFK's eventual primary victory in that state (Waldron and Hartmann, 2005). Here is the alleged situation of a member of America's power elite, Joseph P. Kennedy working side-by-side with some of the country's most notorious and powerful organized crime figures to win the highest office in the land, if not the world, for his son. Just three years later that son, John F. Kennedy would lie in a pool of blood and brain matter after having been assassinated by Lee Harvey Oswald. Or was it Oswald? It is to this issue attention is now directed.

Lee Harvey Oswald: The Lone Assassin: The Argument for Non-Conspiracy

Since 1963 there has been ongoing debate as to who killed President Kennedy. Many theories have been put forth (some identified next section) but there has been support for what has been called *the lone gunman* explanation, meaning that it was one and only one person who killed JFK: Lee Harvey Oswald. Over the years there have been several commissions and committees established to investigate the assassination, however the Warren Commission (1964) remains the most important of these, and it is this body that *first* established it was Lee Harvey Oswald who acted alone in killing President Kennedy. Some major results from this commission are presented.

The Warren Commission

Just six days after JFK was killed in Dallas, President Lyndon B. Johnson authorized Executive Order No. 11130 to investigate the assassination. The Commission was chaired by Chief Justice of the United States Earl Warren and included a future president, Gerald R. Ford who himself would ascend to the presidency via national tragedy (Watergate). The Warren Commission also included the very powerful Representative Hale Boggs, and Senators Richard B. Russell and John Sherman Cooper. In addition, former

Director of the CIA, Allen Dulles was a member of the Commission (JFK fired him after the failed Bay of Pigs invasion) as was current United States Senator Arlen E. Spector, who is credited with developing *the magic bullet theory*, discussed later. The Commission was comprised of over 30 individuals who undertook extensive and exhausting study of the murder, producing over 26,000 pages of evidence and figures. The report was published in the fall of 1964, less than one year after the assassination (1964, v-vii).

The major conclusion of the Warren Commission was Lee Harvey Oswald acted alone in killing President Kennedy. The Commission based this finding on a number of facts including palm and fingerprints on the rifle and pistol used to assassinate the president and police officer J.D. Tippet (respectively); eyewitness reports; the fact that Oswald purchased the rifle and pistol used in the slayings of JFK and Tippit; Oswald's finances; and, his past history of violence and erratic behavior. The extent of the evidence is beyond the scope of this chapter, but some of the most important conclusions derived by the Commission are presented. Before doing this, an overview of Kennedy's reasons for visiting Texas, part of his Texas itinerary, and the composition of the motorcade are presented.

With less than one year until his reelection bid for president, John Kennedy decided to travel to Texas as a move to bolster support from the south for winning a second term. He arrived in San Antonio, Texas at 1:30 pm on November 21, where he was in a motorcade in that city, and then he flew to Houston where he also rode in a motorcade and gave a speech. Kennedy was accompanied by his wife Jacqueline Kennedy, the Governor of Texas, John Connelly, and Vice President Lyndon B. Johnson, among others. On the morning of November 22 Kennedy flew to Dallas, again to ride in a motorcade and to give another speech. The presidential airplane, Air Force One arrived at Love Field (in Dallas) just before noon, and it was from there the motorcade would proceed to weave its way through downtown Dallas, with the intention of ending at the Trade Mart where Kennedy would give a luncheon presentation. The route taken by the motorcade was to pass through a warehouse district that housed the Texas Book Depository Building (TBDB) *where Oswald worked*, located in Dealy Plaza. From there it would proceed to the Trade Mart, just minutes from the plaza. As the president's limousine passed the now famed building, shots rang out at 12:30 pm, and America had its fourth assassinated Commander-in-Chief (1964, 19). The motorcade was comprised of a lead car, a pilot car, the Vice-Presidential car, the Vice-Presidential follow-up car, motorcycles, other vehicles, and of course the Presidential limousine, and the Presidential follow-up car. In the Presidential limousine were President Kennedy; his wife who was seated to his left in the rear seat; Governor Connelly who was seated in the jump seat in front of the president; and his wife who was seated to his left. Driving the limousine was Secret Service Agent William R. Greer, and to his right was another agent, Roy H. Kellerman (1964, 19-20). When it became evident that something terrible had occurred, the limousine sped up to at least 80 miles per hour, now on its way to a new destination, Parkland Memorial Hospital, where the president was pronounced dead at 1:00 pm. The Warren Commission would establish that three shots were fired from the TBDB, and it would claim unequivocally that the shots came from a rifle fired by Lee Harvey Oswald. So what is some of its evidence?

Fingerprints and palmprints were discovered on wrapping paper, boxes, and the rifle used to kill Kennedy. The rifle was a *Mannlicher-Carcano 6.5* millimeter Italian-made rifle that Oswald purchased through a mail order catalog house in Chicago, Illinois. The Dallas police found a latent palmprint from the underside of the barrel of the rifle and identified it as belonging to Oswald. In addition, the police established that the palmprints and fingerprints on a paper bag Oswald used to carry the rifle into the Texas Book Depository Building also were those of Oswald (this is an important conclusion since Oswald claimed the paper bag held curtain rods). As noted previously, the rifle used to kill the president was ordered through the mail and purchased by "A. Hidell." Forensic handwriting analysis of the handwriting on the mail order for the rifle was traced to Lee Harvey Oswald, and the same was found to be the case for the revolver used kill the police officer (1964, 240–241). In addition, the Commission was able to establish that *hairs and fibers* found on a blanket used to wrap the Mannlicher-Carcano rifle on the homemade paper bag found on the sixth floor of the TBDB, and on the shirt worn by Oswald on November 22, all belonged to Oswald. What is more, *two pictures* of Oswald holding the rifle taken prior to the assassination were examined and stated to be authentic, meaning they were actual pictures of the alleged assassin holding the weapon used to murder President Kennedy (1964, 249–250). The Commission took *many routes* in investigating the assassination, too many for our purposes. But one other set of forensic examinations included test firings and reenactments of the assassination, *tests of the penetration power and bullet stability from the rifle, as well as tests simulating President Kennedy's neck and head wounds, and the wounds to Governor Connally*. These tests concluded the rifle was more than capable of exacting the damage it did on the two men, and most saliently they demonstrated the rifle had enough power to send a bullet through two persons (1964, 246–248). *So thus far the evidence includes fingerprints* found in multiple places, hair and fiber samples (found in multiple places), and forensic analyses *of the rifle and revolver, all traced to Lee Harvey Oswald.* In many criminal cases only one of these types of evidence would be necessary to establish guilt, and in addition to the above there were *eye witnesses* who saw a rifle being fired from the sixth floor of the TBDB, and those who saw Oswald kill police officer Tippit, less than one hour after the assassination. *Nine total witnesses* gave positive identification that it was Oswald who killed the policeman (1964, 10–11).

Recently, the *most comprehensive* book written to date in support of the Warren Commission was published by the famed former prosecutor, Vincent Bugliosi, who was instrumental in the sentencing of Charles Manson in the early 1970s. The book, *Reclaiming History: The Assassination of President John F. Kennedy* (2007), over 1,600 pages in length, is an incredibly detailed and in-depth treatise of the assassination, taking it apart from every conceivable angle, and perhaps closing the door on the mysteries surrounding the murder. Much of what is covered in the book is derived from the Warren Commission Report, and what is addressed here is additional information from that and other documents scrutinized and researched by Bugliosi for 20 years. Important evidence in support of the "lone gunman theory" not addressed when discussing the Warren Commission findings is summarized below, *and what is selected from over 1,600 pages is information not usually covered when discussing the assassination* (2007, 955–965):

- Oswald claimed to have carried curtain rods in a package to work with him on November 22, however they were never found, anywhere in the TBDB.

- Atypical of Oswald was on this day he did not bring his lunch to work.
- Before leaving for the TBDB Oswald left his wedding ring and $170 for his wife Marina. The $170 is thought to be all the money he had.
- Oswald was seen on the sixth floor of the building by Charles Givens at 11:55 am, just 35 minutes before the assassination. Oswald claims to have been eating lunch on the first floor of the TBDB and walked up to the second floor to purchase a Coca Cola from a pop machine. Workers in the building said it was rare for anyone to go up to that floor to buy pop, since there was a pop machine on the lunchroom floor that sold mostly Dr. Pepper, a drink that Oswald had with his lunch each day. A police officer, Marion Baker, encountered Oswald on the second floor just two minutes after the shooting and questioned what he was doing there. Shedding doubt on Oswald's story about coming up from the first floor is the comment he made to Givens at 11:55 when Givens asked Oswald if he was going downstairs to eat lunch. Oswald's response was *"No, sir. When you get downstairs, close the gate to the elevator."*
- After the assassination, Oswald worked his way to his rooming house where he picked up his revolver, and he changed trousers. When asked why he picked up his revolver in the middle of a work day Oswald simply responded "You know how boys do when they have a gun, they just carry it." Speaking of a work day, the afternoon of the assassination Oswald was the only employee of the TBDB unaccounted for when the building supervisor took an employee count. Oswald was not known to have left work early any of the previous days he was employed there.

- A clipboard belonging to Oswald for three orders all dated November 22, 1963 was found on the sixth. None of the orders had been filled.

One of the most perplexing situations surrounding the assassination was the murder of Lee Harvey Oswald himself. On the morning of November 24, Oswald was gunned down by Dallas nightclub owner Jack Ruby, as Oswald was being transferred from the Dallas City Hall to the Dallas Sheriff's Office, a murder that has raised suspicions in the eyes of many Americans for years. The shooting was witnessed by millions of Americans (the author of this text who was 15 at the time had his back to the television set when the killing occurred) and there you have it, *three murders in a three-day period in Dallas, Texas*: one, a murder of the President of the United States; the others the killing of the murderer of the president, and the killing of a police officer. It was bizarre and frightening, and over the years the killing of Oswald has been couched in conspiracy theories: that he was murdered because he knew too much; because he was part of a conspiracy, possibly involving organized crime and therefore had to be eliminated, and so forth. *Vincent Bugliosi has examined the killing of Oswald in detail and has concluded, as did the Warren Commission that the killing of the assassin had nothing to do with conspiracy.* Bugliosi uses as evidence some fascinating information that sheds immediate doubt on conspiracy. Jack Ruby killed Oswald at 11:21 am, but just four minutes earlier was at a nearby Western Union sending $25.00 to one of his dancers from his nightclub, the Carousel Club. After completing the transaction, Ruby began walking toward the City Hall building which was *less than 500 feet* from the Western Union, aware that Oswald was to be transferred that same day. As he came closer to the ramp where

Oswald was to be placed in a vehicle for the ride to the sheriff's office, Ruby saw Oswald who was in the protection of Dallas police officers, stepped forward, and in the spare of a moment, without premeditation, pulled a revolver from his coat jacket and shot Oswald in the abdomen (the revolver was given to Ruby by a Dallas police officer, a friend of Ruby's, so he could have it when taking money from his business to deposit it at his bank). Ruby had no clue what time during the day Oswald was to be transferred, and the transfer time was interrupted by officials such as Dallas U.S. Postal Inspector Harry D. Holmes who made a last minute decision that Sunday morning to interview Oswald about purchasing the rifle and handgun through the mail. *No one knew when the transfer was to take place*, and when it occurred came with little advance notice, and Oswald was escorted to the basement of City Hall where he met his fate. In 1963 there were no cell phones, and the claims that some police officers somehow relayed the transfer to Ruby are erroneous, according to Bugliosi. So Bugliosi argues that Ruby's act was out-of-the-blue, and with no knowledge of when the transfer was to take place. It has been said that Ruby killed Oswald because he, Ruby, so admired President Kennedy, and Bugliosi claims when Ruby saw Oswald he simply stepped forward and killed him, allowing his emotions to get the best of him (2007, 1,071–1,078). Bugliosi considers this information critical to his claim that Oswald acted alone, and for the noted prosecutor it helps to shut the door on conspiracy theories, for which we now turn our attention.

The Argument for Conspiracy

Since the assassination of President Kennedy there have been many books claiming the murder was as a result of conspiracy. These books have been all over the place when it comes to the "who," meaning who conspired to kill the president. The conspiracies have included the *mafia; the CIA; the FBI; the military-industrial complex; the Soviet Union; Fidel Castro; right wingers; Lyndon Johnson (LBJ); Gerald Ford; Cuban exiles,* and so on and so forth. Claims have been made that it was actually a combination of Kennedy haters who co-joined to assassinate him, such as LBJ working with the military industrial complex, and the mafia working side-by-side with anti-Castro forces (Cuban exiles). Hundreds of books have been written on this topic, along with numerous articles in newspapers, magazines, and scholarly academic journals. Some of the books have been published by respected journalists and scholars, others have been written by "one-hit wonders" who never published another book, leading Vincent Bugliosi to observe that a *cottage industry* developed that produced book after book relating to the assassination. In addition, the internet has become a huge source of information on the murder, with blogs posted largely by amateurs laying claims to their conspiracy slants. Ironically, the most influential source of conspiracy (author's opinion) came from the movie *JFK* produced by Oliver Stone in 1991. This movie did more to inspire, and perhaps the better word is to incite conspiracy theories and thinking than all previous books on the topic combined (author's opinion). The movie itself was partially based on two books, *Crossfire: The Plot That Killed Kennedy* (1989) by Jim Marrs, and *On the Trail of the Assassins: My Investigation and Prosecution of the Murder of President Kennedy* (1988) by Jim Garrison. Movies are a quick and easy residue of "facts" and can be a powerful influence on how people see and interpret events, and this was the case with *JFK*, to which we turn our attention.

JFK

The 1991 film *JFK* starred Kevin Costner as New Orleans, Louisiana District Attorney Jim Garrison and a host of other big-time names, some just making cameo appearances. Sissy Spacek played the role of Garrison's devoted wife, and Tommy Lee Jones appeared as Clay Shaw who Garrison indicted for the murder of the president. Joe Pesci played right-winger and homosexual David Ferrie, and Ed Asner was former FBI agent Guy Bannister. The cast also included Kevin Bacon who played the role of ex-con and homosexual Willie O'Keefe, and Jack Lemon who was Jack Martin, a friend and sometimes employee of Guy Bannister, an alcoholic, former FBI agent, turned private detective. One of the most interesting roles in the movie was portrayed by Donald Sutherland who played the mysterious "X," a former military man who had inside information on the assassination that he allegedly discussed with Garrison in Washington, D.C. So the cast was a meshing of well-known actors (i.e., Asner, Lemon, Spacek, Sutherland), and those on the rise such as Kevin Bacon and Kevin Costner. The list of stars helped to make the movie all the more believable, and for the younger generation of persons who knew little about the assassination, not to mention those who were around when the murder occurred, *JFK* became the primary and most convincing source of their knowledge of what happened on that fateful November morning in 1963.

The essence of the movie is this: *Clay Shaw* was part of a conspiracy—the mastermind behind the plot to murder President Kennedy that involved David Ferrie, Guy Bannister, a host of anti-Castro exiles, and others. Also entangled in the assassination were Lyndon Baines Johnson, Kennedy's Vice President, the Joint Chiefs of Staff, and former CIA Director John Foster Dulles, who you may recall was fired by President Kennedy. The conspiracy also included the CIA, who Clay Shaw is identified in the postscripts to the movie as having an association, and people "in the know" through their assortment of contacts, such as Willie O' Keefe. *JFK* entails a collage of co-conspirators who wanted Kennedy dead, strange bedfellows if you will, and an ambitious young District Attorney who became convinced that Clay Shaw was the culprit behind a massive conspiracy and government coverup. As the plot thickened and the movie developed, Clay Shaw was revealed as a right winger with ties to David Ferrie, who was friends with Guy Bannister, the latter who hated JFK with a passion. Shaw, Bannister, Ferrie and others were portrayed as strongly connected to anti-Cuban exiles who themselves loathed Kennedy, blaming him for the failed Bay of Pigs invasion (they believed the Cuban refuges and exiles involved in the invasion were left as sitting ducks, and this was an embarrassment to those Cubans stranded in the United States who wanted their country back, minus Fidel Castro). In the process, the military industrial complex comprised of those who could not stand JFK, Lyndon Johnson who became president, and members of the Joint Chiefs of Staff conspired with Shaw and his band of Kennedy haters to assassinate the president. Garrison became convinced of this, tracing Oswald's network back to New Orleans (where he lived as a youth), discovering that Oswald knew Shaw, Ferrie and Bannister, and some Cuban exiles. As his thoughts developed about these connections and as he read through the Warren Commission Report (a document he mistrusted), Garrison became convinced that Oswald was set up to take blame for the assassination (he was a "patsy"). After initial efforts to tie David Ferrie to the murder failed shortly after November 22, 1963, Garrison dropped

interest in the case, but it was *four years later* on March 1, 1967 that the *two-year trial* against Clay Shaw commenced, a trial Garrison would lose based on scanty evidence tying Shaw to the murder, and unreliable witnesses, some of who were ex-convicts and drug addicts. Of course, Oliver Stone brought Jack Ruby into the picture, tying Ruby to Oswald and to others in the conspiracy. One of the opening scenes in JFK shows prostitute and drug addict Rose Cherami (her real name was Melba Christine Marcades) being dumped from a car in rural Louisiana, later lying in a hospital bed crying out loud that Kennedy was to be killed in Dallas in two days. This scene created immediate interest in the movie and set the stage for the much bigger picture to be presented. In short, Oliver Stone put forth one of the most powerful conspiracy theories via screen, a movie claimed by some, including Vincent Bugliosi to be inundated with errors, falsities, and just outright deception. One of the biggest criticisms of *JFK* came from the late television news anchor Peter Jennings, who on the eve of the 40th anniversary of the assassination in November 2003 presented an in-depth television show that was in complete support of the Warren Commission. During the show Jennings claimed that the part of the movie where Garrison gave an emotional closing statement to the jury never occurred. Jennings also through modern technology was able to reenact the path of the second shot fired from the TBDB, the shot that penetrated the president and entered Governor Connally (the trajectories of all three shots were reenacted). This is known as *the magic bullet theory*, a shot that has played an important role in many conspiracy theories. The Warren Commission reported Kennedy "was first struck by a bullet which entered the back of his neck and exited through the lower front portion of the neck . . . Governor Connally was struck by a bullet which entered the right side of his back and traveled downward through the right side of his chest, exiting below his right nipple. This bullet then passed through his right wrist and entered his left thigh where it caused a superficial wound" (1964, 10). The bullet exited the thigh and was later found on a stretcher in Parkland Memorial Hospital. For years there have been many "doubting Thomas's" when it comes to this shot, individuals who have found it simply outlandish and incredible to think that a bullet could travel the path as described, first hitting JFK, next entering Connally, and then doing its zigzag routine. The Jennings report which depicted the possibility of such a shot has been supported elsewhere, and is detailed in *Case Closed* (1993) by Gerald Posner, another book that is in support of the Warren Commission. Not to be withstanding, Oliver Stone remains firm on what he presented in *JFK.*

Credible writers such as Mark North and Lamar Waldron and Thom Hartmann have written two detailed accountings of the assassination which are briefly reviewed. North's provocative book, *Act of Treason* (1991) lays the blame for the murder of President Kennedy on the doorstep of J. Edgar Hoover, Director of the FBI. The subtitle is "The Role of J. Edgar Hoover in the Assassination of President Kennedy" which in itself should make the focus of the book quite clear. North never implicated Hoover directly in the shooting, nor did he ever even insinuate that Hoover had anything to do directly with the assassination. What North did contend is that Hoover intentionally withheld vital information concerning the intentions of mafia figures to have JFK eliminated. For example, North cites as evidence the following intelligence from *ELSUR-Electronic Surveillance*–a statement made by Philadelphia mobster Angelo Bruno: "See what Kennedy done. With Kennedy a guy

should take a knife, like one of them other guys, and stab and kill the fucker . . . somebody should kill the fucker. . . . I mean it. This is truer, honest to God . . . I hope I get a week's notice. I'll kill. Right in…White House. Somebody's got to get rid of this fucker" (1991, 128). North cites other similar statements made by members of organized crime who he claimed were the key players in the assassination. These figures were *Carlos Marcello* from New Orleans, *Santo Traficante* from Miami, and *Sam Giancana* from Chicago. *Act of Treason* also ties the powerful union leader *Jimmy Hoffa* and another Mafiosi, *Johnny Roselli* to the conspiracy. It is North's contention that Hoover had a significant amount of ELSUR pointing to the plan to kill Kennedy by elements of organized crime, but failed to share this information with anyone, especially *Bobby Kennedy, the Attorney General of the United States,* and brother to the president. In the end, according to North, the plan was carried out by organized crime, and JFK lost his life.

In 2005, *Ultimate Sacrifice: John and Robert Kennedy, the Plan for a Coup in Cuba, and the Murder of JFK* was published. Its authors, Lamar Waldron and Thom Hartman spent the better part of 17 years researching the assassination and concluded like North that the mob was involved in the murder. But they assume a different slant by involving Cuban exiles in the plot who were said to have worked side-by-side with figures such as Johnny Roselli in killing Kennedy. The book is over 900 total pages in length and contains an incredible amount of detail, many names, and it is next to impossible to do it justice in a few paragraphs. However, the major positions of the book are now presented.

Waldron and Hartman concluded that Bobby Kennedy had devised a plan to overthrow Fidel Castro in a coup, to be led by an individual within the Castro government who is never identified in the book. President Kennedy was involved with the plan, known only to a handful of individuals. After two major crisis involving Cuba and the United States, the Bay of Pigs fiasco of April 1961 and the Cuban Missile Crisis of October 1962, the two Kennedys wanted to get rid of Castro, once and for all. It was absolutely imperative that this coup, code name *C-Day* or *Coup for Cuba* be kept confidential and highly secretive since the United States had pledged never to invade the island as part of the agreement with the Soviet Union to end the missile crisis. If word leaked that the Kennedy Administration was not only assisting with but planning and funding the coup, which involved Cuban exiles in the United States and anti-Castro forces inside Cuba, this could result in a nuclear confrontation with the Soviets (and at a minimum Castro might have had traitors executed). So how does *organized crime* come into the picture? Waldron and Hartman argue that the CIA had been working with organized crime for several years to have Castro assassinated, therefore the United States government already had its feet wet in the coup business, and it was mobster Johhny Roselli that the CIA was associated with in attempting to pull off a successful coup, which never happened. Prior to the revolution that brought Castro to power in Cuba, the mafia had a significant presence in that nation as a result of owning gambling Casinos in Havana. The mafia knew the island and had contacts in Cuba even after Castro came to power, and was a natural choice to assist in plans to kill Castro. *But critical to understanding C-Day was that the mafia was not involved—it was out of the loop— and the coup was to be strictly the work of Cuban exiles, some CIA operatives, and a small number of people who were close to the President and his brother, Bobby.* Waldron and Hartman con-

cluded the mafia infiltrated the plan, and decided as a result of knowing about the coup that it would be in its best interest if JFK was murdered. Since the book is so detailed and includes hundreds of names, it is never totally clear how the mafia infiltrated the plan, and equally ambiguous is why, as a result of becoming privy to C-Day, some mobsters decided to have JFK murdered. One conclusion that can be reached is during Kennedy's three years in office, his Attorney General brother went after some members of organized crime with a vengeance, and this became reason for them to have Kennedy assassinated. The Mafioso once again are Marcello, Trafficante, Roselli, Giancana and Hoffa, and knowing about C-Day offered them an opportunity to place a hit on JFK, since it could send a message to Bobby Kennedy and others about the power and reach of organized crime. Not only might Bobby know that it was mobsters who killed his brother, *but he could arrive at the conclusion that they were able to infiltrate a major, major secret, for which he would never take any action against them for the murder of his brother.* In essence Waldron and Hartman suggest November 22, 1963 was a matter of *two facts: assassination and blackmail.*

In Recognition: David Simon

David R. Simon is recognized here for keeping the spirit of C. Wright Mills alive and others who have followed in his footstep, such as Williman G. Domhoff. Although he has engaged in other writings, Simon's nine editions of *Elite Deviance* stand out in his career because they help to maintain the study of power from a critical perspective, and because each edition contains new and refreshing reminders that power continues to be corrupted and abused by the elites, a fact reinforcing a number of the assumptions of Mills and his exemplar, Karl

Marx. *Elite Deviance* is a detailed accounting of illegal, unethical, and immoral activities engaged in by the military, corporate, and economic elites of American society. Not only does it explain the nature of power, but it also gives numerous and often heartbreaking examples of its abuses. Examples of this include toxic dumping and other types of pollution allowed by the law, and those not sanctioned legally. Simon addresses the issue of campaign financing and discusses the manners in which campaign finance laws are circumvented and violated. At stake of course is who we elect to office, sometimes the highest offices in the land, and the threat that incompetent individuals may assume political power as a result of the volatility of campaign financing legislation is both scary and real. But it is Simon's application of C. Wright Mills that is of paramount importance in *Elite Deviance.* The ideas of Mills's Simon maintains and energizes include the concept of a power elite itself, and notions such as the higher immorality, specialized vocabularies, and inauthenticity. Over 50 years have passed since Mills wrote *The Power Elite*, and although the United States has undergone significant transformation during this period, much if not all that Mills addressed in 1956 is still relevant today, if not more so. David R. Simon looms as one of the most important individuals to keep the memory of Mills alive, not to mention that his work stands its own ground.

SUMMARY

Elite deviance includes actions taken by the highest ranking members of society. It entails behaviors that are illegal and unethical, normally occurring in the corporate, political, and military sectors of the United States. Power deviance is an extension of elite deviance, and encompasses corruption and damage to individuals and society, for which there is no remorse. Whereas elite deviance depicts deviant and criminal activities engaged in by the elites of society, power deviance is conceptualized as elite deviance that borders on the brutal: it can imply devastation to the environment; it can entail corruption of the United States Constitution and its institutions; it can mean destroying the lives of thousands of people through theft and accounting fraud; all without any feelings of empathy or sympathy for the victims. Power deviance is deviance involving greed taken to the highest exponent. The situations of Enron, Tyco, Worldcom, Watergate, Iran-Contra, the black budget, Chile, and MZM, all entail elements of elite and power deviance. With Enron, for example, the top echelon of the company was involved in eventually bringing havoc to the lives of many people, and these elites participated in the theft of a corporate giant without concern for what that would mean for others. The situations in Chile and Iran demonstrate a total disregard for human life, for the benefit of the few. The many deaths that have occurred in places such as these two countries represent just the tip of the iceberg of elite and power deviance, in the government and military spheres. C. Wright Mills coined the phrase "the power elite" and David Simon is credited with "elite deviance." The power elite are far and few between, have its origins in WASP, and have expanded to include non-WASPS. However, both elites share several things in common: wealth, power and prestige. Simon echoes the great work of Mills by detailing the enormous expansion of the elites in the United States since the 1950s. The assassination of President Kennedy involved the murder of the son of one of America's most powerful elites, Joseph P. Kennedy. It has been argued for years the assassination has been clouded in cover-up and lies from the highest levels of American society, especially the government. Although denied by the Warren Commission and others, a number of individuals have claimed that entities such as the CIA and FBI played a major role in the murder of the president. Perhaps on this issue only time alone will tell.

REFERENCES

A Research Study Conducted by the John Jay College of Criminal Justice. 2004. The Nature and Scope of Sexual Abuse of Catholic Priests and Deacons in the United States 1950–2002. The City University of New York: United States Conference of Catholic Bishops.

ABC News PrimetimeLive Poll: The American Sex Survey. 2004.

Agnew, R. (1985). A revised strain theory of delinquency. *Social Forces, 64* (1): 151–167.

Agnew, R. (1992). Foundation for a general theory of crime and delinquency. *Criminology, 30* (1): 47–87.

Agnew, R. (1993). Why do they do it? An examination of the intervening mechanisms between "social control" variables and delinquency. *Journal of Research in Crime and Delinquency, 30*: 245–266.

Agnew, R. and T. Brezina (1997). Relational problems with peers, gender and delinquency. *Youth and Society, 29*: 84–111.

Agnew, R., T. Brezina, J.P. Wright, and F.T. Cullen (2002). Strain, personality traits, and delinquency: Extending general strain theory. *Criminology 40,* (1): 43–71.

Agnew, R., F.T. Cullen, V.S. Burton, Jr., T.D. Evans, and R.G. Dunaway (1996). A new test of classic strain theory. *Justice Quarterly, 13*: 681–704.

Agnew, R. and H.R. White (1992). An empirical test of general strain theory. *Criminology, 30*: 474–499.

Akers, R.L. (2000). *Criminological theories: Introduction, evaluation, and application* (3rd ed.). Los Angeles: Roxbury.

Akers, R.L. (1977). *Deviant behavior: A social learning approach* (2nd ed.). Belmont, CA: Wadsworth.

Akers, R.L. (1985). *Deviant behavior: A social learning approach.* Belmont, CA: Wadsworth.

Akers, R.L. (1968). Problems in the sociology of deviance: Social definitions and behavior. *Social Forces, 46*: 455–465.

Akers, R.L. (1996). Is differential association/social learning cultural deviance theory? *Criminology, 34*: (2) 229–247.

Akers, R.L. (1998). *Social learning and social structure: A general theory of crime and deviance.* Boston: Northeastern University Press.

Akers, R.L. and J.K. Cochran (1985). Adolescent marijuana use: A test of three theories of deviant behavior. *Deviant Behavior, 6*: 323–346.

Akers, R.L. and G.F. Jensen (2003). *Social learning and the explanation of crime: A guide for the new century.* New Brunswick, NJ: Transaction Publications.

Akers, R.L. and G. Lee (1996). A longitudinal test of social learning theory: Adolescent smoking. *Journal of Drug Issues, 26*: (2) 317–343.

Akers, R.L. and G. Lee (1999). Age, social learning, and social bonding in adolescent substance use. *Deviant Behavior, 19*: 1–25.

Akers, R.L. and C. Sellers (2004). *Criminological theories: Introduction, evaluation, and application.* Los Angeles, CA.: Roxbury Publishing Co.: 81–110.

Albrecht ,G.L. (2006). (ed.). *Encyclopedia of disability.* Volume 1. Thousand Oaks, CA: Sage.

Allen, L.S. and R.A. Gorski (1992). Sexual orientation and the size of the anterior commissure. *Proceedings of the National Academy of Science, 89* (7): 199–202.

American Association of Suicidology Online. 2004.

American Gaming Association. *Building a Better Understanding of Casino Entertainment Through Education and Advocacy.* 2006.

Anglin, D.M. and G. Speckart (1988). Narcotics use and crime: A multisample, multimethod analysis. *Criminology, 29* (May): 197–232.

Anthony, D. and T. Robbins (1997). Religious totalism, exemplary dualism, and the WACO tragedy. In *Millennium, messiahs, and mayhen: Contemporary apocalyptic movements*. T. Robbins and S.J. Palmer. (eds.). 261–284. New York, NY: Routledge.

Arata, C.M. (1998). To tell or not to tell: Current functioning of child sexual abuse survivors who disclosed their victimization. *Child Maltreatment, 3*: 63–71.

Archibold, R.C. (2006). Former congressman sentenced to 8 years in prison. *The New York Times*: March 3.

Arneklev, B.J., H.G. Grasmick, C.R. Tittle, and R.J. Bursik, Jr. (199)3. Low self-control and imprudent behavior. *Journal of Quantitative Criminology, 9*: 225–247.

Arneklev, B.J., H.G. Grasmick, C.R. Tittle, and R.J. Bursik, Jr. (1999). Evaluating the unidimensionality and invariance of low "self-control." *Journal of Quantitative Criminology, 15*: 307–331.

Aseltine, R.H., S. Gore, and J. Gordon (2000). Life stress, anger, and anxiety, and delinquency: An empirical test of general strain theory. *Journal of Health and Social Behavior, 41*: 256–275.

Bandura, A. (1973). *Aggression: A social learning analysis*. Englewood Cliffs, NJ: Prentice-Hall.

Bandura, A. (1977). *Social learning theory*. Englewood Cliffs, NJ: Prentice-Hall.

Baraheni, R. (1976). Terror in Iran. *New York Review of Books*: October 28.

Barkan, S.E. (2005). Criminology: A sociological understanding. 249–250. Upper Saddle River, NJ. Pearson.

Barker, P.R., G. Manderscheid, and I.G. Hendershot (1992). Serious mental illness and disability in the adult household population: United States, 1989. *Advanced Data Vital Health Statistics*. September 16.

Baron, L. and M. Straus (1984). Sexual stratification, pornography, and rape in the United States. In *Pornography and sexual aggression*. N. Malamuth and E. Donnerstein (eds.) 185–209. San Diego, CA: Academic Press.

Baron, L. and M. Straus. (1987). Four theories of rape: A macosociological analysis. Social Problems. 34: 467–488.

Baron, L. and M. Straus (1989). *Four theories of rape in America: A state-level analysis*. New Haven, CT.: Yale University Press.

Baron, S.W. (2003). Self control, social consequences, and criminal behavior: Street youth and the general theory of crime. *Journal of Research in Crime and Delinquency, 40*: 403–425.

Barry, K.B. (1979). *Female sexual slavery*. New York: New York University Press.

Bazemore, G. and L. Walgrave (1999). *Restorative juvenile justice: Repairing the harm of youth crime*. Monsey, NY: Willow Tree Press.

Beal, G., B.D. Skolnik, R.T. Baker, Jr., R.S. Liebman (1978). The United States vs. Spiro Agnew, Vice President. In *Crime in Society*. L.D. Savitz and N. Johnson (eds.). 823–842. New York: John Wiley and Sons.

Bearmon, P.S., J. Moody, and K. Stovel (2004). Chains of affection: The structure of adolescent and sexual networks. *American Journal of Sociology, 110*: 44–91.

Becker, H.S. (1963). *The outsiders: Studies in the sociology of deviance*. New York, NY: Free Press.

Bellair, P.E., F.J. Roscigno, and M.B. Velez. (2003). Occupational Status, social learning, and adolescent violence. In *Social learning theory and the explanation of crime*. R.L. Akers and G.F. Jensen (eds.). 197–225. New Jersey: Transaction Publishers.

Benda, B.B. (1994). Testing competing theoretical concepts: Adolescent alcohol consumption. *Deviant Behavior, 15*: 375–396.

Ben-Veniste, R. (1970). Pornography and sex crime: The Danish experience. *Technical Reports of the Commission on Obscenity and Pornography*. Volume 9. Washington, D.C.: U.S. Government Printing Office.

Bernstein, C. and B. Woodward (1974). *All the President's Men*. New York: Simon and Schuster.

Bierne, P. and J. Messerschmidt (2000). *Criminology*. Boulder, CO. Westview: 203–208.

Blackwell, B.S. (2000). Perceived sanction threats, gender, and crime: A test and elaboration of power control. *Criminology, 38*: 439–488.

Blumstein, A. (2000–2001). Why crime is falling-or is it? National Institute of Justice, *Perspectives on Crime and Justice: 2000–2001 Lecture Series: 16.*

Blumstein, P. and P. Schwartz (1990). Intimate relationships and the creation of sexuality. In *Homosexuality/Heterosexuality.* D.P. McWhirter ,S.A. Sanders, J.M. Reinisch (eds.). New York: Oxford University Press.

Bogard, M. (1988). Feminists perspectives on wife abuse: An introduction. In *Feminists perspectives on wife abuse.* K. Yllo and M. Bogard (eds.) 11–26. Newbury Park, CA, Sage.

Bonger, W. (1969a). *Criminality and economic conditions.* Bloomington: Indiana University Press.

Bonger, W. (1969b). *Race and crime.* Montclair, NJ: Patterson Smith.

Braddock, D.L. and S.L. Parish (2001). An institutional history of disability. In *Handbook of Disability Studies.* G.L Albrecht, K.D. Seelman, and M. Bury (eds.).Thousand Oaks, CA: Sage.

Braithwaite, J. (1989). *Crime, shame, and reintegration.* New York: Cambridge University Press.

Braithwaite, J. (1998). Restorative justice. In *The Handbook of Crime and Punishment.* M. Tonry (ed.). 323–344. Chicago: University of Chicago Press.

Bratihwaite, J. (1999). Restorative justice: Assessing optimistic and pessimistic accounts. In *Crime and Justice: A Review of Research.* M. Tonry (ed.). 25: 1–27. Chicago: University of Chicago Press.

Breault, K.D. and K. Barkey (1982). A comparative analysis of Durkheim's theory of egoistic suicide. *Sociological Quarterly, 24*: 321–331.

Broidy, L.M. (2001). A test of general strain theory. *Criminology, 39* (1): 9–35.

Bromley, D. and E. D. Silver (1995). The Branch Davidians: A social profile and organizational history. In *America's Alternative Religions.* T. Miller (ed.). 149–158. Albany. Suny Press.

Brownmiller, S. (1975). *Against our will: Men, women, and rape.* New York: Bantam Book.

Bugliosi, V. (2007). *Reclaiming history: The assassination of President John F. Kennedy.* New York: W.W. Norton and Company.

Burr, C. (1996). *A separate creation: The search for the biological origins of sexual orientation.* New York: Hyperion.

Burt, C.H., R. Simons, and L.G. Simons (2006). A longititudinal test of the effects of parenting and the stability of self-control: Negative evi-dence for the general theory of crime. *Criminology, 44*: 353–396.

Campbell, A. (1984). *The girls in the gang: A report from New York City.* Oxford, UK: Basil Blackwell.

Campbell, J.C., D. Webster, J. Kozial-McLain, C. Block, D. Campbell, and M. Curry (2003). Risk factors for femicide in abusive relationships. *American Journal of Public Health, 93*: 1,089–1,097.

Catalano, R. and J.D. Hawkins (1996). The social development model: A theory of antisocial behavior. In *Delinquency and crime: Current theories.* J.D. Hawkins (ed.). New York: Cambridge University Press.

Cavan, R.S. (1928). Suicide. Chicago: University of Chicago Press.

Cavan, R.S. (1961). The concepts of tolerance and contraculture as applied to delinquency. *Sociological Quarterly.* 2: 243–258.

Cernkovich, S.A. and P. Giordano (1987). Family relationships and delinquency. *Criminology, 25*: 295–321.

Cernkovich, S.A. and P. Giordano (1992). School bonding, race, and delinquency. *Criminology, 30*: 261–291.

Chamlin, M. and J. Cochran (1995). Assessing Messner and Rosenfled's institutional anomie theory: A partial test. *Criminology, 33* (3): 411–429.

Charlton, J.I. (2006). The dimensions of disability oppression. In The disability studies reader. L.J. Davis (ed.). 217–227. New York Routledge.

Chesney-Lind, M. (2004). Beyond bad girls: Feminists perspectives on female offending. In *The Blackwell companion to female offending.* C. Sumner (ed.) 255–267. Oxford: Blackwell.

Chesney-Lind, M. and R. Shelden (1992). *Girls, delinquency and juvenile justice.* Brooks/Cole.

Child Maltreatment 2005. U.S. Department of Health and Human Services: Administration for Children and Families. Administration on Children, Youth and Familes: Children's Bureau.

Clinard, M.B. and R. Quinney (1973). *Criminal behavior systems.* New York: Holt, Rinehart and Winston.

Clinard, M.B., R. Quinney, and J. Wildeman (1994). *Criminal behavior systems: A typology.* (3rd ed.) Cincinatti: Anderson.

Clinard, M.B. and R. Meier. (2004). *Sociology of deviant behavior*. United States: Thomson.

Clinard, M.B. and R.F. Meier. (2008). *Sociology of deviant behavior*. Australia: Thomson.

Cloward, R. A. and L. E. Ohlin (1960). *Delinquency and opportunity: A theory of delinquent gangs*. New York: Free Press.

Coffman, K. (2007). Qwest ex-CEO gets 6 yrs prison for insider trading. *Reuters*. July 17: Friday.

Cohen, A. (1955). *Delinquent Boys*. Glencoe, IL: The Free Press.

Coleman, E. (1981). Developmental stages in the coming out process. *Journal of Homosexuality, 7*: 31–43.

Colvin, M. (2000). *Crime and coercion: An integrated theory of chronic criminality*. New York: St. Martin's Press.

Commission on Obscenity and Pornograpgy (1967) Report. Washington, D.C.: U. S. Government. Printing Office. 1970: 646 p.

Cooley, C.H. (1902). *Human nature and the social order*. New York: Charles Scribner's Sons.

Cooley, C.H. (1909). *Social organization*. New York: Schocken Books.

Cook, F.F. (1988). The players and the plays: A citizen's guide to Wedtech. *The Nation*. April 2: 458–461.

Covey, H.C. (1998). *Social perceptions of people with disabilities in history*. Springfield, IL. Charles C Thomas.

Crawford, K. (2004). Martha: I cheated no one: Lifestyle diva invokes Mandela as she, broker prepare to appeal 5-month sentences. *CNN Money.com*: July 20.

Curry, T.R. and A.R. Piquero (2003). Control ratios and defiant acts of deviance: Assessing additive and conditional effects with constraints and impulsivity. *Sociological Perspectives, 46*: 397–415.

D'Alession, S.J. and L. Stolzenberg (1993). Socioeconomic status and the sentencing of the traditional offender. *Journal of Criminal Justice, 21*: 73.

Daily Mail: 24 Hours a Day. 2007, December 9.

Daly, K. and M. Chesney-Lind. (1988). Feminism and criminology. *Justice Quarterly, 5*: 497–538.

Danigelis, N. and W. Pope (1979). Durkheim's theory of suicide as applied to the family: An empirical test. *Social Forces, 57*: 1,081–1,106.

Davis, D.J. (2006). Constructing normalcy: The bell shape curve, the novel, and the invention of the disabled body in the nineteenth century. In *The Disability Studies Reader*. L.J. Davis (ed.). 3–31 New York Routledge.

Dekeseredy, W.S. and C. Joseph (2006). Separation/divorce sexual assault in rural Ohio: Preliminary results of an exploratory study. *Violence Against Women, 12*: 301–311.

DeKeseredy, W.S., M.D. Schwarzt, D. Fagen, and M. Hall (2006). Separation/divorce sexual assault: The contribution of male support. *Feminist Criminology, 1* (3): 228–250.

Delisi, M. and A.L. Hochstetler (2002). An exploratory assessment of Tittle's control balance theory: Results from the National Youth Survey. *Justice Professional, 15*: 261–272.

Dell Orto, A.E. and R.P. Martinelli (eds.). (1995). *Encyclopedia of Disability and Rehabilitation*. Macmillan Library Reference U.S.A. New York: Simon and Schuster and Prentice Hall International.

Department of Health , and Human Services: 2005. *Results from the 2005 National Survey on Drug Use and Health: National Findings*. Substance Abuse and Mental Health Services Administration Office of Applied Studies.

Developments in the law-Race and the criminal process. (1988). *Harvard Law Review 101*. 1,496.

Diagnostic and Statistical Manual IV. (1994). American Psychiatric Association.

Dobash, R.E. and R. Dobash. (1979). *Violence against wives: A case against the patriarchy*. London: Open Books.

Douglas, J.D. (1967). *The social meanings of suicide*. Princeton, NJ.: Princeton University Press.

Drug Abuse Warning Network (DAWN) (2002). *Year End 2000 Emergency Department Data from the Drug Abuse Warning Network*. Rockville, MD.: Substance Abuse and Mental Health Services Administration.

Dunaway, R.G., Cullen, V. Burton, and D. Evans (2002). The myth of social class and crime revisited: An examination of adult and class criminality. *Criminology, 38* (2): 600.

Dunsmore, M.W. and H.B. Kaplan (1997). Peer support, adverse effects, and hallucinogenic drug experience. *Applied Behavioral Science Review, 5*: 219–230.

Durkeim, E. (1950). *The rules of sociological method.* New York, NY: Free Press

Durkheim, E. (1951). Suicide: *A study in sociology.* New York, NY: The Free Press.

Durkheim, E. (1956). *The division of labor in society.* New York, NY: The Free Press.

Dworkin, A. (1981). *Pornography: Men possessing women.* New York: Perigee Books.

Emerick, R. and W.A. Dutton. (1993). The effects on polygraphy on the self-report of adolescent sex offenders: Implications for risk assessment. *Annals of Sex Research, 6*: 83–103.

Enron (2007). From Wikipedia. The Free Encyclopedia: Online.

Erickson, K.T. (1962). Notes on the sociology of deviance. *Social Problems 9*: 307–314.

Esbensen, F.A. and L.T. Winfree, Jr. Race and gender differences between gang and non gang youth: Results from a multi-site survey. *Justice Quarterly, 15*: 505–526.

Faris, R.E.L. and H.W. Dunham (1938). *Mental disorders in urban areas.* Chicago: University of Chicago Press.

Farrington. D.P. (2004). Antisocial behavior and youth gang membership: Selection and Socialization. *Criminology, 42*: 55–87.

Feldman, S.S. and D.A. Weinberger (1994). Self-restraint as a mediator of family influences on boys' delinquent behavior: A longitudinal study. *Child Development, 65*: 191–211.

Finkel, E.J. and W.K. Campbell (2001). Self–control and accommodation in close relationships: An interdependence analysis. *Journal of Personality and Social Psychology, 81*: 263–277.

Finkelhor, D. (1984). *Child sexual abuse: New theory and research.* New York: The Free Press.

Finkelhor, D. (1998). Improving research, policy, and practice to understand child sexual abuse. JAMA. *Journal of the American Medical Association, 280*: 1,864–1,865.

Finkelhor, D. and K. Yllo (1985). *License to rape: Sexual abuse of wives.* New York: Holt, Rinehart, and Winston.

Fisher, W.A. and G. Grenier (1994). Violent pornography, antiwoman thoughts, and antiwoman acts: In search of reliable effects. *Journal of Sex Research, 31*: 23–38.

Fleishman, E.G. (1983). Sex role acquisition, sex role behavior, and sexual orientation: Some tentative hypotheses. *Sex Roles, 9*: 1,051–1,059.

Fleury, R.E., C.M. Sullivan, and D.I. Bybee (2000). When ending the relationship does not end the violence: Women's experiences of violence by former partners. *Violence Against Women, 6*: 1,363–1,383.

Fox, J.A. and J. Levin (2005). *Extreme killing.* Thousand Oaks, CA: Sage

French, H.W. (1988). Biaggi sentenced to an 8-year term in Wedtech case. *The New York Times.* November 19.

Fryar, C.A., R. Hirsch, K.S. Porter, B. Kottiri, D.J. Brody, and T. Louis (2007). Drug use and sexual behaviors reported by adults: United States,1999–2002. Advance Data: from *Vital and Health Statistics.* June 28. Number 384: 1–13.

Garbarino, J. (1978). The elusive "crime" of emotional abuse. *Child Abuse and Neglect, 2*: 89–99.

Garbarino, J. and J. Eckenrode (1997). *Understanding abusive families.* San Francisco, CA.: Jossey-Bass Publishers.

Gibbs, J.J. and D. Giever. (1995). Self-control and its mainisfestations among university students: An empirical assessment of Gottfredson and Hirschi's general theory. *Justice Quarterly, 12*: 231–255.

Gibbs, J.J., D. Giever, and G.F. Higgins, (2003). A test of Gottfredson and Hirschi's general theory using structural equation modeling. *Criminal Justice and Behavior, 30*: 441–457.

Gibbs, J.J., D. Giever, and J.S. Martin (1998). Parental management and self-control: An empirical test of Gottfredson and Hirschi's general theory. *Journal of Research in Crime and Delinquency, 35*: 40–70.

Gibbs, J.P. (1966). Conceptions of deviant behavior: The old and the new. *Pacific Sociological Review, 14*: 20–37.

Gibbs, J.P. (1982). Testing the theory of status integration and suicide rates. *American Sociological Review, 47*: 227–337.

J.P. Gibbs and W.L. Martin (1964). *Status integration and suicide: A sociological study.* Eugene, OR: University of Oregon Books.

Gill, C.J. (2001). The social experience of disability. In *Handbook of disability studies.* G.L. Albrecht, K.D. Seelman, and M. Bury (eds.). 351–372. Thousand, Oaks.: Sage.

Goffman, E. (1963). *Stigma: Notes on the management of a spoiled identity.* Englewood Cliffs, NJ: Prentice-Hall, Inc.

Goode, E. (2005). *Drugs in American society*. (6th ed.) Boston: McGraw Hill.

Gottfredson, M.R. and T. Hirschi (1990). A *general theory of crime*. Standford, CA: Standford University Press.

Gouldner, A. (1965). *Enter Plato: Classical Greece and the origins of social theory*. New York: Basic Books, Inc.

Gove, W.R. and M Hughes (1980). Reexamining the ecological fallacy: A study in which aggregate data are critical in investigating the pathological effects of living alone. *Social Forces, 1*, 157–1,177.

Grasmick, H.G., R.J. Bursik, Jr., and B.J. Arneklev (1993). Reduction in drunk driving as a response to increased threats of shame, embarrassment, and legal sanctions. *Criminology, 31*: 41–67.

Grasmick, H.G., J. Hagan, J. Blackwell, and B.J. Arneklev (1996). Risk preferences and patriarch: Extending power-control theory. *Social Forces, 75*: 177–199.

Greenhouse, L. (1997). Court, 9–0, upholds state laws prohibiting assisted suicide; protects speech on internet. *New York Times*. June 27.

Grunbaum, J.A., L. Kann, S. Kinchen, J. Ross, J. Hawkins, R. Lowry, W.A. Harris, T. McManus, D. Chyen, and J. Collins (2003). Youth risk behavior surveillance: United States, 2003. Division of Adolescent and School Health, National Center for Chronic Disease Prevention and Health Promotion. Centers for Disease Control: USA.

Hagan, J. (1989). *Structural Criminology*. New Brunswick, NJ. Rutgers University Press.

Hagan, J., A.R. Gillis, and J. Simpson (1990). Clarifying and extending power-control theory. *American Journal of Sociology, 95*: 1,024–1,037.

Hagan, J. and F. Kay (1990). Gender and delinquency in white-collar families: A control-power perspective. *Crime and Delinquency, 36*: 391–407.

IIahn, P. (1998). *Emerging criminal justice: Three pillars for a proactive justice system*. Thousand Oaks, CA: Sage.

Hamer, D. and P. Copeland (1994). *The science of desire: The search for the gay gene and the biology of behavior*. New York: Simon and Schuster.

Harrell, A., O. Mitchell, A. Hirst, D. Marlowe, and J. Merrill (2002). Breaking the cycle of drugs and crime: Findings from the Birmingham BTC Demonstration. *Criminology and Social Policy, 1*: 189–216.

Harrington, M. (1962). *The other America*. New York: Macmillan Company.

Harris, D.A. (1999). The stories, the statistics, and the law: Why "driving while black" matters. *Minnesota Law Review, 84*: 265–326.

Harris, J.R. (1998). *The nurture assumption: Why children turn out the way they do*. New York: Free Press.

Hay, C. (2001). An exploratory test of Braithwaite's reintegrative shaming theory. *Journal of Research in Crime and Delinquency, 38*: 132–153.

Hay, C. (2001). Parenting, self-control and delinquency: A test of self-control theory. *Criminology, 39*: 707–736.

Haynie, D. L. (2001). Delinquent peers revisited: Does network structure matter? *American Journal of Sociology, 106*: 1,013–1,057.

Heidensohn, F. (1968). The deviance of women: A critique and an inquiry. *British Journal of Sociology, 19*: 160–175.

Herd, D. (2005). Drinking patterns in the black population. In *Alcohol in America*. W.B. Clark and M.E. Hilton (eds.). Albany, NY: State University of New York Press.

Hester, M., L.. Kelley, and J. Radford (1996). *Women, violence, and male power: Feminist activism, research, and practice*. Buckingham, UK.: Open University.

Hickman, M. and A.R. Piquero (2001). Exploring the relationships between gender, control ratios, and deviance. *Deviant Behavior, 22*: 323–351.

Higgins, G.E. and C. Lauterbach. (2004). Control balance theory and exploitation: An examination of contingencies. *Criminal Justice Studies, 17*: 291–310.

Hirschi, T. (1969). *Causes of Delinquency*. Berkeley: University of California Press.

Hite, S. (2003). *The Hite Report: A national study of female sexuality*. New York: Seven Stories Press.

Hoffman, J. and A. Miller. (1998). A latent variable analysis of general strain theory. *Journal of Quantitative Criminology, 14*: 83–111.

Hollingshead, A.B. and F.C. Redlich (1958). *Social class and mental illness*. New York: Wiley.

Homans, G.C. (1962). *Sentiments and activities: Essays in social science.* New York: Free Press.

Horwitz, A.V. and T.L. Scheid (eds.). (1996). *A handbook for the study of mental health.* New York: Cambridge University Press.

Humphrey, J.A. (2006). *Deviant Behavior.* Pearson.

Humphreys. L. (1970). Tearoom trade: Impersonal sex in public places. *Transaction, 7*: 17–18.

Humphreys, L. (1972). *Out of the closets: The sociology of homosexual liberation.* Englewood Cliffs, NJ: Prentice Hall.

Hwang, S. and R.L. Akers (2003). Substance use by Korean adolescents: A cross-cultural test of social learning, social bonding, and self-control theories. In *Social learning and the explanation of crime.* R.L. Akers and G.F. Jensen (eds.) New Brunswick, NJ: Transaction Publishers: 39–63.

Jacobs, J. (1967). A phenomenological study of suicide notes. *Social Problems, 15*: 60–72.

Jellinek, E.M. (1946). Phases in the drinking history of alcoholics. *Quarterly Journal of on Alcohol, 7*:1–88.

Jensen, G. F. (1972). Parents, peers, and delinquent action: A test of the differential association perspective. *The American Journal of Sociology, 78*: (3) 562–575.

Jensen, G. F. (1990). The lingering promise of structural criminology. *Contemporary Sociology, 19*: 12–14.

Jensen, G. F. (1993a). Power-control vs. social control theories of common delinquency: A comparative analysis. *New directions in criminology.* eds. Freda Adler and William Laufer. New Brunswick, NJ: Transaction Publishers: 363–380.

Jensen, G. (1993b). Social class and juvenile delinquency. *Paper Presented at the Annual Meeting of the American Society of Criminology.*

Jensen, G. F. and D.G. Rojek (1998). *Delinquency and youth crime.* Prospect Heights, IL: Waveland Press.

Jensen, G.F. and K. Thompson (1990). What's class got to do with it? A further examination of power-control theory. *American Journal of Sociology, 95*: 1,009–1,023.

JFK (1991). Written by Z. Sklar and O. Stone: Warner Bros. Pictures.

John F. Kennedy. Inaugural Address. (1961): January 20.

Jones, L. and D. Finkelhor (2001). The decline in child sexual abuse cases. *Juvenile Justice Bulletin. January.* Washington, D.C.: U.S. Department of Justice.

Junger, M. and I.H. Marshall (1997). The interethnic generalizability of social control theory: An empirical test. *Journal of Research in Crime and Delinquency, 34*: 79–112.

Kaiser, H.J. Family Foundation (2006). *HIV/AIDS. HIV/AIDS Policy Fact Sheet. The Global HIV/AIDS Epidemic.* November.

Kandel, D. and M. Davies (1991). Friendship networks, intimacy, and illicit drug use in young adulthood: A comparison of two competing theories. *Criminology, 29*: 441–469.

Kantrowitz, B. (1996). Gay families come out. *Newsweek.* November 4: 50–57.

Kappeler, V.E., M. Blumberg, and G.W. Potter (2000). *The mythology of crime and justice.* Prospect Heights, IL.: Waveland Press.

Katz, R.S. (2000). Explaining girls' and womens' crime and desistance in the context of their victimization experiences. *Violence Against Women, 6*: 633–660.

Kelly, M. and J. Drinkard (2005). Secret military spending gets little oversight. *USA Today: Washington/Politics:* November 9.

Kilpatrick, D.G., C.N. Edmunds, and A.K. Seymour (1992). *Rape in America: A report to the Nation.* Arlington, VA.: National Center for Victims of Crime: Charleston, SC: Medical University of South Carolina.

Kilpatrick, D.G., K.J. Rugerrio, R. Acierno, B.E. Saunders, H.S. Resnick, and C.L. Best. (2003). Violence and risk of PTSD, major depression, substanceabuse/dependence, and comorbidity: Results from the national survey of adolescents. *Journal of Consulting and Child Psychology, 71*: 692–700.

Kimmel, M.S. and A. Linders (1996). Does censorship make a difference: An aggregate empirical analysis of pornography and rape. *Journal of Psychology and Human Sexuality, 8* (3): 1–20.

Kinsey, A., et al. (1948). *Sexual behavior in the human male.* Philadelphia: Saunders.

Kinsey, A., et al. (1953). *Sexual behavior in the human female.* Philidelphia: Saunders.

Kitsue, J.I. (1962). Societal reaction to deviant behavior: Problems of theory and method. *Social Problems, 9*: 247–256.

Kituse, J.I. and D.C. Dietrick (1959). Delinquent boys: A critique. *American Sociological Review, 24*: 208–215.

Kramer, J. (2007). Former contractor to be sentenced early next year. www.citizensforethics.org.

Krohn, M.D. and J.L. Massey (1980). Social control and delinquent behavior. An examination of social learning and social bonding theories. *Sociological Quarterly, 25*: 353–371.

Kupperstein, L. and W.C. Wilson (1970). Erotica and anti-social behavior: An analysis of social indicator statistics. *Technical Reports of the Commission on Obscenity and Pornography*. Volume 7. Washington, D.C: U.S. Government Printing Office.

Kutchinsky, B. Pornography and rape: Theory and practice. *International Journal of Law and Psychiatry, 14*: 47–67.

Lagrange, T.C. and R.A. Silverman (1999). Low self-control and opportunity: Testing the general theory of crime as an explanation for gender differences in delinquency. *Criminology, 37*: 41–72.

Lanctot, N. and M. Le Blanc (2002). Explaining deviance by adolescents. *Crime and Justice: A review of research, 29*: 113–202.

Lanza-Kaduce, L. and C. Michael. (2003). Social structure-social learning (SSSL) and binge drinking: A specific test of an integrated theory. In *Social Learning Theory and the Explanation of Crime*. R.L. Akers and G.F. Jensen (eds.). New Jersey: Transaction Publishers: 179–196.

Leighton, D.C, J.S. Harding, D.B. Macklin, A.M. Macmillan, and A.H. Leighton (1963). *The character of danger*. New York: Basic Books.

Lemert, E. M. (1951). *Social Pathology: A systematic approach to the theory of sociopathic behavior*. New York: McGraw-Hill.

Lemert, E.M. (1967). *Human deviance, social problems, and social control*. Englewood Cliffs, NJ: Prentice-Hall.

Lemert, E.M. (1972). *Human deviance, social problems, and social control* (2nd ed.). Englewood Cliffs, NJ: Prentice-Hall.

Leonard, E.B. (1982). *Women, crime, and society: A critique of criminology theory*. New York: Longman.

Lester, D. A test of Durkheim's theory of suicide in primitive societies. *Suicide and Life-Threatening Behavior, 22*: 388–395.

Levant, S., F.T. Cullen, B. Fulton, and J.F. Wozniak (1999). Reconsidering restorative justice: The corruption of benevolence revisited. *Crime and Delinquency, 45*: (3) 3–27.

Levine, S. and L. Montgomery (2003). Large racial disparity found by study of Maryland death penalty. *The Washington Post.* January 8.

Levay, S. (1996). *Queer science: The use and abuse of research into homosexuality*. Cambridge, MA: MIT Press.

Li, W.L. (1972). Suicide and educational attainment in a transitional society. *The Sociological Quarterly, 13*: 253–258.

Liazos, A. (1972). The poverty of the sociology of deviance: Nuts, sluts, and perverts. *Social Problems, 20*: 103–120.

Lilly, R.J., F.T. Cullen, and R.A. Ball (1989). *Criminological theory: Context and consequences*. Newbury Park, CA: Sage.

Lindau, S.T., L.P. Schumm, E.O. Laumann, W. Levinson, C.A O'Muircheataigh, and L.J. Waite (2007). A study of sexuality and healthy among older adults in the United States. *The New England Journal of Medicine, 357*: 762–774.

Lindesmith , A. (1965). *The addict and the law*. Bloomington, IN: Indiana Press.

Link, B.G., M.C. Lennon, and B.P. Dohrenwend (1993). Socioeconomic status and depression: The role of occupations involving direction, control, and planning. *American Journal of Sociology, 98*: 1,351–1,387.

Linton, S. (2006). Reassigning meaning. In *The disability studies reader*. L.J. Davis (ed.). 161–172. New York: Routledge.

Littlejohn, C. (2004). Rediscovering the "social" in the biopsychosocial perspective. *Mental Health Practice, 8*: 14–17.

Longshore, D., E. Chang, S.C. Hsieh, and N. Messina. (2004). Self-control and social bonds: A combined control perspective on deviance. *Crime and Delinquency, 50*: 542–564.

Lyman, M.D. and G. Potter (2004). *Organized crime*. (3rd ed.). Upper Saddle River, NJ: Prentice Hall.

MacKinnon, C.A. (1989). Sexuality, pornography, and method: Pleasure under psychiatry. *Ethics, 99*: 314–346.

Makkai, T. and J. Braithwaite (1991). Criminological theories and regulatory compliance. *Criminology, 29*: 191–220.

Mankoff, M. (1971). Societal reaction and career deviance: A critical analysis. *Sociological Quarterly, 12*: 204–218.

Maris, R. (1969). *Social forces in urban suicide.* Homewood, IL. Dorsey Press.

Marshall, W.L. (1988). The use of sexually explicit stimuli by rapists, child molesters and nonoffenders. *Journal of Sex Research, 25*: 267–288.

Martin, R., R.J. Mutchnick, and W.T. Austin (1990). *Criminological thought: Pioneers past and present.* New York: Macmillan.

Marx, K. and F. Engels (1975). Proceedings of the sixth Rhine Conference Assembly. Debates on the law on thefts of wood. In *Karl Marx/ Frederick Engels: Collected Works, 1*: 224–263 London: Lawrence and Wishart. (originally published in 1842).

Mason, W.A. and M. Windle (2002). Gender, self-control, and informal social control in adolescence: A test of three models of the continuity of delinquent behavior. *Youth and Society, 33*: 479–514.

Mazzerole, P. and J. Maahs (2000). General strain and delinquency: An alternative examination of conditioning influences. *Justice Quarterly, 17*: 753–778.

McCarty, B., J. Hagan, and T.S. Woodward (1999). In the company of women: Structure and agency in a revised power-control theory of gender and delinquency. *Criminology, 37*: 761–788.

McGinn, D. (2004). Mating behavior 101. *Newsweek.* October 4: 44–45.

Mead, G.H. (1834). *Mind, self, and society.* Chicago: The University of Chicago Press.

Menard, S. (1995). A developmental test of anomie theory. *Journal of Research in Crime and Delinquency, 32*: 136–174.

Menard, S., S. Mihalic, and D. Huizinga. Drugs and crime revisted. (2001). *Justice Quarterly, 18*: 269–299.

Merton, R.K. (1938). Social structure and anomie. *American Sociological Review, 3* (5): 672–682.

Merton, R. K. (1968). *Social theory and social structure.* New York, NY: Free Press.

Messner, S.F and R. Rosenfeld (1997). Political restraint of the market and levels of criminal homicide: A cross-national application of institutional anomie theory. *Social Forces, 75* (4): 1393–1416.

Messner, S.F. and R. Rosenfield (1994). *Crime and the American dream.* Belmont, CA: Wadsworth.

Meyer, E. and L. Post (2006). Alone at night: A feminist ecological model of community violence. *Feminist Criminology, 1* (3): 207–227.

Mignon, S.I., C.J. Larson, and W.M. Holmes (2001). *Family abuse: Consequences, theories, and responses.* Boston: Allyn and Bacon.

Miller, E.M., K. Romenesko. and L. Wondolkowski (1993). In *Prostitution: An International Handbook on Trends, Problems, and Policies.* N.J. Davis (ed.). 300–326. Westport, CT. Greenwood Press.

Miller, J. (2000). Feminist theories of women's crime: Robbery as a case study. In *Of crime and criminality: The use of theory in everyday life.* S.S. Simpson (ed.). 25–46. Thousand Oaks, CA. Pine Forge Press:

Miller, J. and S. Decker. (2001). Young women and gang violence: Gender, street offending, and violent victimization in gangs. *Justice Quarterly, 18*: 115–140.

MMWR Weekly. (2008).

Mosher, W.D. (2005). With males in the mix, federal sex survey takes on greater importance. *Contemporary Sexuality, 39*: November, 1–6.

Moyer, I. (2001). *Criminological theories.* Thousand Oaks: Sage Press.

Mulrine, A. (2002). Risky business. *U.S. News and World Report.* May 27: 42–49.

Nagin, D.S. and R. Paternoster (1994). Personal capital and social control: The deterrence implications of a theory of individual differences in criminal offending. *Criminology, 32*: 581–606.

Naffine, N. (1987). *Female crime: The construction of women in criminology.* London: Allen and Bacon.

National Gambling Impact Study Commission (2002). *Gambling Impact and Behavior Study: 1997–1999.* (United States). National Gambling Impact Study Commission: Washington, D.C.

National Gang Crime Research Center (2006).

National Institute on Alcohol Abuse and Alcoholism.

National Victim Awareness Survey (1998).

Nichols, M. (1990). Lesbian relationships: Implications for the study of sexuality and gender.

In *homosexuality/heterosexuality*. D.P. McWhirter, S.A. Sanders, and J.M. Reinisch. (eds.). New York: Oxford University Press.

Nielsen, A.L. and R. Martinez. Jr. (2003). Reassessing the alcohol–violence linkage: Results from a multiethnic city. *Justice Quarterly, 20*: 445–469.

Norris, F.H., et al. (2002). The epidemiology of sex differences in PTSD across developmental, societal, and research contexts. In *Gender and PSTD*. R. Kimerling, P. Ouimette, and J. Wolfe (eds.). New York: Guilford.

North, M. (1991). *Act of Treason: The Role of J. Edgar Hoover in the assassination of President Kennedy*. New York: Carroll and Graf Publishers, Inc.

Office of National Drug Control Policy (ONDCP).

Ohio State University Medical Center (2008).

Parsons, T. (1937). *The structure of social action*. New York: Free Press.

Parsons, T. (1951). *The social system*. New York: Free Press.

Paternoster, R. and P. Mazzerole (1994). General strain theory and delinquency: A replication and extension. *Journal of Research in Crime and Delinquency, 31*: 235–263.

Peralta, R.L. Race and the culture of college drinking. In *Cocktails and dreams: Perspectives on drug and alcohol use*. W.R. Palacios (ed.). Upper Saddle River, NJ: Prentice Hall.

Perret, G. (2001). *Jack: A life like no other*. New York: Random House.

Perrone, D., C.J. Sullivan, T.C. Pratt, S. Margaryan (2004). Parental efficacy, self-control, and delinquency: A test of a general theory of crime on a nationally representative sample of youth. *International Journal of Offender Therapy and Comparative Criminology, 48*: 298–312.

Peter Jennings Reporting; The Kennedy Assassination-Beyond Conspiracy. (2003). Mark Obenhaus: Director.

Peterson, D., J. Miller, and F.A. Esbensen (2001). The impact of sex composition on gangs and gang member delinquency. *Criminology, 39* (2): 411–439.

Piquero, A.R. and M. Hickman (1999). An empirical test of Tittle's control balance theory. *Criminology, 37*: 319–341.

Piquero, A.R. and M. Hickman (2002). The rational choice implications of control balance theory. In *Rational choice and criminal behavior: Recent changes and future challenges*. eds. A.R. Piquero and S.G. Tibbets. New York: Routledge.

Piquero, A.L. and M. Hickman (2003). Extending control balance theory to account for victimization. *Criminal Justice and Behavior, 30*: 282–301.

Piquero, N.L., R. MacIntosh, and M. Hickman (2001). Applying Rasch modeling to the validity of a control balance scale. *Journal of Criminal Justice, 29*: 493–505.

Piquero, N.L. and A.R. Piquero (2006). Control balance and exploitative corporate crime. *Criminology, 44*: 397–429.

Piquero, N.L. and M.D. Sealock (2000). Generalizing general strain theory: An examination of an offending population. *Justice Quarterly, 17*: 448–484.

Pistone, J. with R. Woodley. (1988). *Donnie Brasco: My undercover life in the mafia*. New York, NY and Scarborough, Ontario: New American Library.

Plummer, K. (2002). Continuity and change in Howard S. Becker's work: An interview with Howard S. Becker. *Sociological Perspectives, 46*: (1) 21–39.

Plummer, K. (1979). Misunderstanding labeling perspectives. In *Deviant Interpretations*. D. Downs and P. Rock (eds). 85–121. Oxford: Oxford University Press.

Pope, W. (1976). *Durkheim's "Suicide": A classic analyzed*. Chicago: University of Chicago Press.

Popgun Politics. *U.S. News and World Report*, September 30, 1996: 33.

Porter, R. (1996). Born that way? *New York Times Book Review*. August 11: 8.

Pratt, T.C. and F.T Cullen (2000). The empirical status of Gottfredson and Hirschi's general theory of crime: A meta-analysis. *Criminology, 38*: 931–964.

Quinn, T. (1998). Restorative justice: An interview with visiting fellow Thomas Quinn. In *National Institute of Justice Journal*. March: 10–16.

Quinney, R. (1970). *The social reality of crime*. Boston: Little Brown.

Quinney, R. (1973). Crime control in capitalist society: A critical philosophy of legal order. *Issues in Criminology, 8*: 75–79.

Quinney, R. (1977). *Class, state, and crime*. New

York: Longman.

Quinney, R. (1997). Socialistic Humanism and critical/peacemaking criminology: The continuing project. In *Thinking critically about crime.* B.D. Maclean and D. Milovanovic (eds.) 114–117. Vancouver, B.C.: Collective Press:

Quinney, R. (1991). The way of Peace: On crime, suffering, service. In *Criminology as peacemaking.* H. Pepinsky and R. Quinney (eds.) 3–13. Bloomington, Indiana University Press:

Rape Abuse and Incest National Network. info@rainn.org. 2007.

Reiman, J. (2003). *The rich get richer and the poor get prison.* Class, Ideology, and Criminal Justice. Boston: Pearson.

Reiman, J. (2007). *The rich get richer and the poor get prison: Ideology, class, and criminal justice.* Boston: Pearson.

Results from the 2005 National Survey on Drug Use and Health: National Findings. Department of Health and Human Services. Substance Abuse and Mental health Services Administration: Office of Applied Studies.

Rodgers, B. and S.L. Mann (1993). Rethinking the analysis of intergenerational social mobility: A comment on John W. Fox's "Social class, mental illness, and social mobility." *Journal of health and social behavior, 34*: 165–172.

Roper, W.G. (1996). The etiology of Male homosexuality. *Medical Hypothesis, 46*: 85–88.

Roth, J. (1994). *Psychoactive substances and violence.* Washington, D.C. National Institute of Justice. U.S. Department of Justice.

Russell, D. (1975). *The politics of rape.* New York: Stein and Day.

SAMHSA's National Health Information Center.

Sampson, R.J. and J. Laub (1993). *Crime in the making: Pathways and turning points through life.* Cambridge, MA.: Harvard University Press.

Saunders, (1999). Lolita nation. *The San Francisco Chronicle.* March 28: 7

Savins-Williams, R.C. (2005). Who's gay: Does it matter? *Current Directions in Psychological Science, 15*: 40–44.

Schallet, A., G. Hunt, K. Joe-Laidler (2003). Respect and Autonomy. *Journal of Contemporary Ethnography, 31* (1): 109–143.

Scheff, T.J. (1966). *Being mentally ill: A sociological theory.* Chicago: Aldine and Atherton.

Schrag, C. (1962). Delinquency and Opportunity: Analysis of a theory. *Sociology and Social Research, 46* (2): 167–175.

Schur, E.M. (1965). *Crimes Without Victims: Deviant behavior and public policy-abortion, homosexuality, drug addiction.* Englewood Cliffs, NJ: Prentice Hall/Spectrum.

Schwartz, M.D. and W.S. DeKeseredy (1997). *Sexual assault on the college campus: The role of male peer support.* Thousand Oaks, CA.: Sage.

Schwartz, S. (1991). Women and depression: A Durkheimian perspective. *Social Science and Medicine, 32*: 127.

Scott, J.E. and S.J. Cuvelier (1993). Violence and sexual violence in pornography: Is it really increasing? *Archives of Sexual Behavior, 22*: 357–371.

Seliger, R. V. (1950). Chief Psychiatrist of the Neuropsychiatric Institute of Baltimore.

Sellers, C.S., T.C. Pratt, L.T. Winfree, and F.T. Cullen, Jr. (2000). The empirical status of social learning theory: A meta-analysis. *Paper presented at the meeting of the American Society of Criminology.* San Farancisco.

Shils, E. and H. Finch, eds. (1949). *Max Weber on the methodology of the social sciences.* New York, NY: Free Press.

Shoemaker, D.J. (1996). *Theories of Delinquency: An Examination of Explanations of Delinquent Behavior.* (3rd ed.) New York: Oxford University Press.

Short, J.F. (1960). Differential association as a hypothesis: Problems of empirical testing. *Social Problems, 8*: (1) 14–25.

Silbert, M.H. and M.A. Pines (1984). Pornography and sexual abuse of women. *Sex Roles, 10*: 857–868.

Simon, D.R. (2006). *Elite Deviance.* (8th ed.) Boston: Pearson.

Simon, D.R. (2008). *Elite Deviance.* (9th ed.) Boston: Pearson.

Simpson, S.S. and L. Elis (1995). Doing gender: Sorting out the caste and crime conundrum. *Criminology, 33*: 47–81.

Slade, J.W. (2000). *Pornography in America.* Santa Barbara, CA.: Contemporary World Issues.

Spencer, J.M., G.D. Zimet, M.C. Aalsma, and D.P. Orr (2002). Self-esteem as an initiator of coitus in early adolescents. *Pediatrics, 109*:

581–584.

Spohn, C.C. (2000). Thirty years of sentencing reform: The quest for a racially neutral sentencing process. NIJ. *Criminal Justice 2000, vol. 3: Policies, Processes, and Decisions of the Criminal Justice System:* 427–428.

Srole, L., T.S. Langer, S.T. Michael, P. Kirkpatrick, M.K. Opler, and T.A.C. Rennie (1978). *Mental health in the metropolis: The midtown Manhattan Study.* rev.ed. New York: New York University Press.

Stack, S. (1979). Durkheim's theory of fatalistic suicide: A cross-national approach. *Journal of Social Psychology, 107*: 161–168.

Stinchcombe, A. (1968). *Constructing social theories.* New York: Harcourt Brace Jovanovich.

Sutherland, E.H. (1937). *The professional thief: By a professional thief.* Chicago: University of Chicago Press.

Sutherland, E. H. (1947). *Criminology.* Philadelphia. J.B. Lippincott.

Sutherland E.H. and D. R. Cressey (1975). The theory of differential association. In *Theories of deviance.* S. H. Traub and D. R. Cressey (eds.). Itasca, IL: F. E. Peacock Publishers.

Swabb, D.F. and M.A. Hoffman. (1990). An enlarged suprachiasmatic nucleus in homosexual men. *Brain Research, 537*: 141–148.

Sykes, G. and D. Matza (1961). Juvenile delinquency and subterranean values. *American Sociological Review, 26*: 712–719.

Szasz, T.S. (1960). *The myth of mental illness.* New York: Hoeber–Harper.

Tannebaum, F. (1938). *Crime and the community.* New York: Columbia University Press.

Taylor, I., P. Walton, and J. Young (1973). *The New Criminology: For a Social Theory of Deviance.* New York: Harper and Row.

The Oklahoman (2005). Worldcom's Ebbers given 25 years. Thursday. July 14.

The Warren Report: The Official Report on the Assassination of President John F. Kennedy. 1964. President's Commission on the Assassination of President Kennedy: The Associated Press.

Thio, A. (2006). *Deviant Behavior.* Boston: Pearson.

Thornberry, T.P., A.J. Lizotte, M.D. Krohn, M. Farnworth, and S.J. Jang. Delinquent peers, beliefs, and delinquent behavior: A longitudinal test of interaction theory. *Criminology, 32*:

47–84.

Tittle, C.R. (1995). *Control balance: Toward a general theory of deviance.* Boulder, CO. Westview.

Tittle, C.R. (2004). Refining control balance theory. *Theoretical Criminology, 8*: 395–428.

Tittle, C. R. and E. Botchkovar. (2005). Self-control, criminal motivation and deterrence: An investigation using Russian respondents. *Criminology, 43*: 307–354.

Tittle, C.R., M.J. Burke, and E.F. Jackson (2001). Modeling Sutherland's theory of differential association: Toward an empirical clarification. *Social Forces, 65*: (2) 405–432.

Title, C.R., D.A. Ward., and H.G. Grasmick (2003a). Gender, age, and crime/deviance: A challenge to self-control theory. *Journal of Research in Crime and Delinquency, 40*: 426–453.

Title, C.R., D.A. Ward, and H.G. Grasmick (2003b). Self-control and crime/deviance: Cognitive vs. behavioral measures. *Joural of Quantitative Criminology, 19*: 333–365.

Trenblay, R.E., B. Boulerice, L. Arseneault, M. J. Niscale (1995). Does low self-control during childhood explain the association between delinquency and accidents in early adolescence? *Criminal Behavior and Mental Health, 5*: 439–451.

Troiden, R.R. (1979). Becoming homosexual: A model of gay identity acquisition. *Psychiatry, 42*: 362–373.

Troiden, R.R. (1988). *Gay and lesbian identity: A sociological analysis.* New York: General Hall.

Troiden, R.R. (1989). The formation of homosexual identities. *Journal of Homosexuality, 17*: 43–73.

Turk, A. (1969). *Criminality and the legal order.* Chicago: Rand McNally.

Turner, J.H. (1991). *The structure of sociological theory.* (5th ed.). Belmont, CA: Wadsworth.

Turner, M.G. and A.R. Piquero. (2002). The stability of self-control. *Journal of Criminal Justice, 30*: 457–471.

Unnever, J., T.C. Pratt, and F.T. Cullen (2003). Parental Management, ADHD, and delinquent involvement: Reassesseing Gottfredson and Hirschi's general theory. *Justice Quarterly,* 471–500.

Vagg, J. (1998). Delinquency and shame. Data from Hong Kong. *British Journal of Criminology, 38*: 247–264.

Van Ness, D.W. and K.H. Strong (1997). *Restoring justice.* Cincinatti, OH: Anderson.

Vazsonyi, A.T. and J. M. Crosswhite (2004). A test of Gottfredon and Hirschi's a general theory of crime in African-American adolescents. *Journal of Research in Crime and Delinquency, 41*: 407–432.

Vise, D.A. (2002). *The bureau and the mole.* New York: Grove Press.

Waco-the Inside Story. (1995). Frontline. The Public Broadcasting Service: D. Fanning. Executive Producer. Aired October 17.

Waldron, L. with T. Hartman (2005). *Ultimate sacrifice: John and Robert Kennedy, the plan for a coup in Cuba, and the murder of JFK.* New York: Carroll and Graf Publishers.

Ward, R.H. (1971). The labeling theory: A critical Analysis. *Criminology:* August-November: 268–290.

Warr, M. (1993). Parents, peers, and delinquency. *Social Forces, 72*: 247–264.

Warr, M. (2002). *Comparisons in crime: The social aspects of criminal behavior.* New York: Cambridge University Press.

Weinberg, M.S., C.J. Williams, and D.W. Pryor. (2007). Becoming sexual. In *Deviance: The interactionist perspective.* E. Rubington and M.S. Weinberg (eds.). Boston: Allyn and Bacon: 355–363.

Wellford, C. (1975). Labeling theory and criminology: An assessment. *Social Problems, 22*: 335–347.

West, C. and D.H. Zimmerman (1987). Doing gender. *Gender and Society, 1*: 125–151.

West Slope Methamphetamine Symposium. Grand Junction Colorado. June. 2004.

Whaley, R.B. (2001). The paradoxical relationship between gender inequality and rape: Toward a refined theory. *Gender and Society, 15*: 531–555.

White, H.R., V. Johnson, and A. Horowitz (1986). An application of three deviance theories for adolescent substance use. *International Journal of the Addictions, 21*: 347–366.

White, H.R., P.C. Tick., R. Loeber, and M. Stouthamer-Loeber (2002). Illegal acts committed by adolescents under the influence of alcohol and drugs. *Journal of Research in Crime and Delinquency, 39*: 131–152.

Whitmire, K. (2006). Ex-Governor and executive convicted of bribery. *The New York Times.* June 30.

Whitmire, K. Scrushy to pay $81 million to settle S.E.C. lawsuit. (2007). *The New York Times.* April 24.

Wilkinson, W.A. (2004). Religiosity, authoritarianism, and homophobia: A multidimensional approach. *The International Journal for the Psychology of Religion, 14*: 55–67.

Winick, C. (1985). A content analysis of sexually explicit magazines sold in adult bookstores. *Journal of Sex Research, 21*: 206–210.

Winick, C. and J.T. Evans (1996). The relationship between nonenforcement of state pornography laws and rates of sex crime arrests. *Archives of Sexual Behavior, 25*: 439–453.

Winick, C. and P.M. Kinsie (1971). *The Lively Commerce.* Chicago: Quadrangle.

Wong, D. (1999). Culturally specific causes of delinquency: Implications for juvenile justice in Hong Kong. *Asia Pacific Journal of Social Work, 9*: 98–113.

Wong, G. (2005). Kozloski gets up to 25 years: Mark Swartz, former Tyco CFO, also gets 8-1/3 to 25; both men fined, handcuffed, sent to jail. *CNNMoney.com*: September 19.

Wright, R.T. and S. Decker (1998). *Armed robbers in action: Stickups and street culture.* Boston: Northeastern University Press.

www.businessroundtable.org 2006

www.deathpenaltyinfo.org. April 1, 2008.

www.enron.com/corp/pressroom/bios/rick-causey.html 2008.

www.health.state.ok.us/program/injury/Summary/OVDRS 2007.

www.mentalhealth.samhsa.gov/publications/allpubs/SMA06-4195/chp15table.asp.2004.

www.nimh.gov/health/statistics/index/shtml. 2004.

www.ojp.usdoj.gov 2007.

www.potus.com 2004.

www.surgeongeneral.gov/librarymentalhealth/chapter3/sec5.html.

www.watergateinfo.com 2008.

www.who.int 2003.

Yablonsky, L. (1962). *The violent gang.* New York, NY: Macmillan.

Yang, Bijou (1992). The economy and suicide: A time-series study of the U.S.A. *American Journal of Economics and Sociology, 51*: 87–99.

Yodanis, C.L. (2004). Gender inequality, violence against women, and fear: A cross-national test of the feminist theory of violence against women. *Journal of Interpersonal Violence, 14*: 1,070–1,094.

Young, J. (1981). Thinking seriously about crime: Some models of criminology. In *Readings in history and society*. M. Fitzgerald, G. McLennan, and J. Pawson (eds). London: Routledge and Kegan Paul.

Yonkers, K.A. and G. Gurguis, (1995). Gender differences in the prevalence and expression of anxiety disorders. In *Gender and Psychopathology*. M.V. Seeman (ed.). Washington, D.C.: American Psychiatric Press.

Zatz, M. S. (2000). The convergence of ethnicity, gender, and class on court decision making: Looking toward the 21st Century. NIJ, *Criminal Justice 2000, vol. 3: Policies, Processes, and Decisions of the Criminal Justice System* (NCJ 182410): 515.

Zhang, S. X. (1995). Measuring shaming in an ethnic context. *British Journal of Criminology, 35*: 248–262.

Zillman, D. and J. Bryant (1982). Pornography, sexual callousness, and the trivialization of rape. *Journal of Communication.* 10–21.

Zillman, D. and J. Bryant (1986). Shifting preferences in pornography consumption. *Communication Research, 13*: 560–578.

AUTHOR INDEX

A

Aalsma, M.C., 215
Acierno, R., 142
Agnew, R., 43-48, 50, 53, 55, 57, 82
Agnew, S., 240-241
Akers, R.L., 6, 49, 53, 57, 73, 81, 82, 83, 84, 85, 86
Allen, L.S., 229, 241
Ames, A., 43
Anglin, D.M., 167
Anthony, D., 61
Arata, C.M., 141
Archibold, R.C., 249
Arneklev, B.J., 60, 66
Arnsenauly, 60
Aseltine, R.H., 46
Asner, E., 263
Astors, 256
Austin, W.T., 53, 91, 94, 123

B

Bach, B., 173
Bacon, K., 263
Baker, Jr., R.T., 241
Baker, M., 261
Ball, R.A., 53
Bandura, A., 83
Bannister, G., 263, 264
Baraheni, R., 251
Barkan, S.E., 97, 176
Barker, P.R., 191, 239
Barkley, K., 118
Baron, L., 98
Barron, S.W., 59
Barry, K.B., 220, 221
Bazemore, G., 76

Beall, G., 241
Bearmon, P.S., 214
Becker, H.S., 7, 15, 70, 72, 73, 86, 87
Begin, M., 242
Bell, A.G., 203-204
Bellair, P.E., 86
Benda, B.B., 84
Ben-Veniste, R., 226
Bernstein, C., 240
Best, C.L., 142
Biaggi, M., 244, 245
Bierne, P., 97
Bin Laden, O., 89
Blackwell, B.S., 66
Blackwell, J., 65
Block, C., 98
Bluestine, R., 245
Blumberg, M., 166
Blumer, H., 86
Blumstein, A., 125, 128, 166-167
Blumstein, P., 228
Bogard, M., 98
Boggs, H., 259
Bonger, W., 89, 91, 92, 94, 247
Bonta, 84
Botchkovar, E., 59
Boulerice, B., 60
Boye, 181, 182
Braddock, D.L., 198, 199
Bragg, M., 245
Braithwaite, J., 75, 76, 77, 82
Brasco, D., 20
Breault, K.D., 118
Brezina, T., 45, 46
Brody, D.J., 212
Broidy, L.M., 46
Bromley, D., 61
Brown, J., 75

283

SUBJECT INDEX

A

Ability, 197
Ableism, 198
Absolutism, 8
Abuse, 136-137
    Types, 136-137
Addiction, 157-183
    and Illicit Drug Use, 157-164
    and Alcohol Use, 161
    and Tobacco Use, 162
    and age, 163
    and race/ethnicity, 163-164
    and The Addiction Severity Index
      (ASI), 174
    and The Substance Abuse Subtle
      Screening Inventory (SASSI), 181-
      183
Adolescent Prostitutes, 217
Agnew's Types of Strain, 43-45
Alcohol Abuse, 173-177
    and demographics, 175
    and violence, 176
    and effects, 176
Alcoholism, 173-177
    and loss of control, 173
    and symptoms, 174
    and functional/structural damage, 172-
      173
    and therapeutic uses, 173
Americans with Disabilities Act, 196, 199,
    208-209
Anomie, 29, 34-40
Anxiety Disorders, 187-192
Attachment, 46, 55-58, 77, 82, 85, 141
Attitudinal Patriarchy, 66
Audio Computer-Assisted Self-Interviewing,
    18

Autonomy, 62-63

B

Barry's Types of Prostitute Procurement, 220-
    221
Becker's Sequential Model of Deviant
    Behavior, 72-73
Behavioral Coping Strategies, 45
Belief, 55-58, 85
Bisexuals, 231
    and Weinberg, Williams, and Pryor's
      Stages, 231
Bonger's Theory, 89, 91-92

C

Call Girls, 211, 217-218
Cavan's Delinquency Model, 8-10
Child Emotional Abuse, 140
    Rejecting, 140
    Isolating, 140
    Terrorizing, 140
    Ignoring, 140
    Corrupting, 140
Child Prostitutes, 217
Child Sexual Abuse, 140-143
    and Finklehor's preconditions, 141
    and stages, 141
    and effects, 142-143
Child/Adolescent Mental Disorders, 192-193
    and genetic factors, 193
    and gender, 193
    and biological factors, 193
    and cognitive factors, 193
Citizen Reparative Boards, 76
Clustering, 44
Cocaine, 167-169

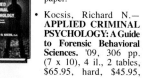
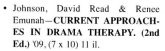

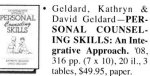